Cases and Materials for an Introduction to American Law

Steve Donweber

Boston University School of Law

Cases and Materials for an Introduction to American Law

Foreword

This book grew from my experiences teaching a class called *Introduction to American Law* for international students at Boston University School of Law and from a series of lectures that I first gave at Fudan University Law School in Shanghai, China and Chuo Law School in Tokyo, Japan in the Summer of 2018. My aim in the class in Boston and in the lectures in China and Japan has always been to provide a clear and concise overview of American law and the American legal system. I found it challenging, however, to find appropriate materials with which to do this. So, I decided to assemble my own. The idea here is to provide—in casebook form—an introduction to American law and legal English for (1) international law students, both those who wish at some point to study or practice in the United States and those who wish to remain in their home countries; (2) English-speaking undergraduate students interested in studying the law and/or going to law school; and (3) anyone else interested in understanding and studying basic concepts in law.

The book presents a general introduction to the study of law in the United States. The book starts with an excerpt from Oliver Wendell Holmes' landmark speech and essay *The Path of the Law*. Why? Holmes succinctly sets forth the reasons for why we study law and the methods for doing so. Can you tell what they are? **Chapter 1** then introduces various aspects of the American political and legal system, including brief discussions of federalism, the branches of government, the judiciary and the caselaw system, precedent, reporters, and citations. When I say brief, I mean *brief*; this is an introduction only. **Chapter 2** begins the first of three chapters on reading, understanding, and using cases in legal argument. This first general caselaw chapter discusses the fine art of briefing cases for use in the classroom. I brief a case called *Nix v. Hedden* by way of example, and I then set forth three additional (and famous) cases—*Palsgraf v. Long Island R.R., Hawkins v. McGee,* and *Burnham v. Superior Court*—for readers to brief themselves by way of practice. The second general caselaw chapter, **Chapter 3**, focuses on the concept of legal reasoning, the method by which judges arrive at conclusions on the facts presented to them by using earlier cases with different, but nevertheless similar, sets of facts. The chapter uses the cases *MacPherson v. Buick Motor, Griswold v. Connecticut, Lawrence v. Texas,* and *Acme v. Federal Armored Express* to show examples of legal reasoning. Finally, in terms of the general discussion of caselaw, comes **Chapter 4**, regarding applying cases to facts. The centerpiece of this chapter is a fact pattern for which I supply three applicable cases. Readers are then tasked with analyzing the three cases and determining how they would apply to the fact pattern and to whose benefit.

Chapter 5 on civil procedure (process) begins the study of the law itself. I start with the litigation process because it is central to understanding what a "case" actually is. Specifically in this chapter, I discuss the federal pleading standard under Rule 8 in the context of *Bell Atlantic v. Twombly* and *Ashcroft v. Iqbal*, and the federal standard for summary judgment under Rule 56 in the context of *Celotex v. Catrett* and *Anderson v. Liberty Lobby*. **Chapter 6** continues the discussion of civil procedure, but this time in the areas of subject matter jurisdiction, personal jurisdiction, and venue.

Then comes a series of five chapters on issues arising under the U.S. Constitution. **Chapter 7** is on Important Early Cases in U.S. Constitutional History, focusing on the role of the judiciary and the relationship between the federal government and the states. Included here are *Calder v. Bull, Marbury v. Madison, Fletcher v. Peck, Martin v. Hunter's Lessee,* and *McCulloch v. Maryland*. **Chapter 8** introduces the Commerce Power and several landmark cases related to it, including *Gibbons v. Ogden* and *Wickard v. Filburn*. **Chapter 9** discusses the First Amendment and freedom of expression and will cover freedom from compelled speech, Holmes' "clear and present danger" test for speech, protection of offensive speech, prior restraints, and the proper standard for finding defamation of a public figure. **Chapter 10** explores America's fraught relationship with race in the context of cases like *Dred Scott v. Sandford, Plessy v. Ferguson, Sweatt v. Painter, Brown v. Board of Education,* and *Heart of Atlanta Motel v. United States*. **Chapter 11** briefly explains the importance of juries in the American system with reference to the amendments in the Bill of Rights related to juries and cases on the "fair cross section of the community" requirement and jury nullification.

Chapters 12 and 13 focus on the substantive law of Contracts and Torts, respectively and discuss many famous cases that are staples of the first year law school curriculum at every law school in the United States. **Chapters 14 and 15**

introduce criminal law and procedure and, finally, **Chapter 16** is devoted to issues in legal ethics and professional responsibility.

The most important skill I hope to foster throughout all this, no matter what the topic, is the reading and understanding of U.S. case law. For students from civil law countries and those unfamiliar with how cases "work" or even what they are, the centrality of cases to the American legal system can seem bewildering. Indeed, getting what cases are, what they do, and why they're important can be difficult at first. I want to make it easier. Therefore, with the exception of the first chapter on the organization of the American political system, the bulk of the book, like any other casebook, consists of key judicial opinions in the development of American law. These opinions, these *cases*, provide the stories that underlie American legal history. Understanding them is vital to the study of law in the United States. They're also supremely interesting and fun to read (Seriously)!

But, why study law in the first place? To me it is the core discipline in any analysis of society as a whole. Indeed, the law relates to the study of the fair resolution of disputes between private individuals, the notions of property ownership and transfer, an understanding of the individual's relation to the state, and a proper theory of governance. In short, it encompasses all human interactions. What could be more important?

So, I congratulate you on your decision to study American law. I hope you find this book interesting and helpful in your endeavors. Good luck!

Many thanks to my amazing students at Boston University School of Law, Fudan University Law School, and Chuo Law School. This is for you!

Steve Donweber
Boston, Massachusetts
August 2019

Table of Contents

Oliver Wendell Holmes, The Path of the Law, 10 Harv. L. Rev. 61 (1897)

Oliver Wendell Holmes (1841-1935) was a legal scholar, Associate Justice and Chief Justice of the Massachusetts Supreme Judicial Court (1882-1902), and Associate Justice of the United States Supreme Court (1902-1932). He was immensely influential and is one of the most famous individuals in all of American legal history.

The excerpt below is from The Path of the Law, a speech delivered by Holmes (and later published in the Harvard Law Review) at the dedication of the new home of Boston University School of Law at 11 Ashburton Place in downtown Boston. Here, Holmes outlines his conception of what the law is, "The prophecies of what the courts will do in fact, and nothing more pretentious, are what I mean by the law." In this way, Holmes separates legal obligations from moral ones. In doing this, he asks the reader to reflect on the "bad man," someone who does not care about morals, but does care about the consequences of violating the law. It is for this "bad man" that the law has its predictive force. For with the law in mind, the "bad man" can now adjust his conduct and modulate his behavior so that he avoids legal consequences. This practical reading of the law was and remains enormously important.

Holmes also describes what we do when we study law; we read cases and then try to predict what a future court will do. This remains today the everyday business of lawyers and law students.

When we study law we are not studying a mystery but a well known profession. We are studying what we shall want in order to appear before judges, or to advise people in such a way as to keep them out of court. The reason why it is a profession, why people will pay lawyers to argue for them or to advise them, is that in societies like ours the command of the public force is intrusted to the judges in certain cases, and the whole power of the state will be put forth, if necessary, to carry out their judgments and decrees. People want to know under what circumstances and how far they will run the risk of coming against what is so much stronger than themselves, and hence it becomes a business to find out when this danger is to be feared. The object of our study, then, is prediction, the prediction of the incidence of the public force through the instrumentality of the courts.

The means of the study are a body of reports, of treatises, and of statutes, in this country and in England, extending back for six hundred years, and now increasing annually by hundreds. In these sibylline leaves are gathered the scattered prophecies of the past upon the cases in which the axe will fall. These are what properly have been called the oracles of the law. Far the most important and pretty nearly the whole meaning of every new effort of legal thought is to make these prophecies more precise, and to generalize them into a thoroughly connected system. The process is one, from a lawyer's statement of a case, eliminating as it does all the dramatic elements with which his client's story has clothed it, and retaining only the facts of legal import, up to the final analyses and abstract universals of theoretic jurisprudence. The reason why a lawyer does not mention that his client wore a white hat when he made a contract ... is that he foresees that the public force will act in the same way whatever his client had upon his head. It is to make the prophecies easier to be remembered and to be understood that the teachings of the decisions of the past are put into general propositions and gathered into text-books, or that statutes are passed in a general form. The primary rights and duties with which jurisprudence busies itself again are nothing but prophecies. One of the many evil effects of the confusion between legal and moral ideas, about which I shall have something to say in a moment, is that theory is apt to get the cart before the horse, and to consider the right or the duty as something existing apart from and independent of the consequences of its breach, to which certain sanctions are added afterward. But, as I shall try to show, a legal duty so called is nothing but a prediction that if a man does or omits certain things he will be made to suffer in this or that way by judgment of the court; — and so of a legal right.

The number of our predictions when generalized and reduced to a system is not unmanageably large. They present themselves as a finite body of dogma which may be mastered within a reasonable time. It is a great mistake to be frightened by the ever increasing number of reports. The reports of a given jurisdiction in the course of a generation take up pretty much the whole body of the law, and restate it from the present point of view. We could reconstruct the corpus from them if all that went before were burned. The use of the earlier reports is mainly historical, a use about which I shall have something to say before I have finished.

I wish, if I can, to lay down some first principles for the study of this body of dogma or systematized prediction which we call the law, for men who want to use it as the instrument of their business to enable them to prophesy in their turn, and, as bearing upon the study, I wish to point out an ideal which as yet our law has not attained. The first thing for a business-like understanding of the matter is to understand its limits, and therefore I think it desirable at once to point out and dispel a confusion between morality and law, which sometimes rises to the height of conscious theory, and more often and indeed constantly is making trouble in detail without reaching the point of consciousness. You can see very plainly that a bad man has as much reason as a good one for wishing to avoid an encounter with the public force, and therefore you can see the practical importance of the distinction between morality and law. A man who cares nothing for an ethical rule which is believed and practised by his neighbors is likely nevertheless to care a good deal to avoid being made to pay money, and will want to keep out of jail if he can.

I take it for granted that no hearer of mine will misinterpret what I have to say as the language of cynicism. The law is the witness and external deposit of our moral life. Its history is the history of the moral development of the race. The practice of it, in spite of popular jests, tends to make good citizens and good men. When I emphasize the difference between law and morals I do so with reference to a single end, that of learning and understanding the law. For that purpose you must definitely master its specific marks, and it is for that that I ask you for the moment to imagine yourselves indifferent to other and greater things.

I do not say that there is not a wider point of view from which the distinction between law and morals becomes of secondary or no importance, as all mathematical distinctions vanish in presence of the infinite. But I do say that that distinction is of the first importance for the object which we are here to consider, — a right study and mastery of the law as a business with well understood limits, a body of dogma enclosed within definite lines. I have just shown the practical reason for saying so. If you want to know the law and nothing else, you must look at it as a bad man, who cares only for the material consequences which such knowledge enables him to predict, not as a good one, who finds his reasons for conduct, whether inside the law or outside of it, in the vaguer sanctions of conscience. The theoretical importance of the distinction is no less, if you would reason on your subject aright. The law is full of phraseology drawn from morals, and by the mere force of language continually invites us to pass from one domain to the other without perceiving it, as we are sure to do unless we have the boundary constantly before our minds. The law talks about rights, and duties, and malice, and intent, and negligence, and so forth, and nothing is easier, or, I may say, more common in legal reasoning, than to take these words in their moral sense, at some stage of the argument, and so to drop into fallacy. For instance, when we speak of the rights of man in a moral sense, we mean to mark the limits of interference with individual freedom which we think are prescribed by conscience, or by our ideal, however reached. Yet it is certain that many laws have been enforced in the past, and it is likely that some are enforced now, which are condemned by the most enlightened opinion of the time, or which at all events pass the limit of interference as many consciences would draw it. Manifestly, therefore, nothing but confusion of thought can result from assuming that the rights of man in a moral sense are equally rights in the sense of the Constitution and the law.

*   *   *

The confusion with which I am dealing besets confessedly legal conceptions. Take the fundamental question, What constitutes the law? You will find some text writers telling you that it is something different from what is decided by the courts of Massachusetts or England, that it is a system of reason, that it is a deduction from principles of ethics or admitted axioms or what not, which may or may not coincide with the decisions. But if we take the view of our friend the bad man we shall find that he does not care two straws for the axioms or deductions, but that he does want to know what the Massachusetts or English courts are likely to do in fact. I am much of his mind. The prophecies of what the courts will do in fact, and nothing more pretentious, are what I mean by the law.

*   *   *

Chapter 1: Introduction to the American System

Introduction and Definitions

This discussion of the "American System" will encompass the Constitution of the United States, the structure of the American government, and the nature of the American judiciary and the role of cases or "judge-made" law in the U.S.

Definitions relevant to this discussion include the following:

Branch of Government: The major governmental divisions set forth in the Constitution. The branches are Congress, the Executive, and the Judiciary. Each branch has its own powers and role in the governance of the United States. The separate powers of the three branches provide the basis for the doctrine of the separation of powers, which essentially provides that the different powers and roles of the three branches provide a safeguard against tyranny.

Case or opinion: A written decision issued by a judge or panel of judges at either the trial court, intermediate appellate court, or supreme court level regarding a dispute between two or more parties. The decision generally resolves the entire dispute or single/multiple issue(s) that have arisen during the course of the dispute. In resolving the dispute, the judge will state and bring to bear applicable legal principles.

Common Law System: A system where judges make law through writing opinions resolving disputes between two or more parties.

Congress: The national legislature, responsible for enacting law. It consists of two houses, the House of Representatives and the Senate.

Constitution: The document that established the United States and its government.

Executive: The branch of government responsible for enforcing the law. The President is the head of the Executive Branch.

Federalism: The system of dual sovereignty and shared powers as between the states and the national government in the United States.

Judiciary: The branch of government responsible for resolving disputes and interpreting the law. Judges make up the judiciary.

Precedent: An earlier decided case that furnishes a basis for deciding later cases involving similar facts or issues.

Stare Decisis: Stare decisis is Latin for "to stand by things decided." In short, it is the doctrine of precedent. Courts cite to stare decisis when an issue has been previously brought to the court and a ruling already issued.

Federalism

The term (and concept) "federalism" describes the relationship between the state and federal governments in the United States of America. Specifically, federalism describes a system of dual sovereignty where the federal government possesses certain limited powers of governance and the states possess others. In this mixed government scheme, the powers of the state and federal governments can be exclusive or they can overlap. Even though the U.S. has a strong central government and federal law is supreme, the powers of the central government are limited and the states possess all other powers of governance unless prohibited by the Constitution.

The concept of federalism is embodied in the 10th Amendment to the Constitution, which provides that "powers not delegated to the United States by the Constitution, nor prohibited by it to the states, are reserved to the states respectively, or to the people."

Federalism is the mixed or compound mode of government, combining a general government (the central or "federal" government) with regional governments (provincial, state, cantonal, territorial or other subunit governments) in a single political system. Its distinctive feature, exemplified in the founding example of modern federalism by the United States under the Constitution of 1787, is a relationship of parity between the two levels of government established. It can thus be defined as a form of government in which there is a division of powers between two levels of government of equal status.   *https://en.wikipedia.org/wiki/Federalism*

Branches of the U.S. Government

The United States Constitution established three branches of government: the legislature, the judiciary, and the executive. Each of the 50 states has a more-or-less parallel system. Primary legal authority flows from all three branches.

The legislature—whether federal or state—produces statutes, which are laws passed by a legislative body following introduction of a bill, a complex deliberative process, and interaction between and among both houses of the legislature and the executive branch. Statutes often, but not always, frame their requirements in general language that is subject to interpretation by courts or amplification by executive agencies.

The executive branch, or more precisely executive agencies, promulgate regulations. In one sense, regulations provide the details for the broad policy mandates set forth in statutes. Put another way, regulations are the rules an agency writes to explain how a statute will be implemented. In some situations, the rules relate to a specific statute and in other cases to the statute establishing an agency. These rules have the legal force of the statute behind them. Rules too are often interpreted by case law.

The judiciary, i.e. our system of courts, produces case law. Case law is comprised of written opinions by judges resolving all or part of a dispute between two or more parties in the course of a civil or criminal proceeding. Case law will often interpret the common law or a statute in the context of an individual dispute. The interpretation creates precedent, which will then shape future interpretations of the common law or the applicable statute in other disputes.

The Judiciary and the Caselaw System

What is a Case?

A case is a written decision issued by a judge or panel of judges at either the trial court, intermediate appellate court, or supreme court level regarding a dispute between two or more parties. The decision generally resolves the entire dispute or single/multiple issue(s) that have arisen during the course of the dispute.

In resolving the dispute, the judge will state and bring to bear applicable legal principles. These principles will for the most part derive from federal or state statutory (or regulatory) sources or the common law. It is the judge's duty to apply these legal principles to the facts of the case before her.

In a common law system like the United States, much law is not based in statute (that is, enacted by the legislature) but rather in judicial decisions. Any court, at any level, can issue a judicial decision. The decision, or case, is binding on the parties and serves as precedent for future cases with similar facts.

The Federal and State Court Systems

Cases come from courts. The United States has one court system for the country as a whole (the federal system) and then parallel systems in each of the 50 states. Cases may be brought in either of the two systems. State courts generally can hear any case brought before them while federal courts are limited to hearing cases raising a question of federal law or cases involving a dispute between citizens of different states, or between a citizen of a state and a citizen of a foreign country, where the amount in controversy exceeds $75,000.

The organization of the federal and state systems is exactly parallel. Both systems consist of the following:

Trial Court (called the District Court in the federal system). The trial court is the first court in which a lawsuit, usually initiated with the filing of a document called a complaint, is brought. This court, presided over by a single judge, will frame the dispute; shepherd the dispute through the pretrial process, which includes motion practice and the exchange of information between the parties (know as "discovery"); determine whether the case should go to trial; and then at trial, generally with the aid of a jury as the finder of fact, resolve the dispute in favor of one of the parties.

Intermediate Appellate Court (called the Court of Appeals in the federal system). The party that loses in the trial court has an automatic right of appeal to the intermediate appellate court. Essentially, the appealing party (known as the "appellant") argues that the trial court did something wrong or "erred" in the application of the law to the facts, and if the appellate court were to correct this error, the appellant would end up the winner.

Supreme Court. The federal system and each state have a supreme court. A state supreme court is the final arbiter for all cases brought within its state (except for certain circumstances where a case from a state supreme court can be appealed to the United States Supreme Court). The United States Supreme Court is the final arbiter for all cases arising under federal law, including the United States Constitution, and the federal statutory and regulatory schemes. Parties have only a discretionary right of appeal from the intermediate appellate court to a supreme court. That means that a supreme court chooses the cases that it wants to hear, usually those it regards as particularly important.

Hierarchy of Case Authority and the Role Of Precedent

Cases are important to the parties to the dispute in question, of course, but to others as well because they have precedential value. For our purposes, precedent means a "decided case that furnishes a basis for determining later cases involving similar facts or issues." The decided case can be binding precedent, which means a "precedent that a court must follow," because it is from a higher court within the same jurisdiction, or the decided case can be persuasive precedent, which is a "precedent that is not binding on a court, but that is entitled to respect and careful consideration." This could be a decided case from a court at the same level in the same jurisdiction or from a court in a neighboring jurisdiction. Either way, the court is not bound by the earlier case, but may use its reasoning in deciding the case before it.

For example, all federal trial courts in the First Circuit (covering Maine, Massachusetts, New Hampshire, Puerto Rico, and Rhode Island) must adhere to applicable precedent from the First Circuit Court of Appeals, as decisions from that court are binding precedent on them. On the other hand the federal trial court in the District of Massachusetts may follow the reasoning from a case in the District of Maine if it finds that reasoning persuasive. Similarly, all courts in the First Circuit, including the Court of Appeals, must adhere to precedent from the United States Supreme Court, and may follow persuasive precedent in the form of decided cases from outside the circuit if they choose.

Recognizing that cases have precedential value provides the key reason for why lawyers research and use them. Simply, lawyers look for prior decided cases that have outcomes favorable to their clients and that are most similar in terms of facts and legal issues to the situations facing their clients. Once these cases are located, the lawyer argues that the result in the earlier case, as either binding or persuasive precedent, should control or inform the outcome for her client in the present case.

In other words, the "best" case you can find is normally, (1) binding precedent from your jurisdiction that is (2) similar in facts and issues to your case, and (3) where the outcome of the case is favorable to your client. By "favorable outcome", I mean that if you're seeking dismissal of a case based on a particular issue, you want a case that dismisses on that issue, etc. Once you find that "best" case, simply compare it to your client's situation and argue that the outcome for your client should be the same as that in the earlier decided case.

Excerpt from William Cleary Sullivan, What is a Precedent?, 11 Geo. L.J. 1 (1922-23)

In this excerpt, Sullivan discusses the importance of precedent and how it works. Precedent is important because once a matter is resolved in a particular way that is seen as the "right" way, future disputes can be resolved in far less time and future actors will understand how to avoid violating the law. Precedent "works" due to the relationship between the court in the current case and the court in the past case (is the court in the past case on a higher level?) and the similarity between the facts in the current case and the facts in the past case; the more similar the facts, the more likely the rule in the past case will be applied in the current one.

In common parlance a precedent is that which we follow because the same thing has been done before in the same way, and it has become recognized as the proper thing to do and way to do it. It may have been done but once before, or it may have been many times, but when used as something to follow it is a precedent. Such is the meaning of the term in common parlance, and it has no different meaning in legal language.

When in the law we speak of a precedent, we may mean either a form of contract, will, pleading or the like, or the decision of a court. In these pages, however, we shall deal only with the latter phase.

Of course, every court decision is not a precedent of equal value or application. Much depends upon the relations of the court in which it is cited to that which rendered it, of the facts of the one case to those of the other, and of the parties litigant to the respective cases.

Courts have been established for the purpose of putting an end to controversies between man and man. The primary purpose of their creation is to settle such matters. Of course, the aim is to settle them properly, according to right and justice, but that is a secondary consideration. The public welfare requires that they be settled once and for all, whether rightly or wrongly, and the public welfare is superior to all matters of private concern. The major purpose, therefore, in establishing courts of justice is to settle controversies and to prevent them arising. The latter purpose, the prevention of controversies, is accomplished by making the rules of law as definite and as certain as possible, and this end is served in court decisions by allowing them to become precedents.

When a court has once fully considered any question, and rendered its decision thereupon, there is little likelihood of a different decision each time that question again comes before the same court. To leave the matter open for reargument on every occasion, therefore, necessarily wastes the time of the court and delays other litigants in bringing their cases to a hearing, and serves also to greatly increase the cost of litigation. These considerations alone are more than sufficient to justify the courts in acting to overcome them. But they are nevertheless of minor importance in comparison with the real, outstanding object of the court in following precedents, which is to effect the purposes of their creation, namely, to terminate and prevent controversies and enable the people to know by what rules they may govern and regulate their affairs with an assurance that in so doing they are conforming to the requirements of the law. Indeed, any other mode of procedure would produce endless confusion. If the subject-matter of each court decision should be left open for reconsideration on every occasion upon which it arises in court, the situation would be intolerable in any business community.

Excerpt from H.W. Humble, Departure from Precedent, 19 Mich. L. Rev. 608 (1920-21)

The author here discusses why rules set forth in precedent should sometimes change.

Aside from the vague speculations in the previous paragraph on the question of the future of society, it is obvious that in many instances a precedent, no matter how illogical and arbitrary, becomes, in the course of time, like beauty, "its own excuse for being." It is not a case of following precedent for precedent's sake, but for society's sake. Members of the legal profession, to say nothing of laymen learned in the law, become accustomed to settled principles and regulate their conduct accordingly. And, in the opening words of Justice Benson, dissenting, in Thurston v. Fritz, "The rule that dying declarations are only admissible where the death of the declarant is the subject of the investigation is settled as firmly in the jurisprudence of this state as any rule can be which is not established by constitution or statute." Probably no lawyer would attempt to name any principle of the common law better settled than the one in question. Hence, it is submitted that such a principle should be overturned only when the good of society will be promoted thereby, taking into account the fact that laws which are settled and certain are one of society's most priceless assets, and that even unfairness, as the old maxim goes, is, often at least, preferable to uncertainty. In the earlier days, when parliament met but rarely, and the calling of such meeting was little short of a mobilization of troops to engage in civil war, there was great reason for resort to fictions, equity, and the various back-door methods of changing the law. But today, with frequent sessions of the legislature, is not the departure from judicial precedents less necessary? Moreover, the test of social utility is involved in the language of the majority of the court as quoted at the beginning of this article, namely, that the rule of stare decisis does not preclude a departure therefrom, "unless * * * a reversal would work a greater injury and injustice than would ensue by following the rule."

Maki v. Frelk, 40 Ill. 2d 193 (1968)

This case is not important for its own sake, but rather for its discussion of the importance of precedent and stare decisis, *the reason for following rules, and the circumstances under which rules should change.*

Where it is clear that the court has made a mistake it will not decline to correct it, even though the rule may have been reasserted and acquiesced in for a long number of years. No person has a vested right in any rule of law entitling him to insist that it shall remain unchanged for his benefit. But when a rule of law has once been settled, contravening no statute or constitutional principle, such rule ought to be followed unless it can be shown that serious detriment is thereby likely to arise prejudicial to public interests. The rule of Stare decisis is founded upon sound principles in the administration of justice, and rules long recognized as the law should not be departed from merely because the court is of the opinion that it might decide otherwise were the question a new one.

Alvis v. Ribar, 85 Ill. 2d 1 (1981)

In a follow up to the case above, the Supreme Court of Illinois overrules it, explaining that precedent or stare decisis *cannot stand in the way of the law's development.*

Defendants urge us to abide by the doctrine of stare decisis and follow the holding in Maki v. Frelk (1968), 40 Ill.2d 193, 239 N.E.2d 445. They contend that it is crucial to the due administration of justice, especially in a court of last resort, that a question once deliberately examined and decided be closed to further scrutiny. It must first be pointed out that the Maki decision, filed 13 years ago, did not, as claimed by defendants, address the merits of the case. On the contrary, the court avoided the merits by holding that the problem was one for the legislature.

It is interesting to observe that if Illinois courts had, in fact, rigidly adhered to the stare decisis rule throughout this State's legal history, the comparative standard could not have been adopted in Galena & Chicago Union R. R. Co. v. Jacobs (1858), 20 Ill. 478. Similarly, the comparative rule could not have been later discarded in [later cases].

The tenets of stare decisis cannot be so rigid as to incapacitate a court in its duty to develop the law. Clearly, the need for stability in law must not be allowed to obscure the changing needs of society or to veil the injustice resulting from a doctrine in need of reevaluation. This court can no longer ignore the fact that Illinois is currently out of step with the majority of States and with the common law countries of the world. We cannot continue to ignore the plight of plaintiffs who, because of some negligence on their part, are forced to bear the entire burden of their injuries. Neither can we condone the policy of allowing defendants to totally escape liability for injuries arising from their own negligence on the pretext that another party's negligence has contributed to such injuries. We therefore hold that in cases involving negligence the common law doctrine of contributory negligence is no longer the law in the State of Illinois, and in those instances where applicable it is replaced by the doctrine of comparative negligence.

Reporters

Cases are published in reporters. A reporter is a print set of books, organized by volume number, in which a particular jurisdiction's cases are collected in chronological order. There are separate reporter systems for the federal judiciary and also for each of the states. State cases are also published in regional reporters, which collect cases decided by the courts of several different states.

Federal Reporters

Reporter	Years Covered	Abbreviation
District Court		
Federal Supplement	1932-1998	F. Supp.
Federal Supplement 2d	1998-date	F. Supp. 2d
Federal Rules Decisions	1938-date	F.R.D.
West's Bankruptcy Reporter	1979-date	B.R.
Circuit Court		

Federal Reporter	1891-1924	F.
Federal Reporter 2d	1924-1993	F.2d
Federal Reporter 3d	1993-date	F.3d
Federal Appendix (unpub cases)	2001-date	F. App'x
Supreme Court		
United States Reports (official reporter)	1790-date	U.S.
Supreme Court Reporter (unofficial; published by West)	1882-date	S. Ct.
Lawyer's Edition (unofficial; published by Lexis)	1790-date	L. Ed., L. Ed. 2d

Regional (State) Reporters

Reporter	Abbreviation	States Covered
Atlantic	A., A.2d, A.3d	CT, DC, DE, MD, ME, NH, NJ, PA, RI, VT
North Eastern	N.E., N.E.2d	IL, IN, MA, NY, OH
North Western	N.W., N.W.2d	IA, MI, MN, ND, NE, SD, WI
Pacific	P., P.2d, P.3d	AK, AZ, CA, CO, HI, ID, KS, MT, NM, NV, OK, OR, UT, WA, WY
Southern	So., So. 2d, So. 3d	AL, FL, LA, MS
South Eastern	S.E., S.E.2d	GA, NC, SC, VA, WV
South Western	S.W., S.W.2d, S.W.3d	AR, KY, MO, TN, TX

Citations to Cases

Legal citation is the method by which lawyers, law students, professors, and judges refer to the sources, whether primary or secondary, that they rely upon when drafting court documents or legal memoranda, law school assignments, law review articles, and judicial opinions. Primary sources include cases, statutes, and regulations. Secondary sources include hornbooks, monographs, legal encyclopedias, law review articles, and treatises.

Citations are shorthand notations that permit the identification and location of a particular source. Elements of a citation generally include the identity of the source, where it can be found, the year it was created or went into effect, and for all primary sources and some secondary sources, the jurisdiction to which the source applies.

Because we rely on different sources for different reasons, legal citation also includes the use of signals, which introduce citations and explain to the reader the citation's purpose, and explanatory parentheticals, which follow the citation and provide further details on a source's relevance to the author's proposition.

Mastering legal citation takes practice, patience, and strict attention to detail. It means mastering the profession-wide standards for legal citation, which are set forth in *The Bluebook: A Uniform System of Citation*, published by the Columbia, Harvard, and University of Pennsylvania Law Reviews, and the Yale Law Journal. Every student of law must learn *The Bluebook*.

A case's citation consists of information following the name of the case that shows where the case can be found in the relevant print reporter, the court that decided the case, and when the case was decided. Examples of case citations are below. Make sure you know how to identify each component of the citation.

First is citation information from a case decided by the state intermediate appellate court in Pennsylvania. The dots indicate spaces. The first number is the volume number of the relevant reporter. The abbreviation "A.2d" refers to the name of the reporter, *Atlantic Reporter, 2d series*. The second number is the page on which the case begins. The parenthetical contains the abbreviation for the court that decided the case and the year the case was decided.

648•A.2d•1218•(Pa.•Super.•Ct.•1994)

Next is a citation from the federal district court in Massachusetts. Same shorthand as above.

112•F.•Supp.•2d•89•(D.•Mass.•2000)

*   *   *

Chapter 2: Reading and Briefing Cases

Introduction and Definitions

The study of cases forms the cornerstone of legal education in the United States. Rather than lecturing on doctrine, American law professors question students on the particulars of selected cases in order to illustrate the relevant legal principles involved. This permits students to understand not only the legal rules, but also the application of those rules to facts.

Because professors expect students to have read the cases prior to class and answer questions on the cases during class, it is vital that students "brief" cases in order to help with studying and preparation.

What's in a case brief?

It's like a summary of the case!
Include…
Case Name
Facts of the Case
Procedural History
Issue
Holding
Rationale for the Holding

More on briefing cases below.

Here are some *definitions* that pertain to this chapter.

Case: A written decision by a judge that resolves a dispute between 2 or more parties. Also referred to as an *opinion*.

Case Name: The parties to a case set forth in the following format, Nix v. Hedden. This is how a case is identified.

Facts of the Case: The details of the situation that gave rise to the dispute that the judge is being asked to resolve. To resolve the dispute the judge will apply the law to the facts.

Issue: The issue in a case is the question that the court is answering. Resolving the issue involves the application of the law to the facts of the case. In particular, resolving this issue may involve a determination of *how* the law applies to the facts of the case.

Holding: The holding in a case is the answer to the question posed by the issue. The holding often serves as the basis for the rule of law or precedent going forward.

Procedural History: Litigation begins with the filing of a complaint and ends with a verdict and possible appeals. A case's procedural history describes this process. A case's procedural posture describes at what point the case is at in the litigation process.

Rationale: The basis for or reasoning behind the court's holding. The rationale for the holding can be precedent, statutes, other authority, or policy.

How to Read a Case

Reading a case properly involves finding and isolating the various parts of the case noted in the *Definitions* section above.

For example, when reading Justice Cardozo's classic opinion in *Palsgraf v. Long Island R.R.*, 248 N.Y. 339 (1928), the student discovers the important facts of the case in the very first paragraph.

> *Plaintiff was standing on a platform of defendant's railroad after buying a ticket to go to Rockaway Beach. A train stopped at the station, bound for another place. Two men ran forward to catch it. One of the men reached the platform of the car without mishap, though the train was already moving. The other man, carrying a package, jumped aboard the car, but seemed unsteady as if about to fall. A guard on the car, who had held the door open, reached forward to help him in, and another guard on the*

platform pushed him from behind. In this act, the package was dislodged, and fell upon the rails. It was a package of small size, about fifteen inches long, and was covered by a newspaper. In fact it contained fireworks, but there was nothing in its appearance to give notice of its contents. The fireworks when they fell exploded. The shock of the explosion threw down some scales at the other end of the platform many feet away. The scales struck the plaintiff, causing injuries for which she sues.

Similarly, in the case of *Marbury v. Madison*, 5 U.S. 137 (1803), Chief Justice Marshall sets forth the issues facing the Court at the outset of his opinion.

In the order in which the court has viewed this subject, the following questions have been considered and decided.

1st. Has the applicant a right to the commission he demands?

2dly. If he has a right, and that right has been violated, do the laws of his country afford him a remedy?

3dly. If they do afford him a remedy, is it a mandamus issuing from this court?

Here is a look at a complete opinion, annotated to show the relevant parts.

Nix v. Hedden, 149 U.S. 304 (1893)

Gray, J., delivered the opinion of the court.

This was an action brought February 4, 1887, against the collector of the port of New York to recover back duties paid under protest on tomatoes imported by the plaintiff from the West Indies in the spring of 1886, which the collector assessed under 'Schedule G.-Provisions,' of the tariff act of March 3, 1883, (chapter 121,) imposing a duty on 'vegetables in their natural state, or in salt or brine, not specially enumerated or provided for in this act, ten per centum ad valorem;' and which the plaintiffs contended came within the clause in the free list of the same act, 'Fruits, green, ripe, or dried, not specially enumerated or provided for in this act.' . . .

The paragraph immediately above describes the facts that led to this dispute. A tax or tariff was imposed on a shipment of tomatoes under the Tariff Act of 1883 based on the assessment of the collector for the Port of New York that tomatoes were vegetables. The plaintiff brought suit because as a matter of botany tomatoes are not vegetables; they're fruit.

The Court also notes the beginning of case's procedural history by stating that the action was brought on February 4, 1887.

The single question in this case is whether tomatoes, considered as provisions, are to be classed as "vegetables" or as "fruit," within the meaning of the tariff act of 1883.

This is the issue or question that the court must decide. Are tomatoes vegetables or fruit for the purpose of the Tariff Act of 1883?

The only witnesses called at the trial testified that neither "vegetables" nor "fruit" had any special meaning in trade or commerce different from that given in the dictionaries, and that they had the same meaning in trade to-day that they had in March, 1883.

The passages cited from the dictionaries define the word "fruit" as the seed of plaints, or that part of plaints which contains the seed, and especially the juicy, pulpy products of certain plants, covering and containing the seed. These definitions have no tendency to show that tomatoes are 'fruit,' as distinguished from "vegetables," in common speech, or within the meaning of the tariff act.

There being no evidence that the words "fruit" and "vegetables" have acquired any special meaning in trade or commerce, they must receive their ordinary meaning. Of that meaning the court is bound to take judicial notice, as it does in regard to all words in our own tongue; and upon such a question dictionaries are admitted, not as evidence, but only as aids to the memory and understanding of the court.

In the three paragraphs set forth above, the Court describes how it is going to reach its decision, by determining the "ordinary meaning" of the word "tomato." This is vital to the ultimate holding, that tomatoes are vegetables.

Botanically speaking, tomatoes are the fruit of a vine, just as are cucumbers, squashes, beans, and peas. But in the common language of the people, whether sellers or consumers of provisions, all these are vegetables which are grown in kitchen gardens, and which, whether eaten cooked or raw, are, like potatoes, carrots, parsnips, turnips, beets, cauliflower, cabbage, celery, and lettuce, usually served at dinner in, with, or after the soup, fish, or meats which constitute the principal part of the repast, and not, like fruits generally, as dessert.

Here, the Court describes its holding, that tomatoes should be considered vegetables, and part of its rationale for deciding that tomatoes are vegetables under the ordinary meaning of the word tomato. Namely, people consider them to be vegetables because they are grown in a garden, eaten like vegetables during the meal, and not served as dessert like fruit would be.

The attempt to class tomatoes as fruit is not unlike a recent attempt to class beans as seeds, of which Mr. Justice Bradley, speaking for this court, said: "We do not see why they should be classified as seeds, any more than walnuts should be so classified. Both are seeds, in the language of botany or natural history, but not in commerce nor in common parlance. On the other hand in speaking generally of provisions, beans may well be included under the term 'vegetables.' As an article of food on our tables, whether baked or boiled, or forming the basis of soup, they are used as a vegetable, as well when ripe as when green. This is the principal use to which they are put. Beyond the common knowledge which we have on this subject, very little evidence is necessary, or can be produced."

Here the Court describes another part of its rationale, an earlier case that held that beans, although botanically seeds, should be considered vegetables in "common parlance."

Judgment affirmed.

By stating that the judgment is "affirmed," the Court is declaring that it is in agreement with the lower court that tomatoes should be considered vegetables. Plaintiff's appeal has therefore failed.

How to Brief a Case

We've asked this question before. What's in a case brief?

It's like a summary of the case!
Include...
Case Name
Facts of the Case
Procedural History
Issue
Holding
Rationale for the Holding

Here is a step-by-step discussion on how to brief a case using *Nix v. Hedden*, which was discussed above, as an example.

Case Name

Nix v. Hedden

Facts of the Case

When setting forth the facts of the case, it is important to identify the parties, the incident that triggered the dispute, the important facts, and what the parties want. In *Nix v. Hedden*, the facts are as follows:

The plaintiff is an importer of tomatoes. The defendant is the Collector of the Port of New York.

The Tariff Act of March 3, 1883 required a tax to be paid on imported vegetables, but not fruit.

The dispute was triggered when the Collector classified plaintiffs' tomatoes as vegetables and imposed a duty.

The plaintiff paid the duty under protest and then filed the case to recover the duties paid.

The basis of the plaintiff's argument is that botanically tomatoes are fruit, not vegetables.

Procedural History

The lower court found for the defendant and held that the duty was properly imposed because tomatoes were considered vegetables in common usage.

The plaintiffs appealed because a tomato is a fruit, not a vegetable.

Issue

Are tomatoes fruits or vegetables under the Tariff Act of 1883?

Holding

Tomatoes are vegetables under the Tariff Act of 1883.

Rationale

"Tomato" had no special meaning in trade or commerce.

Therefore, must refer to ordinary meaning.

Dictionaries did not help in understanding ordinary meaning.

Everyone considers tomatoes to be vegetables.

So, vegetables they are.

Earlier case: Beans are vegetables, even though botanically speaking they are seeds.

*   *   *

I have set forth three famous cases below. Using the techniques discussed above, draft a brief for each case.

Palsgraf v. Long Island R.R., 248 N.Y. 339 (1928)

Palsgraf is a very famous case involving the scope of the duty of care in negligence cases. As you brief the case, make sure to answer the following questions:

(1) To whom does the duty extend and why?

(2) Why was the plaintiff unable to recover in this case?

(3) What does this mean? "What the plaintiff must show is a wrong to herself; i.e., a violation of her own right, and not merely a wrong to someone else."

(4) What about this? "The risk reasonably to be perceived defines the duty to be obeyed, and risk imports relation; it is risk to another or to others within the range of apprehension."

CARDOZO, C. J., delivered the opinion of the court.

Plaintiff was standing on a platform of defendant's railroad after buying a ticket to go to Rockaway Beach. A train stopped at the station, bound for another place. Two men ran forward to catch it. One of the men reached the platform of the car without mishap, though the train was already moving. The other man, carrying a package, jumped aboard the car, but seemed unsteady as if about to fall. A guard on the car, who had held the door open, reached forward to help him in, and another guard on the platform pushed him from behind. In this act, the package was dislodged, and fell upon the rails. It was a package of small size, about fifteen inches long, and was covered by a newspaper. In fact it contained fireworks, but there was nothing in its appearance to give notice of its contents. The fireworks when they fell exploded. The shock of the explosion threw down some scales at the other end of the platform many feet away. The scales struck the plaintiff, causing injuries for which she sues.

The conduct of the defendant's guard, if a wrong in its relation to the holder of the package, was not a wrong in its relation to the plaintiff, standing far away. Relatively to her it was not negligence at all. Nothing in the situation gave notice that the falling package had in it the potency of peril to persons thus removed. Negligence is not actionable unless it involves the invasion of a legally protected interest, the violation of a right. Proof of negligence in the air, so to speak, will not do. Negligence is the absence of care, according to the circumstances.

The plaintiff, as she stood upon the platform of the station, might claim to be protected against intentional invasion of her bodily security. Such invasion is not charged. She might claim to be protected against unintentional invasion by conduct involving in the thought of reasonable men an unreasonable hazard that such invasion would ensue. These, from the point of view of the law, were the bounds of her immunity, with perhaps some rare exceptions, survivals for the most part of ancient forms of liability, where conduct is held to be at the peril of the actor.

If no hazard was apparent to the eye of ordinary vigilance, an act innocent and harmless, at least to outward seeming, with reference to her, did not take to itself the quality of a tort because it happened to be a wrong, though apparently not one involving the risk of bodily insecurity, with reference to someone else. In every instance, before negligence can be predicated of a given act, back of the act must be sought and found a duty to the individual complaining, the observance of which would have averted or avoided the injury. The ideas of negligence and duty are strictly correlative. The plaintiff sues in her own right for a wrong personal to her, and not as the vicarious beneficiary of a breach of duty to another.

A different conclusion will involve us, and swiftly too, in a maze of contradictions. A guard stumbles over a package which has been left upon a platform. It seems to be a bundle of newspapers. It turns out to be a can of dynamite. To the eye of ordinary vigilance, the bundle is abandoned waste, which may be kicked or trod on with impunity. Is a passenger at the other end of the platform protected by the law against the unsuspected hazard concealed beneath the waste? If not, is the result to be any different, so far as the distant passenger is concerned, when the guard stumbles over a valise which a truckman or a porter has left upon the walk? The passenger far away, if the victim of a wrong at all, has a cause of action, not derivative, but original and primary. His claim to be protected against invasion of his bodily security is neither greater nor less because the act resulting in the invasion is a wrong to another far removed. In this case, the rights that are said to have been violated, are not even of the same order. The man was not injured in his person nor even put in danger. The purpose of the act, as well as its effect, was to make his person safe.

If there was a wrong to him at all, which may very well be doubted it was a wrong to a property interest only, the safety of his package. Out of this wrong to property, which threatened injury to nothing else, there has passed, we are told, to the plaintiff by derivation or succession a right of action for the invasion of an interest of another order, the right to bodily security.

The diversity of interests emphasizes the futility of the effort to build the plaintiff's right upon the basis of a wrong to someone else. The gain is one of emphasis, for a like result would follow if the interests were the same. Even then, the orbit of the danger as disclosed to the eye of reasonable vigilance would be the orbit of the duty. One who jostles one's neighbor in a crowd does not invade the rights of others standing at the outer fringe when the unintended contact casts a bomb upon the ground. The wrongdoer as to them is the man who carries the bomb, not the one who explodes it without suspicion of the danger. Life will have to be made over, and human nature transformed, before prevision so extravagant can be accepted as the norm of conduct, the customary standard to which behavior must conform.

The argument for the plaintiff is built upon the shifting meanings of such words as wrong and wrongful, and shares their instability. What the plaintiff must show is a wrong to herself; i.e., a violation of her own right, and not merely a wrong to someone else, nor because unsocial. We are told that one who drives at reckless speed through a crowded city street is guilty of a negligent act and therefore of a wrongful one, irrespective of the consequences. Negligent the act is, and wrongful in the sense that it is unsocial, but wrongful and unsocial in relation to other travelers, only because the eye of vigilance perceives the risk of damage. If the same act were to be committed on a speedway or a race course, it would lose its wrongful quality. The risk reasonably to be perceived defines the duty to be obeyed, and risk imports relation; it is risk to another or to others within the range of apprehension.

This does not mean, of course, that one who launches a destructive force is always relieved of liability, if the force, though known to be destructive, pursues an unexpected path. It was not necessary that the defendant should have had notice of the particular method in which an accident would occur, if the possibility of an accident was clear to the ordinarily prudent eye.

Some acts, such as shooting, are so imminently dangerous to anyone who may come within reach of the missile however unexpectedly, as to impose a duty of prevision not far from that of an insurer. Even today, and much oftener in earlier stages of the law, one acts sometimes at one's peril. Under this head, it may be, fall certain cases of what is known as transferred intent, an act willfully dangerous to A resulting by misadventure in injury to B. These cases aside, wrong is defined in terms of the natural or probable, at least when unintentional.

The range of reasonable apprehension is at times a question for the court, and at times, if varying inferences are possible, a question for the jury. Here, by concession, there was nothing in the situation to suggest to the most cautious mind that the parcel wrapped in newspaper would spread wreckage through the station. If the guard had thrown it down knowingly and willfully, he would not have threatened the plaintiff's safety, so far as appearances could warn him. His conduct would not have involved, even then, an unreasonable probability of invasion of her bodily security. Liability can be no greater where the act is inadvertent.

Negligence, like risk, is thus a term of relation. Negligence in the abstract, apart from things related, is surely not a tort, if indeed it is understandable at all. Negligence is not a tort unless it results in the commission of a wrong, and the commission of a wrong imports the violation of a right, in this case, we are told, the right to be protected against interference with one's bodily security. But bodily security is protected, not against all forms of interference or aggression, but only against some.

One who seeks redress at law does not make out a cause of action by showing without more that there has been damage to his person. If the harm was not willful, he must show that the act as to him had possibilities of danger so many and apparent as to entitle him to be protected against the doing of it though the harm was unintended. Affront to personality is still the keynote of the wrong. Confirmation of this view will be found in the history and development of the action on the case. Negligence as a basis of civil liability was unknown to mediaeval law. For damage to the person, the sole remedy was trespass, and trespass did not lie in the absence of aggression, and that direct and personal.

Liability for other damage, as where a servant without orders from the master does or omits something to the damage of another, is a plant of later growth. When it emerged out of the legal soil, it was thought of as a variant of trespass, an offshoot of the parent stock. This appears in the form of action, which was known as trespass on the case. The victim does not sue derivatively, or by right of subrogation, to vindicate an interest invaded in the person of another. Thus to view his cause of action is to ignore the fundamental difference between tort and crime. He sues for breach of a duty owing to himself.

The law of causation, remote or proximate, is thus foreign to the case before us. The question of liability is always anterior to the question of the measure of the consequences that go with liability. If there is no tort to be redressed, there is no occasion to consider what damage might be recovered if there were a finding of a tort. We may assume, without deciding, that negligence, not at large or in the abstract, but in relation to the plaintiff, would entail liability for any and all consequences, however novel or extraordinary.

There is room for argument that a distinction is to be drawn according to the diversity of interests invaded by the act, as where conduct negligent in that it threatens an insignificant invasion of an interest in property results in an unforeseeable invasion of an interest of another order, as, e. g., one of bodily security. Perhaps other distinctions may be necessary. We do not go into the question now. The consequences to be followed must first be rooted in a wrong.

The judgment of the Appellate Division and that of the Trial Term should be reversed, and the complaint dismissed, with costs in all courts.

Hawkins v. McGee, 84 N.H. 114 (1929)

Hawkins v. McGee *is a very famous case involving the proper measure of damages in a contract case. While briefing the case, please make sure to answer the following questions:*

(1) Why is this a contract case, rather than a tort case?

(2) What is the proper measure of damages in this contracts case? Contrast that with the damages recoverable in a tort case.

BRANCH, J. delivered the opinion of the court.

The operation in question consisted in the removal of a considerable quantity of scar tissue from the palm of the plaintiff's right hand and the grafting of skin taken from the plaintiff's chest in place thereof. The scar tissue was the result of a severe burn caused by contact with an electric wire, which the plaintiff received about nine years before the time of the transactions here involved. There was evidence to the effect that before the operation was performed the plaintiff and his father went to the defendant's office, and that the defendant, in answer to the question, "How long will the boy be in the hospital?" replied, "Three or four days, not over four; then the boy can go home and it will be just a few days when he will go back to work with a good hand." Clearly this and other testimony to the same effect would not justify a finding that the doctor contracted to complete the hospital treatment in three or four days or that the plaintiff would be able to go back to work within a few days thereafter.

The above statements could only be construed as expressions of opinion or predictions as to the probable duration of the treatment and plaintiff's resulting disability, and the fact that these estimates were exceeded would impose no contractual liability upon the defendant. The only substantial basis for the plaintiff's claim is the testimony that the defendant also said before the operation was decided upon, "I will guarantee to make the hand a hundred per cent perfect hand or a hundred per cent good hand." The plaintiff was present when these words were alleged to have been spoken, and, if they are to be taken at their face value, it seems obvious that proof of their utterance would establish the giving of a warranty in accordance with his contention.

The defendant argues, however, that, even if these words were uttered by him, no reasonable man would understand that they were used with the intention of entering "into any contractual relation whatever," and that they could reasonably be understood only "as his expression in strong language that he believed and expected that as a result of the operation he would give the plaintiff a very good hand." It may be conceded, as the defendant contends, that, before the question of the making of a contract should be submitted to a jury, there is a preliminary question of law for the trial court to pass upon, i.e. "whether the words could possibly have the meaning imputed to them by the party who founds his case upon a certain interpretation," but it cannot be held that the trial court decided this question erroneously in the present case.

It is unnecessary to determine at this time whether the argument of the defendant, based upon "common knowledge of the uncertainty which attends all surgical operations," and the improbability that a surgeon would ever contract to make a damaged part of the human body "one hundred per cent perfect," would, in the absence of countervailing considerations, be regarded as conclusive, for there were other factors in the present case which tended to support the contention of the plaintiff. There was evidence that the defendant repeatedly solicited from the plaintiff's father the opportunity to perform this operation, and the theory was advanced by plaintiff's counsel in cross–examination of defendant that he sought an opportunity to "experiment on skin grafting," in which he had had little previous experience. If the jury accepted this part of plaintiff's contention, there would be a reasonable basis for the further conclusion that, if defendant spoke the words attributed to him, he did so with the intention that they should be accepted at their face value, as an inducement for the granting of consent to the operation by the plaintiff and his father, and there was ample evidence that they were so accepted by them. The question of the making of the alleged contract was properly submitted to the jury.

The substance of the charge to the jury on the question of damages appears in the following quotation: "If you find the plaintiff entitled to anything, he is entitled to recover for what pain and suffering he has been made to endure and for what injury he has sustained over and above what injury he had before." To this instruction the defendant seasonably excepted. By it, the jury was permitted to consider two elements of damage: (1) Pain and suffering due to the operation; and (2) positive ill effects of the operation upon the plaintiff's hand. Authority for any specific rule of damages in cases of this kind seems to be lacking, but, when tested by general principle and by analogy, it appears that the foregoing instruction was erroneous.

By "damages," as that term is used in the law of contracts, is intended compensation for a breach, measured in the terms of the contract. The purpose of the law is to put the plaintiff in as good a position as he would have been in had the defendant kept his contract. The measure of recovery is based upon what the defendant should have given the plaintiff, not what the plaintiff has given the defendant or otherwise expended. The only losses that can be said fairly to come within the terms of a contract are such as the parties must have had in mind when the contract was made, or such as they either knew or ought to have known would probably result from a failure to comply with its terms.

The present case is closely analogous to one in which a machine is built for a certain purpose and warranted to do certain work. In such cases, the usual rule of damages for breach of warranty in the sale of chattels is applied, and it is held that the measure of damages is the difference between the value of the machine, if it had corresponded with the warranty and its actual value, together with such incidental losses as the parties knew, or ought to have known, would probably result from a failure to comply with its terms.

The rule thus applied is well settled in this state. As a general rule, the measure of the vendee's damages is the difference between the value of the goods as they would have been if the warranty as to quality had been true, and the actual value at the time of the sale, including gains prevented and losses sustained, and such other damages as could be reasonably anticipated by the parties as likely to be caused by the vendor's failure to keep his agreement, and could not by reasonable care on the part of the vendee have been avoided. We therefore conclude that the true measure of the plaintiff's damage in the present case is the difference between the value to him of a perfect hand or a good hand, such as the jury found the defendant promised him, and the value of his hand in its present condition, including any incidental consequences fairly within the contemplation of the parties when they made their contract. Damages not thus limited, although naturally resulting, are not to be given.

Burnham v. Superior Court, 495 U.S. 604 (1990)

Burnham v. Superior Court *involves a question of personal jurisdiction. Personal jurisdiction refers to the power of a court over the person of the defendant. While briefing this case, please make sure to answer the following questions:*

(1) What specific issue is the Court deciding?

(2) What is the basis of Mr. Burnham's argument?

(3) What does it mean to be "served with process"?

(4) Why was the exercise of personal jurisdiction over Mr. Burnham proper and fair?

(5) Can you explain Justice Scalia's reasoning?

Justice SCALIA announced the judgment of the Court.

The question presented is whether the Due Process Clause of the Fourteenth Amendment denies California courts jurisdiction over a nonresident, who was personally served with process while temporarily in that State, in a suit unrelated to his activities in the State.

Petitioner Dennis Burnham married Francie Burnham in 1976 in West Virginia. In 1977 the couple moved to New Jersey, where their two children were born. In July 1987 the Burnhams decided to separate. They agreed that Mrs. Burnham, who intended to move to California, would take custody of the children. Shortly before Mrs. Burnham departed for California that same month, she and petitioner agreed that she would file for divorce on grounds of irreconcilable differences.

In October 1987, petitioner filed for divorce in New Jersey state court on grounds of desertion. Petitioner did not, however, obtain an issuance of summons against his wife and did not attempt to serve her with process. Mrs. Burnham, after unsuccessfully demanding that petitioner adhere to their prior agreement to submit to an irreconcilable differences divorce, brought suit for divorce in California state court in early January 1988.

In late January, petitioner visited southern California on business, after which he went north to visit his children in the San Francisco Bay area, where his wife resided. He took the older child to San Francisco for the weekend. Upon returning the child to Mrs. Burnham's home on January 24, 1988, petitioner was served with a California court summons and a copy of Mrs. Burnham's divorce petition. He then returned to New Jersey.

Later that year, petitioner made a special appearance in the California Superior Court, moving to quash the service of process on the ground that the court lacked personal jurisdiction over him because his only contacts with California were a few short visits to the State for the purposes of conducting business and visiting his children. The Superior Court denied the motion, and the California Court of Appeal denied mandamus relief, rejecting petitioner's contention that the Due Process Clause prohibited California courts from asserting jurisdiction over him because he lacked minimum contacts with the State. The court held it to be a valid jurisdictional predicate for *in personam* jurisdiction that the defendant [was] present in the forum state and personally served with process.

The proposition that the judgment of a court lacking jurisdiction is void traces back to the English Year Books and was made settled law by Lord Coke in *Case of the Marshalsea*. American courts invalidated, or denied recognition to, judgments that violated this common-law principle long before the Fourteenth Amendment was adopted. We announced that the judgment of a court lacking personal jurisdiction violated the Due Process Clause of the Fourteenth Amendment as well.

To determine whether the assertion of personal jurisdiction is consistent with due process, we have long relied on the principles traditionally followed by American courts in marking out the territorial limits of each State's authority. That criterion was first announced in *Pennoyer v. Neff*, in which we stated that due process "mean[s] a course of legal proceedings according to those rules and principles which have been established in our systems of jurisprudence for the protection and enforcement of private rights," including the "well-established principles of public law respecting the jurisdiction of an independent State over persons and property," In what has become the classic expression of the criterion, we said in *International Shoe Co. v. Washington* that a state court's assertion of personal jurisdiction satisfies the Due Process Clause if it does not violate " 'traditional notions of fair play and substantial justice.'" Since *International Shoe*, we have only been called upon to decide whether these traditional notions permit States to exercise jurisdiction over absent defendants in a manner that deviates from the rules of jurisdiction applied in the 19th century. We have held such deviations permissible, but only with respect to suits arising out of the absent defendant's contacts with the State. The question we must decide today is whether due process requires a similar connection between the litigation and the defendant's contacts with the State in cases where the defendant is physically present in the State at the time process is served upon him.

Among the most firmly established principles of personal jurisdiction in American tradition is that the courts of a State have jurisdiction over nonresidents who are physically present in the State. The view developed early that each State had the power to hale before its courts any individual who could be found within its borders, and that once having acquired jurisdiction over such a person by properly serving him with process, the State could retain jurisdiction to enter judgment against him, no matter how fleeting his visit.

Recent scholarship has suggested that English tradition was not as clear as Justice Story thought. Accurate or not, however, judging by the evidence of contemporaneous or near-contemporaneous decisions, one must conclude that Story's understanding was shared by American courts at the crucial time for present purposes.

Decisions in the courts of many States in the 19th and early 20th centuries held that personal service upon a physically present defendant sufficed to confer jurisdiction, without regard to whether the defendant was only briefly in the State or whether the cause of action was related to his activities there. Although research has not revealed a case deciding the issue in every State's courts that appears to be because the issue was so well settled that it went unlitigated. Opinions from the courts of other States announced the rule in dictum. Most States, more-over, had statutes or common-law rules that exempted from service of process individuals who were brought into the forum by force or fraud or who were there as a party or witness in unrelated judicial proceedings. These exceptions obviously rested upon the premise that service of process conferred jurisdiction. Particularly striking is the fact that, as far as we have been able to determine, not one American case from the period (or, for that matter, not one American case until 1978) held, or even suggested, that in-state personal service on an individual was insufficient to confer personal jurisdiction. Commentators were also seemingly unanimous on the rule.

This American jurisdictional practice is, moreover, not merely old; it is con-tinuing. It remains the practice of, not only a substantial number of the States, but as far as we are aware *all* the States and the Federal Government—if one disre-gards (as one must for this purpose) the few opinions since 1978 that have erro-neously said, on grounds similar to those that petitioner presses here, that this Court's due process decisions render the practice unconstitutional. We do not know of a single state or federal statute, or a single judicial decision resting upon state law, that has abandoned in-state service as a basis of jurisdiction. Many re-cent cases reaffirm it.

Despite this formidable body of precedent, petitioner contends, in reliance on our decisions applying the *International Shoe* standard, that in the absence of con-tinuous and systematic contacts with the forum, see a nonresident defendant can be subjected to judgment only as to matters that arise out of or relate to his con-tacts with the forum. This argument rests on a thorough misunderstanding of our cases.

The view of most courts in the 19th century was that a court simply could not exercise *in personam* jurisdiction over a nonresident who had not been personally served with process in the forum. *Pennoyer v. Neff*, while renowned for its statement of the principle that the Fourteenth Amendment prohibits such an exercise of jurisdiction, in fact set that forth only as dictum and decided the case (which in-volved a judgment rendered more than two years before the Fourteenth Amend-ment's ratification) under well-established principles of public law. Those principles, embodied in the Due Process Clause, required (we said) that when

proceedings involve merely a determination of the personal liability of the defendant, he must be brought within the court's jurisdiction by service of process within
the State, or his voluntary appearance. We invoked that rule in a series of subsequent cases, as either a matter of due process or a fundamental principle of jurisprudence.

Later years, however, saw the weakening of the *Pennoyer* rule. In the late 19th
and early 20th centuries, changes in the technology of transportation and communication, and the tremendous growth of interstate business activity, led to an
inevitable relaxation of the strict limits on state jurisdiction over nonresident individuals and corporations. States required, for example, that nonresident corporations appoint an in-state agent upon whom process could be served as a
condition of transacting business within their borders and provided in-state substituted service for nonresident motorists who caused injury in the State and left
before personal service could be accomplished. We initially upheld these laws under the Due Process Clause on grounds that they complied with *Pennoyer's* rigid
requirement of either consent. As many observed, however, the consent and presence were purely fictional. Our opinion in *International Shoe* cast those fictions aside
and made explicit the underlying basis of these decisions: Due process does not
necessarily require the States to adhere to the unbending territorial limits on jurisdiction set forth in *Pennoyer*. The validity of assertion of jurisdiction over a non-
consenting defendant who is not present in the forum depends upon whether the
quality and nature of [his] activity in relation to the forum, renders such jurisdiction consistent with traditional notions of fair play and substantial justice. Subsequent cases have derived from the *International Shoe* standard the general rule that
a State may dispense with in-forum personal service on nonresident defendants
in suits arising out of their activities in the State. As *International Shoe* suggests, the
defendant's litigation-related "minimum contacts" may take the place of physical
presence as the basis for jurisdiction.

Nothing in *International Shoe* or the cases that have followed it, however, offers
support for the very different proposition petitioner seeks to establish today:
that a defendant's presence in the forum is not only unnecessary to validate novel,
nontraditional assertions of jurisdiction, but is itself no longer sufficient to establish jurisdiction. That proposition is unfaithful to both elementary logic and the
foundations of our due process jurisprudence. The distinction between what is

needed to support novel procedures and what is needed to sustain traditional ones is fundamental, as we observed over a century ago:

> "[A] process of law, which is not otherwise forbidden, must be taken to be due process of law, if it can show the sanction of settled usage both in England and in this country; but it by no means follows that nothing else can be due process of law.... [That which], in substance, has been immemorially the actual law of the land ... therefor[e] is due process of law. But to hold that such a characteristic is essential to due process of law, would be to deny every quality of the law but its age, and to render it incapable of progress or improvement. It would be to stamp upon our jurisprudence the unchangeableness attributed to the laws of the Medes and Persians."

The short of the matter is that jurisdiction based on physical presence alone constitutes due process because it is one of the continuing traditions of our legal system that define the due process standard of traditional notions of fair play and substantial justice. That standard was developed by *analogy* to "physical presence," and it would be perverse to say it could now be turned against that touchstone of jurisdiction.

*   *   *

Chapter 3: Legal Reasoning

Introduction

Legal reasoning refers to the method that judges use to resolve the cases that come before them. Generally speaking, legal reasoning involves reference to existing authority—like a constitution, statute, regulation, or case—and then some sort of comparison of the existing authority with the dispute at hand.

As stated in the Stanford Encyclopedia of Authority:

> *Arguments from precedent and analogy are two central forms of reasoning found in many legal systems, especially 'Common Law' systems such as those in England and the United States. Precedent involves an earlier decision being followed in a later case because both cases are the same. Analogy involves an earlier decision being followed in a later case because the later case is similar to the earlier one. The main philosophical problems raised by precedent and analogy are these: (1) when are two cases the 'same' for the purposes of precedent? (2) when are two cases 'similar' for the purposes of analogy? and (3) in both situations, why should the decision in the earlier case affect the decision in the later case?*

This concept of comparison and analogy is explained briefly by Professors Levi and Lawrence below. We will then discuss the process of legal reasoning found in the cases, *MacPherson v. Buick Motor, Griswold v. Connecticut, Lawrence v. Texas,* and *Acme Markets v. Federal Armored Express.* When reading these cases, pay careful attention to the manner in which the judge arrives at a decision. On what does the judge rely and why? Do you agree with the comparisons that the judge is making?

Excerpt from Edward H. Levi, An Introduction to Legal Reasoning, 15 U. Chi. L. Rev. 501 (1948)

The basic pattern of legal reasoning is reasoning by example. It is reasoning from case to case. It is a three-step process described by the doctrine of precedent in which a proposition descriptive of the first case is made into a rule of law and applied to a next similar situation. The steps are these: similarity is seen between cases; next the rule of law inherent in the first case is announced; then the rule of law is made applicable to the second case. ...

The determination of similarity or difference is the function of each judge. Where case law is considered, and there is no statute, he is not bound by the statement of the rule of law made by the prior judge even in the controlling case. The statement is mere dictum, and this means that the judge in the present case may find irrelevant the existence or absence of facts which prior judges thought important. It is not what the prior judge intended that is of any importance; rather it is what the present judge, attempting to see the law as a fairly consistent whole, thinks to be the determining classification. In arriving at his result he will ignore what the past thought important; he will emphasize facts which prior judges would have thought made no difference. ...

Thus it cannot be said that the legal process is the application of known rules to diverse facts. Yet it is a system of rules; the rules are discovered in the process of determining similarity or difference. ... The problem for the law is: When will it be just to treat different cases as though they were the same? A working legal system must therefore be willing to pick out key similarities and to reason from them to the justice of applying a common classification. The existence of some facts in common brings into play the general rule.

Excerpt from Fred F. Lawrence, Precedent vs. Evolution, 12 Maine L. Rev. 169 (1919)

Centuries ago the common law issued to its judicial exponents a stern imperative - stare decisis - and that vital phrase still voices the eternal truth that the aggregate wisdom of the past is the primary guide to present policy, that in law, as in manners and customs, standards are necessary, conformity desirable. Hence precedent, with its resulting authority.

But equally potent was another axiom ... freely translated by the much-quoted couplet:

"New occasions teach new duties;
Time makes ancient good uncouth."

Without this element of adaptability the common law would have gone the way of other institutions which have outlived their usefulness and been thrown by the tides of human progress upon the sands of history.

If these two maxims are not destructive, the one of the other-and the survival of both is the surest proof they are not-what are the factors determining the relative force of each in measuring the authority of a given case?

No more important inquiry confronts the student of law - neophyte or veteran. The only authoritative guide to our "unwritten" law is the specific case. If Smith vs. Jones controls in one instance, affords a mere analogy in another, and becomes a menace in a third, it is of tremendous practical consequence that we form some conception of the underlying criteria. The American intellect recognizes no insoluble problems. At once scientific and practical, abstract and concrete, skilled in the wedding of theory to fact, it insists on making certain that which is capable of rendition to approximate certainty, and at least blazing the trail of the uncertain.

Macpherson v. Buick Motor Co., 217 N.Y. 382 (1916)

Macpherson v. Buick Motor Co., is a very important case in the development of the common law of torts with regard to who can recover for injury caused by a defective product. **The original rule maintained that only the purchaser of a product from the product's manufacturer could recover for injury caused by a defect.** *In other words, in order to recover, an injured party needed to have* **privity of contract** *with the manufacturer. As discussed in* MacPherson *below, that rule changed with the case of* Thomas v. Winchester. *How?*

In Macpherson, *Justice Cardozo traces the development of the rule after* Winchester. *Take note of how the rule progresses and how the various comparisons are made between products in the different cases. Where does the rule end up? Does Justice Cardozo apply the rule of* Thomas v. Winchester *to the case before him, or does he apply a different rule? In thinking about the development of the rule here, think about the roles that legal reasoning and arguing by analogy play in the court's decision in* MacPherson. *Make sure to trace the rule case-by-case.*

CARDOZO, J.

The defendant is a manufacturer of automobiles. It sold an automobile to a retail dealer. The retail dealer resold to the plaintiff. While the plaintiff was in the car, it suddenly collapsed. He was thrown out and injured. One of the wheels was made of defective wood, and its spokes crumbled into fragments. The wheel was not made by the defendant; it was bought from another manufacturer. There is evidence, however, that its defects could have been discovered by reasonable inspection, and that inspection was omitted. There is no claim that the defendant knew of the defect and willfully concealed it. The charge is one, not of fraud, but of negligence. The question to be determined is whether the defendant owed a duty of care and vigilance to anyone but the immediate purchaser.

The foundations of this branch of the law, at least in this state, were laid in *Thomas v. Winchester.* A poison was falsely labeled. The sale was made to a druggist, who in turn sold to a customer. The customer recovered damages from the seller who affixed the label. The defendant's negligence, it was said, put human life in imminent danger. A poison falsely labeled is likely to injure anyone who gets it. Because the danger is to be foreseen, there is a duty to avoid the injury. Cases were cited by way of illustration in which manufacturers were not subject to any duty irrespective of contract. The distinction was said to be that their conduct, though, negligent, was not likely to result in injury to anyone except the purchaser. We are not required to say whether the chance of injury was always as remote as the distinction assumes. Some of the illustrations might be rejected to-day. The principle of the distinction is for present purposes the important thing.

Thomas v. Winchester became quickly a landmark of the law. In the application of its principle there may at times have been uncertainty or even error. There has never in this state been doubt or disavowal of the principle itself. The chief cases are well known, yet to recall some of them will be helpful. *Loop v. Litchfield* is the earliest. It was the case of a defect in a small balance wheel used on a circular saw. The manufacturer pointed out the defect of the buyer, who wished a cheap article and was ready to assume the risk. The risk can hardly have been an imminent one, for the wheel lasted five years before it broke. In the meanwhile the buyer had made a lease of the machinery. It was held that the manufacturer was not answerable to the lessee. *Loop v. Litchfield* was followed in *Losee v. Clute*, the case of the explosion of a steam boiler. That decision has been criticized; but it must be confined to its special facts. It was put upon the ground that the risk of injury was too remote. The buyer in that case had not only accepted the boiler, but had tested it. The manufacturer knew that his own test was not the final one. The finality of the test has a bearing on the measure of diligence owing to persons other than the purchaser.

These early cases suggest a narrow construction of the rule. Later cases, however, evince a more liberal spirit. First in importance is *Devlin v. Smith*. The defendant, a contractor, built a scaffold for a painter. The painter's servants were injured. The contractor was held liable. He knew that the scaffold, if improperly constructed, was a most dangerous trap. He knew that it was to be used by the workmen. He was building it for that very purpose. Building it for their use, he owed them a duty, irrespective of his contract with their master, to build it with care.

From *Devlin v. Smith* we pass over intermediate cases and turn to the latest case in this court in which *Thomas v. Winchester* was followed. That case is *Statler v. Ray Mfg. Co.* The defendant manufactured a large coffee urn. It was installed in a restaurant. When heated, the urn exploded and injured the plaintiff. We held that the manufacturer was liable. We said that the urn was of such a character inherently that, when applied to the purposes for which it was designed, it was liable to become a source of great danger to many people if not carefully and properly constructed. It may be that *Devlin v. Smith* and *Statler v. Ray Mfg. Co.* have extended the rule of *Thomas v. Winchester*. If so, this court is committed to the extension.

The defendant argues that things imminently dangerous to life are poisons, explosives, deadly weapons-things whose normal function it is to injure or destroy. But whatever the rule in *Thomas v. Winchester* may once have been, it has no

longer that restricted meaning. A large coffee urn may have within itself, if negligently made, the potency of danger, yet no one thinks of it as an implement whose
normal function is destruction. What is true of the coffee urn is equally true of
bottles of aerated water. We have mentioned only cases in this court. But the rule
has received a like extension in our courts of intermediate appeal. In *Burke v. Ire-
land*, it was applied to a builder who constructed a defective building; in *Kahner v.
Otis Elevator Co.* to the manufacturer of an elevator; in *Davies v. Pelham Hod Elevating
Co.* to a contractor who furnished a defective rope was to be used. We are not
required at this time either to approve or to disapprove the application of the rule
that was made in these cases. It is enough that they help to characterize the trend
of judicial thought.

Devlin v. Smith was decided in 1882. A year later a very similar case came before
the Court of Appeal in England. We find in the opinion of Brett, M. R., afterwards
Lord, the same conception of a duty, irrespective of contract, imposed upon the
manufacturer by the law itself: "Whenever one person supplies goods, or machinery, or the like, for the purpose of their being used by another person under
such circumstances that every one of ordinary sense would, if he thought, recognize at once that unless he used ordinary care and skill with regard to the condition
of the thing supplied or the mode of supplying it, there will be danger of injury to
the person or property of him for whose use the thing is supplied, and who is to
use it, a duty arises to use ordinary care and skill as the condition or manner of
supplying such thing." He then points out that for a neglect of such ordinary care
or skill whereby injury happens, the appropriate remedy is an action for negligence. The right to enforce this liability is not to be confined to the immediate
buyer. The right, he says, extends to the persons or class of persons for whose
use the thing is supplied. It is enough that the goods would in all probability be
used at once before a reasonable opportunity for discovering any defect which
might exist, and that the thing supplied is of such a nature that a neglect of ordinary care or skill as to its condition or the manner of supplying it would probably
cause danger to the person or property of the person for whose use it was supplied, and who was about to use it.

On the other hand, he would exclude a case in which the goods are supplied
under circumstances in which it would be a chance by whom they would be used
or whether they would be used or not, or whether they would be before there

would probably be means of observing any defect, or where the goods are of such a nature that a want of care or skill as to their condition or the manner of supplying them would not probably produce danger of injury to person or property. What was said by Lord Esher in that case did not command the full assent of his associates. His opinion has been criticised as requiring every man to take affirmative precautions to protect his neighbors as well as to refrain from injuring them. It may not be an accurate exposition of the law of England. Perhaps it may need some qualification even in our own state. Like most attempts at comprehensive definition, it may involve errors of inclusion and of exclusion. But its tests and standards, at least in their underlying principled, with whatever qualifications may be called for as they are applied to varying conditions, are the tests and standards of our law.

We hold, then, that the principle of *Thomas v. Winchester* is not limited to poisons, explosives, and things of like nature, to things which in their normal operation are implements of destruction. If the nature of a thing is such that it is reasonably certain to place and limb in peril when negligently made, it is then a thing of danger. Its nature gives warning of the consequences to be expected. If to the element of danger there is added knowledge that the thing will be used by persons other than the purchaser, and used without new tests then, irrespective of contract, the manufacturer of this thing of danger is under a duty to make it carefully. That is as far as we are required to go for the decision of this case.

There must be knowledge of a danger, not merely possible, but probable. It is possible to use almost anything in a way that will make it dangerous if defective. That is not enough to charge the manufacturer with a duty independent of his contract. Whether a given thing is dangerous may be sometimes a question for the court and sometimes a question for the jury. There must also be knowledge that in the usual course of events the danger will be shared by others than the buyer. Such knowledge may often be inferred from the nature of the transaction.

But it is possible that even knowledge of the danger and of the use will not always be enough. The proximity or remoteness of the relation is a factor to be considered. We are dealing now with the liability of the manufacturer of the finished product, who puts it on the market to be used without inspection by his customers. If he is negligent, where danger is to be foreseen, a liability will follow.

We are not required at this time to say that it is legitimate to go back of the manufacturer of the finished product and hold the manufacturers of the component parts. To make their negligence a cause of imminent danger, an independent cause must often intervene; the manufacturer of the finished product must also fail in his duty of inspection. It may be that in those circumstances the negligence of the earlier members of the series as too remote to constitute, as to the ultimate user, an actionable wrong.

We leave that question open to you. We shall have to deal with it when it arises. The difficulty which it suggests is not present in this case, there is here no break in the chain of cause and effect. In such circumstances, the presence of a known danger, attendant upon a known use, makes vigilance a duty. We have put aside the notion that the duty to safeguard life and limb, when the consequences of negligence may be foreseen, grows out of contract and nothing else. We have put the source of the obligation where it ought to be. We have put its source in the law.

From this survey of the decisions, there thus emerges a definition of the duty of a manufacturer which enables us to measure this defendant's liability. Beyond all question, the nature of an automobile gives warning of probable danger if its construction is defective. This automobile was designed to go fifty miles an hour. Unless its wheels were sound and strong, injury was almost certain. It was as much a thing of danger as a defective engine for a railroad. The defendant knew the danger. It knew also that the care would be used by persons other than the buyer. This was apparent from its size; there were seats for three persons. It was apparent also from the fact that the buyer was a dealer in cars, who bought to resell. The maker of this car supplied it for the use of purchasers from the dealer just as plainly as the contractor in *Devlin v. Smith* supplied the scaffold for use by the servants of the owner. The dealer was indeed the one person of whom it might be said with some approach to certainly that by him the car would not be used. Yet the defendant would have us say that he was the one person whom it was under a legal duty to protect.

The law does not lead us to so inconsequent a conclusion. Precedents drawn from the days of travel by stage coach do not fit the conditions of travel today.

The principle that the danger must be imminent does not change, but the things subject to the principle do change. They are whatever the needs of life in a developing civilization require them to be.

In reaching this conclusion, we do not ignore the decisions to the contrary in other jurisdictions. Some of them, at first sight inconsistent with our conclusion, may be reconciled upon the ground that the negligence was too remote, and that another cause had intervened. But even when they cannot be reconciled, the difference is rather in the application of the principle than in the principle itself. Judge Sanborn says, for example, that the contractor who builds a bridge, or the manufacturer who builds a car, cannot ordinarily foresee injury to other persons than the owner as the probable result.

We take a different view. We think that injury to others is to be foreseen not merely as a possible, but as an almost inevitable result. Indeed Judge Sanborn concedes that his view is not to be reconciled with our decision in *Devlin v. Smith*. The doctrine of that decision has now become the settled law of this state, and we have no desire to depart from it.

In England the limits of the rule are still unsettled. *Winterbottom v. Wright* is often cited. The defendant undertook to provide a mail coach to carry the mail bags. The coach broke down from latent defects in its construction. The defendant, however, was not the manufacturer. The court held that he was not liable for injuries to a passenger. Lord Esher points out in *Heaven v. Pender* that the form of the declaration was subject to criticism. It did not fairly suggest the existence of a duty aside from the special contract which was the plaintiff's main reliance.

At all events, in *Heaven v. Pender* the defendant, a dock owner, who put up a staging outside a ship, was held liable to the servants of the shipowner. In *Elliot v. Hall* the defendant sent out a defective truck laden with goods which he had sold. The buyer's servants unloaded it, and were injured because of the defects. It was held that the defendant was under a duty not to be guilty of negligence with regard to the state and condition of the truck. There seems to have been a return to the doctrine of *Winterbottom v. Wright* in *Earl v. Lubbock*.

In that case, however, as in to the earlier one, the defendant was not the manufacturer. He had merely made a contract to keep the van in repair. A later case, *White v. Steadman*, emphasizes that element. A livery stable keeper who sent put a vicious horse was held liable not merely to his customer but also to another occupant of the carriage, and *Thomas v. Winchester* was cited and followed *White v. Steadman*. It was again cited and followed in *Dominion Natural Gas Co. v. Collins*. From these cases a consistent principle is with difficulty extracted. The English courts, however, agree with ours in holding that one who invites another to make use of an appliance is bound to the exercise of reasonable care.

That at bottom is the underlying principle of *Devlin v. Smith*. The contractor who builds the scaffold invites the owner's work-men to use it. The manufacturer who sells the automobile to the retail dealer invites the dealer's customers to use it. The invitation is addressed in the one case to determinate persons and in the other to an indeterminate class, but in each case it is equally plain, and in each its consequences must be the same.

There is nothing anomalous in a rule which imposes upon A, who has contracted with B, a duty to C and D and others according as he knows or does not know that the subject matter of the contract is intended for their use. We may find an analogy in the law which measures the liability of landlords. If A leases to B a tumble-down house he is not liable, in the absence of fraud, to B's guests who enter it and are injured. This is because B is then under the duty to repair it, the lessor has the right to suppose that he will fulfill that duty, and if he omits to do so, his guests must look to him. But if A leases a building to be used by the lessee at once as a place of public entertainment, the rule is different. There is injury to persons other than the lessee is to be foreseen, and foresight of the consequences involves the creation of a duty.

In this view of the defendant's liability there is nothing in- consistent with the theory of liability on which the case was tried. It is true that the court told the jury that 'an automobile is not an inherently dangerous vehicle.' The meaning, however, is made plain by the context. The meaning is that danger is not to be expected when the vehicle is well constructed. The court left it to the jury to say whether the defendant ought to have foreseen that the car, if negligently constructed, would become 'imminently dangerous.'

Subtle distinctions are drawn by the defendant between things inherently dangerous and things imminently dangerous, but the case does not turn upon these verbal niceties. If danger was to be expected as reasonably certain, there was a duty of vigilance, and this whether you call the danger inherent or imminent. In varying forms that the court would not have been justified in ruling as a matter of law that the car was a dangerous thing. If there was any error, it was none of which the defendant can complain.

We think the defendant was not absolved from a duty of inspection because it bought the wheels from a reputable manufacturer. It was not merely a dealer in automobiles. It was a manufacturer of automobiles. It was responsible for the finished product. It was not at liberty to put the finished product on the market without subjecting the component parts to ordinary and simple tests. Under the charge of the trial judge nothing more was required of it. The obligation to inspect must vary with the nature of the thing to be inspected. The more probable the danger, the greater the need of caution.

There is little analogy between this case and *Carlson v. Phoenix Bridge Co.*, where the defendant bought a tool for a servant's use. The making of tools was not the business on which the master was engaged. Reliance on the skill of the manufacturer was proper and almost inevitable. But that is not the defendant's situation. Both by its relation to the work and by the nature of its business, it is charged with a stricter duty.

Other rulings complained of have been considered, but no error has been found on them.

The judgment should be affirmed.

Griswold v. Connecticut, 85 S. Ct. 1678 (1965)

Griswold *involved the constitutional right of a married couple to purchase contraception. Of course, such a right is not expressly mentioned in the Constitution, yet the Court here found that such a right existed. How? The key to understanding* Griswold *is understanding the relationship between the right at issue and rights that the Court had found in earlier cases and* *rights that **are** expressly set forth in the Constitution. What do they have in common? Please be prepared to discuss Justice Douglas' legal reasoning.*

Mr. Justice DOUGLAS delivered the opinion of the Court.

Appellant Griswold is Executive Director of the Planned Parenthood League of Connecticut. Appellant Buxton is a licensed physician and a professor at the Yale Medical School who served as Medical Director for the League at its Center in New Haven—a center open and operating from November 1 to November 10, 1961, when appellants were arrested.

They gave information, instruction, and medical advice to married persons as to the means of preventing conception. They examined the wife and prescribed the best contraceptive device or material for her use. Fees were usually charged, although some couples were serviced free.

[Using or providing information about contraception was a crime under Connecticut law].

The appellants were found guilty as accessories and fined $100 each, against the claim that the accessory statute as so applied violated the Fourteenth Amendment. The Appellate Division of the Circuit Court affirmed. The Supreme Court of Errors affirmed that judgment. We noted probable jurisdiction.

*   *   *

Coming to the merits, we are met with a wide range of questions that implicate the Due Process Clause of the Fourteenth Amendment. Overtones of some arguments suggest that Lochner v. State of New York should be our guide. But we decline that invitation as we did in West Coast Hotel Co. v. Parrish; Olsen v. State of Nebraska; Lincoln Federal Labor Union v. Northwestern Co.; Williamson v. Lee Optical Co.; Giboney v. Empire Storage Co.

We do not sit as a super-legislature to determine the wisdom, need, and propriety of laws that touch economic problems, business affairs, or social conditions. This law, however, operates directly on an intimate relation of husband and wife and their physician's role in one aspect of that relation.

The association of people is not mentioned in the Constitution nor in the Bill of Rights. The right to educate a child in a school of the parents' choice—whether public or private or parochial—is also not mentioned. Nor is the right to study any particular subject or any foreign language. Yet the First Amendment has been construed to include certain of those rights.

By Pierce v. Society of Sisters the right to educate one's children as one chooses is made applicable to the States by the force of the First and Fourteenth Amendments. By Meyer v. State of Nebraska, the same dignity is given the right to study the German language in a private school. In other words, the State may not, consistently with the spirit of the First Amendment, contract the spectrum of available knowledge. The right of freedom of speech and press includes not only the right to utter or to print, but the right to distribute, the right to receive, the right to read and freedom of inquiry, freedom of thought, and freedom to teach—indeed the freedom of the entire university community. Without those peripheral rights the specific rights would be less secure. And so we reaffirm the principle of the Pierce and the Meyer cases.

In NAACP v. State of Alabama, we protected the 'freedom to associate and privacy in one's associations,' noting that freedom of association was a peripheral First Amendment right. Disclosure of membership lists of a constitutionally valid association, we held, was invalid 'as entailing the likelihood of a substantial restraint upon the exercise by petitioner's members of their right to freedom of association.' In other words, the First Amendment has a penumbra where privacy is protected from governmental intrusion. In like context, we have protected forms of 'association' that are not political in the customary sense but pertain to the social, legal, and economic benefit of the members.

In Schware v. Board of Bar Examiners, we held it not permissible to bar a lawyer from practice, because he had once been a member of the Communist Party. The man's association with that Party was not shown to be anything more than a political faith in a political party and was not action of a kind proving bad moral character.

Those cases involved more than the right of assembly—a right that extends to all irrespective of their race or ideology. The right of association, like the right of belief, is more than the right to attend a meeting; it includes the right to express one's attitudes or philosophies by membership in a group or by affiliation with it or by other lawful means. Association in that context is a form of expression of opinion; and while it is not expressly included in the First Amendment its existence is necessary in making the express guarantees fully meaningful.

The foregoing cases suggest that specific guarantees in the Bill of Rights have penumbras, formed by emanations from those guarantees that help give them life and substance. Various guarantees create zones of privacy. The right of association contained in the penumbra of the First Amendment is one, as we have seen. The Third Amendment in its prohibition against the quartering of soldiers in any house in time of peace without the consent of the owner is another facet of that privacy. The Fourth Amendment explicitly affirms the right of the people to be secure in their persons, houses, papers, and effects, against unreasonable searches and seizures. The Fifth Amendment in its Self-Incrimination Clause enables the citizen to create a zone of privacy which government may not force him to surrender to his detriment. The Ninth Amendment provides: The enumeration in the Constitution, of certain rights, shall not be construed to deny or disparage others retained by the people.

The Fourth and Fifth Amendments were described in Boyd v. United States as protection against all governmental invasions of the sanctity of a man's home and the privacies of life. We recently referred in Mapp v. Ohio to the Fourth Amendment as creating a right to privacy, no less important than any other right carefully and particularly reserved to the people.

We have had many controversies over these penumbral rights of privacy and repose. These cases bear witness that the right of privacy which presses for recognition here is a legitimate one.

The present case, then, concerns a relationship lying within the zone of privacy created by several fundamental constitutional guarantees. And it concerns a law which, in forbidding the use of contraceptives rather than regulating their manufacture or sale, seeks to achieve its goals by means having a maximum destructive impact upon that relationship. Such a law cannot stand in light of the familiar principle, so often applied by this Court, that a 'governmental purpose to control or prevent activities constitutionally subject to state regulation may not be achieved by means which sweep unnecessarily broadly and thereby invade the area of protected freedoms.' Would we allow the police to search the sacred precincts of marital bedrooms for telltale signs of the use of contraceptives? The very idea is repulsive to the notions of privacy surrounding the marriage relationship.

We deal with a right of privacy older than the Bill of Rights—older than our political parties, older than our school system. Marriage is a coming together for better or for worse, hopefully enduring, and intimate to the degree of being sacred. It is an association that promotes a way of life, not causes; a harmony in living, not political faiths; a bilateral loyalty, not commercial or social projects. Yet it is an association for as noble a purpose as any involved in our prior decisions.

Lawrence v. Texas, 539 U.S. 558 (2003)

What right is at issue in Lawrence v. Texas? *Is it in the Constitution? Is it the same right as that in* Griswold? *How does the Court get from* Griswold *to* Lawrence? *In reaching its conclusions, the Court finds it necessary to overrule one of its own cases,* Bowers v. Hardwick. *How come? What principles of legal reasoning does the Court use in overruling* Bowers?

Justice KENNEDY delivered the opinion of the Court.

Liberty protects the person from unwarranted government intrusions into a dwelling or other private places. In our tradition the State is not omnipresent in the home. And there are other spheres of our lives and existence, outside the home, where the State should not be a dominant presence. Freedom extends beyond spatial bounds. Liberty presumes an autonomy of self that includes freedom of thought, belief, expression, and certain intimate conduct. The instant case involves liberty of the person both in its spatial and in its more transcendent dimensions.

The question before the Court is the validity of a Texas statute making it a crime for two persons of the same sex to engage in certain intimate sexual conduct.

In Houston, Texas, officers of the Harris County Police Department were dispatched to a private residence in response to a reported weapons disturbance. They entered an apartment where one of the petitioners, John Geddes Lawrence, resided. The right of the police to enter does not seem to have been questioned. The officers observed Lawrence and another man, Tyron Garner, engaging in a sexual act. The two petitioners were arrested, held in custody overnight, and charged and convicted before a Justice of the Peace.

The complaints described their crime as "deviate sexual intercourse, namely anal sex, with a member of the same sex (man)." The applicable state law is Tex. Penal Code. It provides: "A person commits an offense if he engages in deviate sexual intercourse with another individual of the same sex."

*   *   *

The petitioners exercised their right to a trial de novo in Harris County Criminal Court. They challenged the statute as a violation of the Equal Protection Clause of the Fourteenth Amendment and of a like provision of the Texas Constitution. Those contentions were rejected. The petitioners, having entered a plea of nolo contendere, were each fined $200 and assessed court costs of $141.25.

The Court of Appeals for the Texas Fourteenth District considered the petitioners' federal constitutional arguments under both the Equal Protection and Due Process Clauses of the Fourteenth Amendment. After hearing the case en banc the court, in a divided opinion, rejected the constitutional arguments and affirmed the convictions. The majority opinion indicates that the Court of Appeals considered our decision in Bowers v. Hardwick, to be controlling on the federal due process aspect of the case. Bowers then being authoritative, this was proper.

We granted certiorari to consider three questions:

1. Whether petitioners' criminal convictions under the Texas 'Homosexual Conduct' law—which criminalizes sexual intimacy by same-sex couples, but not identical behavior by different-sex couples—violate the Fourteenth Amendment guarantee of equal protection of the laws,

2. Whether petitioners' criminal convictions for adult consensual sexual intimacy in the home violate their vital interests in liberty and privacy protected by the Due Process Clause of the Fourteenth Amendment.

3. Whether Bowers v. Hardwick should be overruled.

The petitioners were adults at the time of the alleged offense. Their conduct was in private and consensual.

We conclude the case should be resolved by determining whether the petitioners were free as adults to engage in the private conduct in the exercise of their liberty under the Due Process Clause of the Fourteenth Amendment to the Constitution. For this inquiry we deem it necessary to reconsider the Court's holding in Bowers.

There are broad statements of the substantive reach of liberty under the Due Process Clause in earlier cases, including Pierce v. Society of Sisters and Meyer v. Nebraska, but the most pertinent beginning point is our decision in Griswold v. Connecticut.

In Griswold the Court invalidated a state law prohibiting the use of drugs or devices of contraception and counseling or aiding and abetting the use of contraceptives. The Court described the protected interest as a right to privacy and placed emphasis on the marriage relation and the protected space of the marital bedroom.

After Griswold it was established that the right to make certain decisions regarding sexual conduct extends beyond the marital relationship. In Eisenstadt v. Baird, the Court invalidated a law prohibiting the distribution of contraceptives to unmarried persons. The case was decided under the Equal Protection Clause;

but with respect to unmarried persons, the Court went on to state the fundamental proposition that the law impaired the exercise of their personal rights. It quoted from the statement of the Court of Appeals finding the law to be in conflict with fundamental human rights, and it followed with this statement of its own:

> "It is true that in Griswold the right of privacy in question inhered in the marital relationship .... If the right of privacy means anything, it is the right of the individual, married or single, to be free from unwarranted governmental intrusion into matters so fundamentally affecting a person as the decision whether to bear or beget a child."

The opinions in Griswold and Eisenstadt were part of the background for the decision in Roe v. Wade. As is well known, the case involved a challenge to the Texas law prohibiting abortions, but the laws of other States were affected as well. Although the Court held the woman's rights were not absolute, her right to elect an abortion did have real and substantial protection as an exercise of her liberty under the Due Process Clause. The Court cited cases that protect spatial freedom and cases that go well beyond it. Roe recognized the right of a woman to make certain fundamental decisions affecting her destiny and confirmed once more that the protection of liberty under the Due Process Clause has a substantive dimension of fundamental significance in defining the rights of the person.

In Carey v. Population Services Int'l, the Court confronted a New York law forbidding sale or distribution of contraceptive devices to persons under 16 years of age. Although there was no single opinion for the Court, the law was invalidated. Both Eisenstadt and Carey, as well as the holding and rationale in Roe, confirmed that the reasoning of Griswold could not be confined to the protection of rights of married adults. This was the state of the law with respect to some of the most relevant cases when the Court considered Bowers v. Hardwick.

The facts in Bowers had some similarities to the instant case. A police officer, whose right to enter seems not to have been in question, observed Hardwick, in his own bedroom, engaging in intimate sexual conduct with another adult male. The conduct was in violation of a Georgia statute making it a criminal offense to engage in sodomy. One difference between the two cases is that the Georgia statute prohibited the conduct whether or not the participants were of the same sex, while the Texas statute, as we have seen, applies only to participants of the same sex. Hardwick was not prosecuted, but he brought an action in federal court to declare the state statute invalid. He alleged he was a practicing homosexual and that the criminal prohibition violated rights guaranteed to him by the Constitution. The Court, in an opinion by Justice White, sustained the Georgia law. Chief Justice Burger and Justice Powell joined the opinion of the Court and filed separate, concurring opinions. Four Justices dissented.

The Court began its substantive discussion in Bowers as follows: "The issue presented is whether the Federal Constitution confers a fundamental right upon homosexuals to engage in sodomy and hence invalidates the laws of the many States that still make such conduct illegal and have done so for a very long time." That statement, we now conclude, discloses the Court's own failure to appreciate the extent of the liberty at stake. To say that the issue in Bowers was simply the right to engage in certain sexual conduct demeans the claim the individual put forward, just as it would demean a married couple were it to be said marriage is simply about the right to have sexual intercourse. The laws involved in Bowers and here are, to be sure, statutes that purport to do no more than prohibit a particular sexual act. Their penalties and purposes, though, have more far-reaching consequences, touching upon the most private human conduct, sexual behavior, and in the most private of places, the home. The statutes do seek to control a personal relationship that, whether or not entitled to formal recognition in the law, is within the liberty of persons to choose without being punished as criminals.

This, as a general rule, should counsel against attempts by the State, or a court, to define the meaning of the relationship or to set its boundaries absent injury to a person or abuse of an institution the law protects. It suffices for us to acknowledge that adults may choose to enter upon this relationship in the confines of their homes and their own private lives and still retain their dignity as free persons. When sexuality finds overt expression in intimate conduct with another person, the conduct can be but one element in a personal bond that is more enduring. The liberty protected by the Constitution allows homosexual persons the right to make this choice.

Having misapprehended the claim of liberty there presented to it, and thus stating the claim to be whether there is a fundamental right to engage in consensual sodomy, the Bowers Court said: "Proscriptions against that conduct have ancient roots." In academic writings, and in many of the scholarly amicus briefs filed to assist the Court in this case, there are fundamental criticisms of the historical premises relied upon by the majority and concurring opinions in Bowers. We need not enter this debate in the attempt to reach a definitive historical judgment, but the following considerations counsel against adopting the definitive conclusions upon which Bowers placed such reliance.

At the outset it should be noted that there is no longstanding history in this country of laws directed at homosexual conduct as a distinct matter. Beginning in colonial times there were prohibitions of sodomy derived from the English criminal laws passed in the first instance by the Reformation Parliament of 1533. The English prohibition was understood to include relations between men and women as well as relations between men and men. Nineteenth-century commentators similarly read American sodomy, buggery, and crime-against-nature statutes as criminalizing certain relations between men and women and between men and men. The absence of legal prohibitions focusing on homosexual conduct may be explained in part by noting that according to some scholars the concept of the homosexual as a distinct category of person did not emerge until the late 19th century. Thus early American sodomy laws were not directed at homosexuals as such but instead sought to prohibit nonprocreative sexual activity more generally. This does not suggest approval of homosexual conduct. It does tend to show that this particular form of conduct was not thought of as a separate category from like conduct between heterosexual persons.

Laws prohibiting sodomy do not seem to have been enforced against consenting adults acting in private. A substantial number of sodomy prosecutions and convictions for which there are surviving records were for predatory acts against those who could not or did not consent, as in the case of a minor or the victim of an assault. As to these, one purpose for the prohibitions was to ensure there would be no lack of coverage if a predator committed a sexual assault that did not constitute rape as defined by the criminal law. Thus the model sodomy indictments presented in a 19th-century treatise addressed the predatory acts of an adult man against a minor girl or minor boy. Instead of targeting relations between consenting adults in private, 19th-century sodomy prosecutions typically involved relations between men and minor girls or minor boys, relations between adults involving force, relations between adults implicating disparity in status, or relations between men and animals.

To the extent that there were any prosecutions for the acts in question, 19th-century evidence rules imposed a burden that would make a conviction more difficult to obtain even taking into account the problems always inherent in prosecuting consensual acts committed in private. Under then-prevailing standards, a man could not be convicted of sodomy based upon testimony of a consenting partner, because the partner was considered an accomplice. A partner's testimony, however, was admissible if he or she had not consented to the act or was a minor, and therefore incapable of consent. The rule may explain in part the infrequency of these prosecutions. In all events that infrequency makes it difficult to say that society approved of a rigorous and systematic punishment of the consensual acts committed in private and by adults. The longstanding criminal prohibition of homosexual sodomy upon which the Bowers decision placed such reliance is as consistent with a general condemnation of nonprocreative sex as it is with an established tradition of prosecuting acts because of their homosexual character.

The policy of punishing consenting adults for private acts was not much discussed in the early legal literature. We can infer that one reason for this was the very private nature of the conduct. Despite the absence of prosecutions, there may have been periods in which there was public criticism of homosexuals as such and an insistence that the criminal laws be enforced to discourage their practices. But far from possessing "ancient roots," American laws targeting same-sex couples did not develop until the last third of the 20th century. The reported decisions concerning the prosecution of consensual, homosexual sodomy between adults for the years 1880–1995 are not always clear in the details, but a significant number involved conduct in a public place.

It was not until the 1970's that any State singled out same-sex relations for criminal prosecution, and only nine States have done so. Post-Bowers even some of these States did not adhere to the policy of suppressing homosexual conduct. Over the course of the last decades, States with same-sex prohibitions have moved toward abolishing them.

In summary, the historical grounds relied upon in Bowers are more complex than the majority opinion and the concurring opinion by Chief Justice Burger indicate. Their historical premises are not without doubt and, at the very least, are overstated.

It must be acknowledged, of course, that the Court in Bowers was making the broader point that for centuries there have been powerful voices to condemn homosexual conduct as immoral. The condemnation has been shaped by religious beliefs, conceptions of right and acceptable behavior, and respect for the traditional family. For many persons these are not trivial concerns but profound and deep convictions accepted as ethical and moral principles to which they aspire and which thus determine the course of their lives. These considerations do not answer the question before us, however. The issue is whether the majority may use the power of the State to enforce these views on the whole society through operation of the criminal law. "Our obligation is to define the liberty of all, not to mandate our own moral code.

*   *   *

Two principal cases decided after Bowers cast its holding into even more doubt. In Planned Parenthood of Southeastern Pa. v. Casey, the Court reaffirmed the substantive force of the liberty protected by the Due Process Clause. The Casey decision again confirmed that our laws and tradition afford constitutional protection to personal decisions relating to marriage, procreation, contraception, family relationships, child rearing, and education. In explaining the respect the Constitution demands for the autonomy of the person in making these choices, we stated as follows:

> "These matters, involving the most intimate and personal choices a person may make in a lifetime, choices central to personal dignity and autonomy, are central to the liberty protected by the Fourteenth Amendment. At the heart of liberty is the right to define one's own concept of existence, of meaning, of the universe, and of the mystery of human life. Beliefs about these matters could not define the attributes of personhood were they formed under compulsion of the State."

Persons in a homosexual relationship may seek autonomy for these purposes, just as heterosexual persons do. The decision in Bowers would deny them this right.

The second post-Bowers case of principal relevance is Romer v. Evans. There the Court struck down class-based legislation directed at homosexuals as a violation of the Equal Protection Clause. Romer invalidated an amendment to Colorado's Constitution which named as a solitary class persons who were homosexuals, lesbians, or bisexual either by "orientation, conduct, practices or relationships," and deprived them of protection under state antidiscrimination laws. We concluded that the provision was "born of animosity toward the class of persons affected" and further that it had no rational relation to a legitimate governmental purpose.

As an alternative argument in this case, counsel for the petitioners and some amici contend that Romer provides the basis for declaring the Texas statute invalid under the Equal Protection Clause. That is a tenable argument, but we conclude the instant case requires us to address whether Bowers itself has continuing validity. Were we to hold the statute invalid under the Equal Protection Clause some might question whether a prohibition would be valid if drawn differently, say, to prohibit the conduct both between same-sex and different-sex participants.

Equality of treatment and the due process right to demand respect for conduct protected by the substantive guarantee of liberty are linked in important respects, and a decision on the latter point advances both interests. If protected conduct is made criminal and the law which does so remains unexamined for its substantive validity, its stigma might remain even if it were not enforceable as drawn for equal protection reasons. When homosexual conduct is made criminal by the law of the State, that declaration in and of itself is an invitation to subject homosexual persons to discrimination both in the public and in the private spheres. The central holding of Bowers has been brought in question by this case, and it should be addressed. Its continuance as precedent demeans the lives of homosexual persons.

The stigma this criminal statute imposes, moreover, is not trivial. The offense, to be sure, is but a class C misdemeanor, a minor offense in the Texas legal system. Still, it remains a criminal offense with all that imports for the dignity of the persons charged. The petitioners will bear on their record the history of their criminal convictions. Just this Term we rejected various challenges to state laws requiring the registration of sex offenders. We are advised that if Texas convicted an adult for private, consensual homosexual conduct under the statute here in question the convicted person would come within the registration laws of at least four States were he or she to be subject to their jurisdiction. This underscores the consequential nature of the punishment and the state-sponsored condemnation attendant to the criminal prohibition. Furthermore, the Texas criminal conviction carries with it the other collateral consequences always following a conviction, such as notations on job application forms, to mention but one example.

The foundations of Bowers have sustained serious erosion from our recent decisions in Casey and Romer. When our precedent has been thus weakened, criticism from other sources is of greater significance. In the United States criticism of Bowers has been substantial and continuing, disapproving of its reasoning in all respects, not just as to its historical assumptions. The courts of five different States have declined to follow it in interpreting provisions in their own state constitutions parallel to the Due Process Clause of the Fourteenth Amendment.

*   *   *

The doctrine of stare decisis is essential to the respect accorded to the judgments of the Court and to the stability of the law. It is not, however, an inexorable command. In Casey we noted that when a court is asked to overrule a precedent recognizing a constitutional liberty interest, individual or societal reliance on the existence of that liberty cautions with particular strength against reversing course. The holding in Bowers, however, has not induced detrimental reliance comparable to some instances where recognized individual rights are involved. Indeed, there has been no individual or societal reliance on Bowers of the sort that could counsel against overturning its holding once there are compelling reasons to do so. Bowers itself causes uncertainty, for the precedents before and after its issuance contradict its central holding.

The rationale of Bowers does not withstand careful analysis. In his dissenting opinion in Bowers Justice Stevens came to these conclusions:

> "Our prior cases make two propositions abundantly clear. First, the fact that the governing majority in a State has traditionally viewed a particular practice as immoral is not a sufficient reason for upholding a law prohibiting the practice; neither history nor tradition could save a law prohibiting miscegenation from constitutional attack. Second, individual decisions by married persons, concerning the intimacies of their physical relationship, even when not intended to produce offspring, are a form of 'liberty' protected by the Due Process Clause of the Fourteenth Amendment. Moreover, this protection extends to intimate choices by unmarried as well as married persons."

Justice Stevens' analysis, in our view, should have been controlling in Bowers and should control here.

Bowers was not correct when it was decided, and it is not correct today. It ought not to remain binding precedent. Bowers v. Hardwick should be and now is overruled.

The present case does not involve minors. It does not involve persons who might be injured or coerced or who are situated in relationships where consent might not easily be refused. It does not involve public conduct or prostitution. It does not involve whether the government must give formal recognition to any relationship that homosexual persons seek to enter. The case does involve two adults who, with full and mutual consent from each other, engaged in sexual practices common to a homosexual lifestyle. The petitioners are entitled to respect for their private lives. The State cannot demean their existence or control their destiny by making their private sexual conduct a crime. Their right to liberty under the Due Process Clause gives them the full right to engage in their conduct without intervention of the government. "It is a promise of the Constitution that there is a realm of personal liberty which the government may not enter." The Texas statute furthers no legitimate state interest which can justify its intrusion into the personal and private life of the individual.

Had those who drew and ratified the Due Process Clauses of the Fifth Amendment or the Fourteenth Amendment known the components of liberty in its manifold possibilities, they might have been more specific. They did not presume to have this insight. They knew times can blind us to certain truths and later generations can see that laws once thought necessary and proper in fact serve only to oppress. As the Constitution endures, persons in every generation can invoke its principles in their own search for greater freedom.

The judgment of the Court of Appeals for the Texas Fourteenth District is reversed, and the case is remanded for further proceedings not inconsistent with this opinion.

Acme Markets v. Federal Armored Express, 648 A.2d 1218 (Pa. Super. Ct. 1994)

How does the court in the case below apply the relevant rules and cases to reach a decision?

Opinion

Acme Markets, Inc., appeals from the order entered in the Court of Common Pleas of Montgomery County on December 21, 1993, which granted Federal Armored Express, Inc. ("Federal") summary judgment. For the reasons set forth below, we reverse that order and remand the matter for further proceedings.

The procedural history of this case may be summarized as follows. On November 20, 1990, appellant filed a breach of contract complaint against Federal. In that complaint, appellant alleged that the parties had entered into a contract for armored car service and that the agreement later was amended to provide for the timely reimbursement of service-related losses. In addition, appellant averred that a Federal employee was robbed on May 19, 1990, after accepting possession of one of appellant's cashbags. Finally, appellant asserted that even though it had notified Federal promptly of the $62,544.32 loss, Federal had not made the reimbursement required by the agreement. Consequently, appellant requested, among other things, an award of damages equivalent to the amount of the loss.

On September 26, 1991, following the effectuation of service, appellant filed an answer and new matter. In connection with one of the defenses asserted in that document, Federal relied upon the fifth paragraph of the agreement which provides, "Responsibility of Federal under this contract shall begin when said [cash]bags or packages have been accepted and receipted for by Federal or its authorized employees, and shall terminate upon delivery to consignee or upon return to shipper." Specifically, Federal claimed that it bore no responsibility for the loss since neither it nor any of its employees had accepted the bag or provided the necessary receipt prior to the robbery.

On June 30, 1993, claiming that discovery was complete and that an examination of the record revealed no genuine issue of material fact, appellant moved for summary judgment. Federal responded by filing a cross-motion for summary judgment in which it acknowledged that one of its employees possessed appellant's cashbag at the time of the robbery. In addition, Federal noted that neither party disputed the fact that the employee in question had not provided a receipt for the bag prior to its loss. Consequently, relying upon both the fifth paragraph of the agreement and an affidavit demonstrating that the receipt requirement conformed with the custom of the armored car industry, Federal requested the entrance of judgment in its favor. On December 21, 1993, the trial court concluded that the fifth paragraph constituted a condition precedent to Federal's liability under the agreement. Thus, the court denied appellant's summary judgment motion and granted Federal relief. This timely appeal followed.

Preliminarily, we note that our scope of review from a grant of summary judgment is plenary.

In reviewing an order granting a motion for summary judgment, we must view the record in the light most favorable to the non-moving party. All doubts as to the existence of a genuine issue of material fact must be resolved against the moving party. Moreover, in summary judgment proceedings, it is not the court's function to determine the facts, but only to determine if an issue of material fact exists. Summary judgment should only be granted in those cases which are free and clear from doubt.

Summary judgment is proper only where the pleadings, depositions, answers to interrogatories, admissions of record and affidavits on file support the trial court's conclusion that no genuine issue of material fact exists and [that] the moving party is entitled to judgment as a matter of law.

Furthermore, we will not overturn a trial court's grant of summary judgment in the absence of either an error of law or a clear abuse of discretion. Keeping these principles in mind, we consider the propriety of the contested summary judgment grant.

Appellant asserts that the trial court erroneously concluded that the fifth paragraph of the agreement constituted a condition precedent to Federal's liability for the lost bag. Specifically, appellant argues that since the paragraph was not labelled a condition precedent and does not contain other language normally associated with such a condition, "[t]here is no means by which to state with the certainty required by Pennsylvania law that it creates a condition precedent." We find appellant's claim devoid of merit.

Initially, we note that a condition precedent may be defined as a condition which must occur before a duty to perform under a contract arises. While the parties to a contract need not utilize any particular words to create a condition precedent, an act or event designated in a contract will not be construed as constituting one unless that clearly appears to have been the parties' intention. In addition, we note that the purpose of any condition set forth in a contract must be determined in accordance with the general rules of contractual interpretation. Those rules may be summarized as follows.

When construing agreements involving clear and unambiguous terms, this Court need only examine the writing itself to give effect to the parties' understanding. The court must construe the contract only as written and may not modify the plain meaning of the words under the guise of interpretation. When the terms of a written contract are clear, this Court will not re-write it to give it a construction in conflict with the accepted and plain meaning of the language used. Conversely, when the language is ambiguous and the intention of the parties cannot be reasonably ascertained from the language of the writing alone, the parol evidence rule does not apply to the admission of oral testimony to show both the intent of the parties and the circumstances attending the execution of the contract.

In the present case, the contested paragraph indicates that Federal's responsibility under the contract "shall begin when ... bags or packages have been accepted and receipted for by Federal or its employees...." Our reading of this plain language demonstrates that it clearly and unambiguously conditions Federal's performance under the contract upon both the acceptance of bags or packages and the granting of a receipt for them. Thus, it unquestionably delineates a condition precedent involving those requirements.

Since we have found that Federal's liability under the contract was subject to a condition precedent and neither party disputes that the receipt portion of the condition remained unfulfilled at the time of the robbery, we must determine whether satisfaction of that requirement may be excused. Apparently arguing that strict application of the condition would be unfair, appellant asserts that the receipt requirement was immaterial and could only be seen as incidental to the far more significant satisfied requirement of possession and acceptance by Federal's employee of appellant's property.

Restatement (Second) of Contracts discusses the excuse of a condition to avoid unfairness in connection with its strict enforcement. More specifically, that section relates to the excuse of a condition leading to a forfeiture, a term referring to "the denial of compensation that results when the obligee loses his right to the agreed exchange after he has relied substantially, as by preparation or performance on the expectation of that exchange." Restatement (Second) of Contracts provides, "To the extent that the non-occurrence of a condition would cause disproportionate forfeiture, a court may excuse the non-occurrence of that condition unless its occurrence was a material part of the agreed exchange." Since Pennsylvania law "abhors forfeitures and penalties and enforces them with the greatest reluctance when a proper case is presented[,]" Fogel Refrigerator Co. v. Oteri is consistent with the law of this Commonwealth. Consequently, we will apply it in the present case.

There can be little doubt that the operation of the condition in question will lead to a forfeiture since the condition's nonoccurrence results in the denial of compensation for the loss of a cashbag possessed by Federal for transportation in accordance with the contract. Thus, the question becomes whether the forfeiture would be disproportionate.

In determining whether the forfeiture is "disproportionate," [the] court must weigh the extent of the forfeiture by the obligee against the importance to the obligor of the risk from which he sought to be protected and the degree to which that protection will be lost if the nonoccurrence of the condition is excused to the extent required to prevent forfeiture.

In the present case, appellant obviously entered into the armored car service contract so that it would have a secure method of transporting cash and checks to the bank. Strict application of the condition precedent would result in the loss of appellant's ability to recover from Federal for the theft of the bag entrusted to Federal's care. Moreover, we believe that the receipting requirement was intended to provide Federal with proof that it accepted, at a specific time, a certain number of cashbags for shipment. Thus, in our opinion, the requirement probably was little more than an accounting device designed to track bags picked up in accordance with the agreement. Under such circumstances, the receipt primarily would serve to protect Federal rather than Acme from, among other things, theft by its own employees and disputes regarding the number of bags accepted. Those are two risks not at issue herein.

While we believe that the receipt requirement probably was an accounting device which had little impact upon the situation presently at issue, our examination of the certified record reveals that it is devoid of any evidence demonstrating the requirement's actual purpose. Thus, even though we have speculated on the matter, the record is inadequate to determine whether our speculation is accurate. In view of the inadequate record, we may not conduct the critical weighing analysis required by the Restatement or determine whether fulfillment of the condition may be excused. Indeed, we note that the trial court erroneously believed that its analysis ended upon concluding that a receipt was required to fulfill the condition precedent. Thus, the court did not consider whether the forfeiture would be disproportionate, decide if the receipt requirement constituted a material part of the exchange, or require the parties to provide an adequate record either for resolving those issues or deciding whether summary judgment in favor of Federal would be appropriate. Accordingly, we must reverse the trial court's grant of summary judgment and remand the matter for further proceedings.

On remand, the trial court should conduct an evidentiary hearing to determine the purpose of the receipt requirement and engage in the necessary weighing analysis. In addition, the court should determine whether the contested requirement constituted a material part of the agreement. While this determination rests to a large extent on the analysis of the requirement's purpose, it also involves a consideration of the negotiations of the parties along with all other circumstances relevant to the formation of the contract or to the requirement itself, including the circumstances surrounding the theft.

Order reversed. Case remanded for further proceedings. Jurisdiction relinquished.

*   *   *

Chapter 4: Applying Cases to Facts

Introduction

Litigators rely on cases in making legal argument. This is due to the legal reasoning process discussed in an earlier chapter. The first step in this process is effective legal research; finding the cases and other authority that apply to your facts and will support your argument to the court. Once the cases are collected, it is time to assemble them into a persuasive whole. This is done in writing through an analytical and organizational framework called **IRAC; Issue, Rule, Analysis, Conclusion.**

Both of these concepts, legal research and constructing legal argument using IRAC, will be discussed in detail in this chapter.

Legal Research Method

Legal research is a process. It is a process that involves the distillation of key concepts involved in any particular legal problem, the selection of the proper source in which to research those concepts, and then an analysis of research results.

The same four steps are used in legal research whether researching online or in print.

Step One. *Analyze problem and formulate key terms or concepts.*

Legal issues almost always begin with a story, generally one told you by a client or supervisor. The story outlines a problem or challenge. Perhaps your client is being sued in New York in a shareholder derivative action for allegedly improper payments to interested directors. Or, perhaps your supervisor would like to see an analysis of the law related to dog bites in the state of Iowa.

It doesn't really matter what the story is because your approach to it will generally be the same. The first step is to analyze the story told you and distill its key concepts and terms. This is generally the who, what, where, when, and why of the story.

~Who~

In addition to determining which person is likely to be the plaintiff or the defendant, you want to be on the lookout for special relationships between the parties. Common relationships include parent/child, doctor/patient, attorney/client, landlord/tenant, and employer/employee. You may also be interested in fiduciaries, invitees, executors, and others to whom the law assigns special roles.

~What~

Every factual scenario is a story composed of plot points. Your job is to determine which facts in the story are legally significant. You also want to think of legal keywords relating to the plot points and determine potential claims or defenses based on the plot points.

~Where~

The location where the incident took place may be relevant for a couple of reasons. First, the geographic location of the incident may determine which state's law applies and which court has jurisdiction. Additionally, location may be a legally relevant fact. For example, in instances of landlord liability for injuries to tenants' guests, the outcome might differ if the injury took place in the common area of an apartment building as opposed to a tenant's unit.

~When~

The date of the incident is important for statute of limitations purposes, but should also be considered when determining what the law was at the time the incident occurred. For example, if your client had a campfire in his backyard on May 31st, and the state he lived in passed a statute criminalizing this behavior on the following July 1st, the dates would be very relevant if the state attempted to prosecute your client under the statute for the fire he lit before the statute's effective date. The "when" question also includes the order in which particular events occurred. The sequence of events and the amount of time in between them are often crucial when one is trying to prove causation.

~Why~

You are not always going to be able to answer the "why" question, but it is often relevant. In criminal law, offenses are often distinguished based on the intent, or mens rea, that accompanies the act. Intent is also relevant in common law torts and contracts cases as well as in certain statutory rights of action.

We can apply these ideas to the two simple examples noted earlier. In the case of your client sued in New York, the key concepts/terms are "New York," "shareholder derivative action," "payments," and "interested directors." In the case of the supervisor interested in Iowa law, the key concept/terms are "Iowa" and "dog bites." If we were researching these issues online, we would use these terms to search in an appropriate database. If researching in print, we would look these terms up in an applicable index.

Step Two. *Select a jurisdiction when searching for primary authority; know your jurisdiction when searching for secondary.*

Legal authority is jurisdiction specific, whether the jurisdiction is federal or that of an individual state. Researching in the proper jurisdiction is therefore vital. In our examples, the jurisdictions are New York and Iowa.

Step Three. *Use key terms to search an index or a database.*

This step is where the action is. As noted, take your key terms and enter them into the search box in an appropriate online database or look them up in the index to an appropriate print source. This will provide you with a set of potentially relevant results for analysis.

Step Four. *Analyze results.*

The final step is to analyze your set of potentially relevant results and determine which among them is applicable to your legal issue. If your research has been effective, you should be able to answer the question your client or supervisor has asked. Often your results will point you to more sources, which will require more analysis.

Importance of Cases

Cases are important to the parties to the dispute in question, of course, but to others as well because they have precedential value. For our purposes, precedent means a "decided case that furnishes a basis for determining later cases involving similar facts or issues." The decided case can be binding precedent, which means a "precedent that a court must follow," because it is from a higher court within the same jurisdiction, or the decided case can be persuasive precedent, which is a "precedent that is not binding on a court, but that is entitled to respect and careful consideration." This could be a decided case from a court at the same level in the same jurisdiction or from a court in a neighboring jurisdiction. Either way, the court is not bound by the earlier case, but may use its reasoning in deciding the case before it.

For example, all federal trial courts in the First Circuit (covering Maine, Massachusetts, New Hampshire, Puerto Rico, and Rhode Island) must adhere to applicable precedent from the First Circuit Court of Appeals, as decisions from that court are binding precedent on them. On the other hand the federal trial court in the District of Massachusetts may follow the reasoning from a case in the District of Maine if it finds that reasoning persuasive. Similarly, all courts in the First Circuit, including the Court of Appeals, must adhere to precedent from the United States Supreme Court, and may follow persuasive precedent in the form of decided cases from outside the circuit if they choose.

Recognizing that cases have precedential value provides the key reason for why lawyers research and use them. Simply, lawyers look for prior decided cases that have outcomes favorable to their clients and that are most similar in terms of facts and legal issues to the situations facing their clients. Once these cases are located, the lawyer argues that the result in the earlier case, as either binding or persuasive precedent, should control or inform the outcome for her client in the present case.

In other words, the "best" case you can find is normally, (1) binding precedent from your jurisdiction that is (2) similar in facts and issues to your case, and (3) where the outcome of the case is favorable to your client. By "favorable outcome", I mean that if you're seeking dismissal of a case based on a particular issue, you want a case that dismisses on that issue, etc. Once you find that "best" case, simply compare it to your client's situation and argue that the outcome for your client should be the same as that in the earlier decided case.

Researching Cases

This section will discuss solving case law research problems involving different levels of complexity by searching for cases using a legal database like Westlaw or Lexis.

One of the most basic types of case law research problems is the "single issue" problem. This type of problem involves finding the key case on a single issue. Examples of these research problems are below.

• Find the United States Supreme Court case on corporate spending and political speech in elections.

• Find the New York case authored by then Chief Justice Cardozo on causation in tort cases in the context of an accident on a railroad platform.

• Find the federal bankruptcy case involving Bernie Madoff's investment company.

With questions like these, even though the problem is merely "single issue," the research method discussed previously remains the same. Below is application of the method using the first example on corporate spending and political speech.

Step one. Analyze problem and formulate key terms or concepts.

The key concepts here are two; "corporate spending" and "political speech." These will be our search terms.

Step Two. *Select a jurisdiction when searching for primary authority; know your jurisdiction when searching for secondary.*

The jurisdiction or court here is the United States Supreme Court.

Step Three. *Use key terms to search an index or a database.*

Now, using our key terms, it's time search in the relevant database, which is that for the Supreme Court.

Step Four. *Analyze results.*

In our result list, the first case is called *Citizens United*, and it is the one we're looking for.

See how it works? Please try the other single-issue examples yourself.

A second common case law research question is the "elements" question; that is, the lawyer or student is asked to find the elements of a particular cause of action or crime. This type of question is extremely important to a litigator or trial lawyer as it defines the claim the lawyer must ultimately prove or defend against. Examples of this type of question are below.

- Find the elements for a claim of fraud under Massachusetts law.

- Find the elements for a claim of copyright infringement under federal law.

- Find the elements for the crime of burglary under Michigan law.

Here too, we use the four-step research method.

Step One. *Analyze problem and formulate key terms or concepts.*

In the first example, the key concepts/search terms are "fraud" and "elements."

Step Two. *Select a jurisdiction when searching for primary authority; know your jurisdiction when searching for secondary.*

The proper jurisdiction is Massachusetts.

Step Three. *Use key terms to search an index or a database.*

We will search using the terms "fraud" and "elements" in the Massachusetts case law database.

Step Four. *Analyze results.*

The first case is helpful. It sets forth the elements of fraud and provides citations to cases that may also be helpful.

Finally, there is the legal research question that generally involves the lawyer trying to solve or analyze a complex problem presented by a client. An example is below.

> *Marlo Mackintosh is a famous celebrity. As such, she spends a large part of her day "tweeting" photos and descriptions of her various activities to her smallish cohort of followers. Actually, this is pretty much all she does. Anyway, Marlo has sought your counsel regarding her greatest fear; the dreaded "retweet." That is, she fears that some of her paltry band of followers are unscrupulous and will attempt to publish her tweeted photos without attribution or payment. Marlo wants to know what rights she has in her tweeted photos and whether she can stop others from publishing them. Research Marlo's question using federal law. And hurry! Marlo is just dying to tweet photos from her latest mani-pedi!*

Using the above example, follow the four steps of the research method.

Sample Fact Pattern: Ice Skating

Below is a sample fact pattern. Please apply the legal research method set forth above to it. For our purposes, you simply need to analyze the fact pattern, formulate key terms and concepts, and select a jurisdiction.

Now, imagine that you have searched using your key terms and concepts and have found three relevant cases. The cases are set forth immediately following the fact pattern. Read them. You will need to discuss in class how to use these cases in constructing your legal argument for the Bear Lake Country Club.

You represent the Bear Lake Country Club in the following example.

Johnny Hoy was born and raised in Kona on the Big Island of Hawaii. Hoy was a top athlete and student at Kamehakameha High School in Kona. Upon graduating high school, Hoy attended the University of Hawaii where he was captain of the surfing team and a Phi Beta Kappa student. In his senior year, Hoy decided to take the LSAT and scored a perfect 180. Given his outstanding credentials, he was easily admitted to Harvard Law School. In September 2019, Hoy left Kona for Cambridge, Massachusetts. He had never left the Hawaiian Islands before leaving for law school.

Hoy enjoyed his first New England fall, but he was most excited about his first winter. After all, he had never seen snow before. Hoy had grown up a fanatic fan of men's figure skating. Every four years he was glued to Winter Olympics coverage; Scott Hamilton, Paul Wylie, and Johnny Wier were some of his favorites. Hoy could not wait for the ice to freeze so that he could try to skate himself.

December 2019 began with a week of very cold temperatures. The average temperature during that week was 10 degrees Fahrenheit. Hoy was busy drafting his final research and writing class memo that week so he could not get on the ice. The beginning of the next week was quite a bit warmer; temperatures were about 57 degrees Fahrenheit -- which was still a bit chilly for Hoy. Hoy finished his memo and decided to go for his first skate on Wednesday of that week. A friend in his section from Buffalo offered him a pair of skates and told him about a lake that was part of the Bear Lake Country Club in Brookline, Massachusetts.

Hoy borrowed his friend's skates, put on his spandex skating outfit and took the "T" to the Bear Lake Country Club. The Club had a sign posted stating "Skaters Welcome." The ice was empty as Hoy approached, but Hoy was so excited that he just kept on going. Three feet onto the ice, Hoy heard cracking and fell through. He was submerged for several minutes under the ice and suffered an injury that forced him to withdraw from Harvard.

Hoy has sued the Bear Lake Country Club in Massachusetts Superior Court for failing to warn him about the danger of thin ice.

Is there a duty to warn in this case? Why or why not? To answer this question, please review the three cases set forth below. Don't expect to find a case with facts identical to our situation. You will need to make an argument by analogy. In making your argument, please discuss why each case is helpful or not.

Sweet v. Cieslak, 499 N.E.2d 1218 (Mass. App. Ct. 1986)

As this case has now been tried to conclusion, there is no longer any occasion to consider the propriety of the order denying the defendant's motion for summary judgment. A careful review of all the evidence (and in particular the plaintiff's testimony as to the wet, icy conditions which he observed inside the self service bay of the car wash facility long before he ultimately lost his footing) compels the conclusion that the defendant should have had a directed verdict in the Superior Court because he was under no duty to warn one such as the plaintiff of the open and obvious danger of attempting to wash a car in near zero weather. There is nothing in Mounsey v. Ellard, or in Upham v. Chateau de Ville Dinner Theatre, Inc., which casts doubt on the continued vitality of the rules explicated and adhered to in the cases cited above. Indeed, it is clear from the face of the opinion in the Mounsey case that the court did not enlarge the duty of an owner or occupier of real estate except to the extent that it abolished the distinction between licensees and invitees. In the Upham case the court went no further than to abrogate the rule that a defendant's adherence to a relevant industry standard constituted conclusive proof of no negligence on his part. No such question was presented in this case. We are not persuaded that the concluding ("unless") clause of the Restatement (Second) of Torts reflects the law of this Commonwealth. If that clause does state the law of the Commonwealth, it does not apply in the circumstances of this case.

Greenslade v. Mohawk Park, Inc., 798 N.E.2d 336 (Mass. App. Ct. 2003)

After Arthur Greenslade sustained serious injuries as the result of falling from a rope swing, he commenced an action in Superior Court against Mohawk Park, Inc., the owner of a seasonal campground where Greenslade was camping when he was injured. The rope swing was attached to the limb of a tree on land owned by Joanne and Larry Lemek, located on the river bank opposite Mohawk Park's property. Greenslade appeals the summary judgment in favor of Mohawk Park. We affirm.

These undisputed facts emerge from the summary judgment materials. On land owned by Mohawk Park, which is situated between Route 2 and the banks of the Deerfield River in Charlemont, is a campground, restaurant, and bar. Although bordering the river, the campground has no beach area and no lifeguards.

Greenslade and his companion, Christina Morton, arrived at the Mohawk Park campground on August 29, 1996, the beginning of the Labor Day holiday weekend, and were assigned a campsite located just off the river bank. At that location, according to Greenslade, the Deerfield River was approximately fifty feet wide. On the river bank opposite the Mohawk Park campground was a formation of cliffs and large rocks, either close to or on land owned by Joanne and Larry Lemek. Directly across from the site where Greenslade and Morton had pitched a tent, a rope swing hung from the limb of a tree on the Lemek property. The twenty-foot rope hung about five feet inland from a rock embankment. The embankment itself rose about five feet above the Deerfield River. At the rope's end was a knot the size of a softball. Individuals using the rope swing would grab onto the knot of the rope, jump while holding on and swinging away from the bank and out over the river, then release the rope to plunge into the water below.

Neither party knows the identity of the person who constructed or hung the rope swing. There is also nothing in the record indicating that Paul Fantucchio (who, with his wife Deborah Fantucchio, owned and operated Mohawk Park) or any employees of Mohawk Park had ever witnessed visitors to the campground using the rope swing at any time prior to Greenslade's fall on August 31, 1996. However, we agree with the motion judge that prior to the date of Greenslade's accident, the facts—including the proximity of the rope swing to, and its visibility from, Mohawk Park's premises; and that on at least one occasion prior to the accident Deborah Fantucchio had warned campers who asked if they could use the rope swing that they could not and that it was dangerous—support the reasonable inference that Mohawk Park was aware of the rope swing's existence and that its guests would use it on occasion.

On August 31, Greenslade, Morton and another couple (James and Andrea Molinari) used inner tubes to float on the Deerfield River. As they watched others across the river who were jumping from the cliffs or using the rope swing, Greenslade or James Molinari commented that "[o]ne of these guys is going to break their neck." Greenslade said: "If I see one more of those idiots hit it, I'm going to give it a shot."

After the foursome returned to the campsite, Greenslade made his way across the river to use the rope swing. Greenslade climbed up an embankment onto the Lemeks' property, where he caught the rope swing. He grabbed onto the rope with both hands and, with the knot between his legs, swung out over the river, released his hold, and fell in a backwards flip headfirst into the water. Greenslade climbed back up onto the embankment and attempted a second maneuver with the rope. This time, however, the knot of the rope became entangled in his clothing, causing Greenslade to remain hanging upside down from the rope. As the rope swung back toward the bank, Greenslade fell from the rope headfirst, striking the rocky ledge on the bank below.

Greenslade was airlifted to BayState Medical Center where he remained unconscious for over a month. He sustained a spinal cord injury, leaving him without the use of his legs and with only limited use of his arms.

A Superior Court judge entered a summary judgment in favor of Mohawk Park, ruling that Mohawk Park had no duty to warn its campers or visitors to the camp of the dangers associated with the rope swing, or to advise that the use of the rope swing was not a sanctioned campground activity. Greenslade appeals that ruling, arguing that although the rope swing was not on Mohawk Park's property, it is a disputed question of fact for the jury whether the level of control exercised by Mohawk Park and its employees over the premises on which the rope swing was located nevertheless gave rise to a duty of care owed to campers, such as Greenslade, who made recreational use of the rope swing.

It is a familiar principle that a landowner has a duty to warn of any unreasonable danger of which the owner is or reasonably should have been aware. "The extension of the duty in appropriate circumstances to conditions on adjacent

property derives from the same general obligation to act reasonably to protect
one's invitees from the hazards of which the owner is aware." We need not, however, address whether the plaintiffs are correct that there are material questions
of fact involving the issue of control over the premises on which the swing was
located, because the dispositive issue in this case is whether, as matter of law, the
risks attendant to the rope swinging activity are open and obvious, precluding
liability. That is to say, the outcome in this case would be the same even if it had
been established that the rope swing was located on Mohawk Park's property.

> "[I]t is well established in our law of negligence that a landowner's
> duty to protect lawful visitors against dangerous conditions on his prop-
> erty ordinarily does not extend to damages that would be obvious to per-
> sons of average intelligence." This rule has continued vitality despite the
> Legislature's abolition of the assumption of risk defense. "Landowners are
> relieved of the duty to warn of open and obvious dangers on their prem-
> ises because it is not reasonably foreseeable that a visitor exercising (as the
> law presumes) reasonable care for his own safety would suffer injury from
> such blatant hazards."

The undisputed facts of this case do not overcome the rational conclusion
that would be reached by a person of ordinary intelligence that it is unsafe to
swing on the end of a rope suspended over water, heedless of the potential presence of rocks beneath the water's surface or of the possibility that letting go of
the rope too late or too soon could result in a landing on the rocky embankment.
In this respect, our decision is in accord with those of numerous other jurisdictions, described in the margin, that have concluded that diving into a river from
a cliff or from a rope swing is activity undertaken in conditions that a person of
average intelligence would consider to be dangerous.

Similarly, we need not answer a further question raised by Greenslade,
whether Mohawk Park incurred liability because it exercised a level of control
over the instrumentality, the rope swing, which caused Greenslade's injury. This
is an issue we think is distinct from, although related to, premises liability. There
are, however, no facts present in the record (such as where a defendant constructs
a rope swing, or advertises a rope swing as an amenity available to campers and
promotes its use in a manner that suggests that rope swinging is safe) that would,

if proved, tend to establish any use or control of the rope swing by Mohawk Park sufficient to impose liability. Compare Blythe v. Williams, (plaintiff injured diving into "swimming hole" from cable swing located on campgrounds which had allegedly constructed swing; summary judgment for campground, on ground that risk was open and obvious, reversed where factual issues existed as to whether campground was negligent in providing cable swing at swimming hole extending over area of shallow water, or in failing to provide warnings as to its use); Jackson v. TLC Assocs., Inc., (plaintiff injured when his head hit submerged pipe after diving from shoreline into water of man-made lake; summary judgment for defendants, on ground that diving into murky water of uncertain depth posed risk that was open and obvious, reversed where lake was designed, intended, and used solely for recreational swimming, and where injury stemmed from presence of submerged pipe placed in water by defendants, who periodically changed its location; when defendants opened lake to public and charged fee for admission, patrons had right to assume existence of appropriate safety measures). See Bier v. Leanna Lakeside Property Assn., (summary judgment should not have entered on claim under safety statute establishing and enforcing minimum safety standards for public bathing beaches, where plaintiffs alleged that defendants, shareholders of private lake, had erected and maintained ladder and rope swing connected to tree at its beach adjacent to lake; however, summary judgment properly entered for defendants on claim of common-law duty to warn plaintiff where risk of injury from rope swung is open and obvious).

We conclude that there was no error in applying the open and obvious danger rule to the circumstances of this case and that, under familiar principles set forth in Community Natl. Bank v. Dawes, summary judgment for the defendant was appropriately entered.

Costa v. Boston Red Sox Baseball Club, 809 N.E.2d 1090 (Mass. App. Ct. 2004)

On a September evening in 1998, the plaintiff and three companions attended a Boston Red Sox baseball game at Fenway Park. They arrived late, at the top of the fifth inning. The plaintiff took her seat in an unscreened area in the upper box section on the first base line, more or less behind the Red Sox dugout. Several players from the visiting team, the Detroit Tigers, batted before their side was retired. In the bottom of the fifth, the first batter for the Red Sox was Darren Lewis. On a count of one ball and two strikes, Lewis hit a line drive foul ball into the stands along the first base line. The ball struck the plaintiff in the face, causing severe, permanent injuries. She had been in the ballpark no more than ten minutes when she was hurt.

It is not disputed that, while passively watching the game, the plaintiff's life was forever changed by this tragic event. What is disputed is whether the defendant Boston Red Sox Baseball Club may be compelled to compensate the plaintiff for her injuries. A judge of the Superior Court granted the defendant's motion for summary judgment. We agree that, as matter of law, the plaintiff may not recover on the only theory she advances—negligent failure to warn of the danger of being hit by a foul ball—and, accordingly, we affirm.

We view the summary judgment record, as we are required to do, in the light most favorable to the plaintiff.

In addition to the facts outlined above, the record reveals the following.

Foul ball injuries occur with some regularity at Fenway Park. A spreadsheet produced by the defendant, summarizing five years of data during the 1990's, showed that the annual number of injuries sustained by patrons from foul balls ranged from thirty-six to fifty-three, with a substantial number requiring medical attention. While some of these incidents were listed as involving patrons who were injured while attempting to catch the ball, many others were not. Moreover, avoiding injury from a ball hit into the stands sometimes may be close to impossible. According to a professor of engineering retained by the plaintiff, the plaintiff had virtually no time to react to the ball that came her way. He determined, with the help of a range finder, that the distance from the plaintiff's seat to home plate was forty-seven yards, or 141 feet. By analyzing a videotape of the game, he also determined that the minimum speed of the baseball at the time it struck the plaintiff was ninety miles per hour, or 132 feet per second. Thus, he concluded, the plaintiff had no more than 1.07 seconds from the time Lewis hit the ball to take evasive action.

At her deposition, the plaintiff professed marked ignorance of the sport of baseball. Except for one occasion when she sat in the bleachers with her father when she was eight years old, she had never attended a baseball game prior to the night of the accident. She had not seen baseball on television except while changing channels, and did not watch sports reports or read about sports in the newspaper. Before the evening of her injury, she understood a foul ball to be one that simply rolled off to the side after being hit. As atypical as this may seem in "Red Sox Nation," we accept for present purposes (as we must) that the plaintiff had no subjective understanding of the risks posed by an errant foul ball.

There is an area behind home plate where netting protects approximately 2,511 seats; however, the plaintiff does not contend that the netting should have extended to the area where she was seated, or otherwise question the design of the ballpark. She claims only that she was entitled to an adequate warning of the dangers of sitting in an unprotected location so that she could have made an informed choice whether to remain there. She acknowledges the existence of a disclaimer printed on her admission ticket but maintains that she did not look at the ticket and that, in any event, the disclaimer was not adequate to discharge the defendant's duty to warn, particularly since the print was extremely small. She notes that, after the date of her injury, signage was installed along the first base line reading "BE ALERT. FOUL BALLS AND BATS HURT." Such signage, according to the plaintiff, was feasible and necessary before her accident. She claims that had she been adequately informed of the danger, she would not have exposed herself to the risk of injury presented by the location of her seat.

We turn now to the relevant law. It has been more than fifty years since a case like the plaintiff's has been considered on appeal in Massachusetts. In Shaw v. Boston Am. League Baseball Co., the Supreme Judicial Court held, as matter of law, that a baseball club was not liable to a spectator who was injured by a foul ball. Shaw rested on the doctrine of assumption of risk and therefore turned on the plaintiff's subjective knowledge and appreciation of the danger. The plaintiff in Shaw was an admitted "fan" who had attended many baseball games and who knew that fast-moving foul balls often landed in the stands. On those facts, the court had little difficulty concluding that the defendant was shielded from liability because the "plaintiff's position [was] that of a spectator familiar with the game who was injured by an ordinary risk of the game which she had voluntarily assumed."

The present case stands on a different footing from Shaw, both legally and factually. As to claims arising on or after January 1, 1974, assumption of risk was abolished as an affirmative defense, and here the plaintiff must be taken as ignorant of the danger of being hit by a foul ball. In spite of these distinctions, however, we conclude that the plaintiff still cannot recover.

Before liability for negligence can be imposed, there must first be a legal duty owed by the defendant to the plaintiff, and a breach of that duty proximately resulting in the injury. Here, the asserted duty is the duty to warn of the dangers of foul balls. Although an owner or possessor of land owes to all persons lawfully on the premises a common-law duty of reasonable care to maintain the property in a reasonably safe condition and "to warn visitors of any unreasonable dangers of which the landowner is aware or reasonably should be aware," the duty to warn does not extend to dangers that would be obvious to persons of average intelligence. "[W]here a danger would be obvious to a person of ordinary perception and judgment, a landowner may reasonably assume that a visitor has knowledge of it and, therefore, 'any further warning would be an empty form' that would not reduce the likelihood of resulting harm."

As the Supreme Judicial Court explained, the abolition of assumption of risk as an affirmative defense did "not alter the plaintiff's burden in a negligence action to prove that the defendant owed him a duty of care in the circumstances, and thus [left] intact the open and obvious danger rule, which operates to negate the existence of a duty of care," at least insofar as a duty to warn is concerned.

Viewing the present case through the lens of the defendant's duty, we are persuaded that the potential for a foul ball to enter the stands and injure a spectator who is seated in an unscreened area is, as matter of law, sufficiently obvious that the defendant reasonably could conclude that a person of ordinary intelligence would perceive the risk and need no additional warning. Even someone of limited personal experience with the sport of baseball reasonably may be assumed to know that a central feature of the game is that batters will forcefully hit balls that may go astray from their intended direction. We therefore hold that the defendant had no duty to warn the plaintiff of the obvious danger of a foul ball being hit into the stands.

The result we reach is consistent with the vast majority of reported decisions involving injuries to spectators at baseball games. Although cases in other jurisdictions have turned on a variety of tort doctrines, they reflect a consensus that baseball stadium owners should not be held responsible for injuries to spectators that result from balls leaving the field during play—at least if adequate safety screening has been provided to protect areas of the stadium in the vicinity of home plate, where the danger is thought to be most acute. As a consequence, injured fans like the plaintiff are left to bear the costs of their injuries, even though they played no role in causing them except by choosing to attend the game.

In its amicus brief, the office of the commissioner of baseball, paraphrasing then Chief Judge Cardozo, justifies this result with the cavalier observation that "the timorous may always choose to stay at home." Perhaps a more gracious approach would be for major league baseball to elect to internalize the costs of unavoidable injuries sustained by fans through no fault of their own. On the theory the plaintiff has asserted, however, we do not so require.

Constructing Legal Argument (IRAC)

After finding relevant cases, the goal is to assemble them into a coherent whole in order to persuade a judge that your client should prevail. The best way to do this is through an organizational and analytical framework called IRAC. IRAC stands for Issue, Rule, Analysis, Conclusion. IRAC provides a basis to organize your legal writing. Here's how it works.

Issue

The issue is your client's position on the law and facts with regard to a particular question being argued. By way of example, let's look at a different set of facts. Now, we have a man named Rodriguez who is unable to pay his student loan debt. He would like to discharge his student loan debt in bankruptcy. However, student loan debt, unlike other ordinary debt, is difficult to discharge in bankruptcy. In order to do so, the debtor must show that he will suffer an undue hardship if forced to pay his student loan debt. So, for Rodriguez and his lawyer, their issue or position is that Rodriguez will suffer an undue hardship if he has to repay his loan.

The issue is normally set forth at the beginning of your argument in the form of a heading. A heading is simply the numbered title of the relevant section of your argument. For example:

1. Rodriguez will suffer an undue hardship if forced to repay his student loans.

Following the issue comes the relevant rule of law on the question. In Rodriguez's case the rule of law revolves around what an undue hardship is and what it takes to establish one. For example,

> **To obtain discharge of student loans, a debtor must show that he will suffer "undue hardship" in repaying them. The "undue hardship" test requires that the debtor demonstrate that he "cannot maintain, based on current income and expenses, a 'minimal' standard of living ... if forced to repay the loans." In re Cheesman, 25 F.3d 356, 359 (6th Cir. 1994). Courts have interpreted this rule as calling for a showing of a "current inability to pay." Brunner, 831 F.2d at 396. This encompasses evidence of "low income," a "frugal lifestyle," and a determination if "anything [is] left from the debtor's estimated future income to enable the debtor to make some payment on his/her student loan." Cheesman, 25 F.3d at 359 (quoting Andrews v. South Dakota Student Loan Assist. Corp., 661 F.2d 702, 704 (8th Cir. 1981)).**

Now that he has set forth the relevant law, Rodriguez must establish how it applies to his situation. To do this, Rodriguez must compare the facts of his case with the facts of other earlier decided cases. In essence, he must argue that the facts of his situation are equivalent or similar to other cases where an undue hardship was found to exist. Normally, you would start by discussing the facts of your best case and then compare them to the facts of your case. This is the application or analysis aspect of the IRAC formulation. For example,

> **In Cheesman, the court failed to find "anything left" from the debtor's income to pay his student loans (and thus maintain a minimal standard of living) where the debtor had income in the range of $1600/month and was running a monthly deficit, despite low expenses "consistent" with a "frugal lifestyle." Id. The same is true here with Rodriguez. Rodriguez makes only $1600/month from his job as a handbag salesman. His expenses total just $1500/month, but nevertheless leave him with only $100 left over, or $25/week. Therefore, if forced to make his monthly student loan payment of $325, Rodriguez would run a monthly deficit of $225, putting him in the same position as the debtor in Cheesman. See id. at 360 (holding that monthly deficit of $400 warranted finding that debtor satisfied first element of undue hardship test).**

Then comes the conclusion, which is simply a way of informing the court of the decision you would like it to reach.

> **As a result, this court should find that Rodriguez is unable to repay his student loan and at the same time maintain a minimal standard of living. If forced to do so, he will suffer an undue hardship.**

And that is IRAC, an organizational and analytical framework that uses legal precedent to argue for desired results in current cases.

*　　　*　　　*

Chapter 5: Introduction to Civil Procedure 1: Process

Introduction and Definitions

The American legal system is an adversarial one in which Plaintiff and Defendant or Petitioner and Respondent face off in a court of law in an attempt to persuade judge and/or jury of the merits of their arguments. Unlike a no-holds-bar street fight, however, this legal contest is not a free-for-all. It is governed by certain rules which help guide parties in a number of ways. These rules are known as rules of civil procedure. All references to rules in this chapter refer to the **Federal Rules of Civil Procedure**, which apply in all federal courts. Each state has its own set of rules.

Definitions relevant to this discussion include the following:

Answer: a written pleading filed by a defendant to respond to a complaint in a lawsuit filed and served upon that defendant. An answer generally responds to each allegation in the complaint by denying or admitting it, or admitting in part and denying in part. The answer may also comprise "affirmative defenses" including allegations which contradict the complaint or contain legal theories (like "unclean hands," "contributory negligence" or "anticipatory breach") which are intended to derail the claims in the complaint.

Complaint: the first document filed with the court (actually with the County Clerk or Clerk of the Court) by a person or entity claiming legal rights against another. Complaints are pleadings and must be drafted carefully (usually by an attorney) to properly state the factual as well as legal basis for the claim, although some states have approved complaint forms which can be filled in by an individual.

Discovery: the entire efforts of a party to a lawsuit and his/her/its attorneys to obtain information before trial through demands for production of documents, depositions of parties and potential witnesses, written interrogatories (questions and answers written under oath), written requests for admissions of fact, examination of the scene and the petitions and motions employed to enforce discovery rights

Final Judgment: the written determination of a lawsuit by the judge who presided at trial (or heard a successful motion to dismiss or a stipulation for judgment), which renders (makes) rulings on all issues and completes the case unless it is appealed to a higher court. It is also called a final decree or final decision.

Summary Judgment: a court order ruling that no factual issues remain to be tried and therefore a cause of action or all causes of action in a complaint can be decided upon certain facts without trial.

The Litigation Process

Litigation is a process. It is a process that can be plotted generally on a timeline. The Federal Rules of Civil Procedure govern the litigation process and establish and dictate the timeline of a case. The timeline stretches from the moment of injury (or the moment that the thing happened for which the party is suing) to the entry of final judgment. Along the way, the rules direct the "traffic" of the parties and provide the signposts to show what is required of them, and, very importantly, when it is required.

A lawyer begins work well before the complaint is filed. Indeed, prior to filing, a claim must be investigated and researched pursuant to Rule 11, which governs the signing requirement for papers that are advocated before the court and provides the certifications that a lawyer makes when she signs the paper; namely that the paper (and this includes the complaint) is grounded in law and fact and not filed for any improper purpose. Then the complaint must be drafted with reference to Rules 7-10, which relate to the pleading requirements. The complaint is then filed with the court as directed by Rule 5, and the filing commences the cause of action by virtue of Rule 3. After filing, the plaintiff must serve original process on the defendant(s) pursuant to Rule 4, and the defendant(s) may subsequently move to dismiss the complaint under Rule 12, which sets forth the defenses that may be raised by preliminary motion. Or, rather than attempting to dismiss the complaint, the defendant(s) may choose to answer it under Rule 8 (in any event, if the complaint is not dismissed, an answer will be required eventually). This first stage of the litigation is known as the "pleadings" stage, and its goal is to define the claims and defenses of the parties.

Rule 12 sets forth preliminary defenses that may be raised by motion prior to filing an answer. The Rule 12 motion is thus a test of the complaint. It, in effect, asks the judge to determine if any defects in the court's subject matter jurisdiction, personal jurisdiction, the plaintiff's choice of venue, the method of service of process, or the process itself warrant dismissal of the case prior to discovery. The Rule 12 motion can also ask the judge to determine whether the plaintiff's factual allegations are of sufficient heft to show a plausible, and not merely possible, right to recovery. If the complaint passes these Rule 12 tests, the defendant(s) must formally respond to the complaint's factual allegations in an answer and assert any defenses. Then, the pleadings close and the parties meet among themselves and with the court to discuss the case pursuant to Rules 16 and 26. Once that's done, discovery begins.

Discovery is the voluntary exchange of relevant information and material among the parties. The principal rule governing discovery is Rule 26, which sets forth the scope of discovery; that is, "what" may be discovered during the course of the litigation. Rules 30–36 describe the various methods the parties may employ to obtain information from the other side, that is, the "how" of discovery. Authorized methods of discovery include depositions, interrogatories, document requests, requests for admission, and subpoenas. The methods used and the order in which they are employed are at the lawyer's discretion.

The essential goal of discovery is to adduce facts that will enable a party to prove its case at trial. A more basic purpose is to adduce facts that will enable a party to obtain or, perhaps more importantly, survive summary judgment under Rule 56. As Rule 12 provides the means to test the pleadings, Rule 56 provides the means to test the facts brought forth in discovery to determine if a genuine dispute of material fact exists such that the case (or issue) is appropriate for trial and resolution by a factfinder. The trial, where the claim is finally adjudicated, is then governed by its own set of rules, also found in the Federal Rules of Civil Procedure.

Drafting a Complaint

A lawsuit begins with the filing of a complaint with the court. The complaint sets forth the claims on which the plaintiff seeks relief along with the basic facts that underlie those claims.

Every element of a legal claim ultimately needs facts that match to and support it. A successful lawsuit requires matching the facts to the law at three distinct stages of the litigation. The first matching stage is the pleadings, controlled in a federal case by Rules 7 to 10, with Rule 8 being the most important; the second is summary judgment, controlled by Rule 56; and then finally, there's trial, which is subject to Rules 38 to 53. Each stage requires progressively more factual detail and eventually, at trial, proof.

Factual development begins long before the jury hears any evidence, and the goal of each stage of the litigation—as the record is developed—is to winnow out those cases where the parties cannot connect the facts to the law with the required amount of specificity. Put another way, each stage of litigation defines a mechanism for testing the case to determine if it should go forward, or if it has no hope of success and should therefore be dismissed or subject to summary judgment.

The pleadings stage requires the least specificity. The pleading standard—the statement of the specificity required in a claim for relief—is supplied by Rule 8, unless the claim is subject to Rule 9's pleading with particularity requirements.[1] Rule 8 provides: "A pleading that states a claim for relief must contain…a short and plain statement of the claim showing that the pleader is entitled to relief."[2] This standard was traditionally interpreted as requiring merely that the pleading give notice to the defendant of the nature of the claims asserted;[3] specific legal

---

[1]   *See* Fed. R. Civ. P. 9.

[2]   Fed. R. Civ. P. 8(a)(2). Rule 8 also requires that a pleading stating a claim for relief also contain a "short and plain statement of the grounds for the court's jurisdiction" and a "demand for the relief sought."

[3]   *See, e.g.,* Leavitt v. Cole, 291 F. Supp. 2d 1338, 1341 (M.D. Fla. 2003) ("Generally, a complaint need only give the defendant fair notice of what the plaintiff's claim is and the grounds upon which it rests." (citation omitted)); Temperato v. Rainbolt, 163 F. Supp. 744, 746 (E.D. Ill. 1957) (stating that "it is

theories and other special formats were not required. Once the basic facts were asserted, it was up to the court to apply the law to them.[4]

Perhaps the most widely quoted embodiment of the initial conception of notice pleading[5] was the Supreme Court case of Conley v. Gibson.[6] There, in deciding that black railroad employees had adequately stated a cause of action against their union for intentional discrimination under the Railway Labor Act, Justice Black laid out the Rule 8 standard as he understood it.

> In appraising the sufficiency of the complaint we follow, of course, the accepted rule that a complaint should not be dismissed for failure to state a claim unless it appears beyond doubt that the plaintiff can prove no set of facts in support of his claim which would entitle him to relief.[7]

This was, it seemed, pure notice pleading, with the court pulling the laboring oar at the Rule 12(b)(6) motion stage to determine if it "appear[ed] beyond doubt" that the plaintiff could "prove no set of facts in support of his claim." It is unlikely, however, that Justice Black needed to use language that swept so broadly; the plaintiffs in Conley had sufficiently pled their claim under any standard of pleading. But he did, and the "no set of facts" language remained for decades as a beacon to plaintiffs seeking the widest possible interpretation of the federal pleading standard.

---

generally held that no pleading shall be bad in substance when it reasonably informs the opposition of the nature of a claim or defense which he is called upon to defend").

4   In other words, "the plaintiff states what happened and the court is called upon to apply the law to it." Charles E. Clark & James Wm. Moore, *A New Federal Civil Procedure: II. Pleadings and Parties*, 44 Yale L.J. 1291, 1301 (1935).

5   I say "initial conception" because it is arguable that the Supreme Court tightened the federal pleading standard in the cases *Bell Atlantic v. Twombly*, 550 U.S. 544 (2007), and *Ashcroft v. Iqbal*, 556 U.S. 662 (2009).

6   355 U.S. 41 (1957).

7   *Id.* at 45–46.

In time, however, Justice Black's "no set of facts" language began to trouble some judges,[8] and as the world changed, so too did the law. As explained by Professor Robert Bone:

> It would have made sense in [1938] to assume relatively manageable discovery and trial costs for most cases. Today's world of litigation is very different. There are many more large and complex lawsuits with high stakes, more large law firms and lawyers practicing nationwide who have much weaker incentives to build local reputations, and a much wider range of materials that can be targeted in discovery, including potentially massive electronic records. These changes have fueled a powerful perception of serious litigation cost and frivolous suit problems.[9]

The changes noted by Professor Bone had an enormous impact on amendments to the Federal Rules of Civil Procedure and how the Rules were interpreted. Specifically, changes in the nature of litigation (and society) led, beginning in the 1980s, to restrictions on and changes in discovery practice,[10] clarification that summary judgment is not a "disfavored procedural shortcut,"[11] expanded use of Rule 68 to encourage settlement,[12] and finally, in 2007, these same changes led the Supreme Court seemingly to tighten the federal pleading standard in Bell Atlantic Corp. v. Twombly.[13]

In Twombly, an antitrust case, the Court specifically abrogated the "no set of facts" language from Conley[14] and set in its place a "plausibility" pleading standard which required that the complaint contain enough "[f]actual allegations…to

---

[8]   *See* Bell Atlantic Corp. v. Twombly, 550 U.S. 544, 562 (2007) (noting discontent with "no set of facts" standard).

[9]   Robert G. Bone, Twombly, *Pleading Rules, and the Regulation of Court Access*, 94 Iowa L. Rev. 873, 895–98 (2009) (footnotes omitted).

[10]   *See* Fed. R. Civ. P. 26 advisory committee notes (1980 & 1983 amendments).

[11]   *See* Celotex Corp. v. Catrett, 477 U.S. 317, 327 (1986).

[12]   *See* Robert G. Bone, *"To Encourage Settlement": Rule 68, Offers of Judgment, and the History of the Federal Rules of Civil Procedure*, 102 Nw. U. L. Rev. 1561, 1605–06 (2008).

[13]   550 U.S. 544 (2007).

[14]   *Id.* at 563.

raise a right to relief above the speculative level,"[15] and that the facts alleged "plausibly suggest[]" unlawful conduct.[16] In other words, conclusory allegations were insufficient to state a cause of action without facts that suggested a plausible, and not merely possible, right to relief. What the Court appeared to be saying was that proper notice to the defendant required at least some factual detail to enable a response. It is likely that it always did, and that plaintiffs always needed to plead some factual detail in support of their claims; the Court in Twombly just made the standard explicit. Justice Souter's defense of the Form 9 [now 11] complaint in negligence from the abrogated Federal Appendix of Forms is illustrative in this regard.

> [T]he pleadings [in Twombly] mentioned no specific time, place, or person involved in the alleged conspiracies. This lack of notice contrasts sharply with the model form for pleading negligence, which the dissent says exemplifies the kind of "bare allegation" that survives a motion to dismiss. Whereas the model form alleges that the defendant struck the plaintiff with his car while plaintiff was crossing a particular highway at a specified date and time, the complaint here furnishes no clue as to which of the four ILECs (much less which of their employees) supposedly agreed, or when and where the illicit agreement took place.[17]

In other words, the matching process at the pleading stage requires more than simply a recitation of the elements of the claim. If she has the information, the pleader needs to state, essentially, the who, what, where, and when of her claim; who did this, what did they do, where did they do it, and when did it happen.[18]

There was some question at first as to whether the Twombly analysis applied beyond the antitrust context.[19] The Court answered this question emphatically in

---

15   *Id.* at 555.

16   *See id.* at 557.

17   *Id.* at 564 n.10.

18   I'm not suggesting that this level of detail is required in every case. Ideally, though, if this information is available, you should plead it (unless, of course, strategic considerations dictate otherwise).

19   *See, e.g.*, Iqbal v. Hasty, 490 F.3d 143, 157 (2d Cir. 2007) (stating that "[t]hese conflicting signals create some uncertainty as to the intended scope of

Ashcroft v. Iqbal,[20] where it stated that the Court in Twombly had been construing Rule 8 in general and not just antitrust pleading, and as such the plausibility standard applied to all federal civil cases.[21] In Iqbal, a Muslim Pakistani detainee had brought a Bivens[22] action against Attorney General John Ashcroft and Director of the FBI Robert Mueller (among others, but only these two defendants were before the Court) alleging that Ashcroft and Mueller had discriminated against him on the basis of his race, religion, and national origin by adopting the policy that resulted in his imprisonment following 9/11.[23] Although the plaintiff had alleged in conclusory fashion that Ashcroft's and Mueller's actions were motivated by discriminatory intent, the complaint did not, according to the Court, "contain any factual allegation sufficient to plausibly suggest petitioners' discriminatory state of mind."[24] And, thus, "[u]nder Twombly's construction of Rule 8, [the Court] conclude[d] that respondent's complaint [had] not 'nudged [his] claims' of invidious discrimination across the line from conceivable to plausible,'"[25] and therefore the claims were properly dismissed. As will be discussed, the Court in Iqbal added at least one additional wrinkle to the Twombly analysis by holding that prior to determining if the plaintiff has set forth a plausible cause of action, a district court may disregard all conclusory allegations set forth in the claim for relief.

Of course, what the plausibility standard actually means, the level of factual detail required to meet the standard, and whether Twombly and Iqbal actually changed anything at all are subjects for debate. The ultimate resolution of the debate, however, has little impact on what a litigator must do now to prepare her case. Therefore, because the key for the litigator is crafting a pleading that will survive a motion to dismiss, if you know the facts, you should plead them; you should match them to the elements of your claims, making sure to include the

---

the Court's decision [in Twombly]"), *rev'd sub nom.* Ashcroft v. Iqbal, 556 U.S. 662 (2009).

[20]   556 U.S. 662 (2009).

[21]   *See id.* at 684.

[22]   *See* Bivens v. Six Unknown Fed. Narcotics Agents, 403 U.S. 388 (1971).

[23]   *See* 556 U.S. at 668–69.

[24]   *Id.* at 683.

[25]   *Id.* at 680.

who, what, where, and when. That's the best way to get your claim for relief past the first test in the litigation, the Rule 12(b) motion to dismiss.

Bell Atlantic v. Twombly, 550 U.S. 544 (2007)

In Twombly, the regional legacy companies created in the 1984 divestiture of AT&T were sued in a class action under the Sherman Act for allegedly engaging in a conspiracy to restrain trade. Justice Souter set forth the central issue in the case as follows:

> Liability under § 1 of the Sherman Act, 15 U.S.C. § 1, requires a "contract, combination…, or conspiracy, in restraint of trade or commerce." The question in this putative class action is whether a § 1 complaint can survive a motion to dismiss when it alleges that major telecommunications providers engaged in certain parallel conduct unfavorable to competition, absent some factual context suggesting agreement, as distinct from identical, independent action. We hold that such a complaint should be dismissed.

The resolution of the action was thus a matter of pleading. The specific question was this; can the Sherman Act's requirement of a "contract, combination…, or conspiracy" be satisfied at the pleadings stage with allegations of anticompetitive parallel conduct, but without "factual context suggesting agreement" to engage in such conduct. The complaint's "money" allegation to try and satisfy the "agreement" requirement was as follows:

> In the absence of any meaningful competition between the [ILECs] in one another's markets, and in light of the parallel course of conduct that each engaged in to prevent competition from CLECs within their respective local telephone and/or high speed internet services markets and the other facts and market circumstances alleged above, Plaintiffs allege upon information and belief that [the ILECs] have entered into a contract, combination or conspiracy to prevent competitive entry in their respective local telephone and/or high speed internet services markets and have agreed not to compete with one another and otherwise allocated customers and markets to one another.

To the Court, this simply was not enough because while the conduct alleged could certainly have been the product of an unlawful agreement, the allegations also were—for this particular industry—equally consistent with lawful behavior, as rational market actors could reasonably engage in anticompetitive parallel conduct without an agreement to do so and without violating the Sherman Act. In other words, without facts tending to show an agreement, or from which an agreement could be reasonable inferred, the cause of action was merely "possible," and not "plausible," and thus did not satisfy Rule 8.

The inadequacy of showing parallel conduct or interdependence, without more, mirrors the ambiguity of the behavior: consistent with conspiracy, but just as much in line with a wide swath of rational and competitive business strategy unilaterally prompted by common perceptions of the market....

This case presents the antecedent question of what a plaintiff must plead in order to state a claim under § 1 of the Sherman Act. Federal Rule of Civil Procedure 8(a)(2) requires only "a short and plain statement of the claim showing that the pleader is entitled to relief," in order to "give the defendant fair notice of what the...claim is and the grounds upon which it rests." While a complaint attacked by a Rule 12(b)(6) motion to dismiss does not need detailed factual allegations, a plaintiff's obligation to provide the "grounds" of his "entitle[ment] to relief" requires more than labels and conclusions, and a formulaic recitation of the elements of a cause of action will not do. Factual allegations must be enough to raise a right to relief above the speculative level on the assumption that all the allegations in the complaint are true (even if doubtful in fact).

In applying these general standards to a § 1 claim, we hold that stating such a claim requires a complaint with enough factual matter (taken as true) to suggest that an agreement was made. Asking for plausible grounds to infer an agreement does not impose a probability requirement at the pleading stage; it simply calls for enough fact to raise a reasonable expectation that discovery will reveal evidence of illegal agreement. And, of course, a well-pleaded complaint may proceed even if it strikes a savvy judge that actual proof of those facts is improbable, and "that a recovery is very remote and unlikely." In identifying facts that are suggestive enough to render a § 1 conspiracy plausible, we have the benefit of the prior rulings and considered views of leading commentators, already quoted, that lawful parallel conduct fails to bespeak unlawful agreement. It makes sense to say, therefore, that an allegation of parallel conduct and a bare assertion of conspiracy will not suffice. Without more, parallel conduct does not suggest conspiracy, and a conclusory allegation of agreement at some unidentified point does not supply facts adequate to show illegality. Hence, when allegations of parallel conduct are set out in order to make a § 1 claim, they must be placed in a context that raises a suggestion of a preceding agreement, not merely parallel conduct that could just as well be independent action.

The need at the pleading stage for allegations plausibly suggesting (not merely consistent with) agreement reflects the threshold requirement of Rule 8(a)(2) that the "plain statement" possess enough heft to "sho[w] that the pleader is entitled to relief."

A "plausible" right to relief therefore is not one where a complaint's allegations are balanced on a scale equally between lawful and unlawful conduct. Rather, to render a claim plausible, there must be something that tips the scale, even if ever so slightly, toward unlawful conduct or the reasonable inference of unlawful conduct. The nature of the required something will of course depend on the nature of the claim.

The following questions may help illuminate what the Court meant in Twombly.

1. Is it that the plaintiffs' "ultimate allegation" in Twombly was made "upon information and belief" that doomed their claims? If not, what was it?

2. Please read the following from Arista Records v. Doe.[26]

---

[26]   604 F.3d 110 (2d Cir. 2010).

First, the notion that Twombly imposed a heightened standard that requires a complaint to include specific evidence, factual allegations in addition to those required by Rule 8, and declarations from the persons who collected the evidence is belied by the Twombly opinion itself. The Court noted that Rule 8(a)(2) of the Federal Rules of Civil Procedure "requires only 'a short and plain statement of the claim showing that the pleader is entitled to relief,' in order to give the defendant fair notice of what the…claim is and the grounds upon which it rests."…The Twombly plausibility standard, which applies to all civil actions does not prevent a plaintiff from "pleading facts alleged 'upon information and belief'" where the facts are peculiarly within the possession and control of the defendant or where the belief is based on factual information that makes the inference of culpability plausible. The Twombly Court stated that "[a]sking for plausible grounds to infer an agreement does not impose a probability requirement at the pleading stage; it simply calls for enough fact to raise a reasonable expectation that discovery will reveal evidence of illegal[ity]."[27]

3. Do you agree with this analysis? According to the Court in Arista what are the circumstances where "information and belief" allegations are permitted? In other words, what makes such allegations plausible?

4. Professor Edward A. Hartnett has argued:

    Courts have long held that legal conclusions need not be accepted as true on 12(b)(6) motions, have long insisted that pleaders are not entitled to unreasonable factual inferences, and have long treated "legal conclusions," "unwarranted deductions," "unwarranted inferences," "unsupported conclusions," and "sweeping legal conclusions cast in the form of factual allegations" as "more or less synonymous" terms. So understood, Twombly's insistence that the inference of conspiracy be "plausible" is equivalent to the traditional insistence that an inference be "reasonable."

---

[27]   *Id.* at 119–20.

The Twombly Court concluded that it would be implausible or unreasonable to infer a conspiracy from the factual allegations of the complaint, even assuming that all of those factual allegations were true.[28]

5. If Professor Hartnett is correct, did Twombly change the standard? To think about this question, look at Conley v. Gibson, which was discussed at the outset of this chapter. Were the allegations of discrimination in Conley plausible or the inference of discrimination drawn from the facts reasonable?

6. What makes an inference "reasonable"?

7. Why was the allegation of conspiracy in Twombly not plausible or, to put it another way, an unreasonable inference? What possible facts could the plaintiffs have alleged to render the conclusion plausible or the inference reasonable?

8. Sixteen days after it decided Twombly, the Court decided Erickson v. Pardus,[29] in which it found:

Federal Rule of Civil Procedure 8(a)(2) requires only "a short and plain statement of the claim showing that the pleader is entitled to relief." Specific facts are not necessary; the statement need only "give the defendant fair notice of what the…claim is and the grounds upon which it rests." In addition, when ruling on a defendant's motion to dismiss, a judge must accept as true all of the factual allegations contained in the complaint.

The complaint stated that Dr. Bloor's decision to remove petitioner from his prescribed hepatitis C medication was "endangering [his] life." It alleged this medication was withheld "shortly after" petitioner had commenced a treatment program that would take one year, that he was "still in need of treatment for this disease," and that the prison officials were in

---

[28]   Edward A. Hartnett, *Taming* Twombly, *Even After* Iqbal, 158 U. Pa. L. Rev. 473, 484–86 (2010) (footnotes omitted).

[29]   551 U.S. 89 (2007).

the meantime refusing to provide treatment. This alone was enough to satisfy Rule 8(a)(2).[30]

9.   Is Erickson consistent with Twombly? Can you distinguish the two cases?

The Court revisited the Rule 8 pleading standard two years after Twombly and added at least two additional wrinkles in Ashcroft v. Iqbal.

Ashcroft v. Iqbal, 556 U.S. 662 (2009)

In Iqbal, a former pretrial detainee arrested in the wake of the September 11 attacks sued John Ashcroft, the Attorney General of the United States, and Robert Mueller, the Director of the FBI, claiming that "they adopted an unconstitutional policy that subjected [him] to harsh conditions of confinement on account of his race, religion, or national origin." The case was dismissed for failing to satisfy the Rule 8 pleading standard. Iqbal is important for two reasons: (1) the Court held that the Twombly pleading standard applied to all actions under the federal rules, not just antitrust actions, and (2) the Court arguably added a second prong to the Twombly standard when it held that allegations that a judge labels as conclusory need not be accepted as true (as factual allegations must be) for the purpose of resolving a Rule 12(b)(6) motion to dismiss.

We turn to respondent's complaint. Under Federal Rule of Civil Procedure 8(a)(2), a pleading must contain a "short and plain statement of the claim showing that the pleader is entitled to relief." As the Court held in Twombly, the pleading standard Rule 8 announces does not require "detailed factual allegations," but it demands more than an unadorned, the-defendant-unlawfully-harmed-me accusation. A pleading that offers "labels and conclusions" or "a formulaic recitation of the elements of a cause of action will not do." Nor does a complaint suffice if it tenders "naked assertion[s]" devoid of "further factual enhancement."

To survive a motion to dismiss, a complaint must contain sufficient factual matter, accepted as true, to "state a claim to relief that is plausible on its face." A claim has facial plausibility when the plaintiff pleads factual

---

[30]   *Id.* at 93.

content that allows the court to draw the reasonable inference that the defendant is liable for the misconduct alleged. The plausibility standard is not akin to a "probability requirement," but it asks for more than a sheer possibility that a defendant has acted unlawfully. Where a complaint pleads facts that are "merely consistent with" a defendant's liability, it "stops short of the line between possibility and plausibility of 'entitlement to relief.'"

Two working principles underlie our decision in Twombly. First, the tenet that a court must accept as true all of the allegations contained in a complaint is inapplicable to legal conclusions. Threadbare recitals of the elements of a cause of action, supported by mere conclusory statements, do not suffice. Rule 8 marks a notable and generous departure from the hyper-technical, code-pleading regime of a prior era, but it does not unlock the doors of discovery for a plaintiff armed with nothing more than conclusions. Second, only a complaint that states a plausible claim for relief survives a motion to dismiss. Determining whether a complaint states a plausible claim for relief will, as the Court of Appeals observed, be a context-specific task that requires the reviewing court to draw on its judicial experience and common sense. But where the well-pleaded facts do not permit the court to infer more than the mere possibility of misconduct, the complaint has alleged—but it has not "show[n]"—"that the pleader is entitled to relief."

In keeping with these principles a court considering a motion to dismiss can choose to begin by identifying pleadings that, because they are no more than conclusions, are not entitled to the assumption of truth. While legal conclusions can provide the framework of a complaint, they must be supported by factual allegations. When there are well-pleaded factual allegations, a court should assume their veracity and then determine whether they plausibly give rise to an entitlement to relief.

Our decision in Twombly illustrates the two-pronged approach. There, we considered the sufficiency of a complaint alleging that incumbent telecommunications providers had entered an agreement not to compete and to forestall competitive entry, in violation of the Sherman Act. Recognizing that § 1 enjoins only anticompetitive conduct "effected by a contract, combination, or conspiracy," the plaintiffs in Twombly flatly pleaded that the defendants "ha[d] entered into a contract, combination or conspiracy to prevent competitive entry…and ha[d] agreed not to compete with one another." The complaint also alleged that the defendants' "parallel course of conduct…to prevent competition" and inflate prices was indicative of the unlawful agreement alleged.

The Court held the plaintiffs' complaint deficient under Rule 8. In doing so it first noted that the plaintiffs' assertion of an unlawful agreement was a "'legal conclusion'" and, as such, was not entitled to the assumption of truth. Had the Court simply credited the allegation of a conspiracy, the plaintiffs would have stated a claim for relief and been entitled to proceed perforce. The Court next addressed the "nub" of the plaintiffs' complaint—the well-pleaded, nonconclusory factual allegation of parallel behavior—to determine whether it gave rise to a "plausible suggestion of conspiracy." Acknowledging that parallel conduct was consistent with an unlawful agreement, the Court nevertheless concluded that it did not plausibly suggest an illicit accord because it was not only compatible with, but indeed was more likely explained by, lawful, unchoreographed free-market behavior. Because the well-pleaded fact of parallel conduct, accepted as true, did not plausibly suggest an unlawful agreement, the Court held the plaintiffs' complaint must be dismissed.

*   *   *

Drafting a Motion for Summary Judgment

Just as Rule 12 caps the pleadings, Rule 56 caps discovery. More specifically, just as Rule 12 provides—in the form of a motion to dismiss—the mechanism for testing the sufficiency of the facts alleged in the pleadings to determine if the case should proceed into discovery, Rule 56 provides—in the form of a motion for summary judgment—the mechanism for testing the sufficiency of the facts adduced during discovery to determine if the case should go to trial.

The concept of summary judgment was not new in 1938. It had been used successfully for decades in both Great Britain and the United States.[31] The standard has remained essentially the same over time; summary judgment is appropriate when "there is no genuine dispute as to any material fact and the movant is entitled to judgment as a matter of law."[32] In short, summary judgment provides a method of disposing of cases or issues when the facts are not in dispute.[33] With discovery more liberal, this was an important safeguard against delay and the prosecution of unmeritorious lawsuits. In fact, prevention of delay was the main reason for including a summary judgment provision in the federal rules.

> Thus, the summary judgment procedure becomes very useful in expediting the termination and conclusion of cases in which there is no real controversy on any question of fact and in discouraging the interposition of dilatory and frivolous defenses for the purposes of delay.[34]

Or, as argued by Charles Clark:

> The [summary judgment] is usually advocated because of its effectiveness in preventing delays by defendants, and in securing speedy justice for creditors....Except where a trial is necessary to settle an issue of fact, the whole judicial process is, by this procedure, made to function more quickly and with less complexity than in the ordinary long drawn out suit.[35]

Notwithstanding these arguments and the importance placed on summary judgment by Charles Clark and others, there were those who disagreed; who

---

[31]   Alexander Holtzoff, *Practice Under the Federal Rules of Civil Procedure*, 20 B.U. L. Rev. 179, 232 (1940). Summary judgment was first introduced in England in 1855. States of the United States followed suit thereafter with the procedure being relatively common by the late 1920s. *See* Charles E. Clark & Charles U. Samenow, *The Summary Judgment*, 38 Yale L.J. 423, 424, 440–469 (1928–29).

[32]   Fed. R. Civ. P. 56(a).

[33]   *See* Holtzoff, 20 B.U. L. Rev. at 232–33.

[34]   *Id.* at 233–34.

[35]   Charles E. Clark & Charles U. Samenow, *The Summary Judgment*, 38 Yale L.J. 423, 423 (1928–29).

thought summary judgment "a drastic remedy…to be sparingly used."[36] And, perhaps due to those who thought summary judgment drastic, for several decades it was used sparingly.[37] "This timorous approach obviously reduces the danger of unjust dismissals, but it does so at the cost of permitting at least some useless trials to be conducted."[38] And that was the issue; how could the courts comply with the rules and use summary judgment procedure effectively to weed out cases where the facts were undisputed, while at the same time protecting litigants and permitting meritorious cases to go to trial?

The Supreme Court stepped in and addressed the "timorous approach" in 1986 with a pair of cases decided on the same day: Celotex Corp. v. Catrett[39] and Anderson v. Liberty Lobby, Inc.[40] In Celotex and Liberty Lobby, the Court described the two major analytical methods of moving for summary judgment. First, the Court in Celotex made clear that a moving party may point out to the court a failure of proof with regard to an essential element of the other party's case on which the other party bears the burden of proof.[41] That is, the moving party argues that no facts were adduced during discovery (or supplied by affidavit, etc.) that support a particular element of the nonmoving party's claim, and therefore the claim must fail.[42] In other words, the lack of support is undisputed and all other facts with regard to the particular claim are rendered immaterial, thus making judgment in the moving party's favor appropriate.[43] Second, according to Liberty Lobby, the moving party may look to the facts compiled during discovery and argue to the court that existing undisputed facts mandate judgment in the

---

[36]   Harry J. Lemley, *Summary Judgment Procedure under Rule 56 of The Federal Rules of Civil Procedure—Its Use and Abuse*, 11 Ark. L. Rev. 138, 142 (1956–57). See also Max D. Melville, *Summary Judgment and Discovery: The Amended Rules Will Add To Their Usefulness*, 34 A.B.A. J. 187, 190 (1948) (discussing judicial arguments in favor of using "summary judgment power cautiously").

[37]   *See* John A. Bauman, *A Rationale of Summary Judgment*, 33 Ind. L.J. 467, 467 n.2 (1957–58) (citing statistics).

[38]   Martin B. Louis, *Federal Summary Judgment Doctrine: A Critical Analysis*, 83 Yale L.J. 745, 746 (1973–74).

[39]   477 U.S. 317 (1986).

[40]   477 U.S. 242 (1986).

[41]   *See* Celotex, 477 U.S. at 325.

[42]   *Id.* at 322–23.

[43]   *Id.* at 323.

moving party's favor.[44] This is not the same as a failure of proof, but rather a search for uncontradicted material facts—and so not subject to a finding by the jury—that when subject to the relevant legal standard require that judgment be entered.[45]

Taken together, Celotex and Liberty Lobby freed summary judgment from any past temerity and confirmed Rule 56's place as a vital piece of the procedural landscape.

> The Federal Rules of Civil Procedure have for almost 50 years authorized motions for summary judgment upon proper showings of the lack of a genuine, triable issue of material fact. Summary judgment procedure is properly regarded not as a disfavored procedural shortcut, but rather as an integral part of the Federal Rules as a whole, which are designed "to secure the just, speedy and inexpensive determination of every action."[46]

Or, as put more succinctly in the same opinion, "One of the principal purposes of the summary judgment rule is to isolate and dispose of factually unsupported claims or defenses, and we think it should be interpreted in a way that allows it to accomplish that purpose."[47]

The Supreme Court recently provided a typical application of the summary judgment rule, an application where the material facts were in dispute, but summary judgment was nevertheless entered. In Tolan v. Cotton,[48] the Court summarily vacated an appellate court judgment because the court, in resolving a motion for summary judgment, had failed to view the evidence in the light most favorable to the nonmoving party.

> But under either prong [of the qualified immunity analysis], courts may not resolve genuine disputes of fact in favor of the party seeking summary

---

44   *See* Liberty Lobby, 477 U.S. at 250.
45   *See id.*
46   Celotex, 477 U.S. at 327 (quoting Fed. R. Civ. P. 1).
47   *Id.* at 324.
48   134 S. Ct. 1861 (2014).

judgment. This is not a rule specific to qualified immunity; it is simply an application of the more general rule that a "judge's function" at summary judgment is not "to weigh the evidence and determine the truth of the matter but to determine whether there is a genuine issue for trial." Summary judgment is appropriate only if "the movant shows that there is no genuine issue as to any material fact and the movant is entitled to judgment as a matter of law." In making that determination, a court must view the evidence "in the light most favorable to the opposing party."...

In holding that Cotton's actions did not violate clearly established law, the Fifth Circuit failed to view the evidence at summary judgment in the light most favorable to Tolan with respect to the central facts of this case. By failing to credit evidence that contradicted some of its key factual conclusions, the court improperly "weigh[ed] the evidence" and resolved disputed issues in favor of the moving party....

The witnesses on both sides come to this case with their own perceptions, recollections, and even potential biases. It is in part for that reason that genuine disputes are generally resolved by juries in our adversarial system. By weighing the evidence and reaching factual inferences contrary to Tolan's competent evidence, the court below neglected to adhere to the fundamental principle that at the summary judgment stage, reasonable inferences should be drawn in favor of the nonmoving party.[49]

Celotex Corp. v. Catrett, 477 U.S. 317 (1986)

The Court in Celotex emphasized that summary judgment should be entered when appropriate, and should not be seen as a "disfavored procedural shortcut." Specifically, the Court in Celotex construed Rule 56 to find that a properly supported motion for summary judgment can point to a failure of proof in the record; that is, the absence of a fact supporting an element of the opposing party's claim on which the opposing party bears the burden of proof. If the absence of the fact is undisputed, summary judgment is appropriate. This is different than pointing to an affirmative undisputed fact in the record as in Liberty Lobby below. Rather, the failure of proof

---

[49]   Tolan v. Cotton, 134 S. Ct. 1861, 1866, 1868 (2014) (citations omitted).

involves the absence of a fact in the record. In Celotex, the factual absence that the Court consid-ered was **the absence of a fact** *showing that the plaintiff was exposed to the defendant's asbestos.*

...Under Rule 56(c), summary judgment is proper "if the pleadings, dep-ositions, answers to interrogatories, and admissions on file, together with the affidavits, if any, show that there is no genuine issue as to any material fact and that the moving party is entitled to a judgment as a matter of law." In our view, the plain language of Rule 56(c) mandates the entry of summary judgment, after adequate time for discovery and upon motion, against a party who fails to make a showing sufficient to establish the ex-istence of an element essential to that party's case, and on which that party will bear the burden of proof at trial. In such a situation, there can be "no genuine issue as to any material fact," since a complete failure of proof concerning an essential element of the nonmoving party's case necessarily renders all other facts immaterial. The moving party is "entitled to a judg-ment as a matter of law" because the nonmoving party has failed to make a sufficient showing on an essential element of her case with respect to which she has the burden of proof. "[T]h[e] standard [for granting sum-mary judgment] mirrors the standard for a directed verdict under Federal Rule of Civil Procedure 50(a)...."

Of course, a party seeking summary judgment always bears the initial re-sponsibility of informing the district court of the basis for its motion, and identifying those portions of "the pleadings, depositions, answers to in-terrogatories, and admissions on file, together with the affidavits, if any," which it believes demonstrate the absence of a genuine issue of material fact. But unlike the Court of Appeals, we find no express or implied re-quirement in Rule 56 that the moving party support its motion with affi-davits or other similar materials negating the opponent's claim. On the contrary, Rule 56(c), which refers to "the affidavits, if any" (emphasis added), suggests the absence of such a requirement. And if there were any doubt about the meaning of Rule 56(c) in this regard, such doubt is clearly removed by Rules 56(a) and (b), which provide that claimants and defend-ants, respectively, may move for summary judgment "with or without sup-porting affidavits" (emphasis added). The import of these subsections is that, regardless of whether the moving party accompanies its summary judgment motion with affidavits, the motion may, and should, be granted so long as whatever is before the district court demonstrates that the standard for the entry of summary judgment, as set forth in Rule 56(c), is satisfied. One of the principal purposes of the summary judgment rule is to isolate and dispose of factually unsupported claims or defenses, and we think it should be interpreted in a way that allows it to accomplish this purpose....

In cases like the instant one, where the nonmoving party will bear the burden of proof at trial on a dispositive issue, a summary judgment motion may properly be made in reliance solely on the "pleadings, depositions, answers to interrogatories, and admissions on file." Such a motion, whether or not accompanied by affidavits, will be "made and supported as provided in this rule," and Rule 56(e) therefore requires the nonmoving party to go beyond the pleadings and by her own affidavits, or by the "depositions, answers to interrogatories, and admissions on file," designate "specific facts showing that there is a genuine issue for trial."

We do not mean that the nonmoving party must produce evidence in a form that would be admissible at trial in order to avoid summary judgment. Obviously, Rule 56 does not require the nonmoving party to depose her own witnesses. Rule 56(e) permits a proper summary judgment motion to be opposed by any of the kinds of evidentiary materials listed in Rule 56(c), except the mere pleadings themselves, and it is from this list that one would normally expect the nonmoving party to make the showing to which we have referred....

The Federal Rules of Civil Procedure have for almost 50 years authorized motions for summary judgment upon proper showings of the lack of a genuine, triable issue of material fact. Summary judgment procedure is properly regarded not as a disfavored procedural shortcut, but rather as an integral part of the Federal Rules as a whole, which are designed "to secure the just, speedy and inexpensive determination of every action." Before the shift to "notice pleading" accomplished by the Federal Rules, motions to dismiss a complaint or to strike a defense were the principal tools by which factually insufficient claims or defenses could be isolated and prevented from going to trial with the attendant unwarranted consumption of public and private resources. But with the advent of "notice pleading," the motion to dismiss seldom fulfills this function any more, and its place has been taken by the motion for summary judgment. Rule 56 must be construed with due regard not only for the rights of persons asserting claims and defenses that are adequately based in fact to have those claims and defenses tried to a jury, but also for the rights of persons opposing such claims and defenses to demonstrate in the manner provided by the Rule, prior to trial, that the claims and defenses have no factual basis.

*   *   *

Anderson v. Liberty Lobby, Inc., 477 U.S. 242 (1986)

Anderson v. Liberty Lobby unpacks the Rule 56 summary judgment standard in detail. In particular, the case provides that summary judgment is appropriate "if the pleadings, depositions, answers to interrogatories, and admissions on file, together with the affidavits, if any, show that there is no genuine issue as to any material fact and that the moving party is entitled to a judgment as a matter of law." Material facts are facts that make a difference to the outcome of the action and are determined by reference to the substance law. In a defamation case like Liberty Lobby, the substantive law provides that the level of a reporter's investigation, research, and reliance on a variety of sources is a material fact that if undisputed would preclude a finding of actual malice and thus render summary judgment appropriate. Any dispute of the material fact must be genuine. That is, the facts presented in opposition to summary judgment must show a sufficient disagreement to require submission to a jury. If the facts do not show a sufficient disagreement, one party must prevail as a matter of law. In other words, if a reasonable jury could find for one party or the other under the relevant evidentiary standard, the dispute of fact is genuine.

…Following discovery, petitioners moved for summary judgment pursuant to Rule 56. In their motion, petitioners asserted that because respondents are public figures they were required to prove their case under the standards set forth in New York Times. Petitioners also asserted that summary judgment was proper because actual malice was absent as a matter of law. In support of this latter assertion, petitioners submitted the affidavit of Charles Bermant, an employee of petitioners and the author of the two longer articles. In this affidavit, Bermant stated that he had spent a substantial amount of time researching and writing the articles and that his facts were obtained from a wide variety of sources. He also stated that he had at all times believed and still believed that the facts contained in the articles were truthful and accurate. Attached to this affidavit was an appendix in which Bermant detailed the sources for each of the statements alleged by respondents to be libelous.

Respondents opposed the motion for summary judgment, asserting that there were numerous inaccuracies in the articles and claiming that an issue of actual malice was presented by virtue of the fact that in preparing the articles Bermant had relied on several sources that respondents asserted were patently unreliable. Generally, respondents charged that petitioners had failed adequately to verify their information before publishing. Respondents also presented evidence that William McGaw, an editor of The Investigator, had told petitioner Adkins before publication that the articles were "terrible" and "ridiculous."

In ruling on the motion for summary judgment, the District Court first held that respondents were limited-purpose public figures and that New York Times therefore applied. The District Court then held that Bermant's thorough investigation and research and his reliance on numerous sources precluded a finding of actual malice. Thus, the District Court granted the motion and entered judgment in favor of petitioners....

Rule 56(c) of the Federal Rules of Civil Procedure provides that summary judgment "shall be rendered forthwith if the pleadings, depositions, answers to interrogatories, and admissions on file, together with the affidavits, if any, show that there is no genuine issue as to any material fact and that the moving party is entitled to a judgment as a matter of law." By its very terms, this standard provides that the mere existence of some alleged factual dispute between the parties will not defeat an otherwise properly supported motion for summary judgment; the requirement is that there be no genuine issue of material fact.

As to materiality, the substantive law will identify which facts are material. Only disputes over facts that might affect the outcome of the suit under the governing law will properly preclude the entry of summary judgment. Factual disputes that are irrelevant or unnecessary will not be counted. This materiality inquiry is independent of and separate from the question of the incorporation of the evidentiary standard into the summary judgment determination. That is, while the materiality determination rests on the substantive law, it is the substantive law's identification of which facts are critical and which facts are irrelevant that governs. Any proof or evidentiary requirements imposed by the substantive law are not germane to this inquiry, since materiality is only a criterion for categorizing factual disputes in their relation to the legal elements of the claim and not a criterion for evaluating the evidentiary underpinnings of those disputes.

More important for present purposes, summary judgment will not lie if the dispute about a material fact is "genuine," that is, if the evidence is such that a reasonable jury could return a verdict for the nonmoving party. In First National Bank of Arizona v. Cities Service Co., [391 U.S. 253 (1968)], we affirmed a grant of summary judgment for an antitrust defendant where the issue was whether there was a genuine factual dispute as to the existence of a conspiracy. We noted Rule 56(e)'s provision that a party opposing a properly supported motion for summary judgment "'may not rest upon the mere allegations or denials of his pleading, but...must set forth specific facts showing that there is a genuine issue for trial.'" We observed further that "[i]t is true that the issue of material fact required by Rule 56(c) to be present to entitle a party to proceed to trial is not required to be resolved conclusively in favor of the party asserting its existence; rather, all that is required is that sufficient evidence supporting the claimed factual dispute be shown to require a jury or judge to resolve the parties' differing versions of the truth at trial."

We went on to hold that, in the face of the defendant's properly supported motion for summary judgment, the plaintiff could not rest on his allegations of a conspiracy to get to a jury without "any significant probative evidence tending to support the complaint."...

[I]t is clear enough from our recent cases that at the summary judgment stage the judge's function is not himself to weigh the evidence and determine the truth of the matter but to determine whether there is a genuine issue for trial. [T]here is no issue for trial unless there is sufficient evidence favoring the nonmoving party for a jury to return a verdict for that party. If the evidence is merely colorable or is not significantly probative, summary judgment may be granted....

The Court has said that summary judgment should be granted where the evidence is such that it "would require a directed verdict for the moving party." And we have noted that the "genuine issue" summary judgment standard is "very close" to the "reasonable jury" directed verdict standard: "The primary difference between the two motions is procedural; summary judgment motions are usually made before trial and decided on documentary evidence, while directed verdict motions are made at trial and decided on the evidence that has been admitted." In essence, though, the inquiry under each is the same: whether the evidence presents a sufficient disagreement to require submission to a jury or whether it is so one-sided that one party must prevail as a matter of law....

[W]e are [further] convinced that the inquiry involved in a ruling on a motion for summary judgment or for a directed verdict necessarily implicates the substantive evidentiary standard of proof that would apply at the trial on the merits. If the defendant in a run-of-the-mill civil case moves for summary judgment or for a directed verdict based on the lack of proof of a material fact, the judge must ask himself not whether he thinks the evidence unmistakably favors one side or the other but whether a fair-minded jury could return a verdict for the plaintiff on the evidence presented. The mere existence of a scintilla of evidence in support of the plaintiff's position will be insufficient; there must be evidence on which the jury could reasonably find for the plaintiff. The judge's inquiry, therefore, unavoidably asks whether reasonable jurors could find by a preponderance of the evidence that the plaintiff is entitled to a verdict—"whether there is [evidence] upon which a jury can properly proceed to find a verdict for the party producing it, upon whom the onus of proof is imposed."...

Just as the "convincing clarity" requirement is relevant in ruling on a motion for directed verdict, it is relevant in ruling on a motion for summary judgment. When determining if a genuine factual issue as to actual malice exists in a libel suit brought by a public figure, a trial judge must bear in mind the actual quantum and quality of proof necessary to support liability under New York Times. For example, there is no genuine issue if the evidence presented in the opposing affidavits is of insufficient caliber or quantity to allow a rational finder of fact to find actual malice by clear and convincing evidence.

Thus, in ruling on a motion for summary judgment, the judge must view the evidence presented through the prism of the substantive evidentiary burden. This conclusion is mandated by the nature of this determination....

*   *   *

Chapter 6: Introduction to Civil Procedure 2: Jurisdiction

Introduction

The basic requisites of a federal cause of action are: (1) the court must have subject matter jurisdiction over the claim, (2) the court must have personal jurisdiction over the parties, and (3) the forum for the claim (that is, the claim's venue) must be proper.[50]

When I use the term **jurisdiction**, I am referring to limits on the power of a court. **Subject matter jurisdiction** refers to the power of a federal court to only hear certain types of claims. **Personal jurisdiction** refers to the geographic reach of the court's power; meaning the court's power over the parties to the claim depending on where the parties are located and served with process. **Venue** refers to the proper federal district (trial) court in which the action should be brought.

These concepts are explained in detail below.

Subject Matter Jurisdiction

It is well known that the jurisdiction of the federal courts is limited.[51] This is in contrast to state courts, which are courts of general jurisdiction (meaning they

---

[50]   There are other requisites of a federal cause of action, such as the case or controversy requirement, standing, justiciability, ripeness, and the like, but in litigation involving disputes between private parties, these concepts are generally uncontroversial and their application self-evident. For that reason, discussion of them is beyond the scope of this chapter.

[51]   "From the twin principles discussed above—that Article III of the Constitution delineates the possible range of federal subject-matter jurisdiction and that congressional enactments define the actual scope of jurisdiction at any given time—it follows that federal jurisdiction is limited in nature." JACK H. FRIENDENTHAL ET AL., CIVIL PROCEDURE 13 (4th ed. 2005).

can hear any case brought before them). Given the limits on jurisdiction, all claims filed in federal court must meet certain subject matter requirements before the court can even hear the matter. In other words, the federal court must have subject matter jurisdiction over the claim. Without subject matter jurisdiction, there is no federal judicial power.[52]

The areas over which the federal courts' subject matter jurisdiction extends are set forth in the Constitution, and more specifically in Title 28 of the United

---

Article III of the Constitution specifies the limitations by listing the only areas over which federal judicial power extends:

> The judicial Power shall extend to all Cases, in Law and Equity, arising under this Constitution, the Laws of the United States, and Treaties made, or which shall be made, under their Authority;--to all Cases affecting Ambassadors, other public Ministers and Consuls;--to all Cases of admiralty and maritime Jurisdiction;--to Controversies to which the United States shall be a Party;--to Controversies between two or more States;--between a State and Citizens of another State;--between Citizens of different States;--between Citizens of the same State claiming Lands under Grants of different States, and between a State, or the Citizens thereof, and foreign States, Citizens or Subjects.

U.S. CONST. art. III, § 2.

[52]   The federal courts treat their subject matter jurisdiction with tremendous respect, and may raise the notion of a lack of jurisdiction on their own. *See* Louisiana & Nashville R.R. Co. v. Mottley, 211 U.S. 149, 152 (1908) ("We do not deem it necessary, however, to consider either of these questions, because, in our opinion, the court below was without jurisdiction of the cause. Neither party has questioned that jurisdiction, but it is the duty of this court to see to it that the jurisdiction of the circuit court, which is defined and limited by statute, is not exceeded. This duty we have frequently performed of our own motion."); Cameron v. Hodges, 127 U.S. 322, 325 (1888) ("This court has always been very particular in requiring a distinct statement of the citizenship of the parties, and of the particular state in which it is claimed, in order to sustain the jurisdiction of those courts; and inasmuch as the only citizenship specifically averred and set out in the case before us is that of the defendant Hodges, at whose instance the cause was removed, and as that is the only ground upon which the removal was placed, it seems clear that the circuit court did not have jurisdiction of it, and that the suit should have been dismissed or remanded for that reason.").

States Code.[53] Generally speaking, the federal courts' subject matter jurisdiction is limited to claims arising under the Constitution or laws of the United States, known as **federal question jurisdiction**, and claims between citizens of different states or between citizens of a state and a foreign country where the amount in controversy exceeds $75,000, known as **diversity jurisdiction**. Federal subject matter jurisdiction is of such importance that its basis must appear on the face of the complaint.[54] This means that the facts that support the exercise of jurisdiction must be affirmatively pled.

Federal Question Jurisdiction

The general federal jurisdiction statute in the United States Code provides as follows:

> The district courts shall have original jurisdiction of all civil actions arising under the Constitution, laws, or treaties of the United States.[55]

Other statutes set forth more specific areas of federal question jurisdiction,[56] but 28 U.S.C. § 1331 is considered the general federal question jurisdiction statute.[57] The key question in determining federal question jurisdiction, of course, is

---

[53]   It is important to note that the subject matter jurisdiction authorized by Congress is more narrow than that set forth in the Constitution. *See* ERWIN CHEMERINSKY, FEDERAL JURISDICTION 266-67 (5th ed. 2007) ("Ever since the first statute creating the federal courts, the Judiciary Act of 1789, federal jurisdiction never has included the authority to adjudicate all matters allowed by Article III.").

[54]   *See* FED. R. CIV. P. 8(a)(1).

[55]   28 U.S.C. § 1331 (2006).

[56]   *See id.* §§ 1333-69.

[57]   Although the Constitution specifies the boundaries of the jurisdiction of the federal courts, and has done so since its adoption, Congress did not enact a "general" federal jurisdiction statute until 1875. That statute provided: "[T]he circuit courts of the United States shall have original cognizance, concurrent with the courts of the several States, of all suits of a civil nature at common law or in equity, where the matter in dispute exceeds, exclusive of costs, the sum or value of five hundred dollars, and arising under the Constitution or laws of the United States, or treaties made, or which shall be made, under their authority." Act of March 3, 1875, ch. 137, 18 Stat. 470. This statute, with the exception of

whether the action in question "arises under" the Constitution, laws or treaties of the United States. Erwin Chemerinsky has argued that the "arising under" requirement is best understood in the context of three rules or principles.[58]

1. The Well-Pleaded Complaint Rule.

The Well-Pleaded Complaint Rule is something of a misnomer as the rule really has nothing to do with how "well" the plaintiff has pled her cause of action; that is, it has nothing to do with the "quality" of the pleading. Rather, the Well-Pleaded Complaint Rule refers to the necessity that the plaintiff's complaint, and not any subsequent pleading, contain the basis for federal question jurisdiction. In other words, federal question jurisdiction cannot arise out of allegations raised in a defendant's answer; the basis for the exercise of jurisdiction must be set forth in the plaintiff's complaint itself.

Louisiana & Nashville R.R. Co. v. Mottley, 211 U.S. 149 (1908).

In Mottley, the plaintiffs' cause of action was for specific performance of a contract that, it was alleged, the defendant failed to perform due to application of an Act of Congress. The Supreme Court held, even though jurisdiction was not questioned by either party, that it lacked jurisdiction over the case because it is the plaintiff's cause of action that must arise under federal law in order for jurisdiction to be proper, and in the case before it, the plaintiffs' claim arose under state law and it was only an anticipated defense that implicated federal law.

> It would be wholly unnecessary and improper, in order to prove complainant's cause of action, to go into any matters of defense which the defendants might possibly set up, and then attempt to reply to such defense, and thus, if possible, to show that a Federal question might or probably would arise in the course of the trial of the case. To allege such

---

the amount in controversy requirement (with regard to federal question cases), is the direct ancestor of the modern general federal question jurisdiction statute, which is codified at 28 U.S.C. § 1331.

[58]	*See* ERWIN CHEMERINSKY, FEDERAL JURISDICTION 282-95 (5th ed. 2007).

defense and then make an answer to it before the defendant has the opportunity to itself plead or prove its own defense is inconsistent with any
known rule of pleading, so far as we are aware, and is improper.

The rule is a reasonable and just one that the complainant in the first instance shall be confined to a statement of its cause of action, leaving to
the defendant to set up in his answer what his defense is, and, if anything
more than a denial of complainant's cause of action, imposing upon the
defendant the burden of proving such defense.

Conforming itself to that rule, the complainant would not, in the assertion
or proof of its cause of action, bring up a single Federal question. The
presentation of its cause of action would not show that it was one arising
under the Constitution or laws of the United States.[59]

2.   Claim Based on Federal Law.

The most straightforward basis for federal question jurisdiction is when the
cause of action itself was created by federal law or, more generally, when the right
for which the plaintiff seeks vindication was created by federal law.

3.   Claim Based on State Law.

The most difficult interpretations of the "arising under" language occur when
the plaintiff brings a state law claim that implicates federal law. Does such a claim
arise under the Constitution, laws, or treaties of the United States? In making this
determination, the Supreme Court has stated that "determinations about federal
jurisdiction require sensitive judgments about congressional intent, judicial power,
and the federal system."[60]

---

[59]   211 U.S. 149, 153 (1908) (quoting Boston & Montana Consol. Copper &
Silver Min. Co. v. Montana Ore Purch. Co., 188 U.S. 632, 638-39 (1903)).
[60]   Merrell Dow Pharmaceuticals, Inc. v. Thompson, 478 U.S. 804, 810
(1986).

Smith v. Kansas City Title & Trust Co., 255 U.S. 180 (1921).

The Smith case involved a state law cause of action.

No objection is made to the federal jurisdiction, either original or appellate, by the parties to this suit, but that question will be first examined. The company is authorized to invest its funds in legal securities only. The attack upon the proposed investment in the bonds described is because of the alleged unconstitutionality of the acts of Congress undertaking to organize the banks and authorize the issue of the bonds. No other reason is set forth in the bill as a ground of objection to the proposed investment by the board of directors acting in the company's behalf. As diversity of citizenship is lacking, the jurisdiction of the District Court depends upon whether the cause of action set forth arises under the Constitution or laws of the United States.

The general rule is that, where it appears from the bill or statement of the plaintiff that the right to relief depends upon the construction or application of the Constitution or laws of the United States, and that such federal claim is not merely colorable, and rests upon a reasonable foundation, the District Court has jurisdiction under this provision. ...

The jurisdiction of this court is to be determined upon the principles laid down in the cases referred to. In the instant case the averments of the bill show that the directors were proceeding to make the investments in view of the act authorizing the bonds about to be purchased, maintaining that the act authorizing them was constitutional and the bonds valid and desirable investments. The objecting shareholder avers in the bill that the securities were issued under an unconstitutional law, and hence of no validity. It is therefore apparent that the controversy concerns the constitutional validity of an act of Congress which is directly drawn in question. The decision depends upon the determination of this issue. The general allegations as to the interest of the shareholder, and his right to have an injunction to prevent the purchase of the alleged unconstitutional securities by misapplication of the funds of the corporation, [provides the District Court with] jurisdiction . . . .[61]

Diversity Jurisdiction

Diversity jurisdiction permits the bringing of purely state law claims in federal court. As with federal question jurisdiction, diversity jurisdiction—though Constitutionally-based—is defined by statute. There are two components to this type of jurisdiction, (1) the diversity of citizenship of the parties on either side of the lawsuit, and (2) the amount in controversy. The diversity jurisdiction statute provides:

> The district courts shall have original jurisdiction of all civil actions where the matter in controversy exceeds the sum or value of $75,000, exclusive of interest and costs, and is between—
>
> (1) citizens of different States;
>
> (2) citizens of a State and citizens or subjects of a foreign state;
>
> (3) citizens of different States and in which citizens or subjects of a foreign state are additional parties; and
>
> (4) a foreign state, defined in section 1603(a) of this title, as plaintiff and citizens of a State or of different States.[62]

Capron v. Van Noorden, 6 U.S. 126 (1804).

A plaintiff may assign for error the want of jurisdiction in that court to which he has chosen to resort.

A party may take advantage of an error in his favor, if it be an error of the Court.

The Courts of the U.S. have not jurisdiction unless the record shews that the parties are citizens of different states, or that one is an alien, &c.

---

[61]   255 U.S. 180, 199, 201-02 (1921).

[62]   28 U.S.C. § 1332 (2006).

Error to the Circuit Court of North Carolina. The proceedings stated Van Noorden to be late of Pitt county, but did not allege Capron, the plaintiff, to be an alien, nor a citizen of any state, nor the place of his residence.

Upon the general issue, in an action of trespass on the case, a verdict was found for the defendant, Van Noorden, upon which judgment was rendered.

The writ of Error was sued out by Capron, the plaintiff below, who assigned for error, among other things, first "That the circuit court aforesaid is a court of limited jurisdiction, and that by the record aforesaid it doth not appear, as it ought to have done, that either the said George Capron, or the said Hadrianus Van Noorden was an alien at the time of the commencement of said suit, or at any other time, or that one of the said parties was at that or any other time, a citizen of the state of North Carolina where the suit was brought, and the other a citizen of another state; or that they the said George and Hadrianus were for any cause whatever, persons within the jurisdiction of the said court, and capable of suing and being sued there."

And secondly, "That by the record aforesaid it manifestly appeareth that the said Circuit Court had not any jurisdiction of the cause aforesaid, nor ought to have held plea thereof, or given judgment therein, but ought to have dismissed the same, whereas the said Court hath proceeded to final judgment therein."

Harper, for the plaintiff in error, stated the only question to be whether the plaintiff had a right to assign for error, the want of jurisdiction in that Court to which he had chosen to resort.

It is true, as a general rule, that a man cannot reverse a judgment for error in process or delay, unless he can shew that the error was to his disadvantage; but it is also a rule, that he may reverse a judgment for an error of the Court, even though it be for his advantage. As if a verdict be found for the debt, damages, and costs; and the judgment be only for the debt and damages, the defendant may assign for error that the judgment was not also for costs, although the error is for his advantage.

Here it was the duty of the Court to see that they had jurisdiction, for the consent of parties could not give it.

It is therefore an error of the Court, and the plaintiff has a right to take advantage of it.

The defendant in error did not appear, but the citation having been duly served, the judgment was reversed.

Questions

1. Waaaaait a minute here. This was the plaintiff's lawsuit, the plaintiff's choice of court, and the plaintiff's allegations at issue. How can the plaintiff benefit from his own mistake? Hasn't he waived any objection?

2. Why was federal jurisdiction not proper here?

3. Wasn't there any easy way to cure the problem here? Why wasn't that route taken?

Coury v. Prot, 85 F.3d 244 (5th Cir. 1996).

This case discussed the method for determining the citizenship of an individual for the purpose of diversity.

> What makes a person a citizen of a state? The fourteenth amendment to the Constitution provides that: "All persons born or naturalized in the United States, and subject to the jurisdiction thereof, are citizens of the United States and of the State wherein they reside." However, "reside" has been interpreted to mean more than to be temporarily living in the state; it means to be "domiciled" there. Thus, to be a citizen of a state within the meaning of the diversity provision, a natural person must be both (1) a citizen of the United States, and (2) a domiciliary of that state. Federal common law, not the law of any state, determines whether a person is a citizen of a particular state for purposes of diversity jurisdiction.
>
> ...

A person's domicile persists until a new one is acquired or it is clearly abandoned. There is a presumption in favor of the continuing domicile which requires the party seeking to show a change in domicile to come forward with enough evidence to that effect to withstand a directed verdict. While some opinions seem to imply that the burden of persuasion rests with the party attempting to show a change of domicile, this is an overstatement. The proper rule is that the party attempting to show a change assumes the burden of going forward on that issue. The ultimate burden on the issue of jurisdiction rests with the plaintiff or the party invoking federal jurisdiction.

In determining a litigant's domicile, the court must address a variety of factors. No single factor is determinative. The court should look to all evidence shedding light on the litigant's intention to establish domicile. The factors may include the places where the litigant exercises civil and political rights, pays taxes, owns real and personal property, has driver's and other licenses, maintains bank accounts, belongs to clubs and churches, has places of business or employment, and maintains a home for his family. A litigant's statement of intent is relevant to the determination of domicile, but it is entitled to little weight if it conflicts with the objective facts.[63]

Dimmitt & Owens Financial v. United States, 787 F.2d 1186 (7th Cir. 1986).

This case discussed corporate citizenship. For the purpose of determining diversity, a corporation is deemed a citizen of the both the state where it is incorporated and the state where it has its principal place of business.

The purpose of [the diversity jurisdiction statute] in making a corporation a citizen of the state where it has its principal place of business as well as the state where it is incorporated is to exclude from the federal diversity jurisdiction cases between a citizen of a state and a corporation

---

[63]   85 F.3d 244, 248, 250-51 (5th Cir. 1996).

whose center of gravity is in the same state even though it may be incorporated elsewhere; for such a corporation should be sufficiently "local"— sufficiently identified with the state—to avoid the obloquy that may attach to a "foreign" corporation in litigation with a local resident and that provides the modern rationale of the diversity jurisdiction. The words "principal place of business" are to be construed with this purpose in mind.[64]

Freeland v. Liberty Mutual Fire Ins. Co., 632 F.3d 250 (6th Cir. 2011).

In Freeland, the case had been fully litigated in the district court. Nevertheless, the appellate court dismissed for a lack of subject matter jurisdiction because the amount in controversy was $75,000.00 exactly and therefore did not "exceed" 75,000.00, as required by the diversity jurisdiction statute. Key takeaway? The statutory language matters; make sure your amount in controversy is over $75,000.00 for purposes of diversity jurisdiction in the federal courts.

This insurance coverage case arises out of a tragic car accident. Despite the resources that have been invested in litigating this action, we must dismiss it to start anew in state court because the amount in controversy is one penny short of our jurisdictional minimum. ...

When Congress first established the lower federal courts in the Judiciary Act of 1789, the required amount in controversy was $500. That figure has increased over the years, and today "the matter in controversy [must] exceed[ ] the sum or value of $75,000, exclusive of interest and costs."

Yet in this case the amount in controversy is $75,000 exactly-one penny short of the jurisdictional bar that Congress has set. The Freelands seek a declaratory judgment that their insurance policy provides UM/UIM coverage up to $100,000 per accident, instead of the $25,000 per accident maximum that appears on the policy's face. "In actions seeking declaratory or injunctive relief, it is well established that the amount

---

64   787 F.2d 1186, 1190 (7th Cir. 1986).

in controversy is measured by the value of the object of the litigation." Applying this principle, this Court has said that, "[w]here a party seeks a declaratory judgment, 'the amount in controversy is not necessarily the money judgment sought or recovered, but rather the value of the consequences which may result from the litigation.'" If the Freelands prevail in this case, they will receive a declaration that their policy provides up to $100,000 in UM/UIM coverage. If they do not prevail, their policy will remain as-is, with only $25,000 in UM/UIM coverage. The "value of the consequences which may result from the litigation," id.-that is, the monetary consequences that would result from a victory for the Freelands-is the difference between $100,000 and $25,000. That amount is $75,000 exactly.

This conclusion flows from the text of the jurisdictional statute itself. In order for the district court to have original jurisdiction, "the matter in controversy " must "exceed[ ] the sum or value of $75,000." The words "in controversy" have to mean something.[65]

Questions

1. A penny. A lousy penny. Are you serious?

2. If you are serious, why?

3. What explains the absurd inefficiency the court endorses here?

4. Does anyone benefit from the court's ruling? Does the court?

Personal Jurisdiction

Generally

While subject matter jurisdiction defines the court's power to hear the claim, personal jurisdiction defines the court's power over the litigants. This power,

---

[65]   632 F.3d 250, 251-53 (6th Cir. 2011).

which is geographically based, enables the court to enforce its orders, command the parties to appear, enter judgment, and in short, do all the things a court needs to do to resolve disputes.[66]

Like subject matter jurisdiction, the personal jurisdiction limitations are derived from the Constitution. As Justice Brennan explained in Burger King v. Rudzewicz:[67]

> The Due Process Clause protects an individual's liberty interest in not being subject to the binding judgments of a forum with which he has established no meaningful "contacts, ties, or relations." By requiring that individuals have "fair warning that a particular activity may subject [them] to the jurisdiction of a foreign sovereign," the Due Process Clause "gives a degree of predictability to the legal system that allows potential defendants to structure their primary conduct with some minimum assurance as to where that conduct will and will not render them liable to suit."[68]

When I say that the power of the court over the litigants is "geographically based," I mean that generally speaking, it extends to the boundaries of the state in which the district court sits.

A basic idea of state court personal jurisdiction is that a state court has authority to enter judgment against a person who is in the state, and

---

[66] The exercise of judicial jurisdiction implies the authority to enter legally binding judgments and to use the coercive powers of executive agencies (for example, the sheriff) to compel compliance with those judgments. In this sense, judicial jurisdiction is dependent on the "power" of the state.

FLEMING JAMES, JR. ET AL., CIVIL PROCEDURE 60 (2001) (footnote omitted).

Other types of jurisdiction of this nature are *in rem* jurisdiction, where the claim is directed against a piece of personal or real property, and *quasi in rem*, which is often used to attach or seize property belonging to a defendant or other individual.

[67] 471 U.S. 462 (1985).

[68] *Id.* at 471-72 (footnotes and citations omitted).

served with process, against property located in the state and involved in a transaction in the state, and against one who consents to jurisdiction.[69]

This idea of "presence" within a state being the source of judicial power applies, of course, to those parties actually within the borders of the state when served with process. And, it also applies to those parties who have sufficient contacts with the state to render proper the exercise of jurisdiction over them. As stated by the Supreme Court in International Shoe v. Washington:[70]

> [N]ow . . . due process requires only that in order to subject a defendant to a judgment in personam, if he be not present within the territory of the forum, he have certain minimum contacts with it such that the maintenance of the suit does not offend "traditional notions of fair play and substantial justice." . . . The terms "present" or "presence" are used merely to symbolize those activities of the corporation's agent within the state which courts will deem sufficient to satisfy the demands of due process....[71]

International Shoe's examination of the reach of a state's jurisdiction beyond the borders of the state in effect authorized states to enact laws known as "long-arm statutes," which specified the lengths to which the state's jurisdiction extended with regard to those parties not physically present within the state. While many of these statutes extended the state's jurisdiction to the full extent authorized by the Constitution, others did not, and instead placed more stringent limits on the reach of the state's power. When analyzing questions of personal jurisdiction, the court must therefore be mindful of both the Constitutional and the state statutory dimensions; the court must determine if the exercise of jurisdiction would satisfy (1) the Constitution's due process clause, and (2) the state's long-arm statute.[72]

------

[69]   *Id.* at 463.

[70]   326 U.S. 310 (1945).

[71]   *Id.* at 316-17.

[72]   *See* Omni Capital Int'l, Ltd. v. Rudolf Wolff & Co., Ltd., 484 U.S. 97, 104 (1987) ("[B]efore a court may exercise personal jurisdiction over a defendant, there must be more than notice to the defendant and a constitutionally sufficient

International Shoe Co. v. Washington, 326 U.S. 310 (1945).

STONE, C.J. The questions for decision are (1) whether, within the limitations of the due process clause of the Fourteenth Amendment, appellant, a Delaware corporation, has by its activities in the State of Washington rendered itself amenable to proceedings in the courts of that state to recover unpaid contributions to the state unemployment compensation fund exacted by state statutes, Washington Unemployment Compensation Act, Washington Revised Statutes, s 9998-103a through s 9998-123a, 1941 Supp., and (2) whether the state can exact those contributions consistently with the due process clause of the Fourteenth Amendment.

The statutes in question set up a comprehensive scheme of unemployment compensation, the costs of which are defrayed by contributions required to be made by employers to a state unemployment compensation fund. The contributions are a specified percentage of the wages payable annually by each employer for his employees' services in the state. The assessment and collection of the contributions and the fund are administered by respondents. [Washington law] authorizes respondent Commissioner to issue an order and notice of assessment of delinquent contributions upon prescribed personal service of the notice upon the employer if found within the state, or, if not so found, by mailing the notice to the employer by registered mail at his last known address. That section also authorizes the Commissioner to collect the assessment by distraint if it is not paid

---

relationship between the defendant and the forum. There also must be a basis for the defendant's amenability to service of summons. Absent consent, this means there must be authorization for service of summons on the defendant.")

This framework applies whether the court is exercising diversity or federal question jurisdiction. However, in certain specific exercises of federal question jurisdiction, Congress may have authorized nationwide personal jurisdiction, where some sort of contacts analysis with the United States as a whole may be employed. *See, e.g.,* 15 U.S.C. § 22 (2006) ("Any suit, action, or proceeding under the antitrust laws against a corporation may be brought not only in the judicial district whereof it is an inhabitant, but also in any district wherein it may be found or transacts business; and all process in such cases may be served in the district of which it is an inhabitant, or wherever it may be found.").

within ten days after service of the notice. By [sections] 14(e) and 6(b) the order of assessment may be administratively reviewed by an appeal tribunal within the office of unemployment upon petition of the employer, and this determination is by s 6(i) made subject to judicial review on questions of law by the state Superior Court, with further right of appeal in the state Supreme Court as in other civil cases.

In this case notice of assessment for the years in question was personally served upon a sales solicitor employed by appellant in the State of Washington, and a copy of the notice was mailed by registered mail to appellant at its address in St. Louis, Missouri. Appellant appeared specially before the office of unemployment and moved to set aside the order and notice of assessment on the ground that the service upon appellant's salesman was not proper service upon appellant; that appellant was not a corporation of the State of Washington and was not doing business within the state; that it had no agent within the state upon whom service could be made; and that appellant is not an employer and does not furnish employment within the meaning of the statute.

The motion was heard on evidence and a stipulation of facts by the appeal tribunal which denied the motion and ruled that respondent Commissioner was entitled to recover the unpaid contributions. That action was affirmed by the Commissioner; both the Superior Court and the Supreme Court affirmed. Appellant in each of these courts assailed the statute as applied, as a violation of the due process clause of the Fourteenth Amendment, and as imposing a constitutionally prohibited burden on interstate commerce. The cause comes here on appeal . . ., appellant assigning as error that the challenged statutes as applied infringe the due process clause of the Fourteenth Amendment and the commerce clause.

The facts as found by the appeal tribunal and accepted by the state Superior Court and Supreme Court, are not in dispute. Appellant is a Delaware corporation, having its principal place of business in St. Louis, Missouri, and is engaged in the manufacture and sale of shoes and other footwear. It maintains places of business in several states, other than Washington, at which its manufacturing is carried on and from which its merchandise is distributed interstate through several sales units or branches located outside the State of Washington.

Appellant has no office in Washington and makes no contracts either for sale or purchase of merchandise there. It maintains no stock of merchandise in that state and makes there no deliveries of goods in intrastate commerce. During the years from 1937 to 1940, now in question, appellant employed eleven to thirteen salesmen under direct supervision and control of sales managers located in St. Louis. These salesmen resided in Washington; their principal activities were confined to that state; and they were compensated by commissions based upon the amount of their sales. The commissions for each year totaled more than $31,000. Appellant supplies its salesmen with a line of samples, each consisting of one shoe of a pair, which they display to prospective purchasers. On occasion they rent permanent sample rooms, for exhibiting samples, in business buildings, or rent rooms in hotels or business buildings temporarily for that purpose. The cost of such rentals is reimbursed by appellant.

The authority of the salesmen is limited to exhibiting their samples and soliciting orders from prospective buyers, at prices and on terms fixed by appellant. The salesmen transmit the orders to appellant's office in St. Louis for acceptance or rejection, and when accepted the merchandise for filling the orders is shipped f.o.b. from points outside Washington to the purchasers within the state. All the merchandise shipped into Washington is invoiced at the place of shipment from which collections are made. No salesman has authority to enter into contracts or to make collections.

The Supreme Court of Washington was of opinion that the regular and systematic solicitation of orders in the state by appellant's salesmen, resulting in a continuous flow of appellant's product into the state, was sufficient to constitute doing business in the state so as to make appellant amenable to suit in its courts. But it was also of opinion that there were sufficient additional activities shown to bring the case within the rule frequently stated, that solicitation within a state by the agents of a foreign corporation plus some additional activities there are sufficient to render the corporation amenable to suit brought in the courts of the state to enforce an obligation arising out of its activities there. The court found such additional activities in the salesmen's display of samples sometimes in permanent display rooms, and the salesmen's residence within the state, continued over a period of years, all resulting in a substantial volume of merchandise regularly shipped by appellant to purchasers within the state. The court also held that the statute as applied did not invade the constitutional power of Congress to regulate interstate commerce and did not impose a prohibited burden on such commerce.

Appellant's argument, renewed here, that the statute imposes an unconstitutional burden on interstate commerce need not detain us. For [federal law] provides that "No person required under a State law to make payments to an unemployment fund shall be relieved from compliance therewith on the ground that he is engaged in interstate or foreign commerce, or that the State law does not distinguish between employees engaged in interstate or foreign commerce and those engaged in intrastate commerce." It is no longer debatable that Congress, in the exercise of the commerce power, may authorize the states, in specified ways, to regulate interstate commerce or impose burdens upon it.

Appellant also insists that its activities within the state were not sufficient to manifest its 'presence' there and that in its absence the state courts were without jurisdiction, that consequently it was a denial of due process for the state to subject appellant to suit. It refers to those cases in which it was said that the mere solicitation of orders for the purchase of goods within a state, to be accepted without the state and filled by shipment of the purchased goods interstate, does not render the corporation seller amenable to suit within the state. And appellant further argues that since it was not present within the state, it is a denial of due process to subject it to taxation or other money exaction. It thus denies the power of the state to lay the tax or to subject appellant to a suit for its collection.

Historically the jurisdiction of courts to render judgment in personam is grounded on their de facto power over the defendant's person. Hence his presence within the territorial jurisdiction of court was prerequisite to its rendition of a judgment personally binding him. But now that the capias ad respondendum has given way to personal service of summons or other form of notice, due process requires only that in order to subject a defendant to a judgment in personam, if he be not present within the territory of the forum, he have certain minimum contacts with it such that the maintenance of the suit does not offend "traditional notions of fair play and substantial justice."

Since the corporate personality is a fiction, although a fiction intended to be acted upon as though it were a fact, it is clear that unlike an individual its 'presence' without, as well as within, the state of its origin can be manifested only by activities carried on in its behalf by those who are authorized to act for it. To say that the corporation is so far 'present' there as to satisfy due process requirements, for purposes of taxation or the maintenance of suits against it in the courts of the state, is to beg the question to be decided. For the terms 'present' or 'presence' are used merely to symbolize those activities of the corporation's agent within the state which courts will deem to be sufficient to satisfy the demands of due process. Those demands may be met by such contacts of the corporation with the state of the forum as make it reasonable, in the context of our federal system of government, to require the corporation to defend the particular suit which is brought there. An 'estimate of the inconveniences' which would result to the corporation from a trial away from its 'home' or principal place of business is relevant in this connection.

"Presence" in the state in this sense has never been doubted when the activities of the corporation there have not only been continuous and systematic, but also give rise to the liabilities sued on, even though no consent to be sued or authorization to an agent to accept service of process has been given. Conversely it has been generally recognized that the casual presence of the corporate agent or even his conduct of single or isolated items of activities in a state in the corporation's behalf are not enough to subject it to suit on causes of action unconnected with the activities there. To require the corporation in such circumstances to defend the suit away from its home or other jurisdiction where it carries on more substantial activities has been thought to lay too great and unreasonable a burden on the corporation to comport with due process.

While it has been held in cases on which appellant relies that continuous activity of some sorts within a state is not enough to support the demand that the corporation be amenable to suits unrelated to that activity, there have been instances in which the continuous corporate operations within a state were thought so substantial and of such a nature as to justify suit against it on causes of action arising from dealings entirely distinct from those activities.

Finally, although the commission of some single or occasional acts of the corporate agent in a state sufficient to impose an obligation or liability on the corporation has not been thought to confer upon the state authority to enforce it, other such acts, because of their nature and quality and the circumstances of their commission, may be deemed sufficient to render the corporation liable to suit. True, some of the decisions holding the corporation amenable to suit have been supported by resort to the legal fiction that it has given its consent to service and suit, consent being implied from its presence in the state through the acts of its authorized agents. But more realistically it may be said that those authorized acts were of such a nature as to justify the fiction.

It is evident that the criteria by which we mark the boundary line between those activities which justify the subjection of a corporation to suit, and those which do not, cannot be simply mechanical or quantitative. The test is not merely, as has sometimes been suggested, whether the activity, which the corporation has seen fit to procure through its agents in another state, is a little more or a little less. Whether due process is satisfied must depend rather upon the quality and nature of the activity in relation to the fair and orderly administration of the laws which it was the purpose of the due process clause to insure. That clause does not contemplate that a state may make binding a judgment in personam against an individual or corporate defendant with which the state has no contacts, ties, or relations.

But to the extent that a corporation exercises the privilege of conducting activities within a state, it enjoys the benefits and protection of the laws of that state. The exercise of that privilege may give rise to obligations; and, so far as those obligations arise out of or are connected with the activities within the state, a procedure which requires the corporation to respond to a suit brought to enforce them can, in most instances, hardly be said to be undue.

Applying these standards, the activities carried on in behalf of appellant in the State of Washington were neither irregular nor casual. They were systematic and continuous throughout the years in question. They resulted in a large volume of interstate business, in the course of which appellant received the benefits and protection of the laws of the state, including the right to resort to the courts for the enforcement of its rights. The obligation which is here sued upon arose out of those very activities. It is evident that these operations establish sufficient contacts or ties with the state of the forum to make it reasonable and just according to our traditional conception of fair play and substantial justice to permit the state to enforce the obligations which appellant has incurred there. Hence we cannot say that the maintenance of the present suit in the State of Washington involves an unreasonable or undue procedure.

We are likewise unable to conclude that the service of the process within the state upon an agent whose activities establish appellant's 'presence' there was not sufficient notice of the suit, or that the suit was so unrelated to those activities as to make the agent an inappropriate vehicle for communicating the notice. It is enough that appellant has established such contacts with the state that the particular form of substituted service adopted there gives reasonable assurance that the notice will be actual. Nor can we say that the mailing of the notice of suit to appellant by registered mail at its home office was not reasonably calculated to apprise appellant of the suit.

Only a word need be said of appellant's liability for the demanded contributions of the state unemployment fund. The Supreme Court of Washington, construing and applying the statute, has held that it imposes a tax on the privilege of employing appellant's salesmen within the state measured by a percentage of the wages, here the commissions payable to the salesmen. This construction we accept for purposes of determining the constitutional validity of the statute. The right to employ labor has been deemed an appropriate subject of taxation in this country and England, both before and since the adoption of the Constitution. And such a tax imposed upon the employer for unemployment benefits is within the constitutional power of the states.

Appellant having rendered itself amenable to suit upon obligations arising out of the activities of its salesmen in Washington, the state may maintain the present suit in personam to collect the tax laid upon the exercise of the privilege of employing appellant's salesmen within the state. For Washington has made one of those activities, which taken together establish appellant's 'presence' there for purposes of suit, the taxable event by which the state brings appellant within the reach of its taxing power. The state thus has constitutional power to lay the tax and to subject appellant to a suit to recover it. The activities which establish its 'presence' subject it alike to taxation by the state and to suit to recover the tax.

Questions

1.   What does it mean to be present in a jurisdiction?

2.   How was the corporation in International Shoe deemed to be present in the State of Washington?

3.   Is the Court's ruling fair?

Burger King v. Rudzewicz, 471 U.S. 462 (1985).

This case involved litigation in federal court in Florida between Michigan franchisees and their franchisor, a Florida corporation. The Michigan franchisees argued that the Florida court lacked personal jurisdiction over them. The Supreme Court disagreed and held that the exercise of jurisdiction by the Florida court over the Michigan franchisees did not offend due process.

> By requiring that individuals have "fair warning that a particular activity may subject [them] to the jurisdiction of a foreign sovereign," the Due Process Clause "gives a degree of predictability to the legal system that allows potential defendants to structure their primary conduct with some minimum assurance as to where that conduct will and will not render them liable to suit."

> Where a forum seeks to assert specific jurisdiction over an out-of-state defendant who has not consented to suit there, this "fair warning" requirement is satisfied if the defendant has "purposefully directed" his activities at residents of the forum and the litigation results from alleged injuries that "arise out of or relate to" those activities. Thus "[t]he forum State does not exceed its powers under the Due Process Clause if it asserts personal jurisdiction over a corporation that delivers its products into the stream of commerce with the expectation that they will be purchased by consumers in the forum State" and those products subsequently injure forum consumers. Similarly, a publisher who distributes magazines in a distant State may fairly be held accountable in that forum for damages resulting there from an allegedly defamatory story. And with respect to

interstate contractual obligations, we have emphasized that parties who "reach out beyond one state and create continuing relationships and obligations with citizens of another state" are subject to regulation and sanctions in the other State for the consequences of their activities. ...

Applying these principles to the case at hand, we believe there is substantial record evidence supporting the District Court's conclusion that the assertion of personal jurisdiction over Rudzewicz in Florida for the alleged breach of his franchise agreement did not offend due process. At the outset, we note a continued division among lower courts respecting whether and to what extent a contract can constitute a "contact" for purposes of due process analysis. If the question is whether an individual's contract with an out-of-state party alone can automatically establish sufficient minimum contacts in the other party's home forum, we believe the answer clearly is that it cannot. The Court long ago rejected the notion that personal jurisdiction might turn on "mechanical" tests or on "conceptualistic ... theories of the place of contracting or of performance." Instead, we have emphasized the need for a "highly realistic" approach that recognizes that a "contract" is "ordinarily but an intermediate step serving to tie up prior business negotiations with future consequences which themselves are the real object of the business transaction." It is these factors-prior negotiations and contemplated future consequences, along with the terms of the contract and the parties' actual course of dealing-that must be evaluated in determining whether the defendant purposefully established minimum contacts within the forum.

In this case, no physical ties to Florida can be attributed to Rudzewicz other than MacShara's brief training course in Miami. Rudzewicz did not maintain offices in Florida and, for all that appears from the record, has never even visited there. Yet this franchise dispute grew directly out of "a contract which had a substantial connection with that State." Eschewing the option of operating an independent local enterprise, Rudzewicz deliberately "reach[ed] out beyond" Michigan and negotiated with a Florida corporation for the purchase of a long-term franchise and the manifold benefits that would derive from affiliation with a nationwide organization. Upon approval, he entered into a carefully structured 20-year relationship that envisioned continuing and wide-reaching contacts with Burger King in Florida. In light of Rudzewicz' voluntary acceptance of the long-term and exacting regulation of his business from Burger King's Miami head-quarters, the "quality and nature" of his relationship to the company in Florida can in no sense be viewed as "random," "fortuitous," or "attenuated." Rudzewicz' refusal to make the contractually required payments in Miami, and his continued use of Burger King's trademarks and confidential business information after his termination, caused foreseeable injuries to the corporation in Florida. For these reasons it was, at the very least, presumptively reasonable for Rudzewicz to be called to account there for such injuries.

J. McIntyre Machinery, Ltd. v. Nicastro, 131 S. Ct. 2780 (2011).

In Nicastro, the Court addressed the continuing viability of notions of fore-seeability and fairness in the personal jurisdiction analysis. Specifically, the Court held that whether it is foreseeable that a defendant's product ends up in the forum state is not the proper analysis. Rather, the proper analysis is whether the defendant has purposefully directed its conduct toward the sovereign state. If so, the state has the authority to exercise jurisdiction and enter judgment.

The principal inquiry in cases of this sort is whether the defendant's activities manifest an intention to submit to the power of a sovereign. In other words, the defendant must "purposefully avai[l] itself of the privilege of conducting activities within the forum State, thus invoking the benefits and protections of its laws." Sometimes a defendant does so by sending its goods rather than its agents. The defendant's transmission of goods permits the exercise of jurisdiction only where the defendant can be said to have targeted the forum; as a general rule, it is not enough that the defendant might have predicted that its goods will reach the forum State. ...

[P]ersonal jurisdiction requires a forum-by-forum, or sovereign-by-sovereign, analysis. The question is whether a defendant has followed a course of conduct directed at the society or economy existing within the jurisdiction of a given sovereign, so that the sovereign has the power to subject the defendant to judgment concerning that conduct. Personal jurisdiction, of course, restricts "judicial power not as a matter of sovereignty, but as a matter of individual liberty," for due process protects the individual's right to be subject only to lawful power. But whether a judicial judgment is lawful depends on whether the sovereign has authority to render it.

General v. Specific Jurisdiction

Generally speaking, a state's exercise of personal jurisdiction falls into one of two categories: specific jurisdiction, which is "when a State exercises personal jurisdiction over a defendant in a suit arising out of or related to the defendant's contacts with the forum,"[73] and general jurisdiction, which is when the state is able to exercise jurisdiction over the defendant with regard to any cause of action, whether pertaining to specific contacts with the forum or not.[74]

The distinction between specific and general jurisdiction is often set forth explicitly in the state's long-arm statute. For example, in Massachusetts, the "general jurisdiction" statute provides:

> A court may exercise personal jurisdiction over a person domiciled in, organized under the laws of, or maintaining his or its principal place of business in, this commonwealth as to any cause of action.[75]

For defendants other than those covered in the general jurisdiction statute, the "specific jurisdiction" statute, by contrast, only permits the exercise of jurisdiction when the claim arises out of certain specified contacts with the state, such as transacting business in the state, contracting to supply services or things in the state, and causing tortious injury in the state by acts either within or without the state.[76]

———————————————

[73]   Helicopteros Nacionales de Colombia v. Hall, 466 U.S. 408, 414 n.8 (1984).

[74]   *See id.* at 414 n.9.

[75]   MASS. GEN. LAWS ch. 223A, § 2 (2008).

[76]   *See id.* § 3.

Personal Jurisdiction Summary

Taking the requirements set forth in the key cases together brings the dimensions of personal jurisdiction in the federal courts into focus. A summary is below.

Two important elements to considering when determining the proper exercise of personal jurisdiction.

1. Due process requirements under the 5th and 14th Amendments to the Constitution.

2. Any state limitations under the long arm statute or otherwise.

    *   It's possible that a state would draft its long-arm statute so that it does not reach to the "due process" level under the Constitution. Massachusetts is such a state.

    *   Remember, in certain exercises of federal question jurisdiction, a federal statute may provide for nationwide service of process and personal jurisdiction.

There are three methods to establish personal jurisdiction over the defendant.

1. Consent

2. Service on defendant within confines of state where the district court sits (transient or "tag" jurisdiction).

3. Service on defendant outside the state when defendant has sufficient contacts with the state to make the service fair.

Specific jurisdiction and general jurisdiction are different. Know the difference.

1. Specific jurisdiction is where the defendant's contacts with the forum are related to the action.

2. General jurisdiction is where the defendant's contacts with the forum are substantial, systematic, and continuous such that the defendant is essentially "at home" in the jurisdiction, and therefore the contacts need not specifically relate to the action. This is most often seen in situations where the forum state is where the defendant resides, is incorporated, or has its principal place of business.

Venue

Venue is a statutory creation, designed for the convenience of the parties. It denotes the proper federal district court in which an action may be brought. It is a concept not derived from the Constitution and is quite distinct from the federal court's subject matter and personal jurisdiction.

> The jurisdiction of the federal courts—their power to adjudicate—is a grant of authority to them by Congress and thus beyond the scope of litigants to confer. But the locality of a law suit—the place where judicial authority may be exercised—though defined by legislation relates to the convenience of litigants and as such is subject to their disposition. This basic difference between the court's power and the litigant's convenience is historic in the federal courts.[77]

Today, 28 U.S.C. § 1391 controls venue in the federal district courts. It provides generally that venue is proper in:

•   A district where any defendant resides, if all defendants reside in same state, or

---

[77]   Neirbo Co. v. Bethlehem Shipbuilding Corp., 308 U.S. 165, 167-68 (1939).

- A district "in which a substantial part of the events or omissions giving rise to the claim occurred, or a substantial part of the property that is the subject of the action is situated," or

- In a diversity action if there is no district in which the action may otherwise be brought, in "a judicial district in which any defendant is subject to personal jurisdiction at the time the action is commenced," or

- In a federal question case if there is no district in which the action may otherwise be brought, in a judicial district where any defendant may be found.

The venue statute exists primarily for the convenience of the defendant and thus the burden is on the defendant to object to venue if she believes it improper. Failure to object results in waiver of the defense. The proper vehicle for raising an objection to venue is a Rule 12(b)(3) motion to dismiss.

Tyson Fresh Meats, Inc. v. Lauer Ltd., LLC, 918 F. Supp. 2d 835 (N.D. Iowa 2013).

… As previously noted, all named Defendants contend that this Court is an improper venue and dismissal is appropriate pursuant to Federal Rule of Civil Procedure 12(b)(3). 28 U.S.C. Section 1391(b), the applicable federal venue statute, provides:

A civil action may be brought in—
(1) a judicial district in which any defendant resides, if all defendants are residents of the State in which the district is located;
(2) a judicial district in which a substantial part of the events or omissions giving rise to the claim occurred, or a substantial part of the property that is the subject of the action is situated; or
(3) if there is no district in which an action may otherwise be brought as provided in this section, any judicial district in which any defendant is subject to the court's personal jurisdiction with respect to such action.

Under 28 U.S.C. Section 1391(b), a court should not "ask which of two or more potential forums is the 'best' venue...." Rather, the question is whether a plaintiff's chosen forum has "a substantial connection to the claim...."

Plaintiff contends that courts making venue determinations in contract disputes look "to such factors as where the contract was negotiated or executed, where it was to be performed, and where the alleged breach occurred." While it is undisputed that the negotiation and much of the execution of the Contracts occurred in Nebraska, the performance and breach of the Contracts occurred in Iowa.

In arguing that performance of the Contracts took place in Nebraska, Defendants note that Lauer Limited purchased and raised their hogs in Nebraska, but this is the execution of the Contract, not the performance. The Contracts at issue did not require Lauer Limited to purchase and raise hogs in a certain manner, they simply required Lauer Limited to deliver hogs to Plaintiff's plant in Storm Lake, Iowa, and then spelled out the terms whereby Plaintiff would be compensated. Clearly, the Contracts were to be performed in the State of Iowa; and "the place of performance is a proper venue for breach of contract claims."

In discussing where the alleged breach occurred, Defendants contend that it occurred at Plaintiff's hog buying facility in Laurel, Nebraska, when Robert Lauer informed Plaintiff's buying agent that Lauer Limited would not be able to fulfill the contracts. While Defendants' argument has a simplistic appeal, legally speaking, a breach of contract occurs where performance was to take place but did not. Thus, Lauer Limited's breach of contract occurred in Iowa.

Finally, 28 U.S.C. Section 1391(b) specifically provides that venue is proper not only where a substantial part of the "events" occurred but also where a substantial part of the "omissions" occurred. It seems clear to this Court that relevant omissions would include a failure to perform within a forum under the terms of a valid contract, such as occurred here. It also seems clear that, in a breach of contract cause of action, a failure to perform is as substantial an omission as can be made. Thus, in as far as it is undisputed that Lauer Limited breached its Contracts to deliver hogs to Plaintiff's facility in Storm Lake, Iowa, this Court is a proper venue.

Chapter 7: Important Early Cases in U.S. Constitutional History

Introduction and Definitions

In the summer of 1787, delegates from each of the 13 original states met in Philadelphia to discuss changes to the system of government set up under the Articles of Confederation in 1781. The Constitutional Convention ended up changing the system of government entirely, drafting an all new founding document, the Constitution of the United States of America.

The Constitution established the structure and powers of the government of the United States.

Article I created the national legislature or Congress, dividing it into two houses, the House of Representatives and the Senate. Members of the House of Representatives were to be elected every two years, and members of the Senate every six. Article I also set forth the limited, enumerated powers of Congress. Theses powers include, among others, the powers to lay and collect taxes, regulate commerce, coin money, establish post offices, and declare war. Laws passed by Congress must pass both houses and be presented to the President for signature.

Article II created the Executive, the offices of the Presidency and Vice Presidency, declaring that the "executive Power shall be vested in a President of the United States of America." The President and Vice President serve four-year terms. The Executive Branch, under the President is vast. It encompasses numerous departments or agencies that are headed by political appointees called "Secretaries." The heads of the major agencies serve as the President's cabinet. Although the Executive Branch is often said to merely "enforce" laws, it actually creates many rules of its own through regulations drafted by the federal agencies in their area of expertise.

Article III created the federal judiciary, establishing that the "judicial power of the United States, shall be vested in one Supreme Court, and in such inferior courts as the Congress may from time to time ordain and establish." Article III also established the limited jurisdiction of the federal courts (federal question and diversity) and set forth the edict that federal judges serve for life.

Article IV discussed the relationship between the states as to the "public acts, records, and judicial proceedings of every other state" (they shall be given "full faith and credit") and as to the "privileges and immunities" of the citizens of each state (they should all be the same). Article IV also permitted the admission of new states by the federal government.

Article V set forth the process for amending the Constitution, providing that "Congress, whenever two thirds of both houses shall deem it necessary, shall propose amendments to this Constitution, or, on the application of the legislatures of two thirds of the several states, shall call a convention for proposing amendments, which, in either case, shall be valid to all intents and purposes, as part of this Constitution, when ratified by the legislatures of three fourths of the several states."

Article VI provided that debts incurred prior to the adoption of the Constitution will be honored under it, that the Constitution and federal laws are the "supreme law of the land", and that public officials "shall be bound by oath or affirmation, to support this Constitution." Article VI also provided that no religious test "shall ever be required as a qualification to any office or public trust under the United States."

Finally, Article VII provided that ratification by nine states shall be sufficient to adopt the Constitution between the states so ratifying.

Following the Introduction, this chapter presents the full text of Federalist No. 1 by Alexander Hamilton, which describes the importance of ratifying the new U.S. Constitution. Then five famous early Supreme Court cases are set forth, *Calder v. Bull, Marbury v. Madison, Fletcher v. Peck, Martin v. Hunter's Lessee,* and *McCulloch v. Maryland.* Each of these cases dealt with an aspect of federal power as granted by the Constitution. *Calder v. Bull* discussed declaring laws unconstitutional and sources of law to which the judiciary should look; *Marbury v. Madison* also discussed judicial review, the power of courts to declare laws unconstitutional, and the Court in *Marbury* actually used the power; *Fletcher v. Peck* declared a state law unconstitutional under the Constitution's Contracts Clause; *Martin v. Hunter's Lessee* discussed the power of the U.S. Supreme Court over state courts; and *McCulloch v. Maryland* discussed the Necessary and Proper Clause, the Supremacy Clause, and the power of the federal government over the states.

The following definitions are relevant to this chapter:

Articles of Confederation: The document that bound the original states together prior to the adoption of the Constitution.

Branch of Government: The major governmental divisions set forth in the Constitution. The branches are Congress, the Executive, and the Judiciary. Each branch has its own powers and role in the governance of the United States. The separate powers of the three branches provide the basis for the doctrine of the **separation of powers**, which essentially provides that the different powers and roles of the three branches provide a safeguard against tyranny.

Congress: The national legislature, responsible for enacting law. It consists of two houses, the House of Representatives and the Senate.

Constitution: The document that established the United States and its government.

Executive: The branch of government responsible for enforcing the law. The President is the head of the Executive Branch.

Federalism: The system of dual sovereignty and shared powers as between the states and the national government in the United States.

Federalist Papers: The Federalist Papers are a series of 84 essays written by John Jay, Alexander Hamilton, and James Madison in support of ratification of the Constitution of the United States.

Judicial Review: The power of courts to declare legislation unconstitutional.

Judiciary: The branch of government responsible for resolving disputes and interpreting the law. Judges make up the judiciary.

The Federalist No. 1 (Alexander Hamilton)

The Federalist Papers are a series of 84 essays written by John Jay, Alexander Hamilton, and James Madison in support of ratification of the Constitution of the United States. Written under the pen name Publius, the essays were published from October 1787 to May 1788.

In Federalist No. 1, set forth below, Alexander Hamilton describes the broad aims and importance of the project.

Please consider the following questions:

- *Why does Hamilton think that the fate of the nation is at stake in the debates over the Constitution?*

- *How does Hamilton characterize the opposition to ratification?*

- *What does Hamilton describe as the purpose of the project?*

To the People of the State of New York:

AFTER an unequivocal experience of the inefficiency of the subsisting federal government, you are called upon to deliberate on a new Constitution for the United States of America. The subject speaks its own importance; comprehending in its consequences nothing less than the existence of the UNION, the safety and welfare of the parts of which it is composed, the fate of an empire in many respects the most interesting in the world. It has been frequently remarked that it seems to have been reserved to the people of this country, by their conduct and example, to decide the important question, whether societies of men are really capable or not of establishing good government from reflection and choice, or whether they are forever destined to depend for their political constitutions on accident and force. If there be any truth in the remark, the crisis at which we are arrived may with propriety be regarded as the era in which that decision is to be made; and a wrong election of the part we shall act may, in this view, deserve to be considered as the general misfortune of mankind. This idea will add the inducements of philanthropy to those of patriotism, to heighten the solicitude which all considerate and good men must feel for the event. Happy will it be if our choice should be directed by a judicious estimate of our true interests, unperplexed and unbiased by considerations not connected with the public good. But this is a thing more ardently to be wished than seriously to be expected. The plan offered to our deliberations affects too many particular interests, innovates upon too many local institutions, not to involve in its discussion a variety of objects foreign to its merits, and of views, passions and prejudices little favorable to the discovery of truth.

Among the most formidable of the obstacles which the new Constitution will have to encounter may readily be distinguished the obvious interest of a certain class of men in every State to resist all changes which may hazard a diminution of the power, emolument, and consequence of the offices they hold under the State establishments; and the perverted ambition of another class of men, who will either hope to aggrandize themselves by the confusions of their country, or will flatter themselves with fairer prospects of elevation from the subdivision of the empire into several partial confederacies than from its union under one government.

It is not, however, my design to dwell upon observations of this nature. I am well aware that it would be disingenuous to resolve indiscriminately the opposition of any set of men (merely because their situations might subject them to suspicion) into interested or ambitious views. Candor will oblige us to admit that even such men may be actuated by upright intentions; and it cannot be doubted that much of the opposition which has made its appearance, or may hereafter make its appearance, will spring from sources, blameless at least, if not respectable--the honest errors of minds led astray by preconceived jealousies and fears. So numerous indeed and so powerful are the causes which serve to give a false bias to the judgment, that we, upon many occasions, see wise and good men on the wrong as well as on the right side of questions of the first magnitude to society. This circumstance, if duly attended to, would furnish a lesson of moderation to those who are ever so much persuaded of their being in the right in any controversy. And a further reason for caution, in this respect, might be drawn from the reflection that we are not always sure that those who advocate the truth are influenced by purer principles than their antagonists. Ambition, avarice, personal animosity, party opposition, and many other motives not more laudable than these, are apt to operate as well upon those who support as those who oppose the right side of a question. Were there not even these inducements to moderation, nothing could be more ill-judged than that intolerant spirit which has, at all times, characterized political parties. For in politics, as in religion, it is equally absurd to aim at making proselytes by fire and sword. Heresies in either can rarely be cured by persecution.

And yet, however just these sentiments will be allowed to be, we have already sufficient indications that it will happen in this as in all former cases of great national discussion. A torrent of angry and malignant passions will be let loose. To judge from the conduct of the opposite parties, we shall be led to conclude that they will mutually hope to evince the justness of their opinions, and to increase the number of their converts by the loudness of their declamations and the bitterness of their invectives. An enlightened zeal for the energy and efficiency of government will be stigmatized as the offspring of a temper fond of despotic power and hostile to the principles of liberty. An over-scrupulous jealousy of danger to the rights of the people, which is more commonly the fault of the head than of the heart, will be represented as mere pretense and artifice, the stale bait for popularity at the expense of the public good. It will be forgotten, on the one hand, that jealousy is the usual concomitant of love, and that the noble enthusiasm of liberty is apt to be infected with a spirit of narrow and illiberal distrust. On the other hand, it will be equally forgotten that the vigor of government is essential to the security of liberty; that, in the contemplation of a sound and well-informed judgment, their interest can never be separated; and that a dangerous ambition more often lurks behind the specious mask of zeal for the rights of the people than under the forbidden appearance of zeal for the firmness and efficiency of government. History will teach us that the former has been found a much more certain road to the introduction of despotism than the latter, and that of those men who have overturned the liberties of republics, the greatest number have begun their career by paying an obsequious court to the people; commencing demagogues, and ending tyrants.

In the course of the preceding observations, I have had an eye, my fellow-citizens, to putting you upon your guard against all attempts, from whatever quarter, to influence your decision in a matter of the utmost moment to your welfare, by any impressions other than those which may result from the evidence of truth. You will, no doubt, at the same time, have collected from the general scope of them, that they proceed from a source not unfriendly to the new Constitution. Yes, my countrymen, I own to you that, after having given it an attentive consideration, I am clearly of opinion it is your interest to adopt it. I am convinced that this is the safest course for your liberty, your dignity, and your happiness. I affect not reserves which I do not feel. I will not amuse you with an appearance of deliberation when I have decided. I frankly acknowledge to you my convictions, and I will freely lay before you the reasons on which they are founded. The consciousness of good intentions disdains ambiguity. I shall not, however, multiply professions on this head. My motives must remain in the depository of my own breast. My arguments will be open to all, and may be judged of by all. They shall at least be offered in a spirit which will not disgrace the cause of truth.

I propose, in a series of papers, to discuss the following interesting particulars:

THE UTILITY OF THE UNION TO YOUR POLITICAL PROSPERITY THE INSUFFICIENCY OF THE PRESENT CONFEDERATION TO PRESERVE THAT UNION THE NECESSITY OF A GOVERNMENT AT LEAST EQUALLY ENERGETIC WITH THE ONE PROPOSED, TO THE ATTAINMENT OF THIS OBJECT THE CONFORMITY OF THE PROPOSED CONSTITUTION TO THE TRUE PRINCIPLES OF REPUBLICAN GOVERNMENT ITS ANALOGY TO YOUR OWN STATE CONSTITUTION and lastly, THE ADDITIONAL SECURITY WHICH ITS ADOPTION WILL AFFORD TO THE PRESERVATION OF THAT SPECIES OF GOVERNMENT, TO LIBERTY, AND TO PROPERTY.

In the progress of this discussion I shall endeavor to give a satisfactory answer to all the objections which shall have made their appearance, that may seem to have any claim to your attention.

It may perhaps be thought superfluous to offer arguments to prove the utility of the UNION, a point, no doubt, deeply engraved on the hearts of the great body of the people in every State, and one, which it may be imagined, has no adversaries. But the fact is, that we already hear it whispered in the private circles of those who oppose the new Constitution, that the thirteen States are of too great extent for any general system, and that we must of necessity resort to separate confederacies of distinct portions of the whole. This doctrine will, in all probability, be gradually propagated, till it has votaries enough to countenance an open avowal of it. For nothing can be more evident, to those who are able to take an enlarged view of the subject, than the alternative of an adoption of the new Constitution or a dismemberment of the Union. It will therefore be of use to begin by examining the advantages of that Union, the certain evils, and the probable dangers, to which every State will be exposed from its dissolution. This shall accordingly constitute the subject of my next address.

PUBLIUS.

Calder v. Bull, 3 U.S. 386, 386–401 (1798)

Calder v. Bull *is an interesting early case from the U.S. Supreme Court. The question at issue was whether a particular act of the Legislature of Connecticut that granted a new hearing in a probate matter amounted to an unconstitutional* ex post facto *law within the meaning of the U.S. Constitution. An* ex post facto *law is a law that, after the fact, renders conduct illegal that was legal at the time of commission. The Court held that the Connecticut act was not a prohibited* ex post law *as* ex post facto *laws relate only to crimes and not to legislative acts affecting private property.*

The case is interesting for several other reasons as well, however.

- *Please note that there is no "opinion of the Court." Rather each Justice writes his own opinion. This is known as issuing opinions **seriatim**, that is individually or in a series, and it was the practice of the Court to do so prior to the time of Chief Justice Marshall. Marshall initiated the practice of issuing opinions from the Court as a whole, with the other Justices free to join the opinion, concur, or dissent.*

- *Justices Chase, Paterson, and Iredell each set out in their respective opinions two very important points: **first**, the circumstances under which a court can or should declare an act of the legislature void, and **second**, the actual sources of law that a court may refer* *to when reaching a decision. Compare and contrast the approach of each Justice. Please be prepared to discuss each Justice's approach in class.*

- *Finally, on what basis does Justice Cushing decide the case?*

Opinion

Justice Chase

… The Legislature of Connecticut, on the 2nd Thursday of May 1795, passed a resolution or law, which … set aside a decree of the Court of Probate for Harford … which [had] disapproved of the will of Normand Morrison (the grandson) made the 21st of August 1779, and refused to record the said will; and granted a new hearing by the said Court of Probate, with liberty of appeal therefrom, in six months. A new hearing was [held because] of [the Connecticut] resolution, or law [and the] Court of Probate [then] approved the … will, and ordered it to be recorded. …

[Before this Court, Appellants] contend, that the said resolution or law of the Legislature of Connecticut, granting a new hearing, in the above case, **is an ex post facto law, prohibited by the Constitution of the United States**; that any law of the Federal government, or of any of the State governments, contrary to the Constitution of the United States, is void; and that this court possesses the power to declare such law void.

It appears to me a self-evident proposition, that the several State Legislatures retain all the powers of legislation, delegated to them by the State Constitutions; which are not EXPRESSLY taken away by the Constitution of the United States. The establishing courts of justice, the appointment of Judges, and the making regulations for the administration of justice, within each State, according to its laws, on all subjects not entrusted to the Federal Government, appears to me to be the peculiar and exclusive province, and duty of the State Legislatures: All the powers delegated by the people of the United States to the Federal Government are defined, and NO CONSTRUCTIVE powers can be exercised by it, and all the powers that remain in the State Governments are indefinite …

The effect of the resolution or law of Connecticut, above stated, is to revise a decision of one of its Inferior Courts, called the Court of Probate for Harford, and to direct a new hearing of the case by the same Court of Probate, that passed the decree against the will of Normand Morrison.

By the existing law of Connecticut a right to recover certain property had vested in [the Appellants] in consequence of a decision of a court of justice, but, in virtue of [the] subsequent resolution or law, and the new hearing thereof, and the decision in consequence, this right to recover certain property was divested … The sole enquiry is, whether this resolution or law of Connecticut, having such operation, is an ex post facto law, within the prohibition of the Federal Constitution.

Whether the Legislature of any of the States can revise and correct by law, a decision of any of its Courts of Justice, although not prohibited by the Constitution of the State, is a question of very great importance, and not necessary NOW to be determined; because the resolution or law in question does not go so far. I cannot subscribe to the omnipotence of a State Legislature, or that it is absolute and without control; although its authority should not be expressly restrained by the Constitution, or fundamental law, of the State. **The people of the United States erected their Constitutions, or forms of government, to establish justice, to promote the general welfare, to secure the blessings of liberty; and to protect their persons and property from violence. The purposes for which men enter into society will determine the nature and terms of the social compact; and as they are the foundation of the legislative power, they will decide what are the proper objects of it: The nature, and ends of legislative power will limit the exercise of it. This fundamental principle flows from the very nature of our free Republican governments, that no man should be compelled to do what the laws do not require; nor to refrain from acts which the laws permit. There are acts which the Federal, or State, Legislature cannot do, without exceeding their authority. There are certain vital principles in our free Republican governments, which will determine and over-rule an apparent and flagrant abuse of legislative power; as to authorize manifest injustice by positive law; or to take away that security for**

personal liberty, or private property, for the protection whereof of the government was established. An ACT of the Legislature (for I cannot call it a law) contrary to the great first principles of the social compact, cannot be considered a rightful exercise of legislative authority. The obligation of a law in governments established on express compact, and on republican principles, must be determined by the nature of the power, on which it is founded. ... The Legislature may enjoin, permit, forbid, and punish; they may declare new crimes; and establish rules of conduct for all its citizens in future cases; they may command what is right, and prohibit what is wrong; but they cannot change innocence into guilt; or punish innocence as a crime; or violate the right of an antecedent lawful private contract; or the right of private property. To maintain that our Federal, or State, Legislature possesses such powers, if they had not been expressly restrained; would, in my opinion, be a political heresy, altogether inadmissible in our free republican governments.

I shall endeavour to show what law is to be considered an ex post facto law, within the words and meaning of the prohibition in the Federal Constitution. ... The prohibition ... is not to pass any law concerning, and after the fact; but the plain and obvious meaning and intention of the prohibition is this; that the Legislatures of the several states, shall not pass laws, after a fact done by a subject, or citizen, which shall have relation to such fact, and shall punish him for having done it. The prohibition considered in this light, is an additional bulwark in favour of the personal security of the subject, to protect his person from punishment by legislative acts, having a retrospective operation. I do not think it was inserted to secure the citizen in his private rights, of either property, or contracts. ...

In the present case, there is no fact done by [Appellants that] is in any manner affected by the law or resolution of Connecticut: It does not concern, or relate to, any act done by them. The decree of the Court of Probate of Harford ... was given before the said law or resolution, and in that sense, was affected and set aside by it; and in consequence of the law allowing a hearing and the decision in favor of the will, they have lost, what they would have been entitled to, if the Law or resolution, and the decision in consequence thereof, had not been made. The decree of the Court of probate is the only fact, on which the law or resolution operates. In my judgment the case of the [Appellants] is not within the letter of the prohibition; and, for the reasons assigned, I am clearly of opinion, that it is not within the intention of the prohibition ...

If the term ex post facto law is to be construed to include and to prohibit the enacting any law after a fact, it will greatly restrict the power of the federal and state legislatures; and the consequences of such a construction may not be foreseen. ...

Justice Paterson

... The question is whether the resolution of the Legislature of Connecticut, be an ex post facto law, within the meaning of the Constitution of the United States? I am of opinion, that it is not. **The words, ex post facto, when applied to a law, have a technical meaning, and, in legal phraseology, refer to crimes, pains, and penalties.** Judge Blackstone's description of the terms is clear and accurate. "There is, says he, a still more unreasonable method than this, which is called making of laws, ex post facto, when after an action, indifferent in itself, is committed, the Legislator, then, for the first time, declares it to have been a crime, and inflicts a punishment upon the person who has committed it." ...

[T]he words of the Constitution of the United States are, 'That no State shall pass any bill of attainder, ex post facto law, or law impairing the obligation of contracts.' Article 1st. section 10.

Where is the necessity or use of the latter words, if a law impairing the obligation of contracts, be comprehended within the terms ex post facto law? It is obvious from the specification of contracts in the last member of the clause, that the framers of the Constitution, did not understand or use the words in the sense contended for on the part of the Plaintiffs in Error. **They understood and used the words in their known and appropriate signification, as referring to crimes, pains, and penalties, and no further.** The arrangement of the distinct members of this section, necessarily points to this meaning.

I had an ardent desire to have extended the provision in the Constitution to retrospective laws in general. There is neither policy nor safety in such laws; and, therefore, I have always had a strong aversion against them. It may, in general, be truly observed of retrospective laws of every description, that they neither accord with sound legislation, nor the fundamental principles of the social compact. But on full consideration, I am convinced, that ex post facto laws must be limited in the manner already expressed; they must be taken in their technical, which is also their common and general, acceptation, and are not to be understood in their literal sense.

Justice Iredell

Though I concur in the general result of the opinions, which have been delivered, I cannot entirely adopt the reasons that are assigned upon the occasion. ...

If ... a government, composed of Legislative, Executive and Judicial departments, were established, by a Constitution, which imposed no limits on the legislative power, the consequence would inevitably be, that whatever the legislative power chose to enact, would be lawfully enacted, and the judicial power could never interpose to pronounce it void. **It is true, that some speculative jurists have held, that a legislative act against natural justice must, in itself, be void; but I cannot think that, under such a government, any Court of Justice would possess a power to declare it so. Sir William Blackstone, having put the strong case of an act of Parliament, which should authorise a man to try his own cause, explicitly adds, that even in that case, 'there is no court that has power to defeat the intent of the Legislature, when couched in such evident and express words, as leave no doubt whether it was the intent of the Legislature, or no.'**

[I]t has been the policy of all the American states, which have, individually, framed their state constitutions since the revolution, and of the people of the United States, when they framed the Federal Constitution, to define with precision the objects of the legislative power, and to restrain its exercise within marked and settled boundaries. If any act of Congress, or of the Legislature of a state, violates those constitutional provisions, it is unquestionably void; though, I admit, that as the authority to declare it void is of a delicate and awful nature, the Court will never resort to that authority, but in a clear and urgent case. If, on the other hand, the Legislature of the Union, or the Legislature of any member of the Union, shall pass a law, within the general scope of their constitutional power, **the**

Court cannot pronounce it to be void, merely because it is, in their judgment, contrary to the principles of natural justice. The ideas of natural justice are regulated by no fixed standard: the ablest and the purest men have differed upon the subject; and all that the Court could properly say, in such an event, would be, that the Legislature (possessed of an equal right of opinion) had passed an act which, in the opinion of the judges, was inconsistent with the abstract principles of natural justice. There are then but two lights, in which the subject can be viewed: 1st. If the Legislature pursue the authority delegated to them, their acts are valid. 2nd. If they transgress the boundaries of that authority, their acts are invalid. In the former case, they exercise the discretion vested in them by the people, to whom alone they are responsible for the faithful discharge of their trust: but in the latter case, they violate a fundamental law, which must be our guide, whenever we are called upon as judges to determine the validity of a legislative act.

[I]n the present instance, the act or resolution of the Legislature of Connecticut, cannot be regarded as an ex post facto law; for, the true construction of the prohibition extends to criminal, not to civil, cases. It is only in criminal cases, indeed, in which the danger to be guarded against, is greatly to be apprehended. The history of every country in Europe will furnish flagrant instances of tyranny exercised under the pretext of penal dispensations. ...

The policy, the reason and humanity, of the prohibition, do not, I repeat, extend to civil cases, to cases that merely affect the private property of citizens. Some of the most necessary and important acts of Legislation are, on the contrary, founded upon the principle, that private rights must yield to public exigences. Highways are run through private grounds. Fortifications, Light-houses, and other public edifices, are necessarilly sometimes built upon the soil owned by individuals. In such, and similar cases, if the owners should refuse voluntarily to accommodate the public, they must be constrained, as far as the public necessities require; and justice is done, by allowing them a reasonable equivalent. Without the possession of this power the operations of Government would often be obstructed, and society itself would be endangered. ...

Justice Cushing

The case appears to me to be clear of all difficulty, taken either way. If the act is a judicial act, it is not touched by the Federal Constitution: and, if it is a legislative act, it is maintained and justified by the ancient and uniform practice of the state of Connecticut.

*   *   *

Marbury v. Madison, 5 U.S. 137 (1803)

The situation in Marbury v. Madison presented Chief Justice John Marshall with a significant conflict of interest. Here's why. Marshall was confirmed by the Senate as Chief Justice on January 27, 1801 and officially took office on February 4. He had previously been serving as the Secretary of State under President John Adams. At Adams' request he continued to serve as Secretary of State until the expiration of Adams' term on March 4, 1801.

In the final days of his term, Adams appointed dozens of men to serve as Justices of the Peace in Washington D.C. He then signed the commissions that confirmed the appointments and sent the commissions to the acting Secretary of State, John Marshall, for delivery. Marshall was unable to complete delivery of all the commissions prior to the expiration of Adams' term, however. And, the new president, Thomas Jefferson, refused to deliver those that remained.

One of the disappointed appointees, William Marbury, brought suit in the Supreme Court demanding delivery of his commission. As noted, the Chief Justice of the United States and senior justice on the Supreme Court was John Marshall, the man who had failed to deliver Marbury's commission in the first place. Read on to see how Marshall handled this delicate situation.

While reading Chief Justice Marshall's opinion, consider the following.

- *What is a mandamus?*

- *Do you see how Justice Marshall sets forth the issues before the Court?*

- *If Marbury has a right to the commission, why doesn't he receive it?*

- *If he has a remedy why doesn't the Court act?*

- *How does the Court deem the provision of the Judiciary Act relied upon to be unconstitutional?*

- *What is the difference between **Original** and **Appellate** Jurisdiction?*

- *What are the arguments for the power of judicial review?*

- *What must have been Marshall's concerns when resolving this case?*

- *How does Marshall provide claims to victory to both sides in this case?*

Opinion

At the last term on the affidavits then read and filed with the clerk, a rule was granted in this case, requiring the secretary of state to shew cause why a mandamus should not issue, directing him to deliver to William Marbury his commission as a justice of the peace for the county of Washington, in the district of Columbia.

No cause has been shewn, and the present motion is for a mandamus. The peculiar delicacy of this case, the novelty of some of its circumstances, and the real difficulty attending the points which occur in it, require a complete exposition of the principles, on which the opinion to be given by the court, is founded.

*   *   *

In the order in which the court has viewed this subject, the following questions have been considered and decided.

1st. Has the applicant a right to the commission he demands?

2dly. If he has a right, and that right has been violated, do the laws of his country afford him a remedy?

3dly. If they do afford him a remedy, is it a mandamus issuing from this court?

The first object of inquiry is,

1st. Has the applicant a right to the commission he demands?

His right originates in an act of congress passed in February 1801, concerning the district of Columbia. . . . It appears, from the affidavits, that in compliance with this law, a commission for William Marbury as a justice of peace for the county of Washington, was signed by John Adams, then president of the United States; after which the seal of the United States was affixed to it; but the commission has never reached the person for whom it was made out.

*   *   *

This is an appointment made by the President, by and with the advice and consent of the senate, and is evidenced by no act but the commission itself. In such a case therefore the commission and the appointment seem inseparable; it being almost impossible to shew an appointment otherwise than by proving the existence of a commission; still the commission is not necessarily the appointment; though conclusive evidence of it.

*   *   *

It is therefore decidedly the opinion of the court, that when a commission has been signed by the President, the appointment is made; and that the commission is complete, when the seal of the United States has been affixed to it by the secretary of state.

*   *   *

The discretion of the executive is to be exercised until the appointment has been made. But having once made the appointment, his power over the office is terminated in all cases, where, by law, the officer is not removable by him. The right to the office is then in the person appointed, and he has the absolute, unconditional, power of accepting or rejecting it.

Mr. Marbury, then, since his commission was signed by the President, and sealed by the secretary of state, was appointed; and as the law creating the office, gave the officer a right to hold for five years, independent of the executive, the appointment was not revocable; but vested in the officer legal rights, which are protected by the laws of this country.

To withhold his commission, therefore, is an act deemed by the court not warranted by law, but violative of a vested legal right.

This brings us to the second inquiry; which is,

2dly. If he has a right, and that right has been violated, do the laws of this country afford him a remedy?

The very essence of civil liberty certainly consists in the right of every individual to claim the protection of the laws, whenever he receives an injury. One of the first duties of government is to afford that protection.

*   *   *

The government of the United States has been emphatically termed a government of laws, and not of men. It will certainly cease to deserve this high appellation, if the laws furnish no remedy for the violation of a vested legal right.

*   *   *

By the constitution of the United States, the President is invested with certain important political powers, in the exercise of which he is to use his own discretion, and is accountable only to his country in his political character, and to his own conscience. To aid him in the performance of these duties, he is authorized to appoint certain officers, who act by his authority and in conformity with his orders.

*   *   *

The power of nominating to the senate, and the power of appointing the person nominated, are political powers, to be exercised by the President according to his own discretion. When he has made an appointment, he has exercised his whole power, and his discretion has been completely applied to the case. If, by law, the officer be removable at the will of the President, then a new appointment may be immediately made, and the rights of the officer are terminated. But as a fact which has existed cannot be made never to have existed, the appointment cannot be annihilated; and consequently if the officer is by law not removable at the will of the President; the rights he has acquired are protected by the law, and are not resumable by the President. They cannot be extinguished by executive authority, and he has the privilege of asserting them in like manner as if they had been derived from any other source.

*   *   *

It is then the opinion of the court, ...

That, having this legal title to the office, he has a consequent right to the commission; a refusal to deliver which, is a plain violation of that right, for which the laws of his country afford him a remedy.

It remains to be inquired whether,

3dly. He is entitled to the remedy for which he applies. This depends on,

1st. The nature of the writ applied for, and,

2dly. The power of this court.

1st. The nature of the writ.

*   *   *

This writ, if awarded, would be directed to an officer of government, and its mandate to him would be, to use the words of Blackstone, "to do a particular thing therein specified, which appertains to his office and duty and which the court has previously determined, or at least supposes, to be consonant to right and justice."

*   *   *

Still, to render the mandamus a proper remedy, the officer to whom it is to be directed, must be one to whom, on legal principles, such writ may be directed; and the person applying for it must be without any other specific and legal remedy.

1st. With respect to the officer to whom it would be directed. The intimate political relation, subsisting between the president of the United States and the heads of departments, necessarily renders any legal investigation of the acts of one of those high officers peculiarly irksome, as well as delicate; and excites some hesitation with respect to the propriety of entering into such investigation. . . . The province of the court is, solely, to decide on the rights of individuals, not to enquire how the executive, or executive officers, perform duties in which they have a discretion. Questions, in their nature political, or which are, by the constitution and laws, submitted to the executive, can never be made in this court.

But, if this be not such a question; . . . what is there in the exalted station of the officer, which shall bar a citizen from asserting, in a court of justice, his legal rights, or shall forbid a court to listen to the claim; or to issue a mandamus, directing the performance of a duty, not depending on executive discretion, but on particular acts of congress and the general principles of law?

*   *   *

This, then, is a plain case for a mandamus, either to deliver the commission, or a copy of it from the record; and it only remains to be inquired,

Whether it can issue from this court.

The act to establish the judicial courts of the United States authorizes the supreme court "to issue writs of mandamus, in cases warranted by the principles and usages of law, to any courts appointed, or persons holding office, under the authority of the United States." The secretary of state, being a person holding an office under the authority of the United States, is precisely within the letter of the description; and if this court is not authorized to issue a writ of mandamus to such an officer, it must be because the law is unconstitutional, and therefore absolutely incapable of conferring the authority, and assigning the duties which its words purport to confer and assign.

The constitution vests the whole judicial power of the United States in one supreme court, and such inferior courts as congress shall, from time to time, ordain and establish. This power is expressly extended to all cases arising under the laws of the United States; and consequently, in some form, may be exercised over the present case; because the right claimed is given by a law of the United States.

In the distribution of this power it is declared that "the supreme court shall have original jurisdiction in all cases affecting ambassadors, other public ministers and consuls, and those in which a state shall be a party. In all other cases, the supreme court shall have appellate jurisdiction."

It has been insisted, at the bar, that as the original grant of jurisdiction, to the supreme and inferior courts, is general, and the clause, assigning original jurisdiction to the supreme court, contains no negative or restrictive words; the power remains to the legislature, to assign original jurisdiction to that court in other cases than those specified in the article which has been recited; provided those cases belong to the judicial power of the United States.

If it had been intended to leave it in the discretion of the legislature to apportion the judicial power between the supreme and inferior courts according to the will of that body, it would certainly have been useless to have proceeded further than to have defined the judicial power, and the tribunals in which it should be vested. The subsequent part of the section is mere surplusage, is entirely without meaning, if such is to be the construction. If congress remains at liberty to give this court appellate jurisdiction, where the constitution has declared their jurisdiction shall be original; and original jurisdiction where the constitution has declared it shall be appellate; the distribution of jurisdiction, made in the constitution, is form without substance.

Affirmative words are often, in their operation, negative of other objects than those affirmed; and in this case, a negative or exclusive sense must be given to them or they have no operation at all.

It cannot be presumed that any clause in the constitution is intended to be without effect; and therefore such a construction is inadmissible, unless the words require it.

*   *   *

When an instrument organizing fundamentally a judicial system, divides it into one supreme, and so many inferior courts as the legislature may ordain and establish; then enumerates its powers, and proceeds so far to distribute them, as to define the jurisdiction of the supreme court by declaring the cases in which it shall take original jurisdiction, and that in others it shall take appellate jurisdiction; the plain import of the words seems to be, that in one class of cases its jurisdiction is original, and not appellate; in the other it is appellate, and not original. If any other construction would render the clause inoperative, that is an additional reason for rejecting such other construction, and for adhering to their obvious meaning.

To enable this court then to issue a mandamus, it must be shewn to be an exercise of appellate jurisdiction, or to be necessary to enable them to exercise appellate jurisdiction.

It has been stated at the bar that the appellate jurisdiction may be exercised in a variety of forms, and that if it be the will of the legislature that a mandamus should be used for that purpose, that will must be obeyed. This is true, yet the jurisdiction must be appellate, not original.

It is the essential criterion of appellate jurisdiction, that it revises and corrects the proceedings in a cause already instituted, and does not create that cause. [However, here] to issue . . . a [mandamus] to an officer for the delivery of a paper, is in effect the same as to sustain an original action for that paper, and therefore seems not to belong to appellate, but to original jurisdiction. Neither is it necessary in such a case as this, to enable the court to exercise its appellate jurisdiction.

The authority, therefore, given to the supreme court, by the act establishing the judicial courts of the United States, to issue writs of mandamus to public officers, appears not to be warranted by the constitution; and it becomes necessary to enquire whether a jurisdiction, so conferred, can be exercised.

The question, whether an act, repugnant to the constitution, can become the law of the land, is a question deeply interesting to the United States; but, happily, not of an intricacy proportioned to its interest. It seems only necessary to recognize certain principles, supposed to have been long and well established, to decide it.

That the people have an original right to establish, for their future government, such principles as, in their opinion, shall most conduce to their own happiness, is the basis, on which the whole American fabric has been erected. The exercise of this original right is a very great exertion; nor can it, nor ought it to be frequently repeated. The principles, therefore, so established, are deemed fundamental. And as the authority, from which they proceed, is supreme, and can seldom act, they are designed to be permanent.

This original and supreme will organizes the government, and assigns, to different departments, their respective powers. It may either stop here; or establish certain limits not to be transcended by those departments.

The government of the United States is of the latter description. The powers of the legislature are defined, and limited; and that those limits may not be mistaken, or forgotten, the constitution is written. To what purpose are powers limited, and to what purpose is that limitation committed to writing, if these limits may, at any time, be passed by those intended to be restrained? The distinction, between a government with limited and unlimited powers, is abolished, if those limits do not confine the persons on whom they are imposed, and if acts prohibited and acts allowed, are of equal obligation. It is a proposition too plain to be contested, that the constitution controls any legislative act repugnant to it; or, that the legislature may alter the constitution by an ordinary act.

Between these alternatives there is no middle ground. The constitution is either a superior, paramount law, unchangeable by ordinary means, or it is on a level with ordinary legislative acts, and like other acts, is alterable when the legislature shall please to alter it.

If the former part of the alternative be true, then a legislative act contrary to the constitution is not law: if the latter part be true, then written constitutions are absurd attempts, on the part of the people, to limit a power, in its own nature illimitable.

Certainly all those who have framed written constitutions contemplate them as forming the fundamental and paramount law of the nation, and consequently the theory of every such government must be, that an act of the legislature, repugnant to the constitution, is void.

*   *   *

If an act of the legislature, repugnant to the constitution, is void, does it, notwithstanding its invalidity, bind the courts, and oblige them to give it effect? Or, in other words, though it be not law, does it constitute a rule as operative as if it was a law? This would be to overthrow in fact what was established in theory; and would seem, at first view, an absurdity too gross to be insisted on. It shall, however, receive a more attentive consideration.

It is emphatically the province and duty of the judicial department to say what the law is. Those who apply the rule to particular cases, must of necessity expound and interpret that rule. If two laws conflict with each other, the courts must decide on the operation of each.

So if a law be in opposition to the constitution; if both the law and the constitution apply to a particular case, so that the court must either decide that case conformably to the law, disregarding the constitution; or conformably to the constitution, disregarding the law; the court must determine which of these conflicting rules governs the case. This is of the very essence of judicial duty.

If then the courts are to regard the constitution; and the constitution is superior to any ordinary act of the legislature; the constitution, and not such ordinary act, must govern the case to which they both apply.

Those then who controvert the principle that the constitution is to be considered, in court, as a paramount law, are reduced to the necessity of maintaining that courts must close their eyes on the constitution, and see only the law.

This doctrine would subvert the very foundation of all written constitutions. It would declare that an act, which, according to the principles and theory of our government, is entirely void; is yet, in practice, completely obligatory. It would declare, that if the legislature shall do what is expressly forbidden, such act, notwithstanding the express prohibition, is in reality effectual. It would be giving to the legislature a practical and real omnipotence, with the same breath which professes to restrict their powers within narrow limits. It is prescribing limits, and declaring that those limits may be passed as pleasure.

That it thus reduces to nothing what we have deemed the greatest improvement on political institutions-a written constitution-would of itself be sufficient, in America, where written constitutions have been viewed with so much reverence, for rejecting the construction. But the peculiar expressions of the constitution of the United States furnish additional arguments in favour of its rejection.

The judicial power of the United States is extended to all cases arising under the constitution. Could it be the intention of those who gave this power, to say that, in using it, the constitution should not be looked into? That a case arising under the constitution should be decided without examining the instrument under which it arises?

This is too extravagant to be maintained.

In some cases then, the constitution must be looked into by the judges. And if they can open it at all, what part of it are they forbidden to read, or to obey?

There are many other parts of the constitution which serve to illustrate this subject.

*   *   *

The constitution declares that "no bill of attainder or ex post facto law shall be passed." If, however, such a bill should be passed and a person should be prosecuted under it; must the court condemn to death those victims whom the constitution endeavors to preserve?

"No person," says the constitution, "shall be convicted of treason unless on the testimony of two witnesses to the same overt act, or on confession in open court." Here the language of the constitution is addressed especially to the courts. It prescribes, directly for them, a rule of evidence not to be departed from. If the legislature should change that rule, and declare one witness, or a confession out of court, sufficient for conviction, must the constitutional principle yield to the legislative act?

From these, and many other selections which might be made, it is apparent, that the framers of the constitution contemplated that instrument, as a rule for the government of courts, as well as of the legislature.

Why otherwise does it direct the judges to take an oath to support it? This oath certainly applies, in an especial manner, to their conduct in their official character. How immoral to impose it on them, if they were to be used as the instruments, and the knowing instruments, for violating what they swear to support?

The oath of office, too, imposed by the legislature, is completely demonstrative of the legislative opinion on this subject. It is in these words, "I do solemnly swear that I will administer justice without respect to persons, and do equal right to the poor and to the rich; and that I will faithfully and impartially discharge all the duties incumbent on me as according to the best of my abilities and understanding, agreeably to the constitution, and laws of the United States."

Why does a judge swear to discharge his duties agreeably to the constitution of the United States, if that constitution forms no rule for his government? If it is closed upon him, and cannot be inspected by him?

If such be the real state of things, this is worse than solemn mockery. To prescribe, or to take this oath, becomes equally a crime.

It is also not entirely unworthy of observation, that in declaring what shall be the supreme law of the land, the constitution itself is first mentioned; and not the laws of the United States generally, but those only which shall be made in pursuance of the constitution, have that rank.

Thus, the particular phraseology of the constitution of the United States confirms and strengthens the principle, supposed to be essential to all written constitutions, that a law repugnant to the constitution is void; and that courts, as well as other departments, are bound by that instrument.

The rule must be discharged.

Fletcher v. Peck, 10 U.S. 87 (1810)

The story of Fletcher v. Peck *begins with a fraudulent land deal in which the legislature of Georgia was complicit. The land fraudulently obtained was then conveyed to certain third parties who had no notice of the fraud. Georgia then tried to rectify the situation by annulling both the original fraudulent transactions and the conveyances to third parties. The third parties brought suit, challenging the annulment of the conveyances to themselves. The Supreme Court— declaring a state law unconstitutional for the first time—held that the Georgia law annulling the conveyances violated the Contracts Clause of the U.S. Constitution. Please be prepared to discuss the Court's reasoning in detail. Also note the Court's emphasis on the importance of private property rights and the supremacy of the federal constitution to those of the states.*

Opinion

The importance and the difficulty of the questions, presented by these pleadings, are deeply felt by the court.

The lands in controversy vested absolutely in James Gunn and others, the original grantees, by the conveyance of the governor, made in pursuance of an act of assembly to which the legislature was fully competent. Being thus in full possession of the legal estate, they, for a valuable consideration, conveyed portions of the land to those who were willing to purchase. If the original transaction was infected with fraud, these purchasers did not participate in it, and had no notice of it. They were innocent. Yet the legislature of Georgia has involved them in the fate of the first parties to the transaction, and, if the act be valid, has annihilated their rights also.

The legislature of Georgia was a party to this transaction; and [then later tried] to pronounce its own deed invalid, ...

If a suit be brought to set aside a conveyance obtained by fraud, and the fraud be clearly proved, the conveyance will be set aside, as between the parties; **but the rights of third persons, who are purchasers without notice, for a valuable consideration, cannot be disregarded.** Titles, which, according to every legal test, are perfect, are acquired with that confidence which is inspired by the opinion that the purchaser is safe. If there be any concealed defect, arising from the conduct of those who had held the property long before he acquired it, of which he had no notice, that concealed defect cannot be set up against him. **He has paid his money for a title good at law, he is innocent, whatever may be the guilt of others, and equity will not subject him to the penalties attached to that guilt. All titles would be insecure, and the intercourse between man and man would be very seriously obstructed, if this principle be overturned.** ...

In this case the legislature may have had ample proof that the original grant was obtained by [fraud], and which would have justified its abrogation so far as respected those to whom crime was imputable. But the grant, when issued, conveyed an estate in fee-simple to the grantee, clothed with all the solemnities which law can bestow. This estate was transferrable; and those who purchased parts of it were not stained by that guilt which infected the original transaction. Their case is not distinguishable from the ordinary case of purchasers of a legal estate without knowledge of any secret fraud which might have led to the emanation of the original grant. According to the well known course of equity, their rights could not be affected by such fraud. Their situation was the same, their title was the same, with that of every other member of the community who holds land by regular conveyances from the original patentee.

Is the power of the legislature competent to the annihilation of such title, and to a resumption of the property thus held? ...

When, then, a law is in its nature a contract, when absolute rights have vested under that contract, a repeal of the law cannot devest those rights; and the act of annulling them, if legitimate, is rendered so by a power applicable to the case of every individual in the community. ...

The validity of this rescinding act, then, might well be doubted, were Georgia a single sovereign power. But Georgia cannot be viewed as a single, unconnected, sovereign power, on whose legislature no other restrictions are imposed than may be found in its own constitution. She is a part of a large empire; she is a member of the American union; **and that union has a constitution the supremacy of which all acknowledge, and which imposes limits to the legislatures of the several states, which none claim a right to pass. The constitution of the United States declares that no state shall pass any bill of attainder, *ex post facto* law, or law impairing the obligation of contracts.**

Does the case now under consideration come within this prohibitory section of the constitution?

In considering this very interesting question, we immediately ask ourselves what is a contract? Is a grant a contract?

A contract is a compact between two or more parties, and is either executory or executed. An executory contract is one in which a party binds himself to do, or not to do, a particular thing; such was the law under which the conveyance was made by the governor. A contract executed is one in which the object of contract is performed; and this, says Blackstone, differs in nothing from a grant. The contract between Georgia and the purchasers was executed by the grant. A contract executed, as well as one which is executory, contains obligations binding on the parties. A grant, in its own nature, amounts to an extinguishment of the right of the grantor, and implies a contract not to reassert that right. A party is, therefore, always estopped by his own grant.

Since, then, in fact, a grant is a contract executed, the obligation of which still continues, and since the constitution uses the general term contract, without distinguishing between those which are executory and those which are executed, it must be construed to comprehend the latter as well as the former. A law annulling conveyances between individuals, and declaring that the grantors should stand seized of their former estates, notwithstanding those grants, would be as repugnant to the constitution as a law discharging the vendors of property from the obligation of executing their contracts by conveyances. It would be strange if a contract to convey was secured by the constitution, while an absolute conveyance remained unprotected.

If, under a fair construction the constitution, grants are comprehended under the terms contracts, is a grant from the state excluded from the operation of the provision? Is the clause to be considered as inhibiting the state from impairing the obligation of contracts between two individuals, but as excluding from that inhibition contracts made with itself?

The words themselves contain no such distinction. They are general, and are applicable to contracts of every description. If contracts made with the state are to be exempted from their operation, the exception must arise from the character of the contracting party, not from the words which are employed.

Whatever respect might have been felt for the state sovereignties, it is not to be disguised that the framers of the constitution viewed, with some apprehension, the violent acts which might grow out of the feelings of the moment; and that the people of the United States, in adopting that instrument, have manifested a determination to shield themselves and their property from the effects of those sudden and strong passions to which men are exposed. The restrictions on the legislative power of the states are obviously founded in this sentiment; and the constitution of the United States contains what may be deemed a bill of rights for the people of each state.

No state shall pass any bill of attainder, *ex post facto* law, or law impairing the obligation of contracts.

A bill of attainder may affect the life of an individual, or may confiscate his property, or may do both.

In this form the power of the legislature over the lives and fortunes of individuals is expressly restrained. What motive, then, for implying, in words which import a general prohibition to impair the obligation of contracts, an exception in favour of the right to impair the obligation of those contracts into which the state may enter?

The state legislatures can pass no *ex post facto* law. An *ex post facto* law is one which renders an act punishable in a manner in which it was not punishable when it was committed. Such a law may inflict penalties on the person, or may inflict pecuniary penalties which swell the public treasury. The legislature is then prohibited from passing a law by which a man's estate, or any part of it, shall be seized for a crime which was not declared, by some previous law, to render him liable to that punishment. Why, then, should violence be done to the natural meaning of words for the purpose of leaving to the legislature the power of seizing, for public use, the estate of an individual in the form of a law annulling the title by which he holds that estate? The court can perceive no sufficient grounds for making this distinction. This rescinding act would have the effect of an *ex post facto* law. It forfeits the estate of Fletcher for a crime not committed by himself, but by those from whom he purchased. This cannot be effected in the form of an *ex post facto* law, or bill of attainder; why, then, is it allowable in the form of a law annulling the original grant?

The argument in favour of presuming an intention to except a case, not excepted by the words of the constitution, is susceptible of some illustration from a principle originally ingrafted in that instrument, though no longer a part of it. The constitution, as passed, gave the courts of the United States jurisdiction in suits brought against individual states. A state, then, which violated its own contract was suable in the courts of the United States for that violation. Would it have been a defence in such a suit to say that the state had passed a law absolving itself from the contract? It is scarcely to be conceived that such a defence could be set up. And yet, if a state is neither restrained by the general principles of our political institutions, nor by the words of the constitution, from impairing the obligation of its own contracts, such a defence would be a valid one. This feature is no longer found in the constitution; but it aids in the construction of those clauses with which it was originally associated.

It is, then, the unanimous opinion of the court, that, in this case, the estate having passed into the hands of a purchaser for a valuable consideration, without notice, the state of Georgia was restrained, either by general principles which are common to our free institutions, or by the particular provisions of the constitution of the United States, from passing a law whereby the estate of the plaintiff in the premises so purchased could be constitutionally and legally impaired and rendered null and void.

*   *   *

Martin v. Hunter's Lessee, 14 U.S. 304 (1816)

During the American Revolution, the state of Virginia seized property belonging to individuals who remained loyal to Great Britain. Martin had inherited land from his Loyalist uncle Lord Fairfax, but the Virginia legislature voided that inheritance and transferred the land back to the state. The state then sold the land to Hunter, who leased it to another party. Martin brought suit, but Virginia's highest court, the Court of Appeals, refused to restore title to him. The case was appealed to the Supreme Court in 1813, where Justice Story, writing for the majority, held that the Treaty of Paris, which ended the Revolutionary War, had restored title to Martin and because treaties were considered under the Supremacy Clause to be the supreme law of the land, that trumped the Virginia ruling. The Court than issued a writ ordering Hunter's lessee off the property.

The Virginia Court of Appeals declared the Supreme Court lacked the authority to review state court decisions arguing that the states and the federal government were sovereign equals and thus free to interpret the U.S. Constitution as they saw fit within their respective jurisdictions.

The Supreme Court granted review again and Justice Story established the Court's authority to review state court judgments. Chief Justice Marshall didn't participate because he and his brother had contracted to purchase a large part of the Fairfax estate.

While reading the opinion, please consider the following questions:

- *The Virginia Supreme Court decided that the U.S. Supreme Court did not have authority over cases originating in state court, and thus did not have power over state courts in Virginia. If this were correct, what would be the implications?*

- *Why is the role of people in establishing the Constitution important?*

- *"The constitution unavoidably deals in general language." What does that mean?*

- *How does Justice Story deem the judicial power of the Supreme Court to be supreme to that of the states?*

- *What is the import of the appellate power extending to* **"all"** *cases?*

- *What is the Supremacy Clause? What is its relation to this case?*

- *How does the Supreme Court have appellate jurisdiction over the state law decision at issue here? Isn't this an issue of state law?*

Opinion

STORY, J., delivered the opinion of the court.

This is a writ of error from the court of appeals of Virginia, founded upon the refusal of that court to obey the mandate of this court, requiring the judgment rendered in this very cause, at February term, 1813, to be carried into due execution. The following is the judgment of the court of appeals rendered on the mandate: "The court is unanimously of opinion, that the appellate power of the supreme court of the United States does not extend to this court, under a sound construction of the constitution of the United States; that so much of the 25th section of the act of congress to establish the judicial courts of the United States, as extends the appellate jurisdiction of the supreme court to this court, is not in pursuance of the constitution of the United States; that the writ of error, in this cause, was improvidently allowed under the authority of that act; that the proceedings thereon in the supreme court were, *coram non judice*, in relation to this court, and that obedience to its mandate be declined by the court."

The questions involved in this judgment are of great importance and delicacy. Perhaps it is not too much to affirm, that, upon their right decision, rest some of the most solid principles which have hitherto been supposed to sustain and protect the constitution itself.

*   *   *

The constitution of the United States was ordained and established, not by the states in their sovereign capacities, but emphatically, as the preamble of the constitution declares, by "the people of the United States." There can be no doubt that it was competent to the people to invest the general government with all the powers which they might deem proper and necessary; to extend or restrain these powers according to their own good pleasure, and to give them a paramount and supreme authority. As little doubt can there be, that the people had a right to prohibit to the states the exercise of any powers which were, in their judgment, incompatible with the objects of the general compact; to make the powers of the state governments, in given cases, subordinate to those of the nation, or to reserve to themselves those sovereign authorities which they might not choose to delegate to either. The constitution was not, therefore, necessarily carved out of existing state sovereignties, nor a surrender of powers already existing in state institutions, for the powers of the states depend upon their own constitutions; and the people of every state had the right to modify and restrain them, according to their own views of the policy or principle. On the other hand, it is perfectly clear that the sovereign powers vested in the state governments, by their respective constitutions, remained unaltered and unimpaired, except so far as they were granted to the government of the United States.

. . . The government, then, of the United States, can claim no powers which are not granted to it by the constitution, and the powers actually granted, must be such as are expressly given, or given by necessary implication. . . .

The constitution unavoidably deals in general language. It did not suit the purposes of the people, in framing this great charter of our liberties, to provide for minute specifications of its powers, or to declare the means by which those powers should be carried into execution. It was foreseen that this would be a perilous and difficult, if not an impracticable, task. The instrument was not in-tended to provide merely for the exigencies of a few years, but was to endure through a long lapse of ages, the events of which were locked up in the inscrutable purposes of Providence. It could not be foreseen what new changes and modifi-cations of power might be indispensable to effectuate the general objects of the charter; and restrictions and specifications, which, at the present, might seem sal-utary, might, in the end, prove the overthrow of the system itself. Hence its pow-ers are expressed in general terms, leaving to the legislature, from time to time, to adopt its own means to effectuate legitimate objects, and to mould and model the exercise of its powers, as its own wisdom, and the public interests, should require.

*   *   *

[T]he language of the article creating and defining the judicial power of the United States. . . . is the voice of the whole American people solemnly declared, in establishing one great department of that government which was, in many re-spects, national, and in all, supreme. It is a part of the very same instrument which was to act not merely upon individuals, but upon states; and to deprive them altogether of the exercise of some powers of sovereignty, and to restrain and reg-ulate them in the exercise of others.

Let this article be carefully weighed and considered. The language of the arti-cle throughout is manifestly designed to be mandatory upon the legislature. Its obligatory force is so imperative, that congress could not, without a violation of its duty, have refused to carry it into operation. The judicial power of the United States *shall be vested* (not may be vested) in one supreme court, and in such inferior courts as congress may, from time to time, ordain and establish.

*   *   *

If, then, it is a duty of congress to vest the judicial power of the United States, it is a duty to vest the *whole judicial power.* The language, if imperative as to one part, is imperative as to all. If it were otherwise, this anomaly would exist, that congress might successively refuse to vest the jurisdiction in any one class of cases enumerated in the constitution, and thereby defeat the jurisdiction as to all; for the constitution has not singled out any class on which congress are bound to act in preference to others.

*   *   *

This leads us to the consideration of the great question as to the nature and extent of the appellate jurisdiction of the United States. We have already seen that appellate jurisdiction is given by the constitution to the supreme court in all cases where it has not original jurisdiction; subject, however, to such exceptions and regulations as congress may prescribe. . . .

If the constitution meant to limit the appellate jurisdiction to cases pending in the courts of the United States, it would necessarily follow that the jurisdiction of these courts would, in all the cases enumerated in the constitution, be exclusive of state tribunals. How otherwise could the jurisdiction extend to *all* cases arising under the constitution, laws, and treaties of the United States, or *to all cases* of admiralty and maritime jurisdiction? If some of these cases might be entertained by state tribunals, and no appellate jurisdiction as to them should exist, then the appellate power would not extend to *all*, but to *some*, cases. If state tribunals might exercise concurrent jurisdiction over all or some of the other classes of cases in the constitution without control, then the appellate jurisdiction of the United States might, as to such cases, have no real existence, contrary to the manifest intent of the constitution. Under such circumstances, to give effect to the judicial power, it must be construed to be exclusive; and this not only when the *casus foederis* should arise directly, but when it should arise, incidentally, in cases pending in state courts. This construction would abridge the jurisdiction of such court far more than has been ever contemplated in any act of congress.

*   *   *

But it is plain that the framers of the constitution did contemplate that cases within the judicial cognizance of the United States not only might but would arise in the state courts, in the exercise of their ordinary jurisdiction. With this view the sixth article declares, that 'this constitution, and the laws of the United States which shall be made in pursuance thereof, and all treaties made, or which shall be made, under the authority of the United States, shall be the supreme law of the land, and the judges in every state shall be bound thereby, any thing in the constitution or laws of any state to the contrary notwithstanding.' It is obvious that this obligation is imperative upon the state judges in their official, and not merely in their private, capacities. From the very nature of their judicial duties they would be called upon to pronounce the law applicable to the case in judgment. They were not to decide merely according to the laws or constitution of the state, but according to the constitution, laws and treaties of the United States-'the supreme law of the land.'

*   *   *

It must, therefore, be conceded that the constitution not only contemplated, but meant to provide for cases within the scope of the judicial power of the United States, which might yet depend before state tribunals. It was foreseen that in the exercise of their ordinary jurisdiction, state courts would incidentally take cognizance of cases arising under the constitution, the laws, and treaties of the United States. Yet to all these cases the judicial power, by the very terms of the constitution, is to extend. It cannot extend by original jurisdiction if that was already rightfully and exclusively attached in the state courts, which (as has been already shown) may occur; it must, therefore, extend by appellate jurisdiction, or not at all. It would seem to follow that the appellate power of the United States must, in such cases, extend to state tribunals; and if in such cases, there is no reason why it should not equally attach upon all others within the purview of the constitution.

*   *   *

On the whole, the court are of opinion, that the appellate power of the United States does extend to cases pending in the state courts; and that the 25th section of the judiciary act, which authorizes the exercise of this jurisdiction in the specified cases, by a writ of error, is supported by the letter and spirit of the constitution. We find no clause in that instrument which limits this power; and we dare not interpose a limitation where the people have not been disposed to create one.

*   *   *

The next question which has been argued, is, whether the case at bar be within the purview of the 25th section of the judiciary act, so that this court may rightfully sustain the present writ of error. This section, stripped of passages unimportant in this inquiry, enacts, in substance, that a final judgment or decree in any suit in the highest court of law or equity of a state, where is drawn in question the validity of a treaty or statute of, or an authority excised under, the United States, and the decision is against their validity; or where is drawn in question the validity of a statute of, or an authority exercised under, any state, on the ground of their being repugnant to the constitution, treaties, or laws, of the United States, and the decision is in favour of such their validity; or of the constitution, or of a treaty or statute of, or commission held under, the United States, and *the decision is against the title, right, privilege, or exemption, specially set up or claimed by either party under such* clause of the said constitution, treaty, statute, or commission, may be re-examined and reversed or affirmed in the supreme court of the United States, upon a writ of error, in the same manner, and under the same regulations, and the writ shall have the same effect, as if the judgment or decree complained of had been rendered or passed in a circuit court, and the proceeding upon the reversal shall also be the same, *except that the supreme court, instead of remanding the cause for a final decision, as before provided, may, at their discretion, if the cause shall have been once remanded before, proceed to a final decision of the same, and award execution.* But no other error shall be assigned or regarded as a ground of reversal in any such case as aforesaid, *than such as appears upon the face of the record, and immediately respects the before-mentioned question* of validity or construction of the said constitution, treaties, statutes, commissions, or authorities in dispute. …

McCulloch v. Maryland, 17 U.S. 316 (1819)

The most profound constitutional issue in the years prior to the American Civil War (1861-65) involved the relationship between the individual states and the federal government. States chafed at federal control in many areas and downright revolted against it in others. At its most pernicious, this controversy revolved around slavery; although there were other less despicable manifestations. McCulloch v. Maryland was a less despicable manifestation. It concerned the power of the federal government to charter a bank, and the purported ability of the state of Maryland to then tax it.

While reading the opinion, please consider the following questions.

- *What has caused this dispute?*

- *Why does Justice Marshall believe the question to be so important?*

- *What is the argument of the lawyer for Maryland?*

- *Why does it matter that the Constitution emanates from the people, and not the states?*

- *How does this case involve the conflicting powers of the federal and state governments?*

- *What does this mean? "The government of the United States, then, though limited in its powers, is supreme."*

- *What does this mean? "In considering this question, then, we must never forget that it is a constitution we are expounding."*

- *What is the relationship between powers and means that Chief Justice Marshall discusses?*

- *What is the "necessary and proper" clause?*

- *Does Congress have the power to form a corporation? A bank? How come?*

- *Can Maryland tax the Bank of the United States? Why not?*

Opinion

MARSHALL, Ch. J., delivered the opinion of the court.

In the case now to be determined, the defendant, a sovereign state, denies the obligation of a law enacted by the legislature of the Union, and the plaintiff, on his part, contests the validity of an act which has been passed by the legislature of that state. The constitution of our country, in its most interesting and vital parts, is to be considered; the conflicting powers of the government of the Union and of its members, as marked in that constitution, are to be discussed; and an opinion given, which may essentially influence the great operations of the government. No tribunal can approach such a question without a deep sense of its importance, and of the awful responsibility involved in its decision. But it must be decided peacefully, or remain a source of hostile legislation, perhaps, of hostility of a still more serious nature; and if it is to be so decided, by this tribunal alone can the decision be made. On the supreme court of the United States has the constitution of our country devolved this important duty.

The first question made in the cause is-has congress power to incorporate a bank? It has been truly said, that this can scarcely be considered as an open question, entirely unprejudiced by the former proceedings of the nation respecting it. The principle now contested was introduced at a very early period of our history, has been recognised by many successive legislatures, and has been acted upon by the judicial department, in cases of peculiar delicacy, as a law of undoubted obligation.

*   *   *

The power now contested was exercised by the first congress elected under the present constitution. . . . The original act was permitted to expire; but a short experience of the embarrassments to which the refusal to revive it exposed the government, convinced those who were most prejudiced against the measure of its necessity, and induced the passage of the present law. . . .

In discussing this question, the counsel for the state of Maryland have deemed it of some importance, in the construction of the constitution, to consider that instrument, not as emanating from the people, but as the act of sovereign and independent states. The powers of the general government, it has been said, are delegated by the states, who alone are truly sovereign; and must be exercised in subordination to the states, who alone possess supreme dominion. It would be difficult to sustain this proposition. The convention which framed the constitution was indeed elected by the state legislatures. But the instrument, when it came from their hands, was a mere proposal, without obligation, or pretensions to it. It was reported to the then existing congress of the United States, with a request that it might 'be submitted to a convention of delegates, chosen in each state by the people thereof, under the recommendation of its legislature, for their assent and ratification.' This mode of proceeding was adopted; and by the convention, by congress, and by the state legislatures, the instrument was submitted to the people. They acted upon it in the only manner in which they can act safely, effectively and wisely, on such a subject, by assembling in convention. It is true, they assembled in their several states-and where else should they have assembled? No political dreamer was ever wild enough to think of breaking down the lines which separate the states, and of compounding the American people into one common mass. Of consequence, when they act, they act in their states. But the measures they adopt do not, on that account, cease to be the measures of the people themselves, or become the measures of the state governments.

From these conventions, the constitution derives its whole authority. The government proceeds directly from the people; is 'ordained and established,' in the name of the people; and is declared to be ordained, 'in order to form a more perfect union, establish justice, insure domestic tranquillity, and secure the blessings of liberty to themselves and to their posterity.' The assent of the states, in their sovereign capacity, is implied, in calling a convention, and thus submitting that instrument to the people. But the people were at perfect liberty to accept or reject it; and their act was final. It required not the affirmance, and could not be negatived, by the state governments. The constitution, when thus adopted, was of complete obligation, and bound the state sovereignties.

It has been said, that the people had already surrendered all their powers to the state sovereignties, and had nothing more to give. But, surely, the question whether they may resume and modify the powers granted to government, does not remain to be settled in this country. Much more might the legitimacy of the general government be doubted, had it been created by the states. . . . To the formation of a league, such as was the confederation, the state sovereignties were certainly competent. But when, 'in order to form a more perfect union,' it was deemed necessary to change this alliance into an effective government, possessing great and sovereign powers, and acting directly on the people, the necessity of referring it to the people, and of deriving its powers directly from them, was felt and acknowledged by all. The government of the Union, then . . . is, emphatically and truly, a government of the people. In form, and in substance, it emanates from them. Its powers are granted by them, and are to be exercised directly on them, and for their benefit.

This government is acknowledged by all, to be one of enumerated powers. The principle, that it can exercise only the powers granted to it [is] apparent. . . . But the question respecting the extent of the powers actually granted, is perpetually arising, and will probably continue to arise, so long as our system shall exist. In discussing these questions, the conflicting powers of the general and state governments must be brought into view, and the supremacy of their respective laws, when they are in opposition, must be settled.

If any one proposition could command the universal assent of mankind, we might expect it would be this-that the government of the Union, though limited in its powers, is supreme within its sphere of action. This would seem to result, necessarily, from its nature. It is the government of all; its powers are delegated by all; it represents all, and acts for all. . . . The nation, on those subjects on which it can act, must necessarily bind its component parts. But this question is not left to mere reason: the people have, in express terms, decided it, by saying, 'this constitution, and the laws of the United States, which shall be made in pursuance thereof,' 'shall be the supreme law of the land,' and by requiring that the members of the state legislatures, and the officers of the executive and judicial departments of the states, shall take the oath of fidelity to it. The government of the United States, then, though limited in its powers, is supreme; and its laws, when made in pursuance of the constitution, form the supreme law of the land, 'anything in the constitution or laws of any state to the contrary notwithstanding.'

Among the enumerated powers, we do not find that of establishing a bank or creating a corporation. But there is no phrase in the instrument which, like the articles of confederation, excludes incidental or implied powers; and which requires that everything granted shall be expressly and minutely described. Even the 10th amendment, which was framed for the purpose of quieting the excessive jealousies which had been excited, omits the word 'expressly,' and declares only, that the powers 'not delegated to the United States, nor prohibited to the states, are reserved to the states or to the people;' thus leaving the question, whether the particular power which may become the subject of contest, has been delegated to the one government, or prohibited to the other, to depend on a fair construction of the whole instrument. . . . A constitution, to contain an accurate detail of all the subdivisions of which its great powers will admit, and of all the means by which they may be carried into execution, would partake of the prolixity of a legal code, and could scarcely be embraced by the human mind. . . . Its nature, therefore, requires, that only its great outlines should be marked, its important objects designated, and the minor ingredients which compose those objects, be deduced from the nature of the objects themselves. . . . In considering this question, then, we must never forget that it is a constitution we are expounding.

Although, among the enumerated powers of government, we do not find the word 'bank' or 'incorporation,' we find the great powers, to lay and collect taxes; to borrow money; to regulate commerce; to declare and conduct a war; and to raise and support armies and navies. The sword and the purse, all the external relations, and no inconsiderable portion of the industry of the nation, are intrusted to its government. . . . [I]t may with great reason be contended, that a government, intrusted with such ample powers, on the due execution of which the happiness and prosperity of the nation so vitally depends, must also be intrusted with ample means for their execution. The power being given, it is the interest of the nation to facilitate its execution. It can never be their interest, and cannot be presumed to have been their intention, to clog and embarrass its execution, by withholding the most appropriate means. Throughout this vast republic, from the St. Croix to the Gulf of Mexico, from the Atlantic to the Pacific, revenue is to be collected and expended, armies are to be marched and supported. The exigencies of the nation may require, that the treasure raised in the north should be transported to the south, that raised in the east, conveyed to the west, or that this order should be reversed. Is that construction of the constitution to be preferred, which would render these operations difficult, hazardous and expensive? Can we adopt that construction (unless the words imperiously require it), which would impute to the framers of that instrument, when granting these powers for the public good, the intention of impeding their exercise, by withholding a choice of means? If, indeed, such be the mandate of the constitution, we have only to obey; but that instrument does not profess to enumerate the means by which the powers it confers may be executed; nor does it prohibit the creation of a corporation, if the existence of such a being be essential, to the beneficial exercise of those powers. It is, then, the subject of fair inquiry, how far such means may be employed.

It is not denied, that the powers given to the government imply the ordinary means of execution. That, for example, of raising revenue, and applying it to national purposes, is admitted to imply the power of conveying money from place to place, as the exigencies of the nation may require, and of employing the usual means of conveyance. But it is denied, that the government has its choice of means; or, that it may employ the most convenient means, if, to employ them, it be necessary to erect a corporation. On what foundation does this argument rest? On this alone: the power of creating a corporation, is one appertaining to sovereignty, and is not expressly conferred on congress. This is true. But all legislative powers appertain to sovereignty. The original power of giving the law on any subject whatever, is a sovereign power; and if the government of the Union is restrained from creating a corporation, as a means for performing its functions, on the single reason that the creation of a corporation is an act of sovereignty; if the sufficiency of this reason be acknowledged, there would be some difficulty in sustaining the authority of congress to pass other laws for the accomplishment of the same objects. The government which has a right to do an act, and has imposed on it, the duty of performing that act, must, according to the dictates of reason, be allowed to select the means; and those who contend that it may not select any appropriate means, that one particular mode of effecting the object is excepted, take upon themselves the burden of establishing that exception.

*   *   *

[T]he constitution of the United States has not left the right of congress to employ the necessary means, for the execution of the powers conferred on the government, to general reasoning. To its enumeration of powers is added, that of making 'all laws which shall be necessary and proper, for carrying into execution the foregoing powers, and all other powers vested by this constitution, in the government of the United States, or in any department thereof.' The counsel for the state of Maryland have urged various arguments, to prove that this clause, though, in terms, a grant of power, is not so, in effect; but is really restrictive of the general right, which might otherwise be implied, of selecting means for executing the enumerated powers.

*   *   *

[T]he argument on which most reliance is placed, is drawn from that peculiar language of this clause. Congress is not empowered by it to make all laws, which may have relation to the powers confered on the government, but such only as may be 'necessary and proper' for carrying them into execution. The word 'necessary' is considered as controlling the whole sentence, and as limiting the right to pass laws for the execution of the granted powers, to such as are indispensable, and without which the power would be nugatory. That it excludes the choice of means, and leaves to congress, in each case, that only which is most direct and simple.

Is it true, that this is the sense in which the word 'necessary' is always used? Does it always import an absolute physical necessity, so strong, that one thing to which another may be termed necessary, cannot exist without that other? We think it does not. If reference be had to its use, in the common affairs of the world, or in approved authors, we find that it frequently imports no more than that one thing is convenient, or useful, or essential to another. To employ the means necessary to an end, is generally understood as employing any means calculated to produce the end, and not as being confined to those single means, without which the end would be entirely unattainable. . . .

. . . The subject is the execution of those great powers on which the welfare of a nation essentially depends. It must have been the intention of those who gave these powers, to insure, so far as human prudence could insure, their beneficial execution. This could not be done, by confiding the choice of means to such narrow limits as not to leave it in the power of congress to adopt any which might be appropriate, and which were conducive to the end. This provision is made in a constitution, intended to endure for ages to come, and consequently, to be adapted to the various crises of human affairs. To have prescribed the means by which government should, in all future time, execute its powers, would have been to change, entirely, the character of the instrument, and give it the properties of a legal code. It would have been an unwise attempt to provide, by immutable rules, for exigencies which, if foreseen at all, must have been seen dimly, and which can be best provided for as they occur. To have declared, that the best means shall not be used, but those alone, without which the power given would be nugatory, would have been to deprive the legislature of the capacity to avail itself of experience, to exercise its reason, and to accommodate its legislation to circumstances.

*   *   *

. . . [The necessary and proper] clause, as construed by the state of Maryland, would abridge, and almost annihilate, this useful and necessary right of the legislature to select its means. That this could not be intended [is] too apparent for controversy.

We think so for the following reasons: 1st. The clause is placed among the powers of congress, not among the limitations on those powers. 2d. Its terms purport to enlarge, not to diminish the powers vested in the government. It purports to be an additional power, not a restriction on those already granted. . . . If [the framers'] intention had been, by this clause, to restrain the free use of means which might otherwise have been implied, that intention would have been inserted in another place, and would have been expressed in terms resembling these. 'In carrying into execution the foregoing powers, and all others,' &c., 'no laws shall be passed but such as are necessary and proper.' Had the intention been to make this clause restrictive, it would unquestionably have been so in form as well as in effect.

The result of the most careful and attentive consideration bestowed upon this clause is, that if it does not enlarge, it cannot be construed to restrain the powers of congress, or to impair the right of the legislature to exercise its best judgment in the selection of measures to carry into execution the constitutional powers of the government. If no other motive for its insertion can be suggested, a sufficient one is found in the desire to remove all doubts respecting the right to legislate on that vast mass of incidental powers which must be involved in the constitution, if that instrument be not a splendid bauble.

We admit, as all must admit, that the powers of the government are limited, and that its limits are not to be transcended. But we think the sound construction of the constitution must allow to the national legislature that discretion, with respect to the means by which the powers it confers are to be carried into execution, which will enable that body to perform the high duties assigned to it, in the manner most beneficial to the people. Let the end be legitimate, let it be within the scope of the constitution, and all means which are appropriate, which are plainly adapted to that end, which are not prohibited, but consist with the letter and spirit of the constitution, are constitutional.

That a corporation must be considered as a means not less usual, not of higher dignity, not more requiring a particular specification than other means, has been sufficiently proved. . . .

If a corporation may be employed, indiscriminately with other means, to carry into execution the powers of the government, no particular reason can be assigned for excluding the use of a bank, if required for its fiscal operations. [A bank is necessary for the operation of the country.]

But were its necessity less apparent, none can deny its being an appropriate measure; and if it is, the degree of its necessity, as has been very justly observed, is to be discussed in another place. Should congress, in the execution of its powers, adopt measures which are prohibited by the constitution; or should congress, under the pretext of executing its powers, pass laws for the accomplishment of objects not intrusted to the government; it would become the painful duty of this tribunal, should a case requiring such a decision come before it, to say, that such an act was not the law of the land. But where the law is not prohibited, and is really calculated to effect any of the objects intrusted to the government, to undertake here to inquire into the degree of its necessity, would be to pass the line which circumscribes the judicial department, and to tread on legislative ground. This court disclaims all pretensions to such a power.

*   *   *

After the most deliberate consideration, it is the unanimous and decided opinion of this court, that the act to incorporate the Bank of the United States is a law made in pursuance of the constitution, and is a part of the supreme law of the land.

*   *   *

[The next question is] [w]hether the state of Maryland may, without violating the constitution, tax [a] branch [of the Bank of the United States]? That the power of taxation is one of vital importance; that it is retained by the states; that it is not abridged by the grant of a similar power to the government of the Union; that it is to be concurrently exercised by the two governments-are truths which have never been denied. But such is the paramount character of the constitution, that its capacity to withdraw any subject from the action of even this power, is admitted. The states are expressly forbidden to lay any duties on imports or exports, except what may be absolutely necessary for executing their inspection laws. If the obligation of this prohibition must be conceded-if it may restrain a state from the exercise of its taxing power on imports and exports-the same paramount character would seem to restrain, as it certainly may restrain, a state from such other exercise of this power, as is in its nature incompatible with, and repugnant to, the constitutional laws of the Union. A law, absolutely repugnant to another, as entirely repeals that other as if express terms of repeal were used

*   *   *

The power of congress to create, and of course, to continue, the bank, was the subject of the preceding part of this opinion; and is no longer to be considered as questionable. That the power of taxing it by the states may be exercised so as to destroy it, is too obvious to be denied. But taxation is said to be an absolute power, which acknowledges no other limits than those expressly prescribed in the constitution, and like sovereign power of every other description, is intrusted to the discretion of those who use it. But the very terms of this argument admit, that the sovereignty of the state, in the article of taxation itself, is subordinate to, and may be controlled by the constitution of the United States. How far it has been controlled by that instrument, must be a question of construction. In making this construction, no principle, not declared, can be admissible, which would defeat the legitimate operations of a supreme government. It is of the very essence of supremacy, to remove all obstacles to its action within its own sphere, and so to modify every power vested in subordinate governments, as to exempt its own operations from their own influence. This effect need not be stated in terms. It is so involved in the declaration of supremacy, so necessarily implied in it, that the expression of it could not make it more certain.

*   *   *

The result is a conviction that the states have no power, by taxation or otherwise, to retard, impede, burden, or in any manner control, the operations of the
constitutional laws enacted by congress to carry into execution the powers vested
in the general government. This is, we think, the unavoidable consequence of that
supremacy which the constitution has declared. We are unanimously of opinion,
that the law passed by the legislature of Maryland, imposing a tax on the Bank of
the United States, is unconstitutional and void.

*   *   *

Chapter 8: The Commerce Power

Introduction

The power to regulate commerce is likely the most important power that Congress possesses. The **Commerce Clause** refers to Article 1, Section 8, Clause 3 of the U.S. Constitution, which gives Congress the power "to regulate commerce with foreign nations, and among the several states, and with the Indian Tribes."

Congress has often used the Commerce Clause to justify exercising legislative power over the activities of states and their citizens, leading to significant and ongoing controversy regarding the balance of power between the federal government and the states. The Commerce Clause has historically been viewed as both a grant of congressional authority and as a restriction on the regulatory authority of the States.

The **Dormant Commerce Clause** refers to the prohibition, implicit in the Commerce Clause, against states passing legislation that discriminates against or excessively burdens interstate commerce. Of particular importance here, is the prevention of protectionist state policies that favor state citizens or businesses at the expense of non-citizens conducting business within that state.

The meaning of the word "commerce" is a source of controversy, as the Constitution does not explicitly define the word. Some argue that it refers simply to trade or exchange, while others claim that the Framers of the Constitution intended to describe more broadly commercial and social intercourse between citizens of different states. Thus, the interpretation of "commerce" affects the appropriate dividing line between federal and state power. Moreover, what constitutes "interstate" commercial activity has also been subject to consistent debate.

All the cases in this chapter deal with the nature, scope, and limits of the commerce power. The first case, *Gibbons v. Ogden*, describes a broad reading of the power. The remaining cases, with one exception, also describe broad readings of the commerce power. Which case grants Congress the most power? Which case is the exception? That is, which case limits the commerce power? Why does it do so? Please also note how the opinions in *Wickard, Lopez,* and *Raich* trace the history and development of the Supreme Court's interpretation of the Commerce Clause.

Gibbons v. Ogden, 22 U.S. 1 (1824)

While reading Chief Justice Marshall's opinion, consider the following:

- *The Court said the monopoly granted to Robert Livingston and Robert Fulton over navigation privileges entirely within New York state violated the commerce clause. How so?*

- *How was **interstate** commerce affected?*

- *How did the New York law violate the **dormant commerce clause**?*

- *Is this a **broad** reading of the commerce power?*

Opinion

Mr. Chief Justice MARSHALL delivered the opinion of the Court, and, after stating the case, proceeded as follows:

*   *   *

[The Constitution] contains an enumeration of powers expressly granted by the people to their government. It has been said, that these powers ought to be construed strictly. But why ought they to be so construed? Is there one sentence in the constitution which gives countenance to this rule? In the last of the enumerated powers, that which grants, expressly, the means for carrying all others into execution, Congress is authorized 'to make all laws which shall be necessary and proper' for the purpose. But this limitation on the means which may be used, is not extended to the powers which are conferred; nor is there one sentence in the constitution, which has been pointed out by the gentlemen of the bar, or which we have been able to discern, that prescribes this rule. We do not, therefore, think ourselves justified in adopting it.

*   *   *

The words are, 'Congress shall have power to regulate commerce with foreign nations, and among the several States, and with the Indian tribes.'

The subject to be regulated is commerce; and our constitution being, as was aptly said at the bar, one of enumeration, and not of definition, to ascertain the extent of the power, it becomes necessary to settle the meaning of the word.

The counsel for the appellee would limit it to traffic, to buying and selling, or the interchange of commodities, and do not admit that it comprehends navigation.

This would restrict a general term, applicable to many objects, to one of its significations. Commerce, undoubtedly, is traffic, but it is something more: it is intercourse. It describes the commercial intercourse between nations, and parts of nations, in all its branches, and is regulated by prescribing rules for carrying on that intercourse. The mind can scarcely conceive a system for regulating commerce between nations, which shall exclude all laws concerning navigation, which shall be silent on the admission of the vessels of the one nation into the ports of the other, and be confined to prescribing rules for the conduct of individuals, in the actual employment of buying and selling, or of barter.

If commerce does not include navigation, the government of the Union has no direct power over that subject, and can make no law prescribing what shall constitute American vessels, or requiring that they shall be navigated by American seamen. Yet this power has been exercised from the commencement of the government, has been exercised with the consent of all, and has been understood by all to be a commercial regulation. All America understands, and has uniformly understood, the word 'commerce,' to comprehend navigation. It was so understood, and must have been so understood, when the constitution was framed. The power over commerce, including navigation, was one of the primary objects for which the people of America adopted their government, and must have been contemplated in forming it. The convention must have used the word in that sense, because all have understood it in that sense; and the attempt to restrict it comes too late.

*   *   *

The word used in the constitution, then, comprehends, and has been always understood to comprehend, navigation within its meaning; and a power to regulate navigation, is as expressly granted, as if that term had been added to the word 'commerce.'

To what commerce does this power extend? The constitution informs us, to commerce 'with foreign nations, and among the several States, and with the Indian tribes.'

It has, we believe, been universally admitted, that these words comprehend every species of commercial intercourse between the United States and foreign nations. No sort of trade can be carried on between this country and any other, to which this power does not extend. It has been truly said, that commerce, as the word is used in the constitution, is a unit, every part of which is indicated by the term.

If this be the admitted meaning of the word, in its application to foreign nations, it must carry the same meaning throughout the sentence, and remain a unit, unless there be some plain intelligible cause which alters it.

The subject to which the power is next applied, is to commerce 'among the several States.' The word 'among' means intermingled with. A thing which is among others, is intermingled with them. Commerce among the States, cannot stop at the external boundary line of each State, but may be introduced into the interior.

It is not intended to say that these words comprehend that commerce, which is completely internal, which is carried on between man and man in a State, or between different parts of the same State, and which does not extend to or affect other States. Such a power would be inconvenient, and is certainly unnecessary.

Comprehensive as the word 'among' is, it may very properly be restricted to that commerce which concerns more States than one. The phrase is not one which would probably have been selected to indicate the completely interior traffic of a State, because it is not an apt phrase for that purpose; and the enumeration of the particular classes of commerce, to which the power was to be extended, would not have been made, had the intention been to extend the power to every description. The enumeration presupposes something not enumerated; and that something, if we regard the language or the subject of the sentence, must be the exclusively internal commerce of a State. The genius and character of the whole government seem to be, that its action is to be applied to all the external concerns of the nation, and to those internal concerns which affect the States generally; but not to those which are completely within a particular State, which do not affect other States, and with which it is not necessary to interfere, for the purpose of executing some of the general powers of the government. The completely internal commerce of a State, then, may be considered as reserved for the State itself.

But, in regulating commerce with foreign nations, the power of Congress does not stop at the jurisdictional lines of the several States. It would be a very useless power, if it could not pass those lines. The commerce of the United States with foreign nations, is that of the whole United States. Every district has a right to participate in it. The deep streams which penetrate our country in every direction, pass through the interior of almost every State in the Union, and furnish the means of exercising this right. If Congress has the power to regulate it, that power must be exercised whenever the subject exists. If it exists within the States, if a foreign voyage may commence or terminate at a port within a State, then the power of Congress may be exercised within a State.

This principle is, if possible, still more clear, when applied to commerce 'among the several States.' They either join each other, in which case they are separated by a mathematical line, or they are remote from each other, in which case other States lie between them. What is commerce 'among' them; and how is it to be conducted? Can a trading expedition between two adjoining States, commence and terminate outside of each? And if the trading intercourse be between two States remote from each other, must it not commence in one, terminate in the other, and probably pass through a third? Commerce among the States must, of necessity, be commerce with the States. In the regulation of trade with the Indian tribes, the action of the law, especially when the constitution was made, was chiefly within a State. The power of Congress, then, whatever it may be, must be exercised within the territorial jurisdiction of the several States. The sense of the nation on this subject, is unequivocally manifested by the provisions made in the laws for transporting goods, by land, between Baltimore and Providence, between New-York and Philadelphia, and between Philadelphia and Baltimore.

We are now arrived at the inquiry—What is this power?

It is the power to regulate; that is, to prescribe the rule by which commerce is to be governed. This power, like all others vested in Congress, is complete in itself, may be exercised to its utmost extent, and acknowledges no limitations, other than are prescribed in the constitution. These are expressed in plain terms, and do not affect the questions which arise in this case, or which have been discussed at the bar. If, as has always been understood, the sovereignty of Congress, though limited to specified objects, is plenary as to those objects, the power over commerce with foreign nations, and among the several States, is vested in Congress as absolutely as it would be in a single government, having in its constitution the same restrictions on the exercise of the power as are found in the constitution of the United States. The wisdom and the discretion of Congress, their identity with the people, and the influence which their constituents possess at elections, are, in this, as in many other instances, as that, for example, of declaring war, the sole restraints on which they have relied, to secure them from its abuse. They are the restraints on which the people must often rely solely, in all representative governments.

The power of Congress, then, comprehends navigation, within the limits of every State in the Union; so far as that navigation may be, in any manner, connected with 'commerce with foreign nations, or among the several States, or with the Indian tribes.' It may, of consequence, pass the jurisdictional line of New-York, and act upon the very waters to which the prohibition now under consideration applies.

But it has been urged with great earnestness, that, although the power of Congress to regulate commerce with foreign nations, and among the several States, be co-extensive with the subject itself, and have no other limits than are prescribed in the constitution, yet the States may severally exercise the same power, within their respective jurisdictions. In support of this argument, it is said, that they possessed it as an inseparable attribute of sovereignty, before the formation of the constitution, and still retain it, except so far as they have surrendered it by that instrument; that this principle results from the nature of the government, and is secured by the tenth amendment; that an affirmative grant of power is not exclusive, unless in its own nature it be such that the continued exercise of it by the former possessor is inconsistent with the grant, and that this is not of that description.

The appellant, conceding these postulates, except the last, contends, that full power to regulate a particular subject, implies the whole power, and leaves no residuum; that a grant of the whole is incompatible with the existence of a right in another to any part of it.

*   *   *

It has been contended by the counsel for the appellant, that, as the word 'to regulate' implies in its nature, full power over the thing to be regulated, it excludes, necessarily, the action of all others that would perform the same operation on the same thing. That regulation is designed for the entire result, applying to those parts which remain as they were, as well as to those which are altered. It produces a uniform whole, which is as much disturbed and deranged by changing what the regulating power designs to leave untouched, as that on which it has operated.

There is great force in this argument, and the Court is not satisfied that it has been refuted.

*   *   *

Hall v. Decuir, 95 U.S. 485 (1877)

While reading Justice Waite's opinion, please consider the following:

- *To what end was the commerce power used here?*

- *What was the effect of the Louisiana statute on interstate commerce?*

- *Compare and contrast this case with* Gibbons v. Ogden.

Opinion

For the purposes of this case, we must treat the act of Louisiana of Feb. 23, 1869, as requiring those engaged in inter-state commerce to give all persons travelling in that State, upon the public conveyances employed in such business, equal rights and privileges in all parts of the conveyance, without distinction or discrimination on account of race or color. Such was the construction given to that act in the courts below, and it is conclusive upon us as the construction of a State law by the State courts. It is with this provision of the statute alone that we have to deal. We have nothing whatever to do with it as a regulation of internal commerce, or as affecting anything else than commerce among the States.

There can be no doubt but that exclusive power has been conferred upon Congress in respect to the regulation of commerce among the several States. The difficulty has never been as to the existence of this power, but as to what is to be deemed an encroachment upon it; for, as has been often said, 'legislation may in a great variety of ways affect commerce and persons engaged in it without constituting a regulation of it within the meaning of the Constitution.' Thus, in *Munn v. Illinois*, it was decided that a State might regulate the charges of public warehouses, and in *Chicago, Burlington, & Quincy Railroad Co. v. Iowa*, of railroads situated entirely within the State, even though those engaged in commerce among the States might sometimes use the warehouses or the railroads in the prosecution of their business. So, too, it has been held that States may authorize the construction of dams and bridges across navigable streams situate entirely within their respective jurisdictions. The same is true of turnpikes and ferries. By such statutes the States regulate, as a matter of domestic concern, the instruments of commerce situated wholly within their own jurisdictions, and over which they have exclusive governmental control, except when employed in foreign or inter-state commerce. As they can only be used in the State, their regulation for all purposes may properly be assumed by the State, until Congress acts in reference to their foreign or inter-state relations. When Congress does act, the State laws are superseded only to the extent that they affect commerce outside the State as it comes within the State. It has also been held that health and inspection laws may be passed by the States; and that Congress may permit the States to regulate pilots and pilotage until it shall itself legislate upon the subject, *Cooley v. Board of Wardens.* The line which separates the powers of the States from this exclusive power of Congress is not always distinctly marked, and oftentimes it is not easy to determine on which side a particular case belongs. Judges not unfrequently differ in their reasons for a decision in which they concur. Under such circumstances it would be a useless task to undertake to fix an arbitrary rule by which the line must in all cases be located. It is far better to leave a matter of such delicacy to be settled in each case upon a view of the particular rights involved.

But we think it may safely be said that State legislation which seeks to impose a direct burden upon inter-state commerce, or to interfere directly with its freedom, does encroach upon the exclusive power of Congress. The statute now under consideration, in our opinion, occupies that position. It does not act upon the business through the local instruments to be employed after coming within the State, but directly upon the business as it comes into the State from without or goes out from within. While it purports only to control the carrier when engaged within the State, it must necessarily influence his conduct to some extent in the management of his business throughout his entire voyage. His disposition of passengers taken up and put down within the State, or taken up within to be carried without, cannot but affect in a greater or less degree those taken up without and brought within, and sometimes those taken up and put down without. A passenger in the cabin set apart for the use of whites without the State must, when the boat comes within, share the accommodations of that cabin with such colored persons as may come on board afterwards, if the law is enforced.

It was to meet just such a case that the commercial clause in the Constitution was adopted. The river Mississippi passes through or along the borders of ten different States, and its tributaries reach many more. The commerce upon these waters is immense, and its regulation clearly a matter of a national concern. If each State was at liberty to regulate the conduct of carriers while within its jurisdiction, the confusion likely to follow could not but be productive of great inconvenience and unnecessary hardship. Each State could provide for its own passengers and regulate the transportation of its own freight, regardless of the interests of others. Nay more, it could prescribe rules by which the carrier must be governed within the State in respect to passengers and property brought from without. On one side of the river or its tributaries he might be required to observe one set of rules, and on the other another. Commerce cannot flourish in the midst of such embarrassments. No carrier of passengers can conduct his business with satisfaction to himself, or comfort to those employing him, if on one side of a State line his passengers, both white and colored, must be permitted to occupy the same cabin, and on the other be kept separate. Uniformity in the regulations by which he is to be governed from one end to the other of his route is a necessity in his business, and to secure it Congress, which is untrammelled by State lines, has been invested with the exclusive legislative power of determining what such regulations shall be. If this statute can be enforced against those engaged in inter-state commerce, it may be as well against those engaged in foreign; and the master of a ship clearing from New Orleans for Liverpool, having passengers on board, would be compelled to carry all, white and colored, in the same cabin during his passage down the river, or be subject to an action for damages, 'exemplary as well as actual,' by any one who felt himself aggrieved because he had been excluded on account of his color.

This power of regulation may be exercised without legislation as well as with it. By refraining from action, Congress, in effect, adopts as its own regulations those which the common law or the civil law, where that prevails, has provided for the government of such business, and those which the States, in the regulation of their domestic concerns, have established affecting commerce, but not regulating it within the meaning of the Constitution. In fact, congressional legislation is only necessary to cure defects in existing laws, as they are discovered, and to adapt such laws to new developments of trade. As was said by Mr. Justice Field, speaking for the court in *Welton v. The State of Missouri,* 'inaction [by Congress] . . . is equivalent to a declaration that inter-state commerce shall remain free and untrammelled.' Applying that principle to the circumstances of this case, congressional inaction left Benson at liberty to adopt such reasonable rules and regulations for the disposition of passengers upon his boat, while pursuing her voyage within Louisiana or without, as seemed to him most for the interest of all concerned. The statute under which this suit is brought, as construed by the State court, seeks to take away from him that power so long as he is within Louisiana; and while recognizing to the fullest extent the principle which sustains a statute, unless its unconstitutionality is clearly established, we think this statute, to the extent that it requires those engaged in the transportation of passengers among the States to carry colored passengers in Louisiana in the same cabin with whites, is unconstitutional and void. If the public good requires such legislation, it must come from Congress and not from the States.

We confine our decision to the statute in its effect upon foreign and interstate commerce, expressing no opinion as to its validity in any other respect.

Wickard v. Filburn, 317 U.S. 111 (1942)

While reading Justice Jackson's opinion, please consider the following:

- *Is the statute in question constitutional?*

- *What did the statute here prohibit? Why?*

- *How were the farmer's actions, the growing of wheat for his own personal consumption, deemed to affect interstate commerce?*

Mr. Justice JACKSON delivered the opinion of the Court. ...

In July of 1940, pursuant to the Agricultural Adjustment Act of 1938, as then amended, there were established for the appellee's 1941 crop a wheat acreage allotment of 11.1 acres and a normal yield of 20.1 bushels of wheat an acre. He was given notice of such allotment in July of 1940 before the Fall planting of his 1941 crop of wheat, and again in July of 1941, before it was harvested. He sowed, however, 23 acres, and harvested from his 11.9 acres of excess acreage 239 bushels, which under the terms of the Act as amended on May 26, 1941, constituted farm marketing excess, subject to a penalty of 49 cents a bushel, or $117.11 in all. The appellee has not paid the penalty and he has not postponed or avoided it by storing the excess under regulations of the Secretary of Agriculture, or by delivering it up to the Secretary. The Committee, therefore, refused him a marketing card, which was, under the terms of Regulations promulgated by the Secretary, necessary to protect a buyer from liability to the penalty and upon its protecting lien.

The general scheme of the Agricultural Adjustment Act of 1938 as related to wheat is to control the volume moving in interstate and foreign commerce in order to avoid surpluses and shortages and the consequent abnormally low or high wheat prices and obstructions to commerce. Within prescribed limits and by prescribed standards the Secretary of Agriculture is directed to ascertain and proclaim each year a national acreage allotment for the next crop of wheat, which is then apportioned to the states and their counties, and is eventually broken up into allotments for individual farms. Loans and payments to wheat farmers are authorized in stated circumstances.

*   *   *

It is urged that under the Commerce Clause of the Constitution, Article I, s. 8, clause 3, Congress does not possess the power it has in this instance sought to exercise. The question would merit little consideration since our decision in *United States v. Darby*, sustaining the federal power to regulate production of goods for commerce except for the fact that this Act extends federal regulation to production not intended in any part for commerce but wholly for consumption on the farm. The Act includes a definition of 'market' and its derivatives so that as related to wheat in addition to its conventional meaning it also means to dispose of 'by feeding (in any form) to poultry or livestock which, or the products of which, are sold, bartered, or exchanged, or to be so disposed of.' Hence, marketing quotas not only embrace all that may be sold without penalty but also what may be consumed on the premises. Wheat produced on excess acreage is designated as 'available for marketing' as so defined and the penalty is imposed thereon. Penalties do not depend upon whether any part of the wheat either within or without the quota is sold or intended to be sold. The sum of this is that the Federal Government fixes a quota including all that the farmer may harvest for sale or for his own farm needs, and declares that wheat produced on excess acreage may neither be disposed of nor used except upon payment of the penalty or except it is stored as required by the Act or delivered to the Secretary of Agriculture.

Appellee says that this is a regulation of production and consumption of wheat. Such activities are, he urges, beyond the reach of Congressional power under the Commerce Clause, since they are local in character, and their effects upon interstate commerce are at most 'indirect.' In answer the Government argues that the statute regulates neither production nor consumption, but only marketing; and, in the alternative, that if the Act does go beyond the regulation of marketing it is sustainable as a 'necessary and proper' implementation of the power of Congress over interstate commerce.

The Government's concern lest the Act be held to be a regulation of production or consumption rather than of marketing is attributable to a few dicta and decisions of this Court which might be understood to lay it down that activities such as 'production,' 'manufacturing,' and 'mining' are strictly 'local' and, except in special circumstances which are not present here, cannot be regulated under the commerce power because their effects upon interstate commerce are, as matter of law, only 'indirect.' Even today, when this power has been held to have great latitude, there is no decision of this Court that such activities may be regulated where no part of the product is intended for interstate commerce or intermingled with the subjects thereof. We believe that a review of the course of decision under the Commerce Clause will make plain, however, that questions of the power of Congress are not to be decided by reference to any formula which would give controlling force to nomenclature such as 'production' and 'indirect' and foreclose consideration of the actual effects of the activity in question upon interstate commerce.

At the beginning Chief Justice Marshall described the Federal commerce power with a breadth never yet exceeded. He made emphatic the embracing and penetrating nature of this power by warning that effective restraints on its exercise must proceed from political rather than from judicial processes.

For nearly a century, however, decisions of this Court under the Commerce Clause dealt rarely with questions of what Congress might do in the exercise of its granted power under the Clause and almost entirely with the permissibility of state activity which it was claimed discriminated against or burdened interstate commerce. During this period there was perhaps little occasion for the affirmative exercise of the commerce power, and the influence of the Clause on American life and law was a negative one, resulting almost wholly from its operation as a restraint upon the powers of the states. In discussion and decision the point of reference instead of being what was 'necessary and proper' to the exercise by Congress of its granted power, was often some concept of sovereignty thought to be implicit in the status of statehood. Certain activities such as 'production,' 'manufacturing,' and 'mining' were occasionally said to be within the province of state governments and beyond the power of Congress under the Commerce Clause.

It was not until 1887 with the enactment of the Interstate Commerce Act that the interstate commerce power began to exert positive influence in American law and life. This first important federal resort to the commerce power was followed in 1890 by the Sherman Anti-Trust Act and, thereafter, mainly after 1903, by many others. These statutes ushered in new phases of adjudication, which required the Court to approach the interpretation of the Commerce Clause in the light of an actual exercise by Congress of its power thereunder.

When it first dealt with this new legislation, the Court adhered to its earlier pronouncements, and allowed but little scope to the power of Congress. These earlier pronouncements also played an important part in several of the five cases in which this Court later held that Acts of Congress under the Commerce Clause were in excess of its power.

Even while important opinions in this line of restrictive authority were being written, however, other cases called forth broader interpretations of the Commerce Clause destined to supersede the earlier ones, and to bring about a return to the principles first enunciated by Chief Justice Marshall in *Gibbons v. Ogden*.

Not long after the decision of *United States v. E. C. Knight Co.*, Mr. Justice Holmes, in sustaining the exercise of national power over intrastate activity, stated for the Court that 'commerce among the states is not a technical legal conception, but a practical one, drawn from the course of business.' It was soon demonstrated that the effects of many kinds of intrastate activity upon interstate commerce were such as to make them a proper subject of federal regulation. In some cases sustaining the exercise of federal power over intrastate matters the term 'direct' was used for the purpose of stating, rather than of reaching, a result; in others it was treated as synonymous with 'substantial' or 'material;' and in others it was not used at all. Of late its use has been abandoned in cases dealing with questions of federal power under the Commerce Clause.

In the *Shreveport Rate Cases*, the Court held that railroad rates of an admittedly intrastate character and fixed by authority of the state might, nevertheless, be revised by the Federal Government because of the economic effects which they had upon interstate commerce. The opinion of Mr. Justice Hughes found federal intervention constitutionally authorized because of 'matters having such a close and substantial relation to interstate traffic that the control is essential or appropriate to the security of that traffic, to the efficiency of the interstate service, and to the maintenance of the conditions under which interstate commerce may be conducted upon fair terms and without molestation or hindrance.'

The Court's recognition of the relevance of the economic effects in the application of the Commerce Clause exemplified by this statement has made the mechanical application of legal formulas no longer feasible. Once an economic measure of the reach of the power granted to Congress in the Commerce Clause is accepted, questions of federal power cannot be decided simply by finding the activity in question to be 'production' nor can consideration of its economic effects be foreclosed by calling them 'indirect.' The present Chief Justice has said in summary of the present state of the law: 'The commerce power is not confined in its exercise to the regulation of commerce among the states. It extends to those activities intrastate which so affect interstate commerce, or the exertion of the power of Congress over it, as to make regulation of them appropriate means to the attainment of a legitimate end, the effective execution of the granted power to regulate interstate commerce. The power of Congress over interstate commerce is plenary and complete in itself, may be exercised to its utmost extent, and acknowledges no limitations other than are prescribed in the Constitution. It follows that no form of state activity can constitutionally thwart the regulatory power granted by the commerce clause to Congress. Hence the reach of that power extends to those intrastate activities which in a substantial way interfere with or obstruct the exercise of the granted power.'

Whether the subject of the regulation in question was 'production,' 'consumption,' or 'marketing' is, therefore, not material for purposes of deciding the question of federal power before us. That an activity is of local character may help in a doubtful case to determine whether Congress intended to reach it. The same consideration might help in determining whether in the absence of Congressional action it would be permissible for the state to exert its power on the subject matter, even though in so doing it to some degree affected interstate commerce. But even if appellee's activity be local and though it may not be regarded as commerce, it may still, whatever its nature, be reached by Congress if it exerts a substantial economic effect on interstate commerce and this irrespective of whether such effect is what might at some earlier time have been defined as 'direct' or 'indirect.'

The parties have stipulated a summary of the economics of the wheat industry. Commerce among the states in wheat is large and important. Although wheat is raised in every state but one, production in most states is not equal to consumption. Sixteen states on average have had a surplus of wheat above their own requirements for feed, seed, and food. Thirty-two states and the District of Columbia, where production has been below consumption, have looked to these surplus-producing states for their supply as well as for wheat for export and carryover.

The wheat industry has been a problem industry for some years. Largely as a result of increased foreign production and import restrictions, annual exports of wheat and flour from the United States during the ten-year period ending in 1940 averaged less than 10 per cent of total production, while during the 1920's they averaged more than 25 per cent. The decline in the export trade has left a large surplus in production which in connection with an abnormally large supply of wheat and other grains in recent years caused congestion in a number of markets; tied up railroad cars; and caused elevators in some instances to turn away grains, and railroads to institute embargoes to prevent further congestion.

*   *   *

In the absence of regulation the price of wheat in the United States would be much affected by world conditions. During 1941 producers who cooperated with the Agricultural Adjustment program received an average price on the farm of about $1.16 a bushel as compared with the world market price of 40 cents a bushel.

Differences in farming conditions, however, make these benefits mean different things to different wheat growers. There are several large areas of specialization in wheat, and the concentration on this crop reaches 27 percent of the crop land, and the average harvest runs as high as 155 acres. Except for some use of wheat as stock feed and for seed, the practice is to sell the crop for cash. Wheat from such areas constitutes the bulk of the interstate commerce therein.

On the other hand, in some New England states less than one percent of the crop land is devoted to wheat, and the average harvest is less than five acres per farm. In 1940 the average percentage of the total wheat production that was sold in each state as measured by value ranged from 29 per cent thereof in Wisconsin to 90 per cent in Washington. Except in regions of large-scale production, wheat is usually grown in rotation with other crops; for a nurse crop for grass seeding; and as a cover crop to prevent soil erosion and leaching. Some is sold, some kept for seed, and a percentage of the total production much larger than in areas of specialization is consumed on the farm and grown for such purpose. Such farmers, while growing some wheat, may even find the balance of their interest on the consumer's side.

The effect of consumption of homegrown wheat on interstate commerce is due to the fact that it constitutes the most variable factor in the disappearance of the wheat crop. Consumption on the farm where grown appears to vary in an amount greater than 20 per cent of average production. The total amount of wheat consumed as food varies but relatively little, and use as seed is relatively constant.

The maintenance by government regulation of a price for wheat undoubtedly can be accomplished as effectively by sustaining or increasing the demand as by limiting the supply. The effect of the statute before us is to restrict the amount

which may be produced for market and the extent as well to which one may forestall resort to the market by producing to meet his own needs. That appellee's
own contribution to the demand for wheat may be trivial by itself is not enough
to remove him from the scope of federal regulation where, as here, his contribution, taken together with that of many others similarly situated, is far from trivial.

It is well established by decisions of this Court that the power to regulate
commerce includes the power to regulate the prices at which commodities in that
commerce are dealt in and practices affecting such prices. One of the primary
purposes of the Act in question was to increase the market price of wheat and to
that end to limit the volume thereof that could affect the market. It can hardly be
denied that a factor of such volume and variability as home-consumed wheat
would have a substantial influence on price and market conditions. This may arise
because being in marketable condition such wheat overhangs the market and if
induced by rising prices tends to flow into the market and check price increases.
But if we assume that it is never marketed, it supplies a need of the man who grew
it which would otherwise be reflected by purchases in the open market. Homegrown wheat in this sense competes with wheat in commerce. The stimulation of
commerce is a use of the regulatory function quite as definitely as prohibitions or
restrictions thereon. This record leaves us in no doubt that Congress may properly
have considered that wheat consumed on the farm where grown if wholly outside
the scheme of regulation would have a substantial effect in defeating and obstructing its purpose to stimulate trade therein at increased prices.

It is said, however, that this Act, forcing some farmers into the market to buy
what they could provide for themselves, is an unfair promotion of the markets
and prices of specializing wheat growers. It is of the essence of regulation that it
lays a restraining hand on the self-interest of the regulated and that advantages
from the regulation commonly fall to others. The conflicts of economic interest
between the regulated and those who advantage by it are wisely left under our
system to resolution by the Congress under its more flexible and responsible legislative process. Such conflicts rarely lend themselves to judicial determination.
And with the wisdom, workability, or fairness, of the plan of regulation we have
nothing to do.

*   *   *

United States v. Lopez, 514 U.S. 549 (1995)

While reading Chief Justice Rehnquist's opinion, consider the following:

- *What are the three broad categories of activity that Congress may regulate under its commerce power?*

- *What basis for Congressional regulation exists in* Lopez?

- *The Government argues that guns in school zones affect interstate commerce. How?*

- *What is the basis for the Court's decision that the statute in question exceeds the power granted Congress under the Commerce Clause?*

Chief Justice REHNQUIST delivered the opinion of the Court.

In the Gun–Free School Zones Act of 1990, Congress made it a federal offense "for any individual knowingly to possess a firearm at a place that the individual knows, or has reasonable cause to believe, is a school zone." The Act neither regulates a commercial activity nor contains a requirement that the possession be connected in any way to interstate commerce. We hold that the Act exceeds the authority of Congress "[t]o regulate Commerce ... among the several States...."

On March 10, 1992, respondent, who was then a 12th–grade student, arrived at Edison High School in San Antonio, Texas, carrying a concealed .38–caliber handgun and five bullets. Acting upon an anonymous tip, school authorities confronted respondent, who admitted that he was carrying the weapon. He was arrested and charged under Texas law with firearm possession on school premises. The next day, the state charges were dismissed after federal agents charged respondent by complaint with violating the Gun–Free School Zones Act of 1990.

A federal grand jury indicted respondent on one count of knowing possession of a firearm at a school zone, in violation of § 922(q). Respondent moved to dismiss his federal indictment on the ground that § 922(q) "is unconstitutional as it is beyond the power of Congress to legislate control over our public schools."

The District Court denied the motion, concluding that § 922(q) "is a constitutional exercise of Congress' well-defined power to regulate activities in and affecting commerce, and the 'business' of elementary, middle and high schools ... affects interstate commerce." Respondent waived his right to a jury trial. The District Court conducted a bench trial, found him guilty of violating § 922(q), and sentenced him to six months' imprisonment and two years' supervised release.

On appeal, respondent challenged his conviction based on his claim that § 922(q) exceeded Congress' power to legislate under the Commerce Clause. The Court of Appeals for the Fifth Circuit agreed and reversed respondent's conviction. It held that, in light of what it characterized as insufficient congressional findings and legislative history, "section 922(q), in the full reach of its terms, is invalid as beyond the power of Congress under the Commerce Clause." Because of the importance of the issue, we granted certiorari, and we now affirm.

We start with first principles. The Constitution creates a Federal Government of enumerated powers. As James Madison wrote: "The powers delegated by the proposed Constitution to the federal government are few and defined. Those which are to remain in the State governments are numerous and indefinite." This constitutionally mandated division of authority "was adopted by the Framers to ensure protection of our fundamental liberties." "Just as the separation and independence of the coordinate branches of the Federal Government serve to prevent the accumulation of excessive power in any one branch, a healthy balance of power between the States and the Federal Government will reduce the risk of tyranny and abuse from either front."

The Constitution delegates to Congress the power "[t]o regulate Commerce with foreign Nations, and among the several States, and with the Indian Tribes." The Court, through Chief Justice Marshall, first defined the nature of Congress' commerce power in *Gibbons v. Ogden*:

Commerce, undoubtedly, is traffic, but it is something more: it is intercourse. It describes the commercial intercourse between nations, and parts of nations, in all its branches, and is regulated by prescribing rules for carrying on that intercourse.

The commerce power "is the power to regulate; that is, to prescribe the rule by which commerce is to be governed. This power, like all others vested in congress, is complete in itself, may be exercised to its utmost extent, and acknowledges no limitations, other than are prescribed in the constitution." The Gibbons Court, however, acknowledged that limitations on the commerce power are inherent in the very language of the Commerce Clause.

It is not intended to say that these words comprehend that commerce, which is completely internal, which is carried on between man and man in a State, or between different parts of the same State, and which does not extend to or affect other States. Such a power would be inconvenient, and is certainly unnecessary. Comprehensive as the word 'among' is, it may very properly be restricted to that commerce which concerns more States than one.... The enumeration presupposes something not enumerated; and that something, if we regard the language, or the subject of the sentence, must be the exclusively internal commerce of a State.

*   *   *

[Since *Gibbons v. Ogden*], we have identified three broad categories of activity that Congress may regulate under its commerce power. First, Congress may regulate the use of the channels of interstate commerce. Second, Congress is empowered to regulate and protect the instrumentalities of interstate commerce, or persons or things in interstate commerce, even though the threat may come only from intrastate activities. Finally, Congress' commerce authority includes the power to regulate those activities having a substantial relation to interstate commerce, *Jones & Laughlin Steel*, those activities that substantially affect interstate commerce.

Within this final category, admittedly, our case law has not been clear whether an activity must "affect" or "substantially affect" interstate commerce in order to be within Congress' power to regulate it under the Commerce Clause. We conclude, consistent with the great weight of our case law, that the proper test requires an analysis of whether the regulated activity "substantially affects" interstate commerce.

We now turn to consider the power of Congress, in the light of this framework, to enact § 922(q). The first two categories of authority may be quickly disposed of: § 922(q) is not a regulation of the use of the channels of interstate commerce, nor is it an attempt to prohibit the interstate transportation of a commodity through the channels of commerce; nor can § 922(q) be justified as a regulation by which Congress has sought to protect an instrumentality of interstate commerce or a thing in interstate commerce. Thus, if § 922(q) is to be sustained, it must be under the third category as a regulation of an activity that substantially affects interstate commerce.

First, we have upheld a wide variety of congressional Acts regulating intrastate economic activity where we have concluded that the activity substantially affected interstate commerce. Examples include the regulation of intrastate coal mining, intrastate extortionate credit transactions, restaurants utilizing substantial interstate supplies, inns and hotels catering to interstate guests, and production and consumption of homegrown wheat. These examples are by no means exhaustive, but the pattern is clear. Where economic activity substantially affects interstate commerce, legislation regulating that activity will be sustained.

Even *Wickard* [*v. Filburn*], which is perhaps the most far reaching example of Commerce Clause authority over intrastate activity, involved economic activity in a way that the possession of a gun in a school zone does not. Roscoe Filburn operated a small farm in Ohio, on which, in the year involved, he raised 23 acres of wheat. It was his practice to sow winter wheat in the fall, and after harvesting it in July to sell a portion of the crop, to feed part of it to poultry and livestock on the farm, to use some in making flour for home consumption, and to keep the remainder for seeding future crops. The Secretary of Agriculture assessed a penalty against him under the Agricultural Adjustment Act of 1938 because he harvested about 12 acres more wheat than his allotment under the Act permitted. The Act was designed to regulate the volume of wheat moving in interstate and foreign commerce in order to avoid surpluses and shortages, and concomitant fluctuation in wheat prices, which had previously obtained. The Court said, in an opinion sustaining the application of the Act to Filburn's activity:

One of the primary purposes of the Act in question was to increase the market price of wheat and to that end to limit the volume thereof that could affect the market. It can hardly be denied that a factor of such volume and variability as home-consumed wheat would have a substantial influence on price and market conditions. This may arise because being in marketable condition such wheat overhangs the market and, if induced by rising prices, tends to flow into the market and check price increases. But if we assume that it is never marketed, it supplies a need of the man who grew it which would otherwise be reflected by purchases in the open market. Home-grown wheat in this sense competes with wheat in commerce.

Section 922(q) is a criminal statute that by its terms has nothing to do with "commerce" or any sort of economic enterprise, however broadly one might define those terms. Section 922(q) is not an essential part of a larger regulation of economic activity, in which the regulatory scheme could be undercut unless the intrastate activity were regulated. It cannot, therefore, be sustained under our cases upholding regulations of activities that arise out of or are connected with a commercial transaction, which viewed in the aggregate, substantially affects interstate commerce.

Second, § 922(q) contains no jurisdictional element which would ensure, through case-by-case inquiry, that the firearm possession in question affects interstate commerce. For example, in *United States v. Bass*, the Court interpreted former 18 U.S.C. § 1202(a), which made it a crime for a felon to "receiv[e], posses[s], or transpor[t] in commerce or affecting commerce ... any firearm." The Court interpreted the possession component of § 1202(a) to require an additional nexus to interstate commerce both because the statute was ambiguous and because "unless Congress conveys its purpose clearly, it will not be deemed to have significantly changed the federal-state balance." The *Bass* Court set aside the conviction because, although the Government had demonstrated that Bass had possessed a firearm, it had failed "to show the requisite nexus with interstate commerce." The Court thus interpreted the statute to reserve the constitutional question whether Congress could regulate, without more, the "mere possession" of firearms. Unlike the statute in Bass, § 922(q) has no express jurisdictional element which might limit its reach to a discrete set of firearm possessions that additionally have an explicit connection with or effect on interstate commerce.

*　　　*　　　*

The Government's essential contention, in fine, is that we may determine here that § 922(q) is valid because possession of a firearm in a local school zone does indeed substantially affect interstate commerce. The Government argues that possession of a firearm in a school zone may result in violent crime and that violent crime can be expected to affect the functioning of the national economy in two ways. First, the costs of violent crime are substantial, and, through the mechanism of insurance, those costs are spread throughout the population. Second, violent crime reduces the willingness of individuals to travel to areas within the country that are perceived to be unsafe. The Government also argues that the presence of guns in schools poses a substantial threat to the educational process by threatening the learning environment. A handicapped educational process, in turn, will result in a less productive citizenry. That, in turn, would have an adverse effect on the Nation's economic well-being. As a result, the Government argues that Congress could rationally have concluded that § 922(q) substantially affects interstate commerce.

We pause to consider the implications of the Government's arguments. The Government admits, under its "costs of crime" reasoning, that Congress could regulate not only all violent crime, but all activities that might lead to violent crime, regardless of how tenuously they relate to interstate commerce. Similarly, under the Government's "national productivity" reasoning, Congress could regulate any activity that it found was related to the economic productivity of individual citizens: family law (including marriage, divorce, and child custody), for example. Under the theories that the Government presents in support of § 922(q), it is difficult to perceive any limitation on federal power, even in areas such as criminal law enforcement or education where States historically have been sovereign. Thus, if we were to accept the Government's arguments, we are hard pressed to posit any activity by an individual that Congress is without power to regulate.

*   *   *

These are not precise formulations, and in the nature of things they cannot be. But we think they point the way to a correct decision of this case. The possession of a gun in a local school zone is in no sense an economic activity that might, through repetition elsewhere, substantially affect any sort of interstate commerce.

Respondent was a local student at a local school; there is no indication that he had recently moved in interstate commerce, and there is no requirement that his possession of the firearm have any concrete tie to interstate commerce.

To uphold the Government's contentions here, we would have to pile inference upon inference in a manner that would bid fair to convert congressional authority under the Commerce Clause to a general police power of the sort retained by the States. Admittedly, some of our prior cases have taken long steps down that road, giving great deference to congressional action. The broad language in these opinions has suggested the possibility of additional expansion, but we decline here to proceed any further. To do so would require us to conclude that the Constitution's enumeration of powers does not presuppose something not enumerated and that there never will be a distinction between what is truly national and what is truly local. This we are unwilling to do.

Gonzales v. Raich, 545 U.S. 1 (2005)

While reading Justice Steven's opinion, consider the following:

- *How is Congressional regulation of marijuana cultivation and consumption a valid exercise of federal power?*

- *How is interstate commerce affected?*

Justice STEVENS delivered the opinion of the Court.

California is one of at least nine States that authorize the use of marijuana for medicinal purposes. The question presented in this case is whether the power vested in Congress by Article I, § 8, of the Constitution "[t]o make all Laws which shall be necessary and proper for carrying into Execution" its authority to "regulate Commerce with foreign Nations, and among the several States" includes the power to prohibit the local cultivation and use of marijuana in compliance with California law.

*   *   *

The obvious importance of the case prompted our grant of certiorari. The case is made difficult by respondents' strong arguments that they will suffer irreparable harm because, despite a congressional finding to the contrary, marijuana does have valid therapeutic purposes. The question before us, however, is not whether it is wise to enforce the statute in these circumstances; rather, it is whether Congress' power to regulate interstate markets for medicinal substances encompasses the portions of those markets that are supplied with drugs produced and consumed locally. Well-settled law controls our answer. [Congressional regulation of marijuana cultivation and consumption] is a valid exercise of federal power, even as applied to the troubling facts of this case.

*   *   *

Respondents in this case do not dispute that passage of the CSA, as part of the Comprehensive Drug Abuse Prevention and Control Act, was well within Congress' commerce power. Nor do they contend that any provision or section of the CSA amounts to an unconstitutional exercise of congressional authority. Rather, respondents' challenge is actually quite limited; they argue that the CSA's categorical prohibition of the manufacture and possession of marijuana as applied to the intrastate manufacture and possession of marijuana for medical purposes pursuant to California law exceeds Congress' authority under the Commerce Clause.

In assessing the validity of congressional regulation, none of our Commerce Clause cases can be viewed in isolation. As charted in considerable detail in *United States v. Lopez*, our understanding of the reach of the Commerce Clause, as well as Congress' assertion of authority thereunder, has evolved over time. The Commerce Clause emerged as the Framers' response to the central problem giving rise to the Constitution itself: the absence of any federal commerce power under the Articles of Confederation. For the first century of our history, the primary use of the Clause was to preclude the kind of discriminatory state legislation that had once been permissible. Then, in response to rapid industrial development and an increasingly interdependent national economy, Congress ushered in a new era of federal regulation under the commerce power, beginning with the enactment of the Interstate Commerce Act in 1887 and the Sherman Antitrust Act in 1890.

Cases decided during that "new era," which now spans more than a century, have identified three general categories of regulation in which Congress is authorized to engage under its commerce power. First, Congress can regulate the channels of interstate commerce. Second, Congress has authority to regulate and protect the instrumentalities of interstate commerce, and persons or things in interstate commerce. Third, Congress has the power to regulate activities that substantially affect interstate commerce. Only the third category is implicated in the case at hand.

Our case law firmly establishes Congress' power to regulate purely local activities that are part of an economic "class of activities" that have a substantial effect on interstate commerce. As we stated in *Wickard*, "even if appellee's activity be local and though it may not be regarded as commerce, it may still, whatever its nature, be reached by Congress if it exerts a substantial economic effect on interstate commerce." We have never required Congress to legislate with scientific exactitude. When Congress decides that the "total incidence" of a practice poses a threat to a national market, it may regulate the entire class. In this vein, we have reiterated that when "a general regulatory statute bears a substantial relation to commerce, the de minimis character of individual instances arising under that statute is of no consequence." Our decision in *Wickard* is of particular relevance. In *Wickard*, we upheld the application of regulations promulgated under the Agricultural Adjustment Act of 1938, which were designed to control the volume of wheat moving in interstate and foreign commerce in order to avoid surpluses and consequent abnormally low prices. The regulations established an allotment of 11.1 acres for Filburn's 1941 wheat crop, but he sowed 23 acres, intending to use the excess by consuming it on his own farm. Filburn argued that even though we had sustained Congress' power to regulate the production of goods for commerce, that power did not authorize "federal regulation [of] production not intended in any part for commerce but wholly for consumption on the farm."

Justice Jackson's opinion for a unanimous Court rejected this submission. He wrote:

> The effect of the statute before us is to restrict the amount which may be produced for market and the extent as well to which one may forestall resort to the market by producing to meet his own needs. That appellee's

own contribution to the demand for wheat may be trivial by itself is not enough to remove him from the scope of federal regulation where, as here, his contribution, taken together with that of many others similarly situated, is far from trivial.

Wickard thus establishes that Congress can regulate purely intrastate activity that is not itself "commercial," in that it is not produced for sale, if it concludes that failure to regulate that class of activity would undercut the regulation of the interstate market in that commodity.

The similarities between this case and *Wickard* are striking. Like the farmer in *Wickard*, respondents are cultivating, for home consumption, a fungible commodity for which there is an established, albeit illegal, interstate market.

Just as the Agricultural Adjustment Act was designed "to control the volume [of wheat] moving in interstate and foreign commerce in order to avoid surpluses ..." and consequently control the market price, a primary purpose of the CSA is to control the supply and demand of controlled substances in both lawful and unlawful drug markets. In *Wickard*, we had no difficulty concluding that Congress had a rational basis for believing that, when viewed in the aggregate, leaving home-consumed wheat outside the regulatory scheme would have a substantial influence on price and market conditions. Here too, Congress had a rational basis for concluding that leaving home-consumed marijuana outside federal control would similarly affect price and market conditions.

More concretely, one concern prompting inclusion of wheat grown for home consumption in the 1938 Act was that rising market prices could draw such wheat into the interstate market, resulting in lower market prices. The parallel concern making it appropriate to include marijuana grown for home consumption in the CSA is the likelihood that the high demand in the interstate market will draw such marijuana into that market. While the diversion of homegrown wheat tended to frustrate the federal interest in stabilizing prices by regulating the volume of commercial transactions in the interstate market, the diversion of homegrown marijuana tends to frustrate the federal interest in eliminating commercial transactions in the interstate market in their entirety. In both cases, the regulation is squarely within Congress' commerce power because production of the commodity meant for home consumption, be it wheat or marijuana, has a substantial effect on supply and demand in the national market for that commodity.

Nonetheless, respondents suggest that *Wickard* differs from this case in three respects: (1) the Agricultural Adjustment Act, unlike the CSA, exempted small farming operations; (2) *Wickard* involved a "quintessential economic activity"-a commercial farm-whereas respondents do not sell marijuana; and (3) the *Wickard* record made it clear that the aggregate production of wheat for use on farms had a significant impact on market prices. Those differences, though factually accurate, do not diminish the precedential force of this Court's reasoning.

The fact that Filburn's own impact on the market was "trivial by itself" was not a sufficient reason for removing him from the scope of federal regulation. That the Secretary of Agriculture elected to exempt even smaller farms from regulation does not speak to his power to regulate all those whose aggregated production was significant, nor did that fact play any role in the Court's analysis. Moreover, even though Filburn was indeed a commercial farmer, the activity he was engaged in-the cultivation of wheat for home consumption-was not treated by the Court as part of his commercial farming operation. And while it is true that the record in the *Wickard* case itself established the causal connection between the production for local use and the national market, we have before us findings by Congress to the same effect.

Findings in the introductory sections of the CSA explain why Congress deemed it appropriate to encompass local activities within the scope of the CSA. The submissions of the parties and the numerous amici all seem to agree that the national, and international, market for marijuana has dimensions that are fully comparable to those defining the class of activities regulated by the Secretary pursuant to the 1938 statute. Respondents nonetheless insist that the CSA cannot be constitutionally applied to their activities because Congress did not make a specific finding that the intrastate cultivation and possession of marijuana for medical purposes based on the recommendation of a physician would substantially affect the larger interstate marijuana market. Be that as it may, we have never required Congress to make particularized findings in order to legislate, absent a special concern such as the protection of free speech.

While congressional findings are certainly helpful in reviewing the substance of a congressional statutory scheme, particularly when the connection to commerce is not self-evident, and while we will consider congressional findings in our analysis when they are available, the absence of particularized findings does not call into question Congress' authority to legislate.

In assessing the scope of Congress' authority under the Commerce Clause, we stress that the task before us is a modest one. We need not determine whether respondents' activities, taken in the aggregate, substantially affect interstate commerce in fact, but only whether a "rational basis" exists for so concluding.

Given the enforcement difficulties that attend distinguishing between marijuana cultivated locally and marijuana grown elsewhere and concerns about diversion into illicit channels, we have no difficulty concluding that Congress had a rational basis for believing that failure to regulate the intrastate manufacture and possession of marijuana would leave a gaping hole in the CSA. Thus, as in *Wickard*, when it enacted comprehensive legislation to regulate the interstate market in a fungible commodity, Congress was acting well within its authority to "make all Laws which shall be necessary and proper" to "regulate Commerce ... among the several States." That the regulation ensnares some purely intrastate activity is of no moment. As we have done many times before, we refuse to excise individual components of that larger scheme.

*   *   *

First, the fact that marijuana is used "for personal medical purposes on the advice of a physician" cannot itself serve as a distinguishing factor. The CSA designates marijuana as contraband for any purpose; in fact, by characterizing marijuana as a Schedule I drug, Congress expressly found that the drug has no acceptable medical uses. Moreover, the CSA is a comprehensive regulatory regime specifically designed to regulate which controlled substances can be utilized for medicinal purposes, and in what manner. Indeed, most of the substances classified in the CSA "have a useful and legitimate medical purpose."

Thus, even if respondents are correct that marijuana does have accepted medical uses and thus should be redesignated as a lesser schedule drug, the CSA would still impose controls beyond what is required by California law. The CSA requires manufacturers, physicians, pharmacies, and other handlers of controlled substances to comply with statutory and regulatory provisions mandating registration with the DEA, compliance with specific production quotas, security controls to guard against diversion, recordkeeping and reporting obligations, and prescription requirements. Furthermore, the dispensing of new drugs, even when doctors approve their use, must await federal approval.

Accordingly, the mere fact that marijuana-like virtually every other controlled substance regulated by the CSA-is used for medicinal purposes cannot possibly serve to distinguish it from the core activities regulated by the CSA.

More fundamentally, if, as the principal dissent contends, the personal cultivation, possession, and use of marijuana for medicinal purposes is beyond the " 'outer limits' of Congress' Commerce Clause authority," it must also be true that such personal use of marijuana (or any other homegrown drug) for recreational purposes is also beyond those " 'outer limits,' " whether or not a State elects to authorize or even regulate such use. Justice Thomas' separate dissent suffers from the same sweeping implications. That is, the dissenters' rationale logically extends to place any federal regulation (including quality, prescription, or quantity controls) of any locally cultivated and possessed controlled substance for any purpose beyond the "outer limits" of Congress' Commerce Clause authority. One need not have a degree in economics to understand why a nationwide exemption for the vast quantity of marijuana (or other drugs) locally cultivated for personal use (which presumably would include use by friends, neighbors, and family members) may have a substantial impact on the interstate market for this extraordinarily popular substance. The congressional judgment that an exemption for such a significant segment of the total market would undermine the orderly enforcement of the entire regulatory scheme is entitled to a strong presumption of validity. Indeed, that judgment is not only rational, but "visible to the naked eye," under any commonsense appraisal of the probable consequences of such an open-ended exemption.

Second, limiting the activity to marijuana possession and cultivation "in accordance with state law" cannot serve to place respondents' activities beyond congressional reach. The Supremacy Clause unambiguously provides that if there is any conflict between federal and state law, federal law shall prevail. It is beyond peradventure that federal power over commerce is "superior to that of the States to provide for the welfare or necessities of their inhabitants," however legitimate or dire those necessities may be, just as state acquiescence to federal regulation cannot expand the bounds of the Commerce Clause

Respondents acknowledge this proposition, but nonetheless contend that their activities were not "an essential part of a larger regulatory scheme" because they had been "isolated by the State of California, and [are] policed by the State of California," and thus remain "entirely separated from the market."

The dissenters fall prey to similar reasoning. The notion that California law has surgically excised a discrete activity that is hermetically sealed off from the larger interstate marijuana market is a dubious proposition, and, more importantly, one that Congress could have rationally rejected.

Indeed, that the California exemptions will have a significant impact on both the supply and demand sides of the market for marijuana is not just "plausible" as the principal dissent concedes, it is readily apparent. The exemption for physicians provides them with an economic incentive to grant their patients permission to use the drug. In contrast to most prescriptions for legal drugs, which limit the dosage and duration of the usage, under California law the doctor's permission to recommend marijuana use is open-ended. The authority to grant permission whenever the doctor determines that a patient is afflicted with "any other illness for which marijuana provides relief," is broad enough to allow even the most scrupulous doctor to conclude that some recreational uses would be therapeutic. And our cases have taught us that there are some unscrupulous physicians who overprescribe when it is sufficiently profitable to do so.

The exemption for cultivation by patients and caregivers can only increase the supply of marijuana in the California market. The likelihood that all such production will promptly terminate when patients recover or will precisely match the patients' medical needs during their convalescence seems remote; whereas the danger that excesses will satisfy some of the admittedly enormous demand for recreational use seems obvious. Moreover, that the national and international narcotics trade has thrived in the face of vigorous criminal enforcement efforts suggests that no small number of unscrupulous people will make use of the California exemptions to serve their commercial ends whenever it is feasible to do so. Taking into account the fact that California is only one of at least nine States to have authorized the medical use of marijuana, a fact Justice O'Connor's dissent conveniently disregards in arguing that the demonstrated effect on commerce while admittedly "plausible" is ultimately "unsubstantiated," Congress could have rationally concluded that the aggregate impact on the national market of all the transactions exempted from federal supervision is unquestionably substantial.

So, from the "separate and distinct" class of activities identified by the Court of Appeals (and adopted by the dissenters), we are left with "the intrastate, non-commercial cultivation, possession and use of marijuana."

Thus the case for the exemption comes down to the claim that a locally cultivated product that is used domestically rather than sold on the open market is not subject to federal regulation. Given the findings in the CSA and the undisputed magnitude of the commercial market for marijuana, our decisions in *Wickard v. Filburn* and the later cases endorsing its reasoning foreclose that claim.

Respondents also raise a substantive due process claim and seek to avail themselves of the medical necessity defense. These theories of relief were set forth in their complaint but were not reached by the Court of Appeals. We therefore do not address the question whether judicial relief is available to respondents on these alternative bases. We do note, however, the presence of another avenue of relief. As the Solicitor General confirmed during oral argument, the statute authorizes procedures for the reclassification of Schedule I drugs. But perhaps even more important than these legal avenues is the democratic process, in which the voices of voters allied with these respondents may one day be heard in the halls of Congress. Under the present state of the law, however, the judgment of the Court of Appeals must be vacated. The case is remanded for further proceedings consistent with this opinion.

It is so ordered.

*   *   *

Chapter 9: The First Amendment

Introduction

Freedom of speech is one of the most cherished American rights secured by the Constitution and one of the few that enjoys strong bipartisan support. Importantly, the First Amendment protects not only differences of opinion and opposing political views, but disagreeable and offensive viewpoints as well. As stated by the Supreme Court, "If there is a bedrock principle underlying the First Amendment, it is that the government may not prohibit the expression of an idea simply because society finds the idea itself offensive or disagreeable. *Texas v. Johnson*, 491 U.S. 397, 414 (1989). The First Amendment even protects ideas and viewpoints that are disagreed with by the government. "[T]he government may not prohibit expression simply because it disagrees with its message." *Id.* at 416. In short, the "marketplace of ideas" cannot be regulated by the government, but only by the power of the ideas themselves.

This chapter introduces the First Amendment and the protections it affords. When reading the cases, please think about the importance of speech and why it is protected from government interference. Also, think about the speech at issue in each individual case. Was it protected? Why or why not? Do you agree with each decision? Why or why not?

Text of the First Amendment

"Congress shall make no law respecting an establishment of religion, or prohibiting the free exercise thereof; or abridging the freedom of speech, or of the press; or the right of the people peaceably to assemble, and to petition the Government for a redress of grievances."

West Virginia State Board of Education v. Barnette, 319 U.S. 624 (1943)

In Barnette *Justice Jackson provides a robust defense of freedom of thought and expression in the face of state attempts to compel a salute to the U.S. flag and the saying of the Pledge of*

Allegiance. Why is state compulsion of belief, even in something as seemingly innocuous as the Pledge of Allegiance, so pernicious?

Mr. Justice JACKSON delivered the opinion of the Court.

*   *   *

The Board of Education on January 9, 1942, adopted a resolution … ordering that the salute to the flag become 'a regular part of the program of activities in the public schools,' that all teachers and pupils 'shall be required to participate in the salute honoring the Nation represented by the Flag; provided, however, that refusal to salute the Flag be regarded as an Act of insubordination, and shall be dealt with accordingly.'

The resolution originally required the 'commonly accepted salute to the Flag' which it defined. Objections to the salute as 'being too much like Hitler's' were raised by the Parent and Teachers Association, the Boy and Girl Scouts, the Red Cross, and the Federation of Women's Clubs. Some modification appears to have been made in deference to these objections, but no concession was made to Jehovah's Witnesses. What is now required is the 'stiff-arm' salute, the saluter to keep the right hand raised with palm turned up while the following is repeated: 'I pledge allegiance to the Flag of the United States of America and to the Republic for which it stands; one Nation, indivisible, with liberty and justice for all.'

Failure to conform is 'insubordination' dealt with by expulsion. Readmission is denied by statute until compliance. Meanwhile the expelled child is 'unlawfully absent' and may be proceeded against as a delinquent. His parents or guardians are liable to prosecution, and if convicted are subject to fine not exceeding $50 and jail term not exceeding thirty days.

Appellees, citizens of the United States and of West Virginia, brought suit in the United States District Court for themselves and others similarly situated asking its injunction to restrain enforcement of these laws and regulations against Jehovah's Witnesses. The Witnesses are an unincorporated body teaching that the obligation imposed by law of God is superiod to that of laws enacted by temporal government. Their religious beliefs include a literal version of Exodus, Chapter

20, verses 4 and 5, which says: 'Thou shalt not make unto thee any graven image, or any likeness of anything that is in heaven above, or that is in the earth beneath, or that is in the water under the earth; thou shalt not bow down thyself to them nor serve them.' They consider that the flag is an 'image' within this command. For this reason they refuse to salute it.

Children of this faith have been expelled from school and are threatened with exclusion for no other cause. Officials threaten to send them to reformatories maintained for criminally inclined juveniles. Parents of such children have been prosecuted and are threatened with prosecutions for causing delinquency.

*   *   *

The freedom asserted by these appellees does not bring them into collision with rights asserted by any other individual. It is such conflicts which most frequently require intervention of the State to determine where the rights of one end and those of another begin. But the refusal of these persons to participate in the ceremony does not interfere with or deny rights of others to do so. Nor is there any question in this case that their behavior is peaceable and orderly. The sole conflict is between authority and rights of the individual. The State asserts power to condition access to public education on making a prescribed sign and profession and at the same time to coerce attendance by punishing both parent and child. The latter stand on a right of self-determination in matters that touch individual opinion and personal attitude.

... Here ... we are dealing with a compulsion of students to declare a belief. ...

There is no doubt that, in connection with the pledges, the flag salute is a form of utterance. Symbolism is a primitive but effective way of communicating ideas. The use of an emblem or flag to symbolize some system, idea, institution, or personality, is a short cut from mind to mind. Causes and nations, political parties, lodges and ecclesiastical groups seek to knit the loyalty of their followings to a flag or banner, a color or design. The State announces rank, function, and authority through crowns and maces, uniforms and black robes; the church speaks through the Cross, the Crucifix, the altar and shrine, and clerical reiment.

Symbols of State often convey political ideas just as religious symbols come to convey theological ones. Associated with many of these symbols are appropriate gestures of acceptance or respect: a salute, a bowed or bared head, a bended knee. A person gets from a symbol the meaning he puts into it, and what is one man's comfort and inspiration is another's jest and scorn.

... Here ... the State ... employs a flag as a symbol of adherence to government as presently organized. It requires the individual to communicate by word and sign his acceptance of the political ideas it thus bespeaks. Objection to this form of communication when coerced is an old one, well known to the framers of the Bill of Rights.

It is also to be noted that the compulsory flag salute and pledge requires affirmation of a belief and an attitude of mind. It is not clear whether the regulation contemplates that pupils forego any contrary convictions of their own and become unwilling converts to the prescribed ceremony or whether it will be acceptable if they simulate assent by words without belief and by a gesture barren of meaning. It is now a commonplace that censorship or suppression of expression of opinion is tolerated by our Constitution only when the expression presents a clear and present danger of action of a kind the State is empowered to prevent and punish. It would seem that involuntary affirmation could be commanded only on even more immediate and urgent grounds than silence. But here the power of compulsion is invoked without any allegation that remaining passive during a flag salute ritual creates a clear and present danger that would justify an effort even to muffle expression. To sustain the compulsory flag salute we are required to say that a Bill of Rights which guards the individual's right to speak his own mind, left it open to public authorities to compel him to utter what is not in his mind.

Whether the First Amendment to the Constitution will permit officials to order observance of ritual of this nature does not depend upon whether as a voluntary exercise we would think it to be good, bad or merely innocuous. Any credo of nationalism is likely to include what some disapprove or to omit what others think essential, and to give off different overtones as it takes on different accents or interpretations. If official power exists to coerce acceptance of any patriotic creed, what it shall contain cannot be decided by courts, but must be largely discretionary with the ordaining authority, whose power to prescribe would no doubt include power to amend. Hence validity of the asserted power to force an American citizen publicly to profess any statement of belief or to engage in any ceremony of assent to one presents questions of power that must be considered independently of any idea we may have as to the utility of the ceremony in question.

*   *   *

National unity as an end which officials may foster by persuasion and example is not in question. The problem is whether under our Constitution compulsion as here employed is a permissible means for its achievement.

Struggles to coerce uniformity of sentiment in support of some end thought essential to their time and country have been waged by many good as well as by evil men. Nationalism is a relatively recent phenomenon but at other times and places the ends have been racial or territorial security, support of a dynasty or regime, and particular plans for saving souls. As first and moderate methods to attain unity have failed, those bent on its accomplishment must resort to an ever-increasing severity. As governmental pressure toward unity becomes greater, so strife becomes more bitter as to whose unity it shall be. Probably no deeper division of our people could proceed from any provocation than from finding it necessary to choose what doctrine and whose program public educational officials shall compel youth to unite in embracing. Ultimate futility of such attempts to compel coherence is the lesson of every such effort from the Roman drive to stamp out Christianity as a disturber of its pagan unity, the Inquisition, as a means to religious and dynastic unity, the Siberian exiles as a means to Russian unity, down to the fast failing efforts of our present totalitarian enemies. Those who begin coercive elimination of dissent soon find themselves exterminating dissenters. Compulsory unification of opinion achieves only the unanimity of the graveyard.

It seems trite but necessary to say that the First Amendment to our Constitution was designed to avoid these ends by avoiding these beginnings. There is no mysticism in the American concept of the State or of the nature or origin of its authority. We set up government by consent of the governed, and the Bill of

Rights denies those in power any legal opportunity to coerce that consent. Authority here is to be controlled by public opinion, not public opinion by authority.

The case is made difficult not because the principles of its decision are obscure but because the flag involved is our own. Nevertheless, we apply the limitations of the Constitution with no fear that freedom to be intellectually and spiritually diverse or even contrary will disintegrate the social organization. To believe that patriotism will not flourish if patriotic ceremonies are voluntary and spontaneous instead of a compulsory routine is to make an unflattering estimate of the appeal of our institutions to free minds. We can have intellectual individualism and the rich cultural diversities that we owe to exceptional minds only at the price of occasional eccentricity and abnormal attitudes. When they are so harmless to others or to the State as those we deal with here, the price is not too great. But freedom to differ is not limited to things that do not matter much. That would be a mere shadow of freedom. The test of its substance is the right to differ as to things that touch the heart of the existing order.

If there is any fixed star in our constitutional constellation, it is that no official, high or petty, can prescribe what shall be orthodox in politics, nationalism, religion, or other matters of opinion or force citizens to confess by word or act their faith therein. If there are any circumstances which permit an exception, they do not now occur to us.

We think the action of the local authorities in compelling the flag salute and pledge transcends constitutional limitations on their power and invades the sphere of intellect and spirit which it is the purpose of the First Amendment to our Constitution to reserve from all official control.

*   *   *

Schenck v. United States, 249 U.S. 47 (1919) and Abrams v. United States, 250 U.S. 616 (1919)

The Schenck *and* Abrams *cases must be considered together. They were both decided, within a few months of each other, under the Espionage Act of 1917, which was enacted shortly after the U.S. entered World War I. The Act essentially prohibited interference with the military or the war effort. "Interference" of course can mean many different things, and in* Schenck *and*

Abrams, *the criminal prosecutions in question involved* **speech** *that it was claimed violated the act by (1) encouraging insubordination in the military and interfering with recruitment* (Schenck) *and (2) using language that was abusive toward or contemptuous of the form of government of the United States* (Abrams).

Both cases upheld the application of the Espionage Act to speech. The key difference is that Justice Oliver Wendell Holmes wrote the majority opinion in Schenck *and the dissenting opinion (joined by Justice Brandeis) in* Abrams. *Please consider the following questions:*

- *How would you describe the speech at issue in the 2 cases?*

- *Justice Holmes obviously sees a distinction between the 2 cases. Do you? What is it?*

- *What is the basis for Holmes' majority opinion in* Schenck?

- *What test would Holmes apply to free speech cases?*

- *Why does Holmes dissent in* Abrams?

- *What does Holmes mean by this: "the ultimate good desired is better reached by free trade in ideas - that the best test of truth is the power of the thought to get itself accepted in the competition of the market"*

Schenck v. United States
249 U.S. 47
March 3, 1919

Holmes, J.

This is an indictment in three counts. The first charges a conspiracy to violate the Espionage Act of June 15, 1917 by causing and attempting to cause insubordination ... in the military and naval forces of the United States, and to obstruct the recruiting and enlistment service of the United States, when the United States was at war with the German Empire, to-wit, that the defendant wilfully conspired to have printed and circulated to men who had been called and accepted for military service under … a document set forth and alleged to be calculated to cause such insubordination and obstruction. The count alleges overt acts in pursuance of the conspiracy, ending in the distribution of the document set forth. The second count alleges a conspiracy to commit an offense against the United States … us[ing] the mails for the transmission of … the above mentioned document, with an averment of the same overt acts. The third count charges an unlawful use of the mails for the transmission of the same matter and otherwise as above. The defendants were found guilty on all the counts. They … br[ought] the case here on th[e] ground [that the law in question violates the First Amendment and] have argued some other points also of which we must dispose.

*   *   *

The document in question upon its first printed side recited the first section of the Thirteenth Amendment, said that the idea embodied in it was violated by the conscription act and that a conscript is little better than a convict. In impassioned language it intimated that conscription was despotism in its worst form and a monstrous wrong against humanity in the interest of Wall Street's chosen few. It said, 'Do not submit to intimidation,' but in form at least confined itself to peaceful measures such as a petition for the repeal of the act. The other and later printed side of the sheet was headed 'Assert Your Rights.' It stated reasons for alleging that any one violated the Constitution when he refused to recognize 'your right to assert your opposition to the draft,' and went on, 'If you do not assert and support your rights, you are helping to deny or disparage rights which it is the solemn duty of all citizens and residents of the United States to retain.' It described the arguments on the other side as coming from cunning politicians and a mercenary capitalist press, and even silent consent to the conscription law as helping to support an infamous conspiracy. It denied the power to send our citizens away to foreign shores to shoot up the people of other lands, and added that words could not express the condemnation such cold-blooded ruthlessness deserves, [concluding], 'You must do your share to maintain, support and uphold the rights of the people of this country.' Of course the document would not have been sent unless it had been intended to have some effect, and we do not see what effect it could be expected to have upon persons subject to the draft except to influence them to obstruct the carrying of it out. The defendants do not deny that the jury might find against them on this point.

But it is said, suppose that that was the tendency of this circular, it is protected by the First Amendment to the Constitution. … We admit that in many places and in ordinary times the defendants in saying all that was said in the circular would have been within their constitutional rights. But the character of every act depends upon the circumstances in which it is done. The most stringent protection of free speech would not protect a man in falsely shouting fire in a theatre and causing a panic. It does not even protect a man from an injunction against uttering words that may have all the effect of force. **The question in every case is whether the words used are used in such circumstances and are of such a nature as to create a clear and present danger that they will bring about the substantive evils that Congress has a right to prevent.** It is a question of proximity and degree. When a nation is at war many things that might be said in time of peace are such a hindrance to its effort that their utterance will not be endured so long as men fight and that no Court could regard them as protected by any constitutional right. It seems to be admitted that if an actual obstruction of the recruiting service were proved, liability for words that produced that effect might be enforced.

*   *   *

Abrams v. United States
250 U.S. 616
Nov. 10, 1919

Opinion

Mr. Justice CLARKE delivered the opinion of the Court.

*   *   *

Each of the first three counts [of the indictment under the Espionage Act] charged the defendants with conspiring, when the United States was at war with the Imperial Government of Germany, to unlawfully utter, print, write and publish: In the first count, 'disloyal, scurrilous and abusive language about the form of government of the United States;' in the second count, language 'intended to bring the form of government of the United States into contempt, scorn, contumely, and disrepute;' and in the third count, language 'intended to incite, provoke and encourage resistance to the United States in said war.' The charge in the fourth count was that the defendants conspired 'when the United States was at war with the Imperial German Government, * * * unlawfully and willfully, by utterance, writing, printing and publication to urge, incite and advocate curtailment of production of things and products, to wit, ordnance and ammunition, necessary and essential to the prosecution of the war.' …

It was charged in each count of the indictment that it was a part of the conspiracy that the defendants would attempt to accomplish their unlawful purpose by printing, writing and distributing in the city of New York many copies of a leaflet or circular, printed in the English language, and of another printed in the Yiddish language ….

All of the five defendants were born in Russia. They were intelligent, had considerable schooling, and at the time they were arrested they had lived in the United States terms varying from five to ten years, but none of them had applied for naturalization. Four of them testified as witnesses in their own behalf, and of these three frankly avowed that they were 'rebels,' 'revolutionists,' 'anarchists,' that they did not believe in government in any form, and they declared that they had no interest whatever in the government of the United States. The fourth defendant testified that he was a 'Socialist' and believed in 'a proper kind of government, not capitalistic,' but in his classification the government of the United States was 'capitalistic.'

It was admitted on the trial that the defendants had united to print and distribute the described circulars and that 5,000 of them had been printed and distributed about the 22d day of August, 1918.

*   *   *

On the record thus described it is argued, somewhat faintly, that the acts charged against the defendants were not unlawful because within the protection of that freedom of speech and of the press which is guaranteed by the First Amendment to the Constitution of the United States, and that the entire Espionage Act is unconstitutional because in conflict with that amendment.

This contention is sufficiently discussed and is definitely negatived in *Schenck v. United States* and *Baer v. United States*.

*   *   *

The first of the two articles attached to the indictment is conspicuously headed, "*The Hypocrisy of the United States and her Allies.*" After denouncing President Wilson as a hypocrite and a coward because troops were sent into Russia, it proceeds to assail our government in general, saying:

"His [the President's] shameful, cowardly silence about the intervention in Russia reveals the hypocrisy of the plutocratic gang in Washington and vicinity."

It continues:

"He [the President] is too much of a coward to come out openly and say: 'We capitalistic nations cannot afford to have a proletarian republic in Russia.'"

Among the capitalistic nations Abrams testified the United States was included.

Growing more inflammatory as it proceeds, the circular culminates in:

"The Russian Revolution cries: Workers of the World! Awake! Rise! Put down your enemy and mine!"

"Yes friends, there is only one enemy of the workers of the world and that is CAPITALISM."

This is clearly an appeal to the "workers" of this country to arise and put down by force the government of the United States which they characterize as their "hypocritical," "cowardly" and "capitalistic" enemy.

It concludes:

"Awake! Awake, you Workers of the World! REVOLUTIONISTS."

The second of the articles was printed in the Yiddish language and in the translation is headed, *"Workers-Wake Up."* After referring to "his Majesty, Mr. Wilson, and the rest of the gang, dogs of all colors!" it continues:

"Workers, Russian emigrants, you who had the least belief in the honesty of *our* government,"

--which defendants admitted referred to the United States government—

"must now throw away all confidence, must spit in the face the false, hypocritic, military propaganda which has fooled you so relentlessly, calling forth your sympathy, your help, to the prosecution of the war."

The purpose of this obviously was to persuade the persons to whom it was addressed to turn a deaf ear to patriotic appeals in behalf of the government of the United States, and to cease to render it assistance in the prosecution of the war.

It goes on:

"With the money which you have loaned, or are going to loan them, they will make bullets not only for the Germans, but also for the Workers Soviets of Russia. *Workers in the ammunition factories, you are producing bullets, bayonets, cannon, to murder not only the Germans, but also your dearest, best, who are in Russia and are fighting for freedom."*

It will not do to say, as is now argued, that the only intent of these defendants was to prevent injury to the Russian cause. Men must be held to have intended, and to be accountable for, the effects which their acts were likely to produce. Even if their primary purpose and intent was to aid the cause of the Russian Revolution, the plan of action which they adopted necessarily involved, before it could be realized, defeat of the war program of the United States, for the obvious effect of this appeal, if it should become effective, as they hoped it might, would be to persuade persons of character such as those whom they regarded themselves as addressing, not to aid government loans and not to work in ammunition factories, where their work would produce "bullets, bayonets, cannon" and other munitions of war, the use of which would cause the "murder" of Germans and Russians.

Again, the spirit becomes more bitter as it proceeds to declare that—

"America and her Allies have betrayed [the Workers]. Their robberish aims are clear to all men. The destruction of the Russian Revolution, that is the politics of the march to Russia."

"*Workers, our reply to the barbaric intervention has to be a general strike! An open challenge* only will let the government know that not only the Russian Worker fights for freedom, but also *here in America lives the spirit of Revolution.*"

This is not an attempt to bring about a change of administration by candid discussion, for no matter what may have incited the outbreak on the part of the defendant anarchists, the manifest purpose of such a publication was to create an attempt to defeat the war plans of the government of the United States, by bringing upon the country the paralysis of a general strike, thereby arresting the production of all munitions and other things essential to the conduct of the war.

This purpose is emphasized in the next paragraph, which reads:

"Do not let the government scare you with their wild punishment in prisons, hanging and shooting. We must not and will not betray the splendid fighters of Russia. *Workers, up to fight.*"

After more of the same kind, the circular concludes:

"Woe unto those who will be in the way of progress. Let solidarity live!"

It is signed, "The Rebels."

That the interpretation we have put upon these articles, circulated in the greatest port of our land, from which great numbers of soldiers were at the time taking ship daily, and in which great quantities of war supplies of every kind were at the time being manufactured for transportation overseas, is not only the fair interpretation of them, but that it is the meaning which their authors consciously intended should be conveyed by them to others is further shown by the additional writings found in the meeting place of the defendant group and on the person of one of them. One of these circulars is headed: "Revolutionists! Unite for Action!"

After denouncing the President as "Our Kaiser" and the hypocrisy of the United States and her Allies, this article concludes:

"Socialists, Anarchists, Industrial Workers of the World, Socialists, Labor party men and other revolutionary organizations *Unite for Action* and let us save the Workers' Republic of Russia!"

"Know you lovers of freedom that in order to save the Russian revolution, we must keep the armies of the allied countries busy at home."

Thus was again avowed the purpose to throw the country into a state of revolution, if possible, and to thereby frustrate the military program of the government.

The remaining article, after denouncing the President for what is characterized as hostility to the Russian revolution, continues:

"We, the toilers of America, who believe in real liberty, shall *pledge ourselves*, in case the United States will participate in that bloody conspiracy against Russia, *to create so great a disturbance that the autocrats of America shall be compelled to keep their armies at home, and not be able to spare any for Russia."*

It concludes with this definite threat of armed rebellion:

"If they will use arms against the Russian people to enforce their standard of order, *so will we use arms*, and they shall never see the ruin of the Russian Revolution."

These excerpts sufficiently show, that while the immediate occasion for this particular outbreak of lawlessness, on the part of the defendant alien anarchists, may have been resentment caused by our government sending troops into Russia as a strategic operation against the Germans on the eastern battle front, yet the plain purpose of their propaganda was to excite, at the supreme crisis of the war, disaffection, sedition, riots, and, as they hoped, revolution, in this country for the purpose of embarrassing and if possible defeating the military plans of the government in Europe. A technical distinction may perhaps be taken between disloyal and abusive language applied to the *form* of our government or language intended to bring the *form* of our government into contempt and disrepute, and language of like character and intended to produce like results directed against the President and Congress, the agencies through which that form of government must function in time of war. But it is not necessary to a decision of this case to consider whether such distinction is vital or merely formal, for the language of these circulars was obviously intended to provoke and to encourage resistance to the United States in the war, as the third count runs, and, the defendants, in terms, plainly urged and advocated a resort to a general strike of workers in ammunition factories for the purpose of curtailing the production of ordnance and munitions necessary and essential to the prosecution of the war as is charged in the fourth count. Thus it is clear not only that some evidence but that much persuasive evidence was before the jury tending to prove that the defendants were guilty as charged in both the third and fourth counts of the indictment and under the long established rule of law hereinbefore stated the judgment of the District Court must be

Affirmed.

Mr. Justice HOLMES, dissenting.

This indictment is founded wholly upon the publication of two leaflets which I shall describe in a moment. The first count charges a conspiracy pending the war with Germany to publish abusive language about the form of government of the United States, laying the preparation and publishing of the first leaflet as overt acts. The second count charges a conspiracy pending the war to publish language intended to bring the form of government into contempt, laying the preparation and publishing of the two leaflets as overt acts. The third count alleges a conspiracy to encourage resistance to the United States in the same war and to attempt to effectuate the purpose by publishing the same leaflets. The fourth count lays a conspiracy to incite curtailment of production of things necessary to the prosecution of the war and to attempt to accomplish it by publishing the second leaflet to which I have referred.

[Holmes discusses the content of the leaflets.]

No argument seems to be necessary to show that these pronunciamentos in no way attack the form of government of the United States, or that they do not support either of the first two counts. What little I have to say about the third count may be postponed until I have considered the fourth. With regard to that it seems too plain to be denied that the suggestion to workers in the ammunition factories that they are producing bullets to murder their dearest, and the further advocacy of a general strike, both in the second leaflet, do urge curtailment of production of things necessary to the prosecution of the war within the meaning of the Act of May 16, 1918. But to make the conduct criminal that statute requires that it should be "with intent by such curtailment to cripple or hinder the United States in the prosecution of the war." It seems to me that no such intent is proved.

*   *   *

It seems to me that this statute must be taken to use its words in a strict and accurate sense. They would be absurd in any other. A patriot might think that we were wasting money on aeroplanes, or making more cannon of a certain kind than we needed, and might advocate curtailment with success, yet even if it turned out that the curtailment hindered and was thought by other minds to have been obviously likely to hinder the United States in the prosecution of the war, no one would hold such conduct a crime. I admit that my illustration does not answer all that might be said but it is enough to show what I think and to let me pass to a more important aspect of the case. I refer to the First Amendment to the Constitution that Congress shall make no law abridging the freedom of speech.

I never have seen any reason to doubt that the questions of law that alone were before this Court in the Cases of *Schenck* (249 U. S. 47), *Frohwerk* (249 U. S. 204) and *Debs* (249 U. S. 211), were rightly decided. I do not doubt for a moment that by the same reasoning that would justify punishing persuasion to murder, the United States constitutionally may punish speech that produces or is intended to produce a clear and imminent danger that it will bring about forthwith certain substantive evils that the United States constitutionally may seek to prevent. The power undoubtedly is greater in time of war than in time of peace because war opens dangers that do not exist at other times.

But as against dangers peculiar to war, as against others, the principle of the right to free speech is always the same. It is only the present danger of immediate evil or an intent to bring it about that warrants Congress in setting a limit to the expression of opinion where private rights are not concerned. Congress certainly cannot forbid all effort to change the mind of the country. Now nobody can suppose that the surreptitious publishing of a silly leaflet by an unknown man, without more, would present any immediate danger that its opinions would hinder the success of the government arms or have any appreciable tendency to do so. ...

I do not see how anyone can find the intent required by the statute in any of the defendant's words.

*   *   *

In this case sentences of twenty years imprisonment have been imposed for the publishing of two leaflets that I believe the defendants had as much right to publish as the Government has to publish the Constitution of the United States now vainly invoked by them.

*   *   *

Persecution for the expression of opinions seems to me perfectly logical. If you have no doubt of your premises or your power and want a certain result with all your heart you naturally express your wishes in law and sweep away all opposition. To allow opposition by speech seems to indicate that you think the speech impotent, as when a man says that he has squared the circle, or that you do not care whole heartedly for the result, or that you doubt either your power or your premises. But when men have realized that time has upset many fighting faiths, they may come to believe even more than they believe the very foundations of their own conduct that the ultimate good desired is better reached by free trade in ideas - that the best test of truth is the power of the thought to get itself accepted in the competition of the market, and that truth is the only ground upon which their wishes safely can be carried out. That at any rate is the theory of our Constitution. It is an experiment, as all life is an experiment. Every year if not every day we have to wager our salvation upon some prophecy based upon imperfect knowledge. While that experiment is part of our system I think that we should be eternally vigilant against attempts to check the expression of opinions that we loathe and believe to be fraught with death, unless they so imminently threaten immediate interference with the lawful and pressing purposes of the law that an immediate check is required to save the country. I wholly disagree with the argument of the Government that the First Amendment left the common law as to seditious libel in force. History seems to me against the notion.

*   *   *

Mr. Justice BRANDEIS concurs with the foregoing opinion.

Brandenburg v. Ohio, 395 U.S. 444 (1969)

Brandenburg v. Ohio *dealt with speech that was noxious and offensive, namely that of the Ku Klux Klan, an odious organization that, among other horrifying things, preaches white supremacy, intimidation and violence toward blacks, and anti-semitism. Please consider the following:*

- *Why did the Court rule that the Ohio statute under which the Klan member was prosecuted was unconstitutional?*

- *What type of distinction does the Court make with the advocacy of violence?*

- *Why do we protect speech that we find offensive?*

- *Of particular interest is the concurring opinion of Justice Douglas. Please note how he traces the development of the "clear and present danger" doctrine.*

- *Why does Justice Douglas think that the "clear and present danger" doctrine is incompatible with the First Amendment?*

- *Why does Justice Douglas think that* Whitney v. California *was correctly overruled?*

- *What does Justice Douglas say is <u>not</u> protected by the First Amendment?*

Opinion
PER CURIAM.

The appellant, a leader of a Ku Klux Klan group, was convicted under the Ohio Criminal Syndicalism statute for 'advocat(ing) * * * the duty, necessity, or propriety of crime, sabotage, violence, or unlawful methods of terrorism as a means of accomplishing industrial or political reform' and for 'voluntarily assembl(ing) with any society, group, or assemblage of persons formed to teach or advocate the doctrines of criminal syndicalism.' He was fined $1,000 and sentenced to one to 10 years' imprisonment. The appellant challenged the constitutionality of the criminal syndicalism statute under the First and Fourteenth Amendments to the United States Constitution, but the intermediate appellate court of Ohio affirmed his conviction without opinion. The Supreme Court of Ohio dismissed his appeal, sua sponte, 'for the reason that no substantial constitutional question exists herein.' It did not file an opinion or explain its conclusions. Appeal was taken to this Court.… We reverse.

The record shows that a man, identified at trial as the appellant, telephoned an announcer-reporter on the staff of a Cincinnati television station and invited him to come to a Ku Klux Klan 'rally' to be held at a farm in Hamilton County. With the cooperation of the organizers, the reporter and a cameraman attended the meeting and filmed the events. Portions of the films were later broadcast on the local station and on a national network.

The prosecution's case rested on the films and on testimony identifying the appellant as the person who communicated with the reporter and who spoke at the rally. The State also introduced into evidence several articles appearing in the film, including a pistol, a rifle, a shotgun, ammunition, a Bible, and a red hood worn by the speaker in the films.

One film showed 12 hooded figures, some of whom carried firearms. They were gathered around a large wooden cross, which they burned. No one was present other than the participants and the newsmen who made the film. Most of the words uttered during the scene were incomprehensible when the film was projected, but scattered phrases could be understood that were derogatory of Negroes and, in one instance, of Jews. Another scene on the same film showed the appellant, in Klan regalia, making a speech. The speech, in full, was as follows:

'This is an organizers' meeting. We have had quite a few members here today which are—we have hundreds, hundreds of members throughout the State of Ohio. I can quote from a newspaper clipping from the Columbus, Ohio Dispatch, five weeks ago Sunday morning. The Klan has more members in the State of Ohio than does any other organization. We're not a revengent organization, but if our President, our Congress, our Supreme Court, continues to suppress the white, Caucasian race, it's possible that there might have to be some revengeance taken.

'We are marching on Congress July the Fourth, four hundred thousand strong. From there we are dividing into two groups, one group to march on St. Augustine, Florida, the other group to march into Mississippi. Thank you.'

The second film showed six hooded figures one of whom, later identified as the appellant, repeated a speech very similar to that recorded on the first film. The reference to the possibility of 'revengeance' was omitted, and one sentence was added: 'Personally, I believe the nigger should be returned to Africa, the Jew returned to Israel.' Though some of the figures in the films carried weapons, the speaker did not.

The Ohio Criminal Syndicalism Statute was enacted in 1919. From 1917 to 1920, identical or quite similar laws were adopted by 20 States and two territories. E. Dowell, A History of Criminal Syndicalism Legislation in the United States 21

(1939). In 1927, this Court sustained the constitutionality of California's Criminal Syndicalism Act, Cal. Penal Code ss 11400—11402, the text of which is quite similar to that of the laws of Ohio. *Whitney v. California*, 274 U.S. 357 (1927). The Court upheld the statute on the ground that, without more, 'advocating' violent means to effect political and economic change involves such danger to the security of the State that the State may outlaw it. Cf. *Fiske v. Kansas*, 274 U.S. 380 (1927).

But *Whitney* has been thoroughly discredited by later decisions. See *Dennis v. United States*, 341 U.S. 494, at 507 (1951). These later decisions have fashioned the principle that the constitutional guarantees of free speech and free press do not permit a State to forbid or proscribe advocacy of the use of force or of law violation except where such advocacy is directed to inciting or producing imminent lawless action and is likely to incite or produce such action. As we said in *Noto v. United States*, 367 U.S. 290, 297—298 (1961), "the mere abstract teaching ... of the moral propriety or even moral necessity for a resort to force and violence, is not the same as preparing a group for violent action and steeling it to such action." A statute which fails to draw this distinction impermissibly intrudes upon the freedoms guaranteed by the First and Fourteenth Amendments. It sweeps within its condemnation speech which our Constitution has immunized from governmental control.

Measured by this test, Ohio's Criminal Syndicalism Act cannot be sustained. The Act punishes persons who 'advocate or teach the duty, necessity, or propriety' of violence 'as a means of accomplishing industrial or political reform'; or who publish or circulate or display any book or paper containing such advocacy; or who 'justify' the commission of violent acts 'with intent to exemplify, spread or advocate the propriety of the doctrines of criminal syndicalism'; or who 'voluntarily assemble' with a group formed 'to teach or advocate the doctrines of criminal syndicalism.' Neither the indictment nor the trial judge's instructions to the jury in any way refined the statute's bald definition of the crime in terms of mere advocacy not distinguished from incitement to imminent lawless action.

Accordingly, we are here confronted with a statute which, by its own words and as applied, purports to punish mere advocacy and to forbid, on pain of criminal punishment, assembly with others merely to advocate the described type of action. Such a statute falls within the condemnation of the First and Fourteenth Amendments. The contrary teaching of *Whitney v. California*, supra, cannot be supported, and that decision is therefore overruled.

Mr. Justice BLACK, concurring.

I agree with the views expressed by Mr. Justice DOUGLAS in his concurring opinion in this case that the 'clear and present danger' doctrine should have no place in the interpretation of the First Amendment. I join the Court's opinion, which, as I understand it, simply cites *Dennis v. United States*, 341 U.S. 494 (1951), but does not indicate any agreement on the Court's part with the 'clear and present danger' doctrine on which Dennis purported to rely.

Mr. Justice DOUGLAS, concurring.

While I join the opinion of the Court, I desire to enter a caveat.

The 'clear and present danger' test was adumbrated by Mr. Justice Holmes in a case arising during World War I—a war 'declared' by the Congress, not by the Chief Executive. The case was *Schenck v. United States*, 249 U.S. 47, 52, where the defendant was charged with attempts to cause insubordination in the military and obstruction of enlistment. The pamphlets that were distributed urged resistance to the draft, denounced conscription, and impugned the motives of those backing the war effort. The First Amendment was tendered as a defense. Mr. Justice Holmes in rejecting that defense said:

'The question in every case is whether the words used are used in such circumstances and are of such a nature as to create a clear and present danger that they will bring about the substantive evils that Congress has a right to prevent. It is a question of proximity and degree.'

Frohwerk v. United States, 249 U.S. 204, also authored by Mr. Justice Holmes, involved prosecution and punishment for publication of articles very critical of the war effort in World War I. *Schenck* was referred to as a conviction for obstructing security 'by words of persuasion.' Id., at 206. And the conviction in

Frohwerk was sustained because 'the circulation of the paper was in quarters where a little breath would be enough to kindle a flame.' Id., at 209.

Debs v. United States, 249 U.S. 211 was the third of the trilogy of the 1918 Term. *Debs* was convicted of speaking in opposition to the war where his 'opposition was so expressed that its natural and intended effect would be to obstruct recruiting.' Id., at 215. 'If that was intended and if, in all the circumstances, that would be its probable effect, it would not be protected by reason of its being part of a general program in expressions of a general and conscientious belief.' Ibid.

In the 1919 Term, the Court applied the *Schenck* doctrine to affirm the convictions of other dissidents in World War I. *Abrams v. United States*, 250 U.S. 616 was one instance. Mr. Justice Holmes, with whom Mr. Justice Brandeis concurred, dissented. While adhering to *Schenck*, he did not think that on the facts a case for overriding the First Amendment had been made out: 'It is only the present danger of immediate evil or an intent to bring it about that warrants Congress in setting a limit to the expression of opinion where private rights are not concerned. Congress certainly cannot forbid all effort to change the mind of the country.'

Another instance was *Schaefer v. United States*, 251 U.S. 466, in which Mr. Justice Brandeis, joined by Mr. Justice Holmes, dissented. A third was *Pierce v. United States*, 252 U.S. 239, in which again Mr. Justice Brandeis, joined by Mr. Justice Holmes, dissented.

Those, then, were the World War I cases that put the gloss of 'clear and present danger' on the First Amendment. Whether the war power—the greatest leveler of them all—is adequate to sustain that doctrine is debatable. The dissents in Abrams, Schaefer, and Pierce show how easily 'clear and present danger' is manipulated to crush what Brandeis called '(t)he fundamental right of free men to strive for better conditions through new legislation and new institutions' by argument and discourse (*Pierce v. United States*, supra, at 273) even in time of war. Though I doubt if the 'clear and present danger' test is congenial to the First Amendment in time of a declared war, I am certain it is not reconcilable with the First Amendment in days of peace.

The Court quite properly overrules *Whitney v. California*, 274 U.S. 357, which involved advocacy of ideas which the majority of the Court deemed unsound and dangerous.

Mr. Justice Holmes, though never formally abandoning the 'clear and present danger' test, moved closer to the First Amendment ideal when he said in dissent in *Gitlow* (*Gitlow v. People of State of New York*, 268 U.S. 652):

> 'Every idea is an incitement. It offers itself for belief and if believed it is acted on unless some other belief outweighs it or some failure of energy stifles the movement at its birth. The only difference between the expression of an opinion and an incitement in the narrower sense is the speaker's enthusiasm for the result. Eloquence may set fire to reason. But whatever may be thought of the redundant discourse before us it had no chance of starting a present conflagration. If in the long run the beliefs expressed in proletarian dictatorship are destined to be accepted by the dominant forces of the community, the only meaning of free speech is that they should be given their chance and have their way.'

We have never been faithful to the philosophy of that dissent.

*   *   *

The line between what is permissible and not subject to control and what may be made impermissible and subject to regulation is the line between ideas and overt acts.

The example usually given by those who would punish speech is the case of one who falsely shouts fire in a crowded theatre. This is, however, a classic case where speech is brigaded with action. *See Speiser v. Randall*, 357 U.S. 513, 536—537 (Douglas, J., concurring.) They are indeed inseparable and a prosecution can be launched for the overt acts actually caused. Apart from rare instances of that kind, speech is, I think, immune from prosecution. Certainly there is no constitutional line between advocacy of abstract ideas as in *Yates* and advocacy of political action as in *Scales*. The quality of advocacy turns on the depth of the conviction; and government has no power to invade that sanctuary of belief and conscience.

Near v. Minnesota, 283 U.S. 697 (1931)

Near v. Minnesota *and the case that follows it,* New York Times v. United States, *deal with freedom of the press and a concept known as* **prior restraint**. *Prior restraint refers to efforts by the government to suppress or prohibit speech ahead of time, prior to publication. Under the U.S. Constitution, the government is severely limited in its ability to do this.*

- *How was the Minnesota statute in* Near *deemed an unconstitutional prior restraint?*

- *Why is this type of prior restraint so harmful?*

- *Is there any recourse for harmful and/or false speech published by the press?*

Mr. Chief Justice HUGHES delivered the opinion of the Court.

Chapter 285 of the Session Laws of Minnesota for the year 1925 provides for the abatement, as a public nuisance, of a 'malicious, scandalous and defamatory newspaper, magazine or other periodical.' Section 1 of the act is as follows:

'**Section 1**. Any person who, as an individual, or as a member or employee of a firm, or association or organization, or as an officer, director, member or employee of a corporation, shall be engaged in the business of regularly or customarily producing, publishing or circulating, having in possession, selling or giving away.

'(a) an obscene, lewd and lascivious newspaper, magazine, or other periodical, or

'(b) a malicious, scandalous and defamatory newspaper, magazine or other periodical,

-is guilty of a nuisance, and all persons guilty of such nuisance may be enjoined, as hereinafter provided.

*   *   *

Under this statute, the county attorney of Hennepin county brought this action to enjoin the publication of what was described as a 'malicious, scandalous and defamatory newspaper, magazine or other periodical,' known as *The Saturday Press*, published by the defendants in the city of Minneapolis.

*   *   *

Without attempting to summarize the contents of the voluminous exhibits attached to the complaint, we deem it sufficient to say that the articles charged, in substance, that a Jewish gangster was in control of gambling, bootlegging, and racketeering in Minneapolis, and that law enforcing officers and agencies were not energetically performing their duties. Most of the charges were directed against the chief of police; he was charged with gross neglect of duty, illicit relations with gangsters, and with participation in graft. The county attorney was charged with knowing the existing conditions and with failure to take adequate measures to remedy them. The mayor was accused of inefficiency and dereliction. One member of the grand jury was stated to be in sympathy with the gangsters. A special grand jury and a special prosecutor were demanded to deal with the situation in general, and, in particular, to investigate an attempt to assassinate one Guilford, one of the original defendants, who, it appears from the articles, was shot by gangsters after the first issue of the periodical had been published. There is no question but that the articles made serious accusations against the public officers named and others in connection with the prevalence of crimes and the failure to expose and punish them.

*   *   *

The defendants ... challenged the constitutionality of the statute. The district court ... certified the question of constitutionality to the Supreme Court of the state. The Supreme Court sustained the statute . . . and it is conceded by the appellee that the act was thus held to be valid over the objection that it violated not only the State Constitution, but also the Fourteenth Amendment of the Constitution of the United States.

*   *   *

From the judgment as thus affirmed, the defendant Near appeals to this Court.

This statute, for the suppression as a public nuisance of a newspaper or periodical, is unusual, if not unique, and raises questions of grave importance transcending the local interests involved in the particular action. It is no longer open to doubt that the liberty of the press and of speech is within the liberty safeguarded by the due process clause of the Fourteenth Amendment from invasion by state action. It was found impossible to conclude that this essential personal liberty of the citizen was left unprotected by the general guaranty of fundamental rights of person and property. *Gitlow v. New York*, 268 U. S. 652, 666 (1925). . . . Liberty of speech and of the press is also not an absolute right, and the state may punish its abuse. *Whitney v. California*, 274 U.S. 357 (1927). Liberty, in each of its phases, has its history and connotation, and, in the present instance, the inquiry is as to the historic conception of the liberty of the press and whether the statute under review violates the essential attributes of that liberty.

*   *   *

First. The statute is not aimed at the redress of individual or private wrongs. Remedies for libel remain available and unaffected. The Statute, said the state court . . . 'is not directed at threatened libel but at an existing business which, generally speaking, involves more than libel.' It is aimed at the distribution of scandalous matter as 'detrimental to public morals and to the general welfare,' tending 'to disturb the peace of the community' and 'to provoke assaults and the commission of crime.' . . .

Second. The statute is directed not simply at the circulation of scandalous and defamatory statements with regard to private citizens, but at the continued publication by newspapers and periodical of charges against public officers of corruption, malfeasance in office, or serious neglect of duty. Such charges by their very nature create a public scandal. They are scandalous and defamatory within the meaning of the statute, which has its normal operation in relation to publications dealing prominently and chiefly with the alleged derelictions of public officers.

Third. The object of the statute is not punishment, in the ordinary sense, but suppression of the offending newspaper or periodical. ...

This suppression is accomplished by enjoining publication, and that restraint is the object and effect of the statute.

Fourth. The statute not only operates to suppress the offending newspaper or periodical, but to put the publisher under an effective censorship. ...

If we cut through mere details of procedure, the operation and effect of the statute in substance is that public authorities may bring the owner or publisher of a newspaper or periodical before a judge upon a charge of conducting a business of publishing scandalous and defamatory matter-in particular that the matter consists of charges against public officers of official dereliction-and, unless the owner or publisher is able and disposed to bring competent evidence to satisfy the judge that the charges are true and are published with good motives and for justifiable ends, his newspaper or periodical is suppressed and further publication is made punishable as a contempt. This is of the essence of censorship.

The question is whether a statute authorizing such proceedings in restraint of publication is consistent with the conception of the liberty of the press as historically conceived and guaranteed. In determining the extent of the constitutional protection, it has been generally, if not universally, considered that it is the chief purpose of the guaranty to prevent previous restraints upon publication. ...

The exceptional nature of its limitations places in a strong light the general conception that liberty of the press, historically considered and taken up by the Federal Constitution, has meant, principally although not exclusively, immunity from previous restraints or censorship. The conception of the liberty of the press in this country had broadened with the exigencies of the colonial period and with the efforts to secure freedom from oppressive administration. That liberty was especially cherished for the immunity it afforded from previous restraint of the publication of censure of public officers and charges of official misconduct. ...

The fact that for approximately one hundred and fifty years there has been almost an entire absence of attempts to impose previous restraints upon publications relating to the malfeasance of public officers is significant of the deep-seated conviction that such restraints would violate constitutional right. Public officers, whose character and conduct remain open to debate and free discussion in the press, find their remedies for false accusations in actions under libel laws providing for redress and punishment, and not in proceedings to restrain the publication of newspapers and periodicals. The general principle that the constitutional guaranty of the liberty of the press gives immunity from previous restraints has been approved in many decisions under the provisions of state constitutions.

The importance of this immunity has not lessened. While reckless assaults upon public men, and efforts to bring obloquy upon those who are endeavoring faithfully to discharge official duties, exert a baleful influence and deserve the severest condemnation in public opinion, it cannot be said that this abuse is greater, and it is believed to be less, than that which characterized the period in which our institutions took shape. Meanwhile, the administration of government has become more complex, the opportunities for malfeasance and corruption have multiplied, crime has grown to most serious proportions, and the danger of its protection by unfaithful officials and of the impairment of the fundamental security of life and property by criminal alliances and official neglect, emphasizes the primary need of a vigilant and courageous press, especially in great cities. The fact that the liberty of the press may be abused by miscreant purveyors of scandal does not make any the less necessary the immunity of the press from previous restraint in dealing with official misconduct. ...

For these reasons we hold the statute, so far as it authorized the proceedings in this action under clause (b) of section 1, to be an infringement of the liberty of the press guaranteed by the Fourteenth Amendment. We should add that this decision rests upon the operation and effect of the statute, without regard to the question of the truth of the charges contained in the particular periodical. The fact that the public officers named in this case, and those associated with the charges of official dereliction, may be deemed to be impeccable, cannot affect the conclusion that the statute imposes an unconstitutional restraint upon publication.

*   *   *

New York Times v. United States, 403 U.S. 713 (1971)

New York Times v. United States *is a justly famous case dealing with efforts by the U.S. Government to prohibit publication of a classified study entitled "History of U.S. Decision-Making Process on Viet Nam Policy," also known as the Pentagon Papers. The study revealed details about U.S. decision making in the Vietnam War that were embarrassing to the government and showed the various ways the government sought to mislead the American people about the scope of the war and U.S. success in it.*

The case shows the very dim view that courts take of prior restraints initiated by the government. Take note of the various concurring opinions that discuss the importance of the First Amendment and the reasons for severely restricting government efforts to suppress speech.

Opinion
PER CURIAM.

We granted certiorari . . . in these cases in which the United States seeks to enjoin the *New York Times* and the *Washington Post* from publishing the contents of a classified study entitled 'History of U.S. Decision-Making Process on Viet Nam Policy.'

'**Any system of prior restraints of expression comes to this Court bearing a heavy presumption against its constitutional validity.**' *Bantam Books, Inc. v. Sullivan*, 372 U.S. 58, 70, 83 (1963) . . . The Government 'thus carries a heavy burden of showing justification for the imposition of such a restraint.' *Organization for a Better Austin v. Keefe*, 402 U.S. 415, 419 (1971). The District Court for the Southern District of New York in the *New York Times* case, 328 F.Supp. 324, and the District Court for the District of Columbia and the Court of Appeals for the District of Columbia Circuit, 446 F.2d 1327, in the *Washington Post* case held that the Government had not met that burden. We agree.

The judgment of the Court of Appeals for the District of Columbia Circuit is therefore affirmed. The order of the Court of Appeals for the Second Circuit is reversed, . . . and the case is remanded with directions to enter a judgment affirming the judgment of the District Court for the Southern District of New York. The stays entered June 25, 1971, by the Court are vacated. The judgments shall issue forthwith.

So ordered.

Mr. Justice BLACK, with whom Mr. Justice DOUGLAS joins, concurring.

I believe that every moment's continuance of the injunctions against these newspapers amounts to a flagrant, indefensible, and continuing violation of the First Amendment. Furthermore, after oral argument, I agree completely that we must affirm the judgment of the Court of Appeals for the District of Columbia Circuit and reverse the judgment of the Court of Appeals for the Second Circuit for the reasons stated by my Brothers DOUGLAS and BRENNAN. . . .

Our Government was launched in 1789 with the adoption of the Constitution. The Bill of Rights, including the First Amendment, followed in 1791. Now, for the first time in the 182 years since the founding of the Republic, the federal courts are asked to hold that the First Amendment does not mean what it says, but rather means that the Government can halt the publication of current news of vital importance to the people of this country. . . .

In the First Amendment the Founding Fathers gave the free press the protection it must have to fulfill its essential role in our democracy. The press was to serve the governed, not the governors. The Government's power to censor the press was abolished so that the press would remain forever free to censure the Government. The press was protected so that it could bare the secrets of government and inform the people. Only a free and unrestrained press can effectively expose deception in government. And paramount among the responsibilities of a free press is the duty to prevent any part of the government from deceiving the people and sending them off to distant lands to die of foreign fevers and foreign shot and shell. In my view, far from deserving condemnation for their courageous reporting, the New York Times, the Washington Post, and other newspapers should be commended for serving the purpose that the Founding Fathers saw so clearly. In revealing the workings of government that led to the Vietnam war, the newspapers nobly did precisely that which the Founders hoped and trusted they would do. . . .

[We] are asked to hold that despite the First Amendment's emphatic command, the Executive Branch, the Congress, and the Judiciary can make laws enjoining publication of current news and abridging freedom of the press in the name of 'national security.' The Government does not even attempt to rely on any act of Congress. Instead it makes the bold and dangerously far-reaching contention that the courts should take it upon themselves to 'make' a law abridging freedom of the press in the name of equity, presidential power and national security, even when the representatives of the people in Congress have adhered to the command of the First Amendment and refused to make such a law. *See* concurring opinion of Mr. Justice DOUGLAS, post, at 2145. To find that the President has 'inherent power' to halt the publication of news by resort to the courts would wipe out the First Amendment and destroy the fundamental liberty and security of the very people the Government hopes to make 'secure.' No one can read the history of the adoption of the First Amendment without being convinced beyond any doubt that it was injunctions like those sought here that Madison and his collaborators intended to outlaw in this Nation for all time.

The word 'security' is a broad, vague generality whose contours should not be invoked to abrogate the fundamental law embodied in the First Amendment. The guarding of military and diplomatic secrets at the expense of informed representative government provides no real security for our Republic. The Framers of the First Amendment, fully aware of both the need to defend a new nation and the abuses of the English and Colonial Governments, sought to give this new society strength and security by providing that freedom of speech, press, religion, and assembly should not be abridged. This thought was eloquently expressed in 1937 by Mr. Chief Justice Hughes—great man and great Chief Justice that he was—when the Court held a man could not be punished for attending a meeting run by Communists.

'The greater the importance of safeguarding the community from incitements to the overthrow of our institutions by force and violence, the more imperative is the need to preserve inviolate the constitutional rights of free speech, free press and free assembly in order to maintain the opportunity for free political discussion, to the end that government may be responsive to the will of the people and that changes, if desired, may be obtained by peaceful means. Therein lies the security of the Republic, the very foundation of constitutional government.'

Mr. Justice DOUGLAS, with whom Mr. Justice BLACK joins, concurring.

These disclosures may have a serious impact. But that is no basis for sanctioning a previous restraint on the press. . . .

The dominant purpose of the First Amendment was to prohibit the widespread practice of governmental suppression of embarrassing information. It is common knowledge that the First Amendment was adopted against the widespread use of the common law of seditious libel to punish the dissemination of material that is embarrassing to the powers-that-be . . .The present cases will, I think, go down in history as the most dramatic illustration of that principle. A debate of large proportions goes on in the Nation over our posture in Vietnam. That debate antedated the disclosure of the contents of the present documents. The latter are highly relevant to the debate in progress.

Secrecy in government is fundamentally anti-democratic, perpetuating bureaucratic errors. Open debate and discussion of public issues are vital to our national health. On public questions there should be 'uninhibited, robust, and wide-open' debate. *New York Times Co. v. Sullivan*, 376 U.S. 254, 269—270 (1964).

I would affirm the judgment of the Court of Appeals in the Post case, vacate the stay of the Court of Appeals in the Times case and direct that it affirm the District Court.

The stays is these cases that have been in effect for more than a week constitute a flouting of the principles of the First Amendment as interpreted in *Near v. Minnesota ex rel. Olson.*

Mr. Justice BRENNAN, concurring.

The error that has pervaded these cases from the outset was the granting of any injunctive relief whatsoever, interim or otherwise. The entire thrust of the Government's claim throughout these cases has been that publication of the material sought to be enjoined 'could,' or 'might,' or 'may' prejudice the national interest in various ways. But the First Amendment tolerates absolutely no prior judicial restraints of the press predicated upon surmise or conjecture that untoward consequences may result. Our cases, it is true, have indicated that there is a single, extremely narrow class of cases in which the First Amendment's ban on prior judicial restraint may be overridden. Our cases have thus far indicated that such cases may arise only when the Nation 'is at war,' *Schenck v. United States*, 249 U.S. 47, 52 (1919), during which times '(n)o one would question but that a government might prevent actual obstruction to its recruiting service or the publication of the sailing dates of transports or the number and location of troops.' *Near v. Minnesota ex rel. Olson*, 283 U.S. 697, 716 (1931). Even if the present world situation were assumed to be tantamount to a time of war, or if the power of presently available armaments would justify even in peacetime the suppression of information that would set in motion a nuclear holocaust, in neither of these actions has the Government presented or even alleged that publication of items from or based upon the material at issue would cause the happening of an event of that nature. '(T)he chief purpose of (the First Amendment's) guaranty (is) to prevent previous restraints upon publication.' *Near v. Minnesota ex rel. Olson*, supra, at 713. Thus, only governmental allegation and proof that publication must inevitably, directly, and immediately cause the occurrence of an event kindred to imperiling the safety of a transport already at sea can support even the issuance of an interim restraining order. In no event may mere conclusions be sufficient: for if the Executive Branch seeks judicial aid in preventing publication, it must inevitably submit the basis upon which that aid is sought to scrutiny by the judiciary. And therefore, every restraint issued in this case, whatever its form, has violated the First Amendment—and not less so because that restraint was justified as necessary to afford the courts an opportunity to examine the claim more thoroughly. Unless and until the Government has clearly made out its case, the First Amendment commands that no injunction may issue.

Mr. Justice STEWART, with whom Mr. Justice WHITE joins, concurring.

In the governmental structure created by our Constitution, the Executive is endowed with enormous power in the two related areas of national defense and international relations. This power, largely unchecked by the Legislative and Judicial branches, has been pressed to the very hilt since the advent of the nuclear missile age. For better or for worse, the simple fact is that a President of the United States possesses vastly greater constitutional independence in these two vital areas of power than does, say, a prime minister of a country with a parliamentary form of government.

In the absence of the governmental checks and balances present in other areas of our national life, the only effective restraint upon executive policy and power in the areas of national defense and international affairs may lie in an enlightened citizenry—in an informed and critical public opinion which alone can here protect the values of democratic government. For this reason, it is perhaps here that a press that is alert, aware, and free most vitally serves the basic purpose of the First Amendment. For without an informed and free press there cannot be an enlightened people.

Yet it is elementary that the successful conduct of international diplomacy and the maintenance of an effective national defense require both confidentiality and secrecy. Other nations can hardly deal with this Nation in an atmosphere of mutual trust unless they can be assured that their confidences will be kept. And within our own executive departments, the development of considered and intelligent international policies would be impossible if those charged with their formulation could not communicate with each other freely, frankly, and in confidence. In the area of basic national defense the frequent need for absolute secrecy is, of course, self-evident.

I think there can be but one answer to this dilemma, if dilemma it be. The responsibility must be where the power is.[3] If the Constitution gives the Executive a large degree of unshared power in the conduct of foreign affairs and the maintenance of our national defense, then under the Constitution the Executive must have the largely unshared duty to determine and preserve the degree of internal security necessary to exercise that power successfully. It is an awesome responsibility, requiring judgment and wisdom of a high order. I should suppose that moral, political, and practical considerations would dictate that a very first principle of that wisdom would be an insistence upon avoiding secrecy for its own sake. For when everything is classified, then nothing is classified, and the system becomes one to be disregarded by the cynical or the careless, and to be manipulated by those intent on self-protection or self-promotion. I should suppose, in short, that the hallmark of a truly effective internal security system would be the maximum possible disclosure, recognizing that secrecy can best be preserved only when credibility is truly maintained. But be that as it may, it is clear to me that it is the constitutional duty of the Executive—as a matter of sovereign prerogative and not as a matter of law as the courts know law—through the promulgation and enforcement of executive regulations, to protect the confidentiality necessary to carry out its responsibilities in the fields of international relations and national defense.

This is not to say that Congress and the courts have no role to play. Undoubtedly Congress has the power to enact specific and appropriate criminal laws to protect government property and preserve government secrets. . . .

But in the cases before us we are asked neither to construe specific regulations nor to apply specific laws. We are asked, instead, to perform a function that the Constitution gave to the Executive, not the Judiciary. We are asked, quite simply, to prevent the publication by two newspapers of material that the Executive Branch insists should not, in the national interest, be published. I am convinced that the Executive is correct with respect to some of the documents involved. But I cannot say that disclosure of any of them will surely result in direct, immediate, and irreparable damage to our Nation or its people. That being so, there can under the First Amendment be but one judicial resolution of the issues before us. I join the judgments of the Court.

Mr. Justice WHITE, with whom Mr. Justice STEWART joins, concurring.

I concur in today's judgments, but only because of the concededly extraordinary protection against prior restraints enjoyed by the press under our constitutional system. I do not say that in no circumstances would the First Amendment permit an injunction against publishing information about government plans or operations. Nor, after examining the materials the Government characterizes as the most sensitive and destructive, can I deny that revelation of these documents will do substantial damage to public interests. Indeed, I am confident that their disclosure will have that result. But I nevertheless agree that the United States has not satisfied the very heavy burden that it must meet to warrant an injunction against publication in these cases, at least in the absence of express and appropriately limited congressional authorization for prior restraints in circumstances such as these. . . .

Prior restraints require an unusually heavy justification under the First Amendment; but failure by the Government to justify prior restraints does not measure its constitutional entitlement to a conviction for criminal publication. That the Government mistakenly chose to proceed by injunction does not mean that it could not successfully proceed in another way.

When the Espionage Act was under consideration in 1917, Congress eliminated from the bill a provision that would have given the President broad powers in time of war to proscribe, under threat of criminal penalty, the publication of various categories of information related to the national defense. Congress at that time was unwilling to clothe the President with such far-reaching powers to monitor the press, and those opposed to this part of the legislation assumed that a necessary concomitant of such power was the power to 'filter out the news to the people through some man.' 55 Cong.Rec. 2008 (remarks of Sen. Ashurst). However, these same members of Congress appeared to have little doubt that newspapers would be subject to criminal prosecution if they insisted on publishing information of the type Congress had itself determined should not be revealed. Senator Ashurst, for example, was quite sure that the editor of such a newspaper 'should be punished if he did publish information as to the movements of the fleet, the troops, the aircraft, the location of powder factories, the location of defense works, and all that sort of thing.' Id., at 2009.

The Criminal Code contains numerous provisions potentially relevant to these cases. . . . Section 793(e) makes it a criminal act for any unauthorized possessor of a document 'relating to the national defense' either (1) willfully to communicate or cause to be communicated that document to any person not entitled to receive it or (2) willfully to retain the document and fail to deliver it to an officer of the United States entitled to receive it. . . .

It is thus clear that Congress has addressed itself to the problems of protecting the security of the country and the national defense from unauthorized disclosure of potentially damaging information. Cf. *Youngstown Sheet & Tube Co. v. Sawyer*, 343 U.S. 579, 585—586 (1952); *see also* id., at 593—628 (Frankfurter, J., concurring). It has not, however, authorized the injunctive remedy against threatened publication. It has apparently been satisfied to rely on criminal sanctions and their deterrent effect on the responsible as well as the irresponsible press. I am not, of course, saying that either of these newspapers has yet committed a crime or that either would commit a crime if it published all the material now in its possession. That matter must await resolution in the context of a criminal proceeding if one is instituted by the United States. In that event, the issue of guilt or innocence would be determined by procedures and standards quite different from those that have purported to govern these injunctive proceedings.

Mr. Justice MARSHALL, concurring.

. . . I believe the ultimate issue in this case is even more basic than the one posed by the Solicitor General. The issue is whether this Court or the Congress has the power to make law. . . .

The problem here is whether in these particular cases the Executive Branch has authority to invoke the equity jurisdiction of the courts to protect what it believes to be the national interest. See *In re Debs*, 158 U.S. 564, 584 (1895). The Government argues that in addition to the inherent power of any government to protect itself, the President's power to conduct foreign affairs and his position as Commander in Chief give him authority to impose censorship on the press to protect his ability to deal effectively with foreign nations and to conduct the military affairs of the country. Of course, it is beyond cavil that the President has broad powers by virtue of his primary responsibility for the conduct of our foreign affairs and his position as Commander in Chief. *Chicago & Southern Air Lines v. Waterman S.S. Corp.*, 333 U.S. 103 (1948) . . . . And in some situations it may be that under whatever inherent powers the Government may have, as well as the implicit authority derived from the President's mandate to conduct foreign affairs and to act as Commander in Chief, there is a basis for the invocation of the equity jurisdiction of this Court as an aid to prevent the publication of material damaging to 'national security,' however that term may be defined.

It would, however, be utterly inconsistent with the concept of separation of powers for this Court to use its power of contempt to prevent behavior that Congress has specifically declined to prohibit. . . .The Constitution provides that Congress shall make laws, the President execute laws, and courts interpret laws. *Youngstown Sheet & Tube Co. v. Sawyer*, 343 U.S. 579 (1952). It did not provide for government by injunction in which the courts and the Executive Branch can 'make law' without regard to the action of Congress. It may be more convenient for the Executive Branch if it need only convince a judge to prohibit conduct rather than ask the Congress to pass a law, and it may be more convenient to enforce a contempt order than to seek a criminal conviction in a jury trial. Moreover, it may be considered politically wise to get a court to share the responsibility for arresting those who the Executive Branch has probable cause to believe are violating the law. But convenience and political considerations of the moment do not justify a basic departure from the principles of our system of government.

In these cases we are not faced with a situation where Congress has failed to provide the Executive with broad power to protect the Nation from disclosure of damaging state secrets. Congress has on several occasions given extensive consideration to the problem of protecting the military and strategic secrets of the United States. This consideration has resulted in the enactment of statutes making it a crime to receive, disclose, communicate, withhold, and publish certain documents, photographs, instruments, appliances, and information. The bulk of these statutes is found in chapter 37 of U.S.C., Title 18, entitled Espionage and Censorship. In that chapter, Congress has provided penalties ranging from a $10,000 fine to death for violating the various statutes.

Thus it would seem that in order for this Court to issue an injunction it would require a showing that such an injunction would enhance the already existing power of the Government to act. *See People ex rel. Bennett v. Laman*, 277 N.Y. 368, 14 N.E.2d 439 (1938). It is a traditional axiom of equity that a court of equity will not do a useless thing just as it is a traditional axiom that equity will not enjoin the commission of a crime . . . . Here there has been no attempt to make such a showing. The Solicitor General does not even mention in his brief whether the Government considers that there is probable cause to believe a crime has been committed or whether there is a conspiracy to commit future crimes.

If the Government had attempted to show that there was no effective remedy under traditional criminal law, it would have had to show that there is no arguably applicable statute. Of course, at this stage this Court could not and cannot determine whether there has been a violation of a particular statute or decide the constitutionality of any statute. Whether a good-faith prosecution could have been instituted under any statute could, however, be determined.

At least one of the many statutes in this area seems relevant to these cases. Congress has provided in 18 U.S.C. s 793(e) that whoever 'having unauthorized possession of, access to, or control over any document, writing, code book, signal book * * * or note relating to the national defense, or information relating to the national defense which information the possessor has reason to believe could be used to the injury of the United States or to the advantage of any foreign nation, willfully communicates, delivers, transmits * * * the same to any person not entitled to receive it, or willfully retains the same and fails to deliver it to the officer or employee of the United States entitled to receive it * * * (s)hall be fined not more than $10,000 or imprisoned not more than ten years, or both.' Congress has also made it a crime to conspire to commit any of the offenses listed in 18 U.S.C. s 793(e).

It is true that Judge Gurfein found that Congress had not made it a crime to publish the items and material specified in s 793(e). He found that the words 'communicates, delivers, transmits * * *' did not refer to publication of newspaper stories. And that view has some support in the legislative history and conforms with the past practice of using the statute only to prosecute those charged with ordinary espionage. *But see* 103 Cong.Rec. 10449 (remarks of Sen. Humphrey). Judge Gurfein's view of the Statute is not, however, the only plausible construction that could be given. *See* my Brother WHITE's concurring opinion.

Even if it is determined that the Government could not in good faith bring criminal prosecutions against the New York Times and the Washington Post, it is clear that Congress has specifically rejected passing legislation that would have clearly given the President the power he seeks here and made the current activity of the newspapers unlawful. When Congress specifically declines to make conduct unlawful it is not for this Court to redecide those issues—to overrule Congress. *See Youngtown Sheet & Tube Co. v. Sawyer*, 343 U.S. 579 (1952). . . .

*   *   *

New York Times v. Sullivan, 376 U.S. 254 (1964)

The final case in this chapter, New York Times v. Sullivan, *deals with the proper standard for libel actions when a public official is involved. A libel action involves a claim for damages following the publishing of a reputation damaging statement that is false. Truth of the statement is an absolute defense to the claim. When I say the "proper standard for libel actions" I mean the level of knowledge the defendant has as to the relevant statement's falsity.*

- *State law claims for libel implicate the U.S. Constitution. Do you see why?*

- *What is the reason behind having a more demanding standard for libel when the claimant is a public official?*

- *What does this mean? "That erroneous statement is inevitable in free debate, and that it must be protected if the freedoms of expression are to have the 'breathing space' that they 'need … to survive' [is well supported in our cases and in those of lower federal courts.]"*

- *What standard does the Court articulate? What does it mean?*

- *How does a case like* Sullivan *relate to the cases on prior restraints?*

Mr. Justice BRENNAN delivered the opinion of the Court.

We are required in this case to determine for the first time the extent to which the constitutional protections for speech and press limit a State's power to award damages in a libel action brought by a public official against critics of his official conduct.

Respondent L. B. Sullivan is one of the three elected Commissioners of the City of Montgomery, Alabama. He testified that he was 'Commissioner of Public Affairs and the duties are supervision of the Police Department, Fire Department, Department of Cemetery and Department of Scales.' He brought this civil libel action against the four individual petitioners, who are Negroes and Alabama clergymen, and against petitioner the New York Times Company, a New York corporation which publishes the New York Times, a daily newspaper. A jury in the Circuit Court of Montgomery County awarded him damages of $500,000, the full amount claimed, against all the petitioners, and the Supreme Court of Alabama affirmed.

Respondent's complaint alleged that he had been libeled by statements in a full-page advertisement that was carried in the New York Times on March 29, 1960. Entitled 'Heed Their Rising Voices,' the advertisement began by stating that 'As the whole world knows by now, thousands of Southern Negro students are engaged in widespread non-violent demonstrations in positive affirmation of the right to live in human dignity as guaranteed by the U.S. Constitution and the Bill of Rights.' It went on to charge that 'in their efforts to uphold these guarantees, they are being met by an unprecedented wave of terror by those who would deny and negate that document which the whole world looks upon as setting the pattern for modern freedom."

*   *   *

Of the 10 paragraphs of text in the advertisement, the third and a portion of the sixth were the basis of respondent's claim of libel. They read as follows:

Third paragraph:

'In Montgomery, Alabama, after students sang 'My Country, 'Tis of Thee' on the State Capitol steps, their leaders were expelled from school, and truckloads of police armed with shotguns and tear-gas ringed the Alabama State College Campus. When the entire student body protested to state authorities by refusing to re-register, their dining hall was padlocked in an attempt to starve them into submission.'

Sixth paragraph:

> 'Again and again the Southern violators have answered Dr. King's peaceful protests with intimidation and violence. They have bombed his home almost killing his wife and child. They have assaulted his person. They have arrested him seven times—for 'speeding,' 'loitering' and similar 'offenses.' And now they have charged him with 'perjury'—a felony under which they could imprison him for ten years.'

Although neither of these statements mentions respondent by name, he contended that the word 'police' in the third paragraph referred to him as the Montgomery Commissioner who supervised the Police Department, so that he was being accused of 'ringing' the campus with police. He further claimed that the paragraph would be read as imputing to the police, and hence to him, the padlocking of the dining hall in order to starve the students into submission. As to the sixth paragraph, he contended that since arrests are ordinarily made by the police, the statement 'They have arrested (Dr. King) seven times' would be read as referring to him; he further contended that the 'They' who did the arresting would be equated with the 'They' who committed the other described acts and with the 'Southern violators.' Thus, he argued, the paragraph would be read as accusing the Montgomery police, and hence him, of answering Dr. King's protests with 'intimidation and violence,' bombing his home, assaulting his person, and charging him with perjury. Respondent and six other Montgomery residents testified that they read some or all of the statements as referring to him in his capacity as Commissioner.

It is uncontroverted that some of the statements contained in the two paragraphs were not accurate descriptions of events which occurred in Montgomery.

*   *   *

Because of the importance of the constitutional issues involved, we granted the separate petitions for certiorari … We reverse the judgment. We hold that the rule of law applied by the Alabama courts is constitutionally deficient for failure to provide the safeguards for freedom of speech and of the press that are required by the First and Fourteenth Amendments in a libel action brought by a public official against critics of his official conduct. We further hold that under the proper safeguards the evidence presented in this case is constitutionally insufficient to support the judgment for respondent.

*   *   *

Under Alabama law as applied in this case, a publication is 'libelous per se' if the words 'tend to injure a person ... in his reputation' or to 'bring (him) into public contempt'; the trial court stated that the standard was met if the words are such as to 'injure him in his public office, or impute misconduct to him in his office, or want of official integrity, or want of fidelity to a public trust ....' Once 'libel per se' has been established, the defendant has no defense as to stated facts unless he can persuade the jury that they were true in all their particulars.

*   *   *

The question before us is whether this rule of liability, as applied to an action brought by a public official against critics of his official conduct, abridges the freedom of speech and of the press that is guaranteed by the First and Fourteenth Amendments.

*   *   *

The general proposition that freedom of expression upon public questions is secured by the First Amendment has long been settled by our decisions. The constitutional safeguard, we have said, 'was fashioned to assure unfettered interchange of ideas for the bringing about of political and social changes desired by the people.' ... The First Amendment, said Judge Learned Hand, 'presupposes that right conclusions are more likely to be gathered out of a multitude of tongues, than through any kind of authoritative selection. To many this is, and always will be, folly; but we have staked upon it our all.' Mr. Justice Brandeis, in *Whitney v. California* gave the principle its classic formulation:

> 'Those who won our independence believed ... that public discussion is a political duty; and that this should be a fundamental principle of the

American government. They recognized the risks to which all human institutions are subject. But they knew that order cannot be secured merely through fear of punishment for its infraction; that it is hazardous to discourage thought, hope and imagination; that fear breeds repression; that repression breeds hate; that hate menaces stable government; that the path of safety lies in the opportunity to discuss freely supposed grievances and proposed remedies; and that the fitting remedy for evil counsels is good ones. Believing in the power of reason as applied through public discussion, they eschewed silence coerced by law—the argument of force in its worst form. Recognizing the occasional tyrannies of governing majorities, they amended the Constitution so that free speech and assembly should be guaranteed.'

Thus we consider this case against the background of a profound national commitment to the principle that debate on public issues should be uninhibited, robust, and wide-open, and that it may well include vehement, caustic, and sometimes unpleasantly sharp attacks on government and public officials. **The present advertisement, as an expression of grievance and protest on one of the major public issues of our time, would seem clearly to qualify for the constitutional protection. The question is whether it forfeits that protection by the falsity of some of its factual statements and by its alleged defamation of respondent.**

Authoritative interpretations of the First Amendment guarantees have consistently refused to recognize an exception for any test of truth—whether administered by judges, juries, or administrative officials—and especially one that puts the burden of proving truth on the speaker. The constitutional protection does not turn upon 'the truth, popularity, or social utility of the ideas and beliefs which are offered.'

*   *   *

That erroneous statement is inevitable in free debate, and that it must be protected if the freedoms of expression are to have the 'breathing space' that they 'need ... to survive' [is well supported in our cases and in those of lower federal courts.]

If neither factual error nor defamatory [reputation injuring] content suffices to remove the constitutional shield from criticism of official conduct, the combination of the two elements is no less inadequate.

*   *   *

What a State may not constitutionally bring about by means of a criminal statute is likewise beyond the reach of its civil law of libel. The fear of damage awards under a rule such as that invoked by the Alabama courts here may be markedly more inhibiting than the fear of prosecution under a criminal statute.

*   *   *

The state rule of law is not saved by its allowance of the defense of truth. A defense for erroneous statements honestly made is … essential here ….

A rule compelling the critic of official conduct to guarantee the truth of all his factual assertions—and to do so on pain of libel judgments virtually unlimited in amount—leads to a comparable 'self-censorship.' Allowance of the defense of truth, with the burden of proving it on the defendant, does not mean that only false speech will be deterred. Even courts accepting this defense as an adequate safeguard have recognized the difficulties of adducing legal proofs that the alleged libel was true in all its factual particulars. Under such a rule, would-be critics of official conduct may be deterred from voicing their criticism, even though it is believed to be true and even though it is in fact true, because of doubt whether it can be proved in court or fear of the expense of having to do so. They tend to make only statements which 'steer far wider of the unlawful zone.' The rule thus dampens the vigor and limits the variety of public debate. It is inconsistent with the First and Fourteenth Amendments.

The constitutional guarantees require, we think, a federal rule that prohibits a public official from recovering damages for a defamatory falsehood relating to his official conduct unless he proves that the statement was made with 'actual malice'—that is, with knowledge that it was false or with reckless disregard of whether it was false or not. …

We hold today that the Constitution delimits a State's power to award damages for libel in actions brought by public officials against critics of their official conduct.

*   *   *

Chapter 10: Race and Civil Rights

Introduction

The issue of race has long presented a difficult problem in the United States. This problem existed prior to the founding of the American republic, and in varying degrees of severity has persisted ever since. Unfortunately, in many ways, the treatment of black Americans has been wholly inconsistent with the "promises" of equality and justice set forth in the Declaration of Independence and the Constitution.

It wasn't until the ratification of the 13th Amendment following the U.S. Civil War that the enslavement of black Americans finally came to an end. Nevertheless, hostile and systemic discrimination against blacks, particularly in the South, persisted for another 100 years until major civil rights legislation was enacted in the mid-1960s. The problem has yet to be solved. Racism still exists of course. We see deeply depressing indications of this every day. Like when, for example, police officers mistreat blacks due to the color of their skin or when individuals object to black presence in certain spaces (like coffee shops or rental homes, for example) and summon the authorities to remove them. Like I said, it's a big problem. One we in the U.S. need to work to resolve.

The cases in this chapter include *Dred Scott v. Sandford*, which held that slaves were neither citizens nor even "people" for the purposes of the U.S. Constitution; *Plessy v. Ferguson*, which upheld the constitutionality of the "separate but equal" doctrine; *Sweatt v. Painter*, which held that unequal facilities are unconstitutional; *Brown v. Board of Education*, which finally held the "separate but equal" doctrine unconstitutional; and *Heart of Atlanta Motel v. United States*, which found that the Civil Rights Act of 1964 was a valid exercise of Congressional power under the Commerce Clause.

But first, it is important to review the language of the 13th, 14th, and 15th Amendments to the Constitution. These amendments, enacted after the Civil War, eradicated slavery, granted citizenship to all those born or naturalized within the United States, guaranteed the equal protection of the law, and prohibited deprivation of the right to vote on account of race, color, or previous condition of servitude.

Text of the Thirteenth Amendment

"Neither slavery nor involuntary servitude, except as a punishment for crime whereof the party shall have been duly convicted, shall exist within the United States, or any place subject to their jurisdiction."

Text of the Fourteenth Amendment

"All persons born or naturalized in the United States and subject to the jurisdiction thereof, are citizens of the United States and of the State wherein they reside. No State shall make or enforce any law which shall abridge the privileges or immunities of citizens of the United States; nor shall any State deprive a person of life, liberty, or property, without due process of law; nor deny to any person within its jurisdiction the equal protection of the laws."

Text of the Fifteenth Amendment

"The right of citizens of the United States to vote shall not be denied or abridged by the United States or by any State on account of race, color, or previous condition of servitude."

Dred Scott v. Sandford, 60 U.S. 393 (1857)

The Dred Scott *case is one of the most infamous and despicable decisions ever issued by the U.S. Supreme Court. In it, Chief Justice Taney expressly states that descendants of slaves and of course slaves themselves have no legal or political rights whatsoever. Indeed, Taney denies the humanity of slaves by holding that they are not "people" within the meaning of the U.S. Constitution.*

Mr. Chief Justice TANEY delivered the opinion of the court. …

The question is simply this: Can a negro, whose ancestors were imported into this country, and sold as slaves, become a member of the political community formed and brought into existence by the Constitution of the United States, and as such become entitled to all the rights, and privileges, and immunities, guarantied by that instrument to the citizen? One of which rights is the privilege of suing in a court of the United States in the cases specified in the Constitution.

It will be observed, that the plea applies to that class of persons only whose ancestors were negroes of the African race, and imported into this country, and sold and held as slaves. The only matter in issue before the court, therefore, is, whether the descendants of such slaves, when they shall be emancipated, or who are born of parents who had become free before their birth, are citizens of a State, in the sense in which the word citizen is used in the Constitution of the United States. And this being the only matter in dispute on the pleadings, the court must be understood as speaking in this opinion of that class only, that is, of those persons who are the descendants of Africans who were imported into this country, and sold as slaves.

*   *   *

The words 'people of the United States' and 'citizens' are synonymous terms, and mean the same thing. They both describe the political body who, according to our republican institutions, form the sovereignty, and who hold the power and conduct the Government through their representatives. They are what we familiarly call the 'sovereign people,' and every citizen is one of this people, and a constituent member of this sovereignty. The question before us is, whether the class of persons described in the plea in abatement compose a portion of this people, and are constituent members of this sovereignty? We think they are not, and that they are not included, and were not intended to be included, under the word 'citizens' in the Constitution, and can therefore claim none of the rights and privileges which that instrument provides for and secures to citizens of the United States. On the contrary, they were at that time considered as a subordinate and inferior class of beings, who had been subjugated by the dominant race, and, whether emancipated or not, yet remained subject to their authority, and had no rights or privileges but such as those who held the power and the Government might choose to grant them.

*   *   *

The question then arises, whether the provisions of the Constitution, in relation to the personal rights and privileges to which the citizen of a State should be entitled, embraced the negro African race, at that time in this country, or who might afterwards be imported, who had then or should afterwards be made free in any State; and to put it in the power of a single State to make him a citizen of the United States, and endue him with the full rights of citizenship in every other State without their consent? Does the Constitution of the United States act upon him whenever he shall be made free under the laws of a State, and raised there to the rank of a citizen, and immediately clothe him with all the privileges of a citizen in every other State, and in its own courts?

The court think the affirmative of these propositions cannot be maintained. And if it cannot, the plaintiff in error could not be a citizen of the State of Missouri, within the meaning of the Constitution of the United States, and, consequently, was not entitled to sue in its courts.

*   *   *

Plessy v. Ferguson, 163 U.S. 537 (1896)

In yet another vile opinion on the legal rights and status of Black Americans, the Supreme Court in Plessy v. Ferguson *held that facilities that separated white citizens from black citizens were Constitutional so long as they were "equal." "Equal" they were not, however, and it would take another 60 years, and the Court's decision in* Brown v. Board of Education, *for the "separate but equal" doctrine to be declared unconstitutional. Please pay attention to Justice Harlan's dissent, where he likens the* Plessy *decision to that in* Dred Scott.

Opinion

This case turns upon the constitutionality of an act of the general assembly of the state of Louisiana, passed in 1890, providing for separate railway carriages for the white and colored races.

*   *   *

The constitutionality of this act is attacked upon the ground that it conflicts both with the thirteenth amendment of the constitution, abolishing slavery, and the fourteenth amendment, which prohibits certain restrictive legislation on the part of the states.

That it does not conflict with the thirteenth amendment, which abolished slavery and involuntary servitude, except as a punishment for crime, is too clear for argument. Slavery implies involuntary servitude,—a state of bondage; the ownership of mankind as a chattel, or, at least, the control of the labor and services of one man for the benefit of another, and the absence of a legal right to the disposal of his own person, property, and services. This amendment was said in the *Slaughter-House Cases* to have been intended primarily to abolish slavery, as it had been previously known in this country, and that it equally forbade Mexican peonage or the Chinese coolie trade, when they amounted to slavery or involuntary servitude, and that the use of the word 'servitude' was intended to prohibit the use of all forms of involuntary slavery, of whatever class or name. It was intimated, however, in that case, that this amendment was regarded by the statesmen of that day as insufficient to protect the colored race from certain laws which had been enacted in the Southern states, imposing upon the colored race onerous disabilities and burdens, and curtailing their rights in the pursuit of life, liberty, and property to such an extent that their freedom was of little value; and that the fourteenth amendment was devised to meet this exigency.

So, too, in the *Civil Rights Cases* it was said that the act of a mere individual, the owner of an inn, a public conveyance or place of amusement, refusing accommodations to colored people, cannot be justly regarded as imposing any badge of slavery or servitude upon the applicant, but only as involving an ordinary civil injury, properly cognizable by the laws of the state, and presumably subject to redress by those laws until the contrary appears. 'It would be running the slavery question into the ground,' said Mr. Justice Bradley, 'to make it apply to every act of discrimination which a person may see fit to make as to the guests he will entertain, or as to the people he will take into his coach or cab or car, or admit to his concert or theater, or deal with in other matters of intercourse or business.'

A statute which implies merely a legal distinction between the white and colored races—a distinction which is founded in the color of the two races, and which must always exist so long as white men are distinguished from the other race by color—has no tendency to destroy the legal equality of the two races, or re-establish a state of involuntary servitude. Indeed, we do not understand that the thirteenth amendment is strenuously relied upon by the plaintiff in error in this connection.

By the fourteenth amendment, all persons born or naturalized in the United States, and subject to the jurisdiction thereof, are made citizens of the United States and of the state wherein they reside; and the states are forbidden from making or enforcing any law which shall abridge the privileges or immunities of citizens of the United States, or shall deprive any person of life, liberty, or property without due process of law, or deny to any person within their jurisdiction the equal protection of the laws.

The proper construction of this amendment was first called to the attention of this court in the *Slaughter-House Cases* which involved, however, not a question of race, but one of exclusive privileges. The case did not call for any expression of opinion as to the exact rights it was intended to secure to the colored race, but it was said generally that its main purpose was to establish the citizenship of the negro, to give definitions of citizenship of the United States and of the states, and to protect from the hostile legislation of the states the privileges and immunities of citizens of the United States, as distinguished from those of citizens of the states.

The object of the amendment was undoubtedly to enforce the absolute equality of the two races before the law, but, in the nature of things, it could not have been intended to abolish distinctions based upon color, or to enforce social, as distinguished from political, equality, or a commingling of the two races upon terms unsatisfactory to either. Laws permitting, and even requiring, their separation, in places where they are liable to be brought into contact, do not necessarily imply the inferiority of either race to the other, and have been generally, if not universally, recognized as within the competency of the state legislatures in the exercise of their police power. The most common instance of this is connected with the establishment of separate schools for white and colored children, which have been held to be a valid exercise of the legislative power even by courts of states where the political rights of the colored race have been longest and most earnestly enforced.

*   *   *

The distinction between laws interfering with the political equality of the negro and those requiring the separation of the two races in schools, theaters, and railway carriages has been frequently drawn by this court. Thus, in *Strauder v. West Virginia*, 100 U. S. 303, it was held that a law of West Virginia limiting to white male persons 21 years of age, and citizens of the state, the right to sit upon juries, was a discrimination which implied a legal inferiority in civil society, which lessened the security of the right of the colored race, and was a step towards reducing them to a condition of servility.

*   *   *

[W]e think the enforced separation of the races, as applied to the internal commerce of the state, neither abridges the privileges or immunities of the colored man, deprives him of his property without due process of law, nor denies him the equal protection of the laws, within the meaning of the fourteenth amendment. ...

So far, then, as a conflict with the fourteenth amendment is concerned, the case reduces itself to the question whether the statute of Louisiana is a reasonable regulation, and with respect to this there must necessarily be a large discretion on the part of the legislature. In determining the question of reasonableness, it is at liberty to act with reference to the established usages, customs, and traditions of the people, and with a view to the promotion of their comfort, and the preservation of the public peace and good order. Gauged by this standard, we cannot say that a law which authorizes or even requires the separation of the two races in public conveyances is unreasonable, or more obnoxious to the fourteenth amendment than the acts of congress requiring separate schools for colored children in the District of Columbia, the constitutionality of which does not seem to have been questioned, or the corresponding acts of state legislatures.

We consider the underlying fallacy of the plaintiff's argument to consist in the assumption that the enforced separation of the two races stamps the colored race with a badge of inferiority. If this be so, it is not by reason of anything found in the act, but solely because the colored race chooses to put that construction upon it. The argument necessarily assumes that if, as has been more than once the case, and is not unlikely to be so again, the colored race should become the dominant power in the state legislature, and should enact a law in precisely similar terms, it would thereby relegate the white race to an inferior position. We imagine that the white race, at least, would not acquiesce in this assumption. The argument also assumes that social prejudices may be overcome by legislation, and that equal rights cannot be secured to the negro except by an enforced commingling of the two races. We cannot accept this proposition. If the two races are to meet upon terms of social equality, it must be the result of natural affinities, a mutual appreciation of each other's merits, and a voluntary consent of individuals. As was said by the court of appeals of New York in *People v. Gallagher*, 93 N. Y. 438, 448: 'This end can neither be accomplished nor promoted by laws which conflict with the general sentiment of the community upon whom they are designed to operate. When the government, therefore, has secured to each of its citizens equal rights before the law, and equal opportunities for improvement and progress, it has accomplished the end for which it was organized, and performed all of the functions respecting social advantages with which it is endowed.' Legislation is powerless to eradicate racial instincts, or to abolish distinctions based upon physical differences, and the attempt to do so can only result in accentuating the difficulties of the present situation. If the civil and political rights of both races be equal, one cannot be inferior to the other civilly or politically. If one race be inferior to the other socially, the constitution of the United States cannot put them upon the same plane.

*   *   *

Mr. Justice HARLAN *dissenting*.

*   *   *

In respect of civil rights, common to all citizens, the constitution of the United States does not, I think, permit any public authority to know the race of those entitled to be protected in the enjoyment of such rights. Every true man has pride of race, and under appropriate circumstances, when the rights of others, his equals before the law, are not to be affected, it is his privilege to express such pride and to take such action based upon it as to him seems proper. But I deny that any legislative body or judicial tribunal may have regard to the race of citizens when the civil rights of those citizens are involved. Indeed, such legislation as that here in question is inconsistent not only with that equality of rights which pertains to citizenship, national and state, but with the personal liberty enjoyed by everyone within the United States.

*   *   *

It was said in argument that the statute of Louisiana does not discriminate against either race, but prescribes a rule applicable alike to white and colored citizens. But this argument does not meet the difficulty. Everyone knows that the statute in question had its origin in the purpose, not so much to exclude white persons from railroad cars occupied by blacks, as to exclude colored people from coaches occupied by or assigned to white persons. Railroad corporations of Louisiana did not make discrimination among whites in the matter of accommodation for travelers. The thing to accomplish was, under the guise of giving equal accommodation for whites and blacks, to compel the latter to keep to themselves while traveling in railroad passenger coaches. No one would be so wanting in candor as to assert the contrary. The fundamental objection, therefore, to the statute, is that it interferes with the personal freedom of citizens. 'Personal liberty,' it has been well said, 'consists in the power of locomotion, of changing situation, or removing one's person to whatsoever places one's own inclination may direct, without imprisonment or restraint, unless by due course of law.' If a white man and a black man choose to occupy the same public conveyance on a public highway, it is their right to do so; and no government, proceeding alone on grounds of race, can prevent it without infringing the personal liberty of each.

*   *   *

[I]n view of the constitution, in the eye of the law, there is in this country no superior, dominant, ruling class of citizens. There is no caste here. Our constitution is color-blind, and neither knows nor tolerates classes among citizens. In respect of civil rights, all citizens are equal before the law. The humblest is the peer of the most powerful. The law regards man as man, and takes no account of his surroundings or of his color when his civil rights as guaranteed by the supreme law of the land are involved. It is therefore to be regretted that this high tribunal, the final expositor of the fundamental law of the land, has reached the conclusion that it is competent for a state to regulate the enjoyment by citizens of their civil rights solely upon the basis of race.

In my opinion, the judgment this day rendered will, in time, prove to be quite as pernicious as the decision made by this tribunal in the Dred Scott Case.

*   *   *

Sweatt v. Painter, 339 U.S. 629 (1950)

Things begin to improve with the Court's decision in Sweatt v. Painter. *There the Court held that separate facilities that are not equal are unconstitutional. This was a step in the right direction, but it unfortunately left the "separate but equal" doctrine intact.*

Mr. Chief Justice VINSON delivered the opinion of the Court.

This case and *McLaurin v. Oklahoma State Regents*, 339 U.S. 637, present different aspects of this general question: To what extent does the Equal Protection Clause of the Fourteenth Amendment limit the power of a state to distinguish between students of different races in professional and graduate education in a state university? Broader issues have been urged for our consideration, but we adhere to the principle of deciding constitutional questions only in the context of the particular case before the Court. We have frequently reiterated that this Court will decide constitutional questions only when necessary to the disposition of the case at hand, and that such decisions will be drawn as narrowly as possible.. . . . Because of this traditional reluctance to extend constitutional interpretations to situations or facts which are not before the Court, much of the excellent research and detailed argument presented in these cases is unnecessary to their disposition.

In the instant case, petitioner filed an application for admission to the University of Texas Law School for the February, 1946 term. His application was rejected solely because he is a Negro. Petitioner thereupon brought this suit for mandamus against the appropriate school officials, respondents here, to compel his admission. At that time, there was no law school in Texas which admitted Negroes.

*   *   *

The University of Texas Law School, from which petitioner was excluded, was staffed by a faculty of sixteen full-time and three part-time professors, some of whom are nationally recognized authorities in their field. Its student body numbered 850. The library contained over 65,000 volumes. Among the other facilities available to the students were a law review, moot court facilities, scholarship funds, and Order of the Coif affiliation. The school's alumni occupy the most distinguished positions in the private practice of the law and in the public life of the State. It may properly be considered one of the nation's ranking law schools.

The law school for Negroes which was to have opened in February, 1947, would have had no independent faculty or library. The teaching was to be carried on by four members of the University of Texas Law School faculty, who were to maintain their offices at the University of Texas while teaching at both institutions. Few of the 10,000 volumes ordered for the library had arrived; nor was there any full-time librarian. The school lacked accreditation.

*   *   *

Whether the University of Texas Law School is compared with the original or the new law school for Negroes, we cannot find substantial equality in the educational opportunities offered white and Negro law students by the State. In terms of number of the faculty, variety of courses and opportunity for specialization, size of the student body, scope of the library, availability of law review and similar activities, the University of Texas Law School is superior. What is more important, the University of Texas Law School possesses to a far greater degree those qualities which are incapable of objective measurement but which make for greatness in a law school. Such qualities, to name but a few, include reputation of the faculty, experience of the administration, position and influence of the alumni, standing in the community, traditions and prestige. It is difficult to believe that one who had a free choice between these law schools would consider the question close.

Moreover, although the law is a highly learned profession, we are well aware that it is an intensely practical one. The law school, the proving ground for legal learning and practice, cannot be effective in isolation from the individuals and institutions with which the law interacts. Few students and no one who has practiced law would choose to study in an academic vacuum, removed from the interplay of ideas and the exchange of views with which the law is concerned. The law school to which Texas is willing to admit petitioner excludes from its student body members of the racial groups which number 85% of the population of the State and include most of the lawyers, witnesses, jurors, judges and other officials with whom petitioner will inevitably be dealing when he becomes a member of the Texas Bar. With such a substantial and significant segment of society excluded, we cannot conclude that the education offered petitioner is substantially equal to that which he would receive if admitted to the University of Texas Law School.

*   *   *

In accordance with these cases, petitioner may claim his full constitutional right: legal education equivalent to that offered by the State to students of other races. Such education is not available to him in a separate law school as offered by the State. We cannot, therefore, agree with respondents that the doctrine of *Plessy v. Ferguson*, 163 U.S. 537 (1896) requires affirmance of the judgment below. Nor need we reach petitioner's contention that *Plessy v. Ferguson* should be reexamined in the light of contemporary knowledge respecting the purposes of the Fourteenth Amendment and the effects of racial segregation.

We hold that the Equal Protection Clause of the Fourteenth Amendment requires that petitioner be admitted to the University of Texas Law School. The judgment is reversed and the cause is remanded for proceedings not inconsistent with this opinion.

Brown v. Board of Education, 347 U.S. 483 (1954)

Finally, in Brown v. Board of Education, *the Court held that the "separate but equal" doctrine was unconstitutional. The Court's decision is premised on the notion that separate can* <u>never</u> *be equal. Please take note of the Court's discussion of the history of "separate but equal" doctrine and why its constitutionality is squarely before the Court in* Brown. *Please also note that* Brown *was decided nearly 90 years after the enactment of the 14th Amendment.*

Mr. Chief Justice WARREN delivered the opinion of the Court.

These cases come to us from the States of Kansas, South Carolina, Virginia, and Delaware. They are premised on different facts and different local conditions, but a common legal question justifies their consideration together in this consolidated opinion.

In each of the cases, minors of the Negro race, through their legal representatives, seek the aid of the courts in obtaining admission to the public schools of their community on a nonsegregated basis. In each instance, they have been denied admission to schools attended by white children under laws requiring or permitting segregation according to race. This segregation was alleged to deprive the plaintiffs of the equal protection of the laws under the Fourteenth Amendment. …

The plaintiffs contend that segregated public schools are not 'equal' and cannot be made 'equal,' and that hence they are deprived of the equal protection of the laws. …

In the first cases in this Court construing the Fourteenth Amendment, decided shortly after its adoption, the Court interpreted it as proscribing all state-imposed discriminations against the Negro race. The doctrine of "separate but equal" did not make its appearance in this court until 1896 in the case of *Plessy v. Ferguson*, involving not education but transportation. American courts have since labored with the doctrine for over half a century. In this Court, there have been six cases involving the 'separate but equal' doctrine in the field of public education. In *Cumming v. Board of Education of Richmond County*, 175 U.S. 528, and *Gong Lum v. Rice*, 275 U.S. 78, the validity of the doctrine itself was not challenged. In more recent cases, all on the graduate school level, inequality was found in that specific benefits enjoyed by white students were denied to Negro students of the same educational qualifications. *State of Missouri ex rel. Gaines v. Canada*, 305 U.S. 337; *Sipuel v. Board of Regents of University of Oklahoma*, 332 U.S. 631; *Sweatt v. Painter*, 339 U.S. 629; *McLaurin v. Oklahoma State Regents*, 339 U.S. 637, 70 S.Ct. 851, 94 L.Ed. 1149. **In none of these cases was it necessary to re-examine the doctrine to grant relief to the Negro plaintiff.** And in *Sweatt v. Painter, supra*, the Court expressly reserved decision on the question whether *Plessy v. Ferguson* should be held inapplicable to public education.

In the instant cases, that question is directly presented. Here, unlike *Sweatt v. Painter*, there are findings below that the Negro and white schools involved have been equalized, or are being equalized, with respect to buildings, curricula, qualifications and salaries of teachers, and other 'tangible' factors. **Our decision, therefore, cannot turn on merely a comparison of these tangible factors in the Negro and white schools involved in each of the cases. We must look instead to the effect of segregation itself on public education.**

In approaching this problem, we cannot turn the clock back to 1868 when the Amendment was adopted, or even to 1896 when *Plessy v. Ferguson* was written. We must consider public education in the light of its full development and its present place in American life throughout the Nation. Only in this way can it be determined if segregation in public schools deprives these plaintiffs of the equal protection of the laws.

Today, education is perhaps the most important function of state and local governments. Compulsory school attendance laws and the great expenditures for education both demonstrate our recognition of the importance of education to our democratic society. It is required in the performance of our most basic public responsibilities, even service in the armed forces. It is the very foundation of good citizenship. Today it is a principal instrument in awakening the child to cultural values, in preparing him for later professional training, and in helping him to adjust normally to his environment. In these days, it is doubtful that any child may reasonably be expected to succeed in life if he is denied the opportunity of an education. Such an opportunity, where the state has undertaken to provide it, is a right which must be made available to all on equal terms.

We come then to the question presented: Does segregation of children in public schools solely on the basis of race, even though the physical facilities and other 'tangible' factors may be equal, deprive the children of the minority group of equal educational opportunities? We believe that it does.

In *Sweatt v. Painter, supra* (339 U.S. 629, 70 S.Ct. 850), in finding that a segregated law school for Negroes could not provide them equal educational opportunities, this Court relied in large part on 'those qualities which are incapable of objective measurement but which make for greatness in a law school.' In *McLaurin v. Oklahoma State Regents,* the Court, in requiring that a Negro admitted to a white graduate school be treated like all other students, again resorted to intangible considerations: '* * * his ability to study, to engage in discussions and exchange views with other students, and, in general, to learn his profession.' Such considerations apply with added force to children in grade and high schools. To separate them from others of similar age and qualifications solely because of their race generates a feeling of inferiority as to their status in the community that may affect their hearts and minds in a way unlikely ever to be undone. The effect of this separation on their educational opportunities was well stated by a finding in the Kansas case by a court which nevertheless felt compelled to rule against the Negro plaintiffs:

'Segregation of white and colored children in public schools has a detrimental effect upon the colored children. The impact is greater when it has the sanction of the law; for the policy of separating the races is usually interpreted as denoting the inferiority of the negro group. A sense of inferiority affects the motivation of a child to learn. Segregation with the sanction of law, therefore, has a tendency to (retard) the educational and mental development of Negro children and to deprive them of some of the benefits they would receive in a racial(ly) integrated school system.'

Whatever may have been the extent of psychological knowledge at the time of *Plessy v. Ferguson,* this finding is amply supported by modern authority. Any language in *Plessy v. Ferguson* contrary to this finding is rejected.

We conclude that in the field of public education the doctrine of 'separate but equal' has no place. Separate educational facilities are inherently unequal. Therefore, we hold that the plaintiffs and others similarly situated for whom the actions have been brought are, by reason of the segregation complained of, deprived of the equal protection of the laws guaranteed by the Fourteenth Amendment. This disposition makes unnecessary any discussion whether such segregation also violates the Due Process Clause of the Fourteenth Amendment.

Excerpt from the Civil Rights Act of 1964

With the Civil Rights Act of 1964, Congress, among other things, finally took action to prohibit private discrimination on the basis of race in places of public accommodation.

SEC. 201. (a) All persons shall be entitled to the full and equal enjoyment of the goods, services, facilities, and privileges, advantages, and accommodations of any place of public accommodation, as defined in this section, without discrimination or segregation on the ground of race, color, religion, or national origin.

(b) Each of the following establishments which serves the public is a place of public accommodation within the meaning of this title if its operations affect commerce, or if discrimination or segregation by it is supported by State action:

(1) any inn, hotel, motel, or other establishment which provides lodging to transient guests, other than an establishment located within a building which contains not more than five rooms for rent or hire and which is actually occupied by the proprietor of such establishment as his residence;

(2) any restaurant, cafeteria, lunchroom, lunch counter, soda fountain, or other facility principally engaged in selling food for consumption on the premises, including, but not limited to, any such facility located on the premises of any retail establishment; or any gasoline station;

(3) any motion picture house, theater, concert hall, sports arena, stadium or other place of exhibition or entertainment; and

(4) any establishment (A)(i) which is physically located within the premises of any establishment otherwise covered by this subsection, or (ii) within the premises of which is physically located any such covered establishment, and (B) which holds itself out as serving patrons of such covered establishment.

Heart of Atlanta Motel v. United States, 379 U.S. 241 (1964)

Once the Civil Rights Act of 1964 was enacted, the question became whether it was consti-tutional. In other words, the question became on what basis could Congress regulate private activities? After all, there is no express power in the Constitution that permits Congress to prohibit private discrimination. So, how did they do it? The Court answered the question in Heart of Atlanta Motel v. United States.

Mr. Justice CLARK delivered the opinion of the Court

This is a declaratory judgment action attacking the constitutionality of Title II of the Civil Rights Act of 1964.

* * *

Appellant owns and operates the Heart of Atlanta Motel which has 216 rooms available to transient guests. The motel is located on Courtland Street, two blocks from downtown Peachtree Street. It is readily accessible to interstate highways 75 and 85 and state highways 23 and 41. Appellant solicits patronage from outside the State of Georgia through various national advertising media, including maga-zines of national circulation; it maintains over 50 billboards and highway signs within the State, soliciting patronage for the motel; it accepts convention trade from outside Georgia and approximately 75% of its registered guests are from out of State. Prior to passage of the Act the motel had followed a practice of refusing to rent rooms to Negroes, and it alleged that it intended to continue to do so. In an effort to perpetuate that policy this suit was filed.

The appellant contends that Congress in passing this Act exceeded its power to regulate commerce under Art. I, s 8, cl. 3, of the Constitution of the United States; that the Act violates the Fifth Amendment because appellant is deprived of the right to choose its customers and operate its business as it wishes, resulting in a taking of its liberty and property without due process of law and a taking of its property without just compensation; and, finally, that by requiring appellant to rent available rooms to Negroes against its will, Congress is subjecting it to involuntary servitude in contravention of the Thirteenth Amendment.

The appellees counter that the unavailability to Negroes of adequate accommodations interferes significantly with interstate travel, and that Congress, under the Commerce Clause, has power to remove such obstructions and restraints; that the Fifth Amendment does not forbid reasonable regulation and that consequential damage does not constitute a 'taking' within the meaning of that amendment; that the Thirteenth Amendment claim fails because it is entirely frivolous to say that an amendment directed to the abolition of human bondage and the removal of widespread disabilities associated with slavery places discrimination in public accommodations, beyond the reach of both federal and state law.

*   *   *

Title [II of the Civil Rights Act of 1964 regarding public accommodations] is divided into seven sections beginning with s 201(a) which provides that:

> 'All persons shall be entitled to the full and equal enjoyment of the goods, services, facilities, privileges, advantages, and accommodations of any place of public accommodation, as defined in this section, without discrimination or segregation on the ground of race, color, religion, or national origin.'

*   *   *

It is admitted that the operation of the motel brings it within the provisions of s 201(a) of the Act and that appellant refused to provide lodging for transient Negroes because of their race or color and that it intends to continue that policy unless restrained.

The sole question posed is, therefore, the constitutionality of the Civil Rights Act of 1964 as applied to these facts. The legislative history of the Act indicates

that Congress based the Act on s 5 and the Equal Protection Clause of the Fourteenth Amendment as well as its power to regulate interstate commerce under
Art. I, s 8, cl. 3, of the Constitution.

The Senate Commerce Committee made it quite clear that the fundamental
object of Title II was to vindicate 'the deprivation of personal dignity that surely
accompanies denials of equal access to public establishments.' At the same time,
however, it noted that such an objective has been and could be readily achieved
'by congressional action based on the commerce power of the Constitution.' ...

*   *   *

While the Act as adopted carried no congressional findings the record of its
passage through each house is replete with evidence of the burdens that discrimination by race or color places upon interstate commerce. This testimony included
the fact that our people have become increasingly mobile with millions of people
of all races traveling from State to State; that Negroes in particular have been the
subject of discrimination in transient accommodations, having to travel great dis-
tances to secure the same; that often they have been unable to obtain accommodations and have had to call upon friends to put them up overnight; and that these
conditions had become so acute as to require the listing of available lodging for
Negroes in a special guidebook which was itself 'dramatic testimony to the difficulties' Negroes encounter in travel. These exclusionary practices were found to
be nationwide, the Under Secretary of Commerce testifying that there is 'no question that this discrimination in the North still exists to a large degree' and in the
West and Midwest as well. This testimony indicated a qualitative as well as quantitative effect on interstate travel by Negroes. The former was the obvious impairment of the Negro traveler's pleasure and convenience that resulted when he
continually was uncertain of finding lodging. As for the latter, there was evidence
that this uncertainty stemming from racial discrimination had the effect of dis-
couraging travel on the part of a substantial portion of the Negro community.
This was the conclusion not only of the Under Secretary of Commerce but also
of the Administrator of the Federal Aviation Agency who wrote the Chairman of
the Senate Commerce Committee that it was his 'belief that air commerce is adversely affected by the denial to a substantial segment of the traveling public of
adequate and desegregated public accommodations.' We shall not burden this

opinion with further details since the voluminous testimony presents overwhelming evidence that discrimination by hotels and motels impedes interstate travel. …

The power of Congress to deal with these obstructions depends on the meaning of the Commerce Clause. …

In short, the determinative test of the exercise of power by the Congress under the Commerce Clause is simply whether the activity sought to be regulated is 'commerce which concerns more States than one' and has a real and substantial relation to the national interest. …

It is said that the operation of the motel here is of a purely local character. But, assuming this to be true, '(i)f it is interstate commerce that feels the pinch, it does not matter how local the operation which applies the squeeze.' *United States v. Women's Sportswear Mfg. Ass'n*, 336 U.S. 460, 464 (1949). As Chief Justice Stone put it in *United States v. Darby*: 'The power of Congress over interstate commerce is not confined to the regulation of commerce among the states. It extends to those activities intrastate which so affect interstate commerce or the exercise of the power of Congress over it as to make regulation of them appropriate means to the attainment of a legitimate end, the exercise of the granted power of Congress to regulate interstate commerce.'

Thus the power of Congress to promote interstate commerce also includes the power to regulate the local incidents thereof, including local activities in both the States of origin and destination, which might have a substantial and harmful effect upon that commerce. One need only examine the evidence which we have discussed above to see that Congress may—as it has—prohibit racial discrimination by motels serving travelers, however 'local' their operations may appear.

*   *   *

Chapter 11: Juries

Introduction

The right to a trial in front of a jury is one of the cornerstones of the American legal system. The right is embodied in no less than three amendments in the Bill of Rights. Why is the right to a jury trial so important? The first case set forth below, *Taylor v. Louisiana*, answers that question in detail. You should summarize the Court's reasoning prior to coming to class.

The second case, *United States v. Dougherty*, involves two somewhat related issues, the right of the criminal defendant to proceed *pro se* (without counsel) if he wishes and the power of the jury to issue a verdict that is at odds with both the facts and the law, known as "jury nullification." When reading *Dougherty*, think about how the two issues are related.

The final case, *Merced v. McGrath*, also involves jury nullification. How is it different than *Dougherty*?

Text of the Fifth Amendment

*This amendment mandates that a **Grand Jury** must deliver an indictment prior to any conviction of a defendant in a **federal criminal matter**. The Fifth Amendment also contains the Double Jeopardy clause, the right against self-incrimination, and a "takings" provision providing that the state may not take private property for public use without just compensation.*

"No person shall be held to answer for a capital, or otherwise infamous crime, unless on a presentment or indictment of a Grand Jury, except in cases arising in the land or naval forces, or in the Militia, when in actual service in time of War or public danger; nor shall any person be subject for the same offence to be twice put in jeopardy of life or limb; nor shall be compelled in any criminal case to be a witness against himself, nor be deprived of life, liberty, or property without due process of law; nor shall private property be taken for public use, without just compensation."

Text of the Sixth Amendment

The Sixth Amendment mandates that all criminal defendants are entitled to a speedy and public trial by an impartial jury, to be confronted by the witnesses against him, and to the effective assistance of counsel.

"In all criminal prosecutions, the accused shall enjoy the right to a speedy and public trial, by an impartial jury of the State and district wherein the crime shall have been committed, which district shall have been previously ascertained by law, and to be informed of the nature and cause of the accusation; to be confronted with the witnesses against him; to have compulsory process for obtaining witnesses in his favor, and to have the Assistance of Counsel for his defence."

Text of the Seventh Amendment

The right to trial by jury is also preserved, although not mandated, in civil cases. Please note that in many small cases there is no right to a jury trial.

"In Suits at common law, where the value in controversy shall exceed twenty dollars, the right of trial by jury shall be preserved, and no fact tried by a jury, shall be otherwise re-examined in any Court of the United States, than according to the rules of the common law."

Taylor v. Louisiana, 419 U.S. 522 (1975)

In Taylor v. Louisiana, *the Supreme Court discussed the constitutional requirement that a jury pool be drawn from a fair cross section of the community. What does a "fair cross section of the community" mean? Why is it so important that a jury be drawn from a fair cross section of the community? In particular, why is it so important in* criminal *trials?*

Opinion

When this case was tried, Art. VII, § 41, of the Louisiana Constitution, and Art. 402 of the Louisiana Code of Criminal Procedure provided that a woman should not be selected for jury service unless she had previously filed a written declaration of her desire to be subject to jury service. The constitutionality of these provisions is the issue in this case.

*   *   *

The Louisiana jury-selection system does not disqualify women from jury service, but in operation its conceded systematic impact is that only a very few women, grossly disproportionate to the number of eligible women in the community, are called for jury service. In this case, no women were on the venire from which the petit jury was drawn. The issue we have, therefore, is whether a jury-selection system which operates to exclude from jury service an identifiable class of citizens constituting 53% of eligible jurors In the community comports with the Sixth and Fourteenth Amendments.

The State first insists that Taylor, a male, has no standing to object to the exclusion of women from his jury. But Taylor's claim is that he was constitutionally entitled to a jury drawn from a venire constituting a fair cross section of the community and that the jury that tried him was not such a jury by reason of the exclusion of women. Taylor was not a member of the excluded class; but there is no rule that claims such as Taylor presents may be made only by those defendants who are members of the group excluded from jury service. In *Peters v. Kiff*, 407 U.S. 493 (1972), the defendant, a white man, challenged his conviction on the ground that Negroes had been systematically excluded from jury service. Six Members of the Court agreed that petitioner was entitled to present the issue and concluded that he had been deprived of his federal rights. Taylor, in the case before us, was similarly entitled to tender and have adjudicated the claim that the exclusion of women from jury service deprived him of the kind of factfinder to which he was constitutionally entitled.

*   *   *

Our inquiry is whether the presence of a fair cross section of the community on venires, panels, or lists from which petit juries are drawn is essential to the fulfillment of the Sixth Amendment's guarantee of an impartial jury trial in criminal prosecutions.

The Court's prior cases are instructive. Both in the course of exercising its supervisory powers over trials in federal courts and in the constitutional context, the Court has unambiguously declared that the American concept of the jury trial contemplates a jury drawn from a fair cross section of the community. A unanimous Court stated in *Smith v. Texas*, 311 U.S. 128, 130 (1940), that "[i]t is part of the established tradition in the use of juries as instruments of public justice that the jury be a body truly representative of the community." To exclude racial groups from jury service was said to be "at war with our basic concepts of a democratic society and a representative government." A state jury system that resulted in systematic exclusion of Negroes as jurors was therefore held to violate the Equal Protection Clause of the Fourteenth Amendment. ...

The unmistakable import of this Court's opinions ... is that the selection of a petit jury from a representative cross section of the community is an essential component of the Sixth Amendment right to a jury trial. ...

We accept the fair-cross-section requirement as fundamental to the jury trial guaranteed by the Sixth Amendment and are convinced that the requirement has solid foundation. The purpose of a jury is to guard against the exercise of arbitrary power - to make available the commonsense judgment of the community as a hedge against the overzealous or mistaken prosecutor and in preference to the professional or perhaps overconditioned or biased response of a judge. [This purpose is not served] if the jury pool is made up of only special segments of the populace or if large, distinctive groups are excluded from the pool. Community participation in the administration of the criminal law, moreover, is not only consistent with our democratic heritage but is also critical to public confidence in the fairness of the criminal justice system. Restricting jury service to only special groups or excluding identifiable segments playing major roles in the community cannot be squared with the constitutional concept of jury trial. "Trial by jury presupposes a jury drawn from a pool broadly representative of the community as well as impartial in a specific case. [T]he broad representative character of the jury should be maintained, partly as assurance of a diffused impartiality and partly because sharing in the administration of justice is a phase of civic responsibility."

We are also persuaded that the fair-cross-section requirement is violated by the systematic exclusion of women, who in the judicial district involved here amounted to 53% of the citizens eligible for jury service. ...

Louisiana's special exemption for women operates to exclude them from petit juries, which in our view is contrary to the command of the Sixth and Fourteenth Amendments.

It should also be emphasized that in holding that petit juries must be drawn from a source fairly representative of the community we impose no requirement that petit juries actually chosen must mirror the community and reflect the various distinctive groups in the population. Defendants are not entitled to a jury of any particular composition, but the jury wheels, pools of names, panels, or venires from which juries are drawn must not systematically exclude distinctive groups in the community and thereby fail to be reasonably representative thereof.

*   *   *

United States v. Dougherty, 473 F.2d 1113 (D.C. Cir. 1972)

United States v. Dougherty, *involves two somewhat related issues, the right of the criminal defendant to proceed pro se (without counsel) if he wishes and the power of the jury to issue a verdict that is at odds with both the facts and the law, known as "jury nullification." Think about the following while reading the case:*

- *Why is it important for a criminal defendant to proceed* pro se *if he wishes? How does it relate to the fairness and legitimacy of the proceedings?*

- *What is the power of jury nullification? Its basis is in the U.S. Constitution's double jeopardy clause. How so?*

- *If juries have the power of nullification, why not instruct them on that right?*

LEVENTHAL, Circuit Judge:

Seven of the so-called "D.C. Nine" bring this joint appeal from convictions arising out of their unconsented entry into the Washington offices of the Dow Chemical Company, and their destruction of certain property therein. ...

Appellants urge three grounds for reversal as follows: (1) The trial judge erred in denying defendants' timely motions to dispense with counsel and represent themselves. (2) The judge erroneously refused to instruct the jury of its right to acquit appellants without regard to the law and the evidence, and refused to permit appellants to argue that issue to the jury. (3) The instructions actually given by the court coerced the jury into delivering a verdict of guilty. On the basis of defendants' first contention we reverse and remand for new trial. To provide an appropriate mandate governing the new trial, we consider the second and third contentions, and conclude that these cannot be accepted.

*   *   *

Initially, the court appointed separate counsel for each defendant. [All defendants then requested to proceed without counsel. The court denied the defendants' requests. The defendants went to trial represented by court-appointed counsel].

In defendants' view, Judge Pratt violated their constitutional and statutory rights when he refused to permit them to represent themselves. They say the right to dispense with counsel is correlative to the guarantee of the right to counsel and is therefore "implicit" in the Sixth Amendment. ...

*   *   *

In guaranteeing counsel for the accused, the Sixth Amendment conferred a right for the benefit of the accused. As implemented by Congress, this right is not an imperative requirement that may be thrust upon him when in his judgment, as a person without impaired mental capacity, it is against his interest. Even if the defendant will likely lose the case anyway, he has the right–as he suffers whatever consequences there may be–to the knowledge that it was the claim that he put forward that was considered and rejected, and to the knowledge that in our free society, devoted to the ideal of individual worth, he was not deprived of his free will to make his own choice, in his hour of trial, to handle his own case.

In the case at bar defendants believed they would be vindicated by their peers by presenting their positions without law-trained counsel as intermediary. They may or may not be right about the relative effectiveness of a lawyer's presentation of their case. Ordinarily representation by an attorney has structure and clarity that enables a jury to better understand defendants' positions. Presentation of a case *pro se* will often be artless and confusing. Yet the normal disadvantage of confusion may be offset by the enhanced intensity and appearance of greater sincerity of a defendant's presentation.

*   *   *

[The court now discussed the defendants' second claim of error, the refusal to instruct the jury on the issue of jury nullification]. The pages of history shine on instances of the jury's exercise of its prerogative to disregard uncontradicted evidence and instructions of the judge. Most often commended are the 18th century acquittal of Peter Zenger of seditious libel, on the plea of Andrew Hamilton, and the 19th century acquittals in prosecutions under the fugitive slave law. The values involved drop a notch when the liberty vindicated by the verdict relates to the defendant's shooting of his wife's paramour, or purchase during Prohibition of alcoholic beverages.

Even the notable Dean Pound commented in 1910 on positive aspects of "such jury lawlessness." ...

> Reflective opinions upholding the necessity for the jury as a protection against arbitrary action, such as prosecutorial abuse of power, stress fundamental features like the jury "common sense judgment" and assurance of "community participation in the determination of guilt or innocene." Human frailty being what it is, a prosecutor disposed by unworthy motives could likely establish some basis in fact for bringing charges against anyone he wants to book, but the jury system operates in fact, so that the jury will not convict when they empathize with the defendant, as when the offense is one they see themselves as likely to commit, or consider generally acceptable or condonable under the mores of the community.

The existence of an unreviewable and unreversible power in the jury, to acquit in disregard of the instructions on the law given by the trial judge, has for many years co-existed with legal practice and precedent upholding instructions to the jury that they are required to follow the instructions of the court on all matters of law.

*   *   *

We are aware of the number and variety of expressions at that time from respected sources–John Adams; Alexander Hamilton; prominent judges–that jurors had a duty to find a verdict according to their own conscience, though in opposition to the direction of the court; that their power signified a right; that they were judges both of law and of fact in a criminal case, and not bound by the opinion of the court.

*   *   *

The crucial legal ruling came in [1835]. Justice Story's strong opinion supported the conception that the jury's function lay in accepting the law given to it by the court and applying that law to the facts. This considered ruling of an influential jurist won increasing acceptance in the nation. The youthful passion for independence accommodated itself to the reality that the former rebels were now in control of their own destiny, that the practical needs of stability and sound growth outweighed the abstraction of centrifugal philosophy, and that the judges in the courts, were not the colonial appointees projecting royalist patronage and influence but were themselves part and parcel of the nation's intellectual mainstream, subject to the checks of the common law tradition and professional opinion, and capable, in Roscoe Pound's words, of providing "true judicial justice" standing in contrast with the colonial experience.

*   *   *

The breadth of the continuing prerogative of the jury, however, perseveres, as appears from the rulings permitting inconsistent verdicts. These reflect, in the words of Justice Holmes, an acknowledgment that "the jury has the power to bring in a verdict in the teeth of both law and facts," or as Judge Learned Hand said: "We interpret the acquittal as no more than their assumption of a power which they had no right to exercise, but to which they were disposed through lenity."

*   *   *

This so-called right of jury nullification is put forward in the name of liberty and democracy, but its explicit avowal risks the ultimate logic of anarchy.

*   *   *

The way the jury operates may be radically altered if there is alteration in the way it is told to operate. The jury knows well enough that its prerogative is not limited to the choices articulated in the formal instructions of the court. The jury gets its understanding as to the arrangements in the legal system from more than one voice. There is the formal communication from the judge. There is the informal communication from the total culture–literature (novel, drama, film, and television); current comment (newspapers, magazines and television); conversation; and, of course, history and tradition. The totality of input generally convey adequately enough the idea of prerogative, of freedom in an occasional case to depart from what the judge says. Even indicators that would on their face seem too weak to notice–like the fact that the judge tells the jury it must acquit (in case of reasonable doubt) but never tells the jury in so many words that it must convict–are a meaningful part of the jury's total input. Law is a system, and it is also a language, with secondary meanings that may be unrecorded yet are part of its life.

When the legal system relegates the information of the jury's prerogative to an essentially informal input, it is not being duplicitous, chargeable with chicane and intent to deceive. The limitation to informal input is, rather a governor to avoid excess: the prerogative is reserved for the exceptional case, and the judge's instruction is retained as a generally effective constraint. We "recognize a constraint as obligatory upon us when we require not merely reason to defend our rule departures, but damn good reason." The practicalities of men, machinery and rules point up the danger of articulating discretion to depart from a rule, that the breach will be more often and casually invoked. We cannot gainsay that occasionally jurors uninstructed as to the prerogative may feel themselves compelled to the point of rigidity. The danger of the excess rigidity that may now occasionally exist is not as great as the danger of removing the boundaries of constraint provided by the announced rules.

*   *   *

In the last analysis, our rejection of the request for jury nullification doctrine is a recognition that there are times when logic is not the only or even best guide to sound conduct of government. For machines, one can indulge the person who likes to tinker in pursuit of fine tuning. When men and judicial machinery are involved, one must attend to the many and complex mechanisms and reasons that lead men to change their conduct–when they know they are being studied; when they are told of the consequences of their conduct; and when conduct exercised with restraint as an unwritten exception is expressly presented as a legitimate option.

What makes for health as an occasional medicine would be disastrous as a daily diet. The fact that there is widespread existence of the jury's prerogative, and approval of its existence as a "necessary counter to casehardened judges and arbitrary prosecutors," does not establish as an imperative that the jury must be informed by the judge of that power. On the contrary, it is pragmatically useful to structure instructions in such wise that the jury must feel strongly about the values involved in the case, so strongly that it must itself identify the case as establishing a call of high conscience, and must independently initiate and undertake an act in contravention of the established instructions. This requirement of independent jury conception confines the happening of the lawless jury to the occasional instance that does not violate, and viewed as an exception may even enhance, the over-all normative effect of the rule of law. An explicit instruction to a jury conveys an implied approval that runs the risk of degrading the legal structure requisite for true freedom, for an ordered liberty that protects against anarchy as well as tyranny.

*   *   *

Merced v. McGrath, 426 F.3d 1076 (9th Cir. 2005)

Like Dougherty, McGrath *also involves jury nullification. What is the difference between the 2 cases?*

Opinion

Juan Merced, a California state prisoner, appeals the district court's denial of his petition for habeas corpus. In his petition, Merced makes several assignments of error, only one of which we discuss here: whether the trial court violated Merced's constitutional rights when it excused a prospective juror based on his belief in exercising the power of jury nullification in appropriate circumstances. We affirm the district court's denial of the habeas petition with respect to this assignment of error.

*   *   *

At trial, the jury questionnaire contained an open-ended question, asking jurors to volunteer anything else that they feel that they should mention at this time that might affect their ability to be fair and impartial jurors in this case. Prospective alternate juror Andrew B. answered as follows: "I recognize and believe in jury nullification where appropriate." After reviewing the questionnaires, the trial judge called Mr. B. into the box and the following colloquy ensued:

THE COURT: Mr. B_____, ... I appreciate your candor, particularly No. 64 about jury nullification. I mean, that's your right. I have no problem with that. My question is this: If you are selected on this jury, and if I instructed you as to the law that implies[sic] in the state of California and it went against your conscience for whatever reason, is it reasonable for me to assume that you would not follow the law as I dictate it to you?

MR. B_____: It's reasonable for you to assume that.

THE COURT: I'm going to excuse you then Mr. B_____. Thank you very much.

*   *   *

A juror's ability to acquit "in the teeth of both law and facts" is a well-established power that defense counsel correctly observed "ha[s] been with us since Common Law England." Importantly, while jurors have the power to nullify a verdict, they have no right to do so. If jurors had a right to nullify, then a court would have a correlative duty to safeguard their ability to exercise this right. But courts manifestly do not have a duty to ensure a jury's free exercise of this power. In fact, "it is the duty of juries in criminal cases to take the law from the court, and apply that law to the facts as they find them to be from the evidence."

The power to nullify is reinforced by a jury's freedom from recrimination or sanction for exercising this power after the verdict has been reached. Notwithstanding the unassailability of jury verdicts of acquittal, [i]nasmuch as no juror has a right to engage in nullification-and, on the contrary, it is a violation of a juror's sworn duty to follow the law as instructed by the court-trial courts have the duty to forestall or prevent such conduct, whether by firm instruction or admonition or, where it does not interfere with guaranteed rights or the need to protect the secrecy of jury deliberations, ... by dismissal of an offending juror from the venire or the jury.

With this backdrop in place, we turn to a consideration of the following question: was the California Court of Appeal's decision contrary to or an unreasonable application of the appropriate federal standard for the removal of a juror for cause? The court of appeal, in affirming the trial court, relied upon *People v. Holt* to conclude that "a prospective juror may be excused if the juror's voir dire responses convey a 'definite impression' that the juror's views 'would prevent or substantially impair the performance of his duties as a juror in accordance with his instructions and his oath.'" In articulating this standard, *Holt* relied upon the Supreme Court's holding in *Wainwright v. Witt*. We hold that the court of appeal's decision neither contravened nor unreasonably applied clearly established federal law.

Witt dealt with the removal for cause of a prospective juror in a capital case because of her personal beliefs in opposition to the death penalty. *Witt* is no less applicable here, even though this is not a capital case. As Chief Justice Rehnquist, writing for the majority in *Witt*, made clear:

> [T]here is nothing talismanic about juror exclusion under *Witherspoon* merely because it involves capital sentencing juries. *Witherspoon* is not grounded in the Eighth Amendment's prohibition against cruel and unusual punishment, but in the Sixth Amendment. Here, as elsewhere, the quest is for jurors who will conscientiously apply the law and find the facts.

A juror's refusal to inflict the death penalty because of the personal demands of conscience over the firm dictates of law is, of course, an example of juror nullification. Witt clarified that the standard for removal for cause in *Witherspoon* should not be understood to require a finding that the juror would "automatically" nullify-i.e., vote against the death penalty no matter the facts of the case. Rather, "whether or not a venireman might vote for death under certain personal standards, the State still may properly challenge that venireman if he refuses to follow the statutory scheme and truthfully answer the questions put by the trial judge." But if the case before the venireman were one in which his or her personal standards happened to coincide with the requirements of the law, the venireman could not be properly excused for cause.

Importantly, "it cannot be assumed that a juror who describes himself as having 'conscientious or religious scruples' against the infliction of the death penalty or against its infliction 'in a proper case' thereby affirmed that he could never vote in favor of it or that he would not consider doing so in the case before him." Similarly, it cannot be assumed that a prospective juror who describes himself as believing in jury nullification "where appropriate" thereby affirmed that he could not refrain from doing so in the case before him.

However, the fact that Mr. B. volunteered this information in response to a question about his ability to remain impartial "in this case" reasonably gave rise to a definite impression of serious potential juror bias. Notwithstanding the trial judge's own inadequate justification-"[t]he [mere] fact that he believes in jury nullification is enough for me as a challenge for cause"-it was reasonable for the court of appeal to find that the challenge was proper in this case. We disagree with the court of appeal that a trial judge is never required to ask a potentially nullifying prospective juror further questions about the circumstances under which he would nullify-including questions about the juror's attitudes toward the relevant statutory scheme under which the defendant was charged-before excusing him for cause. We note, however, that it is the state court's decision, as opposed to its reasoning, that is judged under the "unreasonable application" standard. We therefore conclude that the California Court of Appeal's decision neither contravened nor unreasonably applied clearly established federal law.

The extent to which a trial court should question a prospective juror who has expressed a willingness to follow his or her conscience, come what may, depends upon the circumstances. In this case, the trial judge never asked Mr. B. to explain what, if any, particular circumstances he considered "appropriate" for jury nullification. Rather, the judge simply posed a hypothetical question, the answer to which revealed no more information about Mr. B.'s likelihood to nullify in the case before him than Mr. B.'s questionnaire did. Notwithstanding the trial judge's failure to glean more information about whether Mr. B. was inclined to follow the dictates of his own conscience rather than those of the law in the particular case at hand, the fact that Mr. B. volunteered his belief in jury nullification in response to a question about his ability to be an impartial juror "in this case" was enough to create a definite impression of potential bias.

In other contexts of potential nullification, as in the death penalty context, judges often carefully explore a prospective juror's possible willingness to nullify a verdict before excusing him or her. On the facts of the present case, the trial judge was not obligated to ask Mr. B. to flesh out in greater detail his volunteered remark about his belief in jury nullification for the reasons already discussed. But the judge was mistaken in assuming that the mere fact of Mr. B.'s general belief in jury nullification was enough to justify excusing him for cause. Suppose the trial judge had independent knowledge of Mr. B.'s belief in jury nullification-say, because he had written an article on the subject or because he had appeared before the same judge on a previous venire panel and had disclosed his belief then. If Mr. B. had not said anything that would have indicated his inability to be fair and impartial in this case, the judge could not then have pointed to his independent knowledge of Mr. B.'s belief in jury nullification "where appropriate" as a legitimate reason for excusing him for cause. Witt's requirement of a "definite impression" of juror bias demands more.

*   *   *

Because the trial judge reasonably had a definite impression that the prospective juror's views "would prevent or substantially impair the performance of his duties as a juror in accordance with his instructions and his oath," we affirm the district court's denial of Merced's petition for habeas corpus.

*   *   *

Chapter 12: Introduction to the Law of Contracts

Introduction and Definitions

The law of contracts is perhaps best described as the law of enforceable promises. A promise is *enforceable* by a court when it meets the requirements set forth by the law. Generally, those requirements include a valid **offer, acceptance,** and the support of **consideration.** These concepts are all interrelated.

An **offeror** is a person who makes an **offer**. An **offeree** is the recipient of the offer and is able to **accept** it. For our purposes, the terms **promisor** and **promisee** mean the same as **offeror** and **offeree**.

"[A]n **offer** is, in effect, a **promise** by the offeror to do or abstain from doing something, provided that the offeree will accept the offer and pay or promise to pay the 'price' of the offer. The price, of course, need not be a monetary one. In fact, in bilateral contracts, as we explained earlier, the mere promise of payment of the price suffices to conclude the contract, while in a unilateral contract it is the actual payment of the price which is required."[78]

An **acceptance** then is "[a]n offeree's assent **[agreement]**, either by express act or by implication from conduct, to the terms of an offer in a manner authorized or requested by the offeror, so that a binding contract is formed. • If an acceptance modifies the terms or adds new ones, it generally operates as a **counteroffer**."[79]

---

[78]   P.S. Atiyah, *An Introduction to the Law of Contract* 44 (3d ed. 1981) (emphasis supplied).

[79]   ACCEPTANCE, Black's Law Dictionary (11th ed. 2019) (emphasis supplied).

Consideration is the glue that binds the offer and acceptance together and forms a contract. In essence, consideration is the **exchange** of promises or performance between offeror and offeree. "Something (such as an act, a forbearance, or a return promise) bargained for and received by a promisor from a promisee; that which motivates a person to do something, esp. to engage in a legal act. • Consideration, or a substitute such as promissory estoppel, is necessary for an agreement to be enforceable."[80]

Performance is the successful completion of a contractual duty or, more generally, the fulfillment of a promise.

Finally, the term **damages** refers to the amount of money or **remedy** that the non-breaching party may recover in a breach of contract action.

Some questions to consider.

- What is a contract?

- What function do contracts serve?

- Why are certain promises enforceable?

- What does it mean to enforce a promise?

- What are the elements of an enforceable promise or contract?

What to Look for While Reading a Case Involving Contracts

Remember, the study of contracts is the study of enforceable promises. Therefore, the typical contracts case involves questions as to whether a valid contract exists (that is, whether a promise is enforceable), whether the contract has been breached, and if so the determination of a proper remedy or the correct measure of damages.

---

[80]   CONSIDERATION, Black's Law Dictionary (11th ed. 2019).

Therefore, when reading a contracts case, *always look first for the underlying agreement or contract.* Is it enforceable? Have the requirements of offer, acceptance, and consideration been met? If the contract is valid, what are its terms? Has there been a breach of any terms or a failure to perform? If so, what is the proper measure of damages?

Nebraska Seed Co. v. Harsh, 98 Neb. 89 (1915)

*This case involved questions as to the validity of a purported **offer**. The plaintiff thought it had accepted an offer and formed a contract. The court said no. How come?*

Some questions to help understand the case.

- *What is an offer? What is an acceptance?*

- *What happened here?*

- *Why isn't the plaintiff entitled to damages?*

- *Why did the letter **not** constitute an offer?*

- *What are the requirements of a valid offer?*

Opinion

Plaintiff, a corporation, engaged in buying and selling seed in the city of Omaha, Neb., brought this action against the defendant, a farmer residing at Lowell, Kearney county, Neb. The petition alleges:

That on the 26th day of April, 1912, the plaintiff purchased of and from the defendant 1,800 bushels of millet seed at the agreed price of $2.25 per hundredweight, F. O. B. Lowell, Neb., which said purchase and contract was evidenced by writing and correspondence passing between the respective parties of which the following is a copy:

Lowell, Nebraska, 4—24—1912.

Neb. Seed Co., Omaha, Neb.—Gentlemen: I have about 1800 bu. or thereabouts of millet seed of which I am mailing you a sample. This millet is recleaned and was grown on sod and is good seed. I want $2.25 per cwt. for this seed f. o. b. Lowell.

Yours truly,

H. F. Harsh.

Said letter was received by the plaintiff at its place of business in Omaha, Neb., on the 26th day of April, 1912, and immediately thereafter the plaintiff telegraphed to the defendant at Lowell, Neb., a copy of which is as follows:

4—26—12.

H. F. Harsh, Lowell, Nebr. Sample and letter received. Accept your offer. Millet like sample two twenty–five per hundred. Wire how soon can load.

The Nebraska Seed Co.

On the same day, to wit, April 26, 1912, the plaintiff, in answer to the letter of the said defendant, wrote to him a letter and deposited the same in the United States mail, directed to the said defendant at Lowell, Neb., which said letter was duly stamped, and which the plaintiff charges that the defendant in due course of mail received. That a copy of said letter is as follows:

4—26—12.

Mr. H. F. Harsh, Lowell, Neb.—Dear Sir: We received your letter and sample of millet seed this morning and at once wired you as follows: "Sample and letter received. Accept your offer. Millett like sample two twenty–five per hundred, wire how soon can load." We confirm this message have booked purchase of you 1800 bushels of millet seed to be fully equal to sample you sent us at $2.25 per cwt. your track. Please be so kind as to load this seed at once and ship to us at Omaha. We thank you in advance for prompt attention. When anything further in the line of millet to offer, let us have samples.

Yours truly, The Nebraska Seed Co.

It alleges that defendant refused to deliver the seed, after due demand and tender of the purchase price, and prays judgment in the sum of $900. Defendant filed a demurrer, which was overruled. He saved an exception to the ruling and answered, denying that the petition stated a cause of action; that the correspondence set out constituted a contract, etc. There was a trial to a jury with verdict and judgment for plaintiff, and defendant appeals.

In our opinion the letter of defendant cannot be fairly construed into an offer to sell to the plaintiff. After describing the seed, the writer says, "I want $2.25 per cwt. for this seed f. o. b. Lowell." He does not say, "I offer to sell to you." The language used is general, and such as may be used in an advertisement, or circular addressed generally to those engaged in the seed business, and is not an offer by which he may be bound, if accepted, by any or all of the persons addressed.

If a proposal is nothing more than an invitation to the person to whom it is made to make an offer to the proposer, it is not such an offer as can be turned into an agreement by acceptance. Proposals of this kind, although made to definite persons and not to the public generally, are merely invitations to trade; they go no further than what occurs when one asks another what he will give or take for certain goods. Such inquiries may lead to bargains, but do not make them. They ask for offers which the proposer has a right to accept or reject as he pleases.

The letter as a whole shows that it was not intended as a final proposition, but as a request for bids. It did not fix a time for delivery, and this seems to have been regarded as one of the essentials by plaintiff, for in his telegram he requests defendant to "wire how soon can load."

The mere statement of the price at which property is held cannot be understood as an offer to sell. The letter of acceptance is not in the terms of the offer.

Defendant stated that he had 1,800 bushels or thereabouts. He did not fix a definite and certain amount. It might be 1,800 bushels; it might be more; it might be less; but plaintiff undertook to make an acceptance for 1,800 bushels—no more, no less. Defendant might not have this amount, and therefore be unable to deliver, or he might have a greater amount, and, after filling plaintiff's order, have a quantity of seed left for which he might find no market. We may assume that when he wrote the letter he did not contemplate the sale of more seed than he had, and that he fixed the price on the whole lot whether it was more or less than 1,800 bushels.

We do not think the correspondence made a complete contract. To so hold where a party sends out letters to a number of dealers would subject him to a suit by each one receiving a letter, or invitations to bid, even though his supply of seed were exhausted. In *Lyman v. Robinson*, the Supreme Court of Massachusetts has sounded the warning: Care should always be taken not to construe as an agreement letters which the parties intended only as a preliminary negotiation.

Holding, as we do, that there was no binding contract between the parties, it is unnecessary to discuss the other questions presented.

The judgment of the district court is reversed.

Dickinson v. Dodds, 2 Ch. Div. 463 (Ct. App. 1876)

In this case there most certainly was a valid offer. But, for some reason, the plaintiff's "acceptances" were not effective to form a valid contract. How come?

Questions.

- *Can an offer be revoked?*

- *What happened here?*

- *Why were the various "acceptances" ineffective?*

- *What is the rule on revocation of an offer?*

- *What is an option contract?*

- *Why was the option here unenforceable?*

Opinion

On Wednesday, the 10th of June, 1874, the Defendant John Dodds signed and delivered to the Plaintiff, George Dickinson, a memorandum, of which the material part was as follows:

> I hereby agree to sell to Mr. George Dickinson the whole of the dwelling- houses, garden ground, stabling, and outbuildings thereto belonging, situate at Croft, belonging to me, for the sum of £800. As witness my hand this tenth day of June, 1874.
>
> (Signed) John Dodds.
>
> P.S.-This offer to be left over until Friday, 9 o'clock, a.m. J.D. (the twelfth), 12th June, 1874.
>
> (Signed) J. Dodds.

The bill alleged that Dodds understood and intended that the Plaintiff should have until Friday 9 A.M. within which to determine whether he would or would not purchase, and that he should absolutely have until that time the refusal of the property at the price of £800, and that the Plaintiff in fact determined to accept the offer on the morning of Thursday, the 11th of June, but did not at once signify his acceptance to Dodds, believing that he had the power to accept it until 9 A.M. on the Friday.

In the afternoon of the Thursday the Plaintiff was informed by a Mr. Berry that Dodds had been offering or agreeing to sell the property to Thomas Allan, the other Defendant. Thereupon the Plaintiff, at about half-past seven in the evening, went to the house of Mrs. Burgess, the mother-in-law of Dodds, where he was then staying, and left with her a formal acceptance in writing of the offer to sell the property. According to the evidence of Mrs. Burgess this document never in fact reached Dodds, she having forgotten to give it to him.

On the following (Friday) morning, at about seven o'clock, Berry, who was acting as agent for Dickinson, found Dodds at the Darlington railway station, and handed to him a duplicate of the acceptance by Dickinson, and explained to Dodds its purport. He replied that it was too late, as he had sold the property. A few minutes later Dickinson himself found Dodds entering a railway carriage, and handed him another duplicate of the notice of acceptance, but Dodds declined to receive it, saying, "You are too late. I have sold the property."

It appeared that on the day before, Thursday, the 11th of June, Dodds had signed a formal contract for the sale of the property to the Defendant Allan for £800, and had received from him a deposit of £40.

The bill in this suit prayed that the Defendant Dodds might be decreed specifically to perform the contract of the 10th of June, 1874; that he might be restrained from conveying the property to Allan; that Allan might be restrained from taking any such conveyance; that, if any such conveyance had been or should be made, Allan might be declared a trustee of the property for, and might be directed to convey the property to, the Plaintiff; and for damages.

The cause came on for hearing before Vice Chancellor Bacon on the 29th of January, 1876 [who decreed specific performance for the plaintiff. From this decision the defendants appeal].

James, L.J., after referring to the document of the 10th of June, 1874, continued:

The document, though beginning, "I hereby agree to sell," was nothing but an offer, and was only intended to be an offer, for the Plaintiff himself tells us that he required time to consider whether he would enter into an agreement or not.

Unless both parties had then agreed there was no concluded agreement then made; it was in effect and substance only an offer to sell. The plaintiff being minded not to complete the bargain at that time adds this memorandum: "This offer is to be left over until Friday, 9 o'clock a.m. 12th June 1874. "That shows it was only an offer. There was no consideration given for the undertaking or promise, to whatever extent it may be considered binding, to keep the property unsold until 9 o'clock on Friday morning; but apparently Dickinson was of opinion, and probably Dodds was of the same opinion, that he (Dodds) was bound by that promise, and could not in any way withdraw from it, or retract it, until 9 o'clock on Friday morning, and this probably explains a good deal of what afterwards took place. But it is clear settled law, on one of the clearest principles of law, that this promise, being a mere *nudum pactum*, was not binding, and that at any moment before a complete acceptance by Dickinson of the offer, Dodds was as free as Dickinson himself. Well, that being the state of things, it is said that the only mode in which Dodds could assert that freedom was by actually and distinctly saying to Dickinson, "Now I withdraw my offer." It appears to me that there is neither principle nor authority for the proposition that there must be an express and actual withdrawal of the offer, or what is called a retractation. It must, to constitute a contract, appear that the two minds were at one, at the same moment of time, that is, that there was an offer continuing up to the time of the acceptance. If there was not such a continuing offer, then the acceptance comes to nothing. Of course it may well be that the one man is bound in some way or other to let the other man know that his mind with regard to the offer has been changed; but in this case, beyond all question, the Plaintiff knew that Dodds was no longer minded to sell the property to him as plainly and clearly as if Dodds had told him in so many words, "I withdraw the offer." This is evidence from the Plaintiff's own statements in the bill.

The Plaintiff says in effect that, having heard and knowing that Dodds was no longer minded to sell to him, and that he was selling or had sold to some one else, thinking that he could not in point of law withdraw his offer, meaning to fix him to it, and endeavoring to bind him, "I went to the house where he was lodging, and saw his mother-in-law, and left with her an acceptance of the offer, knowing all the while that he had entirely changed his mind. I got an agent to watch for him at 7 o'clock the next morning, and I went to the train just before 9 o'clock, in order that I might catch him and give him my notice of acceptance just before 9 o'clock, and when that occurred he told my agent, and he told me, you are too late, and he then threw back the paper." It is to my mind quite clear that before there was any attempt at acceptance by the Plaintiff, he was perfectly well aware that Dodds had changed his mind, and that he had in fact agreed to sell the property to Allan. It is impossible, therefore, to say that there was ever that existence of the same mind between the two parties which is essential in point of law to the making of an agreement. I am of opinion, therefore, that the Plaintiff has failed to prove that there was any binding contract between Dodds and himself.

Ardente v. Horan, 366 A.2d 162 (R.I. 1976)

Here too there was a valid offer that the plaintiff thought he had accepted. But, the court said that a binding contract was not formed. How come?

Questions.

- *What constitutes an acceptance?*

- *What are the facts here?*

- *Was an offer made? Was it valid?*

- *Did the plaintiff accept the offer? Why not? What did the plaintiff actually do?*

- *What should the plaintiff have done?*

Opinion

Ernest P. Ardente, the plaintiff, brought this civil action in Superior Court to specifically enforce an agreement between himself and William A. and Katherine L. Horan, the defendants, to sell certain real property. The defendants filed an answer together with a motion for summary judgment pursuant to Super.R.Civ.P. 56. Following the submission of affidavits by both the plaintiff and the defendants and a hearing on the motion, judgment was entered by a Superior Court justice for the defendants. The plaintiff now appeals.

In August 1975, certain residential property in the city of Newport was offered for sale by defendants. The plaintiff made a bid of $250,000 for the property which was communicated to defendants by their attorney. After defendants' attorney advised plaintiff that the bid was acceptable to defendants, he prepared a purchase and sale agreement at the direction of defendants and forwarded it to plaintiff's attorney for plaintiff's signature. After investigating certain title conditions, plaintiff executed the agreement. Thereafter plaintiff's attorney returned the document to defendants along with a check in the amount of $20,000 and a letter dated September 8, 1975, which read in relevant part as follows:

My clients are concerned that the following items remain with the real estate: a) dining room set and tapestry wall covering in dining room; b) fireplace fixtures throughout; c) the sun parlor furniture. I would appreciate your confirming that these items are a part of the transaction, as they would be difficult to replace.

The defendants refused to agree to sell the enumerated items and did not sign the purchase and sale agreement. They directed their attorney to return the agreement and the deposit check to plaintiff and subsequently refused to sell the property to plaintiff. This action for specific performance followed.

In Superior Court, defendants moved for summary judgment on the ground that the facts were not in dispute and no contract had been formed as a matter of law. The trial justice ruled that the letter quoted above constituted a conditional acceptance of defendants' offer to sell the property and consequently must be construed as a counteroffer. Since defendants never accepted the counteroffer, it followed that no contract was formed, and summary judgment was granted.

Summary judgment is a drastic remedy and should be cautiously applied; nevertheless, where there is no genuine issue as to any material fact and the moving party is entitled to judgment as a matter of law, summary judgment properly issues. On appeal this court is bound by the same rules as the trial court. With these rules is mind we address ourselves to the facts.

The plaintiff assigns several grounds for appeal in his brief. He urges first that summary judgment was improper because there existed a genuine issue of fact. The factual question, according to plaintiff, was whether the oral agreement which preceded the drafting of the purchase and sale agreement was intended by the parties to take effect immediately to create a binding oral contract for the sale of the property.

We cannot agree with plaintiff's position. A review of the record shows that the issue was never raised before the trial justice. The plaintiff did not, in his affidavit in opposition to summary judgment or by any other means, bring to the attention of the trial court any facts which established the existence of a relevant factual dispute. Indeed, at the hearing on the motion plaintiff did not even mention the alleged factual dispute which he now claims the trial justice erred in overlooking. The only issue plaintiff addressed was the proper interpretation of the language used in plaintiff's letter of acceptance. This was solely a question of law.

It is well-settled that one who opposes a motion for summary judgment may not rest upon the mere allegations or denials of his pleading. He has an affirmative duty to set forth specific facts which show that there is a genuine issue of fact to be resolved at trial. If he does not do so, summary judgment, if appropriate, will be entered against him. Accordingly, since no genuine issue of fact was presented to the trial justice, we hold that he did not err in ruling that summary judgment was appropriate.

The plaintiff's second contention is that the trial justice incorrectly applied the principles of contract law in deciding that the facts did not disclose a valid acceptance of defendants' offer. Again we cannot agree.

The trial justice proceeded on the theory that the delivery of the purchase and sale agreement to plaintiff constituted an offer by defendants to sell the property. Because we must view the evidence in the light most favorable to the party against whom summary judgment was entered, in this case plaintiff, we assume as the trial justice did that the delivery of the agreement was in fact an offer.

The question we must answer next is whether there was an acceptance of that offer. The general rule is that where, as here, there is an offer to form a bilateral contract, the offeree must communicate his acceptance to the offeror before any contractual obligation can come into being. A mere mental intent to accept the offer, no matter how carefully formed, is not sufficient. The acceptance must be transmitted to the offeror in some overt manner. A review of the record shows that the only expression of acceptance which was communicated to defendants was the delivery of the executed purchase and sale agreement accompanied by the letter of September 8. Therefore it is solely on the basis of the language used in these two documents that we must determine whether there was a valid acceptance. Whatever plaintiff's unexpressed intention may have been in sending the documents is irrelevant. We must be concerned only with the language actually used, not the language plaintiff thought he was using or intended to use.

There is no doubt that the execution and delivery of the purchase and sale agreement by plaintiff, without more, would have operated as an acceptance. The terms of the accompanying letter, however, apparently conditioned the acceptance upon the inclusion of various items of personality. In assessing the effect of the terms of that letter we must keep in mind certain generally accepted rules. To be effective, an acceptance must be definite and unequivocal. An offeror is entitled to know in clear terms whether the offeree accepts his proposal. It is not enough that the words of a reply justify a probable inference of assent. The acceptance may not impose additional conditions on the offer, nor may it add limitations. An acceptance which is equivocal or upon condition or with a limitation is a counteroffer and requires acceptance by the original offeror before a contractual relationship can exist.

However, an acceptance may be valid despite conditional language if the acceptance is clearly independent of the condition. Many cases have so held. Williston states the rule as follows:

Frequently an offeree, while making a positive acceptance of the offer, also makes a request or suggestion that some addition or modification be made. So long as it is clear that the meaning of the acceptance is positively and unequivocally to accept the offer whether such request is granted or not, a contract is formed.

Corbin is in agreement with the above view. Thus our task is to decide whether plaintiff's letter is more reasonably interpreted as a qualified acceptance or as an absolute acceptance together with a mere inquiry concerning a collateral matter.

In making our decision we recognize that, as one text states, the question whether a communication by an offeree is a conditional acceptance or counter-offer is not always easy to answer. It must be determined by the same common-sense process of interpretation that must be applied in so many other cases. In our opinion the language used in plaintiff's letter of September 8 is not consistent with an absolute acceptance accompanied by a request for a gratuitous benefit. We interpret the letter to impose a condition on plaintiff's acceptance of defendants' offer. The letter does not unequivocally state that even without the enumerated items plaintiff is willing to complete the contract. In fact, the letter seeks confirmation that the listed items are a part of the transaction. Thus, far from being an independent, collateral request, the sale of the items in question is explicitly referred to as a part of the real estate transaction. Moreover, the letter goes on to stress the difficulty of finding replacements for these items. This is a further indication that plaintiff did not view the inclusion of the listed items as merely collateral or incidental to the real estate transaction.

A review of the relevant case law discloses that those cases in which an acceptance was found valid despite an accompanying conditional term generally involved a more definite expression of acceptance than the one in the case at bar.

Accordingly, we hold that since the plaintiff's letter of acceptance dated September 8 was conditional, it operated as a rejection of the defendants' offer and no contractual obligation was created.

The plaintiff's appeal is denied and dismissed, the judgment appealed from is affirmed and the case is remanded to the Superior Court.

Wood v. Lucy, Lady Duff Gordon, 118 N.E. 214 (N.Y. 1917)

In this famous case, there is most certainly a contract, but we wonder at its terms. What did the plaintiff agree to do? How does Cardozo resolve the case?

- *What is the contract at issue?*

- *What went wrong?*

- *What is plaintiff's theory of recovery?*

- *What is Lady Duff Gordon's defense?*

- *What does Justice Cardozo say?*

- *What are the implied promises or terms here? What effect do they have on the agreement?*

CARDOZO, J.

The defendant styles herself 'a creator of fashions.' Her favor helps a sale. Manufacturers of dresses, millinery, and like articles are glad to pay for a certificate of her approval. The things which she designs, fabrics, parasols, and what not, have a new value in the public mind when issued in her name. She employed the plaintiff to help her to turn this vogue into money. He was to have the exclusive right, subject always to her approval, to place her indorsements on the designs of others. He was also to have the exclusive right to place her own designs on sale, or to license others to market them. In return she was to have one-half of 'all profits and revenues' derived from any contracts he might make. The exclusive right was to last at least one year from April 1, 1915, and thereafter from year to year unless terminated by notice of 90 days. The plaintiff says that he kept the contract on his part, and that the defendant broke it. She placed her indorsement on fabrics, dresses, and millinery without his knowledge, and withheld the profits. He sues her for the damages, and the case comes here on demurrer.

The agreement of employment is signed by both parties. It has a wealth of recitals. The defendant insists, however, that it lacks the elements of a contract. She says that the plaintiff does not bind himself to anything. It is true that he does not promise in so many words that he will use reasonable efforts to place the defendant's indorsements and market her designs. We think, however, that such a promise is fairly to be implied. The law has outgrown its primitive stage of formalism when the precise word was the sovereign talisman, and every slip was fatal. It takes a broader view today. A promise may be lacking, and yet the whole writing may be 'instinct with an obligation,' imperfectly expressed. If that is so, there is a contract.

The implication of a promise here finds support in many circumstances. The defendant gave an exclusive privilege. She was to have no right for at least a year to place her own indorsements or market her own designs except through the agency of the plaintiff. The acceptance of the exclusive agency was an assumption of its duties. Many other terms of the agreement point the same way. We are told at the outset by way of recital that:

The said Otis F. Wood possesses a business organization adapted to the placing of such indorsements as the said Lucy, Lady Duff-Gordon, has approved.

The implication is that the plaintiff's business organization will be used for the purpose for which it is adapted. But the terms of the defendant's compensation are even more significant. Her sole compensation for the grant of an exclusive agency is to be one-half of all the profits resulting from the plaintiff's efforts. Unless he gave his efforts, she could never get anything. Without an implied promise, the transaction cannot have such business efficacy, as both parties must have intended that at all events it should have. But the contract does not stop there. The plaintiff goes on to promise that he will account monthly for all moneys received by him, and that he will take out all such patents and copyrights and trade-marks as may in his judgment be necessary to protect the rights and articles affected by the agreement. It is true, of course, as the Appellate Division has said, that if he was under no duty to try to market designs or to place certificates of indorsement, his promise to account for profits or take out copyrights would be valueless. But in determining the intention of the parties the promise has a value. It helps to enforce the conclusion that the plaintiff had some duties. His promise to pay the defendant one-half of the profits and revenues resulting from the exclusive agency and to render accounts monthly was a promise to use reasonable efforts to bring profits and revenues into existence. For this conclusion the authorities are ample.

The judgment of the Appellate Division should be reversed, and the order of the Special Term affirmed, with costs in the Appellate Division and in this court.

Hamer v. Sidway, 124 N.Y. 538 (1891)

This case is about **consideration**, *its definition and components.*

- *What is sufficient consideration?*

- *What is the promise or offer in this case?*

- *Does the nephew accept? How?*

- *Does the uncle agree to pay?*

- *What happens when the uncle dies?*

- *What is the defendant's/estate's theory of the case [the defense]?*

- *What does the court say?*

- *So, what is sufficient consideration?*

Opinion

APPEAL from order of the General Term of the Supreme Court in the fourth judicial department, made July 1, 1890, which reversed a judgment in favor of plaintiff entered upon a decision of the court on trial at Special Term and granted a new trial.

This action was brought upon an alleged contract.

The plaintiff presented a claim to the executor of William E. Story, Sr., for $5,000 and interest from the 6th day of February, 1875. She acquired it through several mesne assignments from William E. Story, 2d. The claim being rejected by the executor, this action was brought. It appears that William E. Story, Sr., was the uncle of William E. Story, 2d; that at the celebration of the golden wedding of Samuel Story and wife, father and mother of William E. Story, Sr., on the 20th day of March, 1869, in the presence of the family and invited guests he promised his nephew that if he would refrain from drinking, using tobacco, swearing and playing cards or billiards for money until he became twenty-one years of age he would pay him a sum of $5,000. The nephew assented thereto and fully performed the conditions inducing the promise. When the nephew arrived at the age of twenty-one years and on the 31st day of January, 1875, he wrote to his uncle informing him that he had performed his part of the agreement and had thereby become entitled to the sum of $5,000. The uncle received the letter and a few days later and on the sixth of February, he wrote and mailed to his nephew the following letter:

BUFFALO, Feb. 6, 1875.

W. E. STORY, Jr.:

DEAR NEPHEW--Your letter of the 31st ult. came to hand all right, saying that you had lived up to the promise made to me several years ago. I have no doubt but you have, for which you shall have five thousand dollars as I promised you. I had the money in the bank the day you was 21 years old that I intend for you, and you shall have the money certain. Now, Willie I do not intend to interfere with this money in any way till I think you are capable of taking care of it and the sooner that time comes the better it will please me. I would hate very much to have you start out in some adventure that you thought all right and lose this money in one year. The first five thousand dollars that I got together cost me a heap of hard work. You would hardly believe me when I tell you that to obtain this I shoved a jackplane many a day, butchered three or four years, then came to this city, and after three months' perseverence I obtained a situation in a grocery store. I opened this store early, closed late, slept in the fourth story of the building in a room 30 by 40 feet and not a human being in the building but myself. All this I done to live as cheap as I could to save something. I don't want you to take up with this kind of fare. I was here in the cholera season '49 and '52 and the deaths averaged 80 to 125 daily and plenty of small-pox. I wanted to go home, but Mr. Fisk, the gentleman I was working for, told me if I left then, after it got healthy he probably would not want me. I stayed. All the money I have saved I know just how I got it. It did not come to me in any mysterious way, and the reason I speak of this is that money got in this way stops longer with a fellow that gets it with hard knocks than it does when he finds it. Willie, you are 21 and you have many a thing to learn yet. This money you have earned much easier than I did besides acquiring good habits at the same time and you are quite welcome to the money; hope you will make good use of it. I was ten long years getting this together after I was your age. Now, hoping this will be satisfactory, I stop. One thing more. Twenty-one years ago I bought you 15 sheep. These sheep were put out to double every four years. I kept track of them the first eight years; I have not heard much about them since. Your father and grandfather promised me that they would look after them till you were of age. Have they done so? I hope they have. By this time you have between five and six hundred sheep, worth a nice little income this spring. Willie, I have said much more than I expected to; hope you can make out what I have written. To-day is the seventeenth day that I have not been out of my room, and have had the doctor as many days. Am a little better to-day; think I will get out next week. You need not mention to father, as he always worries about small matters.

Truly Yours,

W. E. STORY.

P. S.--You can consider this money on interest.

The nephew received the letter and thereafter consented that the money should remain with his uncle in accordance with the terms and conditions of the letters. The uncle died on the 29th day of January, 1887, without having paid over to his nephew any portion of the said $5,000 and interest.

The question which provoked the most discussion by counsel on this appeal, and which lies at the foundation of plaintiff's asserted right of recovery, is whether by virtue of a contract defendant's testator William E. Story became indebted to his nephew William E. Story, 2d, on his twenty-first birthday in the sum of five thousand dollars. The trial court found as a fact that 'on the 20th day of March, 1869, William E. Story agreed to and with William E. Story, 2d, that if he would refrain from drinking liquor, using tobacco, swearing, and playing cards or billiards for money until he should become 21 years of age then he, the said William E. Story, would at that time pay him, the said William E. Story, 2d, the sum of $5,000 for such refraining, to which the said William E. Story, 2d, agreed, and that he in all things fully performed his part of said agreement.

The defendant contends that the contract was without consideration to support it, and, therefore, invalid. He asserts that the promisee by refraining from the use of liquor and tobacco was not harmed but benefited; that that which he did was best for him to do independently of his uncle's promise, and insists that it follows that unless the promisor was benefited, the contract was without consideration. A contention, which if well founded, would seem to leave open for controversy in many cases whether that which the promisee did or omitted to do was, in fact, of such benefit to him as to leave no consideration to support the enforcement of the promisor's agreement. Such a rule could not be tolerated, and is without foundation in the law. The Exchequer Chamber, in 1875, defined consideration as follows: A valuable consideration in the sense of the law may consist either in some right, interest, profit or benefit accruing to the one party, or some forbearance, detriment, loss or responsibility given, suffered or undertaken by the other. Courts will not ask whether the thing which forms the consideration does in fact benefit the promisee or a third party, or is of any substantial value to anyone. It is enough that something is promised, done, forborne or suffered by the party to whom the promise is made as consideration for the promise made to him.

In general a waiver of any legal right at the request of another party is a sufficient consideration for a promise.

Any damage, or suspension, or forbearance of a right will be sufficient to sustain a promise.

Pollock, in his work on contracts [. . .] says: The second branch of this judicial description is really the most important one. Consideration means not so much that one party is profiting as that the other abandons some legal right in the present or limits his legal freedom of action in the future as an inducement for the promise of the first.

Now, applying this rule to the facts before us, the promisee used tobacco, occasionally drank liquor, and he had a legal right to do so. That right he abandoned for a period of years upon the strength of the promise of the testator that for such forbearance he would give him $5,000. We need not speculate on the effort which may have been required to give up the use of those stimulants. It is sufficient that he restricted his lawful freedom of action within certain prescribed limits upon the faith of his uncle's agreement, and now having fully performed the conditions imposed, it is of no moment whether such performance actually proved a benefit to the promisor, and the court will not inquire into it, but were it a proper subject of inquiry, we see nothing in this record that would permit a determination that the uncle was not benefited in a legal sense. Few cases have been found which may be said to be precisely in point, but such as have been support the position we have taken.

*   *   *

Hadley v. Baxendale, 156 Eng. Rep. 145 (1854)

*This case is about the proper measure of **damages**.*

- *What happened?*

- *Was there a contract? Between whom? Was it breached?*

- *What damages did the mill suffer because of the breach?*

- *What damages did the mill seek? To what damages was the mill entitled?*

- *What was the defendant's argument?*

- *What rule did the court establish?*

Opinion

At the trial before Crompton, J., at the last Gloucester Assizes, it appeared that the plaintiffs carried on an extensive business as millers at Gloucester; and that on the 11th on May, their mill was stopped by a breakage of the crank shaft by which the mill was worked. The steam-engine was manufactured by Messrs. Joyce & Co., the engineers, at Greenwich, and it became necessary to send the shaft as a pattern for a new one to Greenwich. The fracture was discovered on the 12th, and on the 13th the plaintiffs sent one of their servants to the office of the defendants, who are the well-known carriers trading under the name of Pickford & Co., for the purpose of having the shaft carried to Greenwich. The plaintiffs' servant told the clerk that the mill was stopped, and that the shaft must be sent immediately; and in answer to the inquiry when the shaft would be taken, the answer was, that if it was sent up by twelve o'clock any day, it would be delivered at Greenwich on the following day. On the following day the shaft was taken by the defendants, before noon, for the purpose of being conveyed to Greenwich, and the sum was paid for its carriage for the whole distance; at the same time the defendants' clerk was told that a special entry, if required, should be made to hasten its delivery. The delivery of the shaft at Greenwich was delayed by some neglect; and the consequence was, that the plaintiffs did not receive the new shaft for several days after they would otherwise have done, and the working of their mill was thereby delayed, and they thereby lost the profits they would otherwise have received.

On the part of the defendants, it was objected that these damages were too remote, and that the defendants were not liable with respect to them. The learned Judge left the case generally to the jury, who found a verdict with £25 damages beyond the amount paid into Court.

*   *   *

We think that there ought to be a new trial in this case; but, in so doing, we deem it to be expedient and necessary to state explicitly the rule which the Judge, at the next trial, ought, in our opinion, to direct the jury to be governed by when they estimate the damages.

It is, indeed, of the last importance that we should do this; for, if the jury are left without any definite rule to guide them, it will, in such cases as these, manifestly lead to the greatest injustice. The Courts have done this on several occasions; and, in *Blake v. Midland Railway Company*, the Court granted a new trial on this very ground, that the rule had not been definitely laid down to the jury by the learned Judge at Nisi Prius.

"There are certain established rules," this Court says, in *Alder v. Keighley*,"according to which the jury ought to find." And the Court, in that case, adds: "and here there is a clear rule, that the amount which would have been received if the contract had been kept, is the measure of damages if the contract is broken."

Now we think the proper rule in such a case as the present is this:-- Where two parties have made a contract which one of them has broken, the damages which the other party ought to receive in respect of such breach of contract should be such as may fairly and reasonably be considered either arising naturally, i.e., according to the usual course of things, from such breach of contract itself, or such as may reasonably be supposed to have been in the contemplation of both parties, at the time they made the contract, as the probable result of the breach of it. Now, if the special circumstances under which the contract was actually made were communicated by the plaintiffs to the defendants, and thus known to both parties, the damages resulting from the breach of such a contract, which they would reasonably contemplate, would be the amount of injury which would ordinarily follow from a breach of contract under these special circumstances so known and communicated. But, on the other hand, if these special circumstances were wholly unknown to the party breaking the contract, he, at the most, could only be supposed to have had in his contemplation the amount of injury which would arise generally, and in the great multitude of cases not affected by any special circumstances, from such a breach of contract. For, had the special circumstances been known, the parties might have specially provided for the breach of contract by special terms as to the damages in that case; and of this advantage it would be very unjust to deprive them. Now the above principles are those by which we think the jury ought to be guided in estimating the damages arising out of any breach of contract. It is said, that other cases such as breaches of contract in the nonpayment of money, or in the not making a good title of land, are to be treated as exceptions from this, and as governed by a conventional rule. But as, in such cases, both parties must be supposed to be cognizant of that well-known rule, these cases may, we think, be more properly classed under the rule above enunciated as to cases under known special circumstances, because there both parties may reasonably be presumed to contemplate the estimation of the amount of damages according to the conventional rule. Now, in the present case, if we are to apply the principles above laid down, we find that the only circumstances here communicated by the plaintiffs to the defendants at the time of the contract was made, were, that the article to be carried was the broken shaft of a mill, and that the plaintiffs were the millers of the mill.

But how do these circumstances shew reasonably that the profits of the mill must be stopped by an unreasonable delay in the delivery of the broken shaft by the carrier to the third person? Suppose the plaintiffs had another shaft in their possession put up or putting up at the time, and that they only wished to send back the broken shaft to the engineer who made it; it is clear that this would be quite consistent with the above circumstances, and yet the unreasonable delay in the delivery would have no effect upon the intermediate profits of the mill. Or, again, suppose that, at the time of the delivery to the carrier, the machinery of the mill had been in other respects defective, then, also, the same results would follow. Here it is true that the shaft was actually sent back to serve as a model for the new one, and that the want of a new one was the only cause of the stoppage of the mill, and that the loss of profits really arose from not sending down the new shaft in proper time, and that this arose from the delay in delivering the broken one to serve as a model. But it is obvious that, in the great multitude of cases of millers sending off broken shafts to third persons by a carrier under ordinary circumstances, such consequences would not, in all probability, have occurred; and these special circumstances were here never communicated by the plaintiffs to the defendants. It follows therefore, that the loss of profits here cannot reasonably be considered such a consequence of the breach of contract as could have been fairly and reasonably contemplated by both the parties when they made this contract. For such loss would neither have flowed naturally from the breach of this contract in the great multitude of such cases occurring under ordinary circumstances, nor were the special circumstances, which, perhaps, would have made it a reasonable and natural consequence of such breach of contract, communicated to or known by the defendants. The Judge ought, therefore, to have told the jury that upon the facts then before them they ought not to take the loss of profits into consideration at all in estimating the damages. There must therefore be a new trial in this case.

*   *   *

Chapter 13: Introduction to the Law of Torts

Introduction and Definitions

A tort action seeks to recover damages for some type of injury, normally physical, but also sometimes reputational or economic. Tort actions are not based on any sort of agreement or contract, but rather on the actions of the defendant. Meaning that the defendant may have *intentionally* done something that caused injury to another or the defendant may have acted *carelessly* and his careless actions caused injury to another. Thus, torts are generally divided into intentional torts and negligence or carelessness.[81]

The cases below discuss both intentional torts and negligence. For example, the first case *Vosburg v. Putney* deals with the intentional tort of battery. Other cases deal with the intentional torts of false imprisonment and the intentional infliction of emotional distress. Then, the cases *U.S. v. Carroll Towing, Warner v. Santa Catalina Island Co., Petition of Kinsman, Dellwo v. Perason,* and *Ford v. Trident Fisheries Co.* deal with negligence.

Whether dealing with intentional torts or negligence, courts must analyze and discuss the **elements** of the tort. A tort's elements are the factual matters that a plaintiff must prove in order to recover. For example, *Vosburg v. Putney,* as noted, involved the intentional tort of battery. The elements of tortious battery are as follows:

1. *Intent* (not criminal intent to cause injury, necessarily, but intent to commit the act)
2. *Contact* (non-consensual contact with the individual or his/her effects, such as clothing)

---

[81] There are other tort actions, such as those for strict or products liability, but they are beyond the scope of these materials.

3. *Harm* (the battery caused actual harm meaning physical, mental, or emotional, not limited to just physical harm)

This means that at trial, a plaintiff would need to present evidence (facts) to persuade a jury that each of the elements existed. All torts have elements of this type.

While reading the cases, please pay attention to the elements of each tort.

Vosburg v. Putney, 80 Wis. 523 (1891)

When reading Judge Lyon's opinion, please consider the following:

- *What did the jury find?*

- *What did the defendant argue regarding the jury's finding that he did not intend to cause injury?*

- *Why does it make a difference that this is a claim for battery as opposed to assault?*

- *What does this mean? — "if the intended act is unlawful, the intention to commit it must necessarily be unlawful."*

- *Why does it matter that the act here happened in the classroom, and not on the playground?*

- *Why is the act in question here "necessarily unlawful"?*

- *What is the defendant's argument as to damages?*

- *How does the court respond to that argument?*

Opinion

The jury having found that the defendant, in touching the plaintiff with his foot, did not intend to do him any harm, counsel for defendant maintain that the plaintiff has no cause of action, and that defendant's motion for judgment on the special verdict should have been granted. In support of this proposition, counsel quotes the rule that "the intention to do harm is of the essence of an assault."

Such is the rule, no doubt, in actions or prosecutions for mere assaults. But this is an action to recover damages for an alleged assault and battery. In such case the rule is correctly stated, in many of the authorities cited by counsel, that plaintiff must show either that the intention was unlawful, or that the defendant is in fault. If the intended act is unlawful, the intention to commit it must necessarily be unlawful. Hence, as applied to this case, if the kicking of the plaintiff by the defendant was an unlawful act, the intention of defendant to kick him was also unlawful. Had the parties been upon the play-grounds of the school, engaged in the usual boyish sports, the defendant being free from malice, wantonness, or negligence, and intending no harm to plaintiff in what he did, we should hesitate to hold the act of the defendant unlawful, or that he could be held liable in this action. Some consideration is due to the implied license of the play-grounds. But it appears that the injury was inflicted in the school, after it had been called to order by the teacher, and after the regular exercises of the school had commenced. Under these circumstances, no implied license to do the act complained of existed, and such act was a violation of the order and decorum of the school, and necessarily unlawful. Hence we are of the opinion that, under the evidence and verdict, the action may be sustained.

The plaintiff testified, as a witness in his own behalf, as to the circumstances of the alleged injury inflicted upon him by the defendant, and also in regard to the wound he received in January, near the same knee, mentioned in the special verdict. The defendant claimed that such wound was the proximate cause of the injury to plaintiff's leg, in that it produced a diseased condition of the bone, which disease was in active progress when he received the kick, and that such kick did nothing more than to change the location, and perhaps somewhat hasten the progress, of the disease. The testimony of Dr. Bacon, a witness for plaintiff, (who was plaintiff's attending physician,) elicited on cross-examination, tends to some extent to establish such claim. Dr. Bacon first saw the injured leg on February 25th, and Dr. Philler, also one of plaintiff's witnesses, first saw it March 8th. Dr. Philler was called as a witness after the examination of the plaintiff and Dr. Bacon.

On his direct examination he testified as follows: "I heard the testimony of Andrew Vosburg in regard to how he received the kick, February 20th, from his playmate. I heard read the testimony of Miss More, and heard where he said he received this kick on that day." (Miss More had already testified that she was the teacher of the school, and saw defendant standing in the aisle by his seat, and kicking across the aisle, hitting the plaintiff.)

The following question was then propounded to Dr. Philler: "After hearing that testimony, and what you know of the case of the boy, seeing it on the 8th day of March, what, in your opinion, was the exciting cause that produced the inflammation that you saw in that boy's leg on that day?" An objection to this question was overruled, and the witness answered: "The exciting cause was the injury received at that day by the kick on the shin-bone." It will be observed that the above question to Dr. Philler calls for his opinion as a medical expert, based in part upon the testimony of the plaintiff, as to what was the proximate cause of the injury to plaintiff's leg. The plaintiff testified to two wounds upon his leg, either of which might have been such proximate cause.

Without taking both of these wounds into consideration, the expert could give no intelligent or reliable opinion as to which of them caused the injury complained of; yet, in the hypothetical question propounded to him, one of these probable causes was excluded from the consideration of the witness, and he was required to give his opinion upon an imperfect and insufficient hypothesis,--one which excluded from his consideration a material fact essential to an intelligent opinion. A consideration by the witness of the wound received by the plaintiff in January being thus prevented, the witness had but one fact upon which to base his opinion, to-wit, the fact that defendant kicked plaintiff on the shin-bone. Based, as it necessarily was, on that fact alone, the opinion of Dr. Philler that the kick caused the injury was inevitable, when, had the proper hypothesis been submitted to him, his opinion might have been different. The answer of Dr. Philler to the hypothetical question put to him may have had, probably did have, a controlling influence with the jury, for they found by their verdict that his opinion was correct. Surely there can be no rule of evidence which will tolerate a hypothetical question to an expert, calling for his opinion in a matter vital to the case, which excludes from his consideration facts already proved by a witness upon whose testimony such hypothetical question is based, when a consideration of such facts by the expert is absolutely essential to enable him to form an intelligent opinion concerning such matter. The objection to the question put to Dr. Philler should have been sustained. The error in permitting the witness to answer the question is material, and necessarily fatal to the judgment.

Certain questions were proposed on behalf of defendant to be submitted to the jury, founded upon the theory that only such damages could be recovered as the defendant might reasonably be supposed to have contemplated as likely to result from his kicking the plaintiff. The court refused to submit such questions to the jury. The ruling was correct. The rule of damages in actions for torts was held in *Brown v. Railway Co.*, to be that the wrongdoer is liable for all injuries resulting directly from the wrongful act, whether they could or could not have been foreseen by him. The chief justice and the writer of this opinion dissented from the judgment in that case, chiefly because we were of the opinion that the complaint stated a cause of action *ex contractu,* and not *ex delicto,* and hence that a different rule of damages--the rule here contended for -- was applicable. We did not question that the rule in actions for tort was correctly stated. That case rules this on the question of damages. The remaining errors assigned are upon the rulings of the court on objections to testimony. These rulings are not very likely to be repeated on another trial, and are not of sufficient importance to require a review of them on this appeal. The judgment of the circuit court must be reversed, and the cause will be remanded for a new trial.

Coblyn v. Kennedy's Inc., 359 Mass. 319 (1971)

This case involved the intentional tort of false imprisonment. Please consider the following:

- *What happened?*

- *How was the plaintiff detained?*

- *How was the plaintiff injured?*

- *What is defendant's argument? How does the court respond?*

- *Explain the court's discussion as to whether there were "reasonable grounds" for the detention.*

- *Explain the court's discussion regarding using an objective, rather than a subjective, standard.*

Opinion

This is an action of tort for false imprisonment. At the close of the evidence the defendants filed a motion for directed verdicts which was denied. The jury returned verdicts for the plaintiff in the sum of $12,500. The case is here on the defendants' exceptions to the denial of their motion and to the refusal of the trial judge to give certain requested instructions to the jury.

We state the pertinent evidence most favorable to the plaintiff. On March 5, 1965, the plaintiff went to Kennedy's, Inc. (Kennedy's), a store in Boston. He was seventy years of age and about five feet four inches in height. He was wearing a woolen shirt, which was 'open at the neck,' a topcoat and a hat. '(A)round his neck' he wore an ascot which he had 'purchased previously at Filenes.' He proceeded to the second floor of Kennedy's to purchase a sport coat. He removed his hat, topcoat and ascot, putting the ascot in his pocket. After purchasing a sport coat and leaving it for alterations, he put on his hat and coat and walked downstairs. Just prior to exiting through the outside door of the store, he stopped, took the ascot out of his pocket, put it around his neck, and knotted it. The knot was visible 'above the lapels of his shirt.' The only stop that the plaintiff made on the first floor was immediately in front of the exit in order to put on his ascot.

Just as the plaintiff stepped out of the door, the defendant Goss, an employee, 'loomed up' in front of him with his hand up and said: 'Stop. Where did you get that scarf?' The plaintiff responded, 'Why?' Goss firmly grasped the plaintiff's arm and said: 'You better go back and see the manager.' Another employee was standing next to him. Eight or ten other people were standing around and were staring at the plaintiff. The plaintiff then said, 'Yes, I'll go back in the store' and proceeded to do so. As he and Goss went upstairs to the second floor, the plaintiff paused twice because of chest and back pains. After reaching the second floor, the salesman from whom he had purchased the cost recognized him and asked what the trouble was. The plaintiff then asked: 'Why 'these two gentlemen stop me?'' The salesman confirmed that the plaintiff had purchased a sport coat and that the ascot belonged to him. The salesman became alarmed by the plaintiff's appearance and the store nurse was called. She brought the plaintiff into the nurse's room and gave him a soda mint tablet. As a direct result of the emotional upset caused by the incident, the plaintiff was hospitalized and treated for a 'myocardial infarct.'

Initially, the defendants contend that as a matter of law the plaintiff was not falsely imprisoned. They argue that no unlawful restraint was imposed by either force or threat upon the plaintiff's freedom of movement. However, 'the law is well settled that 'any genuine restraint is sufficient to constitute an imprisonment' and 'any demonstration of physical power which, to all appearances, can be avoided only by submission, operates as effectually to constitute an imprisonment, if submitted to, as if any amount of force had been exercised.' 'If a man is restrained of his personal liberty by fear of a personal difficulty, that amounts to a false imprisonment' within the legal meaning of such term.'

We think it is clear that there was sufficient evidence of unlawful restraint to submit this question to the jury. Just as the plaintiff had stepped out of the door of the store, the defendant Goss stopped him, firmly grasped his arm and told him that he had 'better go back and see the manager.' There was another employee at his side. The plaintiff was an elderly man and there were other people standing around staring at him. Considering the plaintiff's age and his heart condition, it is hardly to be expected that with one employee in front of him firmly grasping his arm and another at his side the plaintiff could do other than comply with Goss's 'request' that he go back and see the manager. The physical restraint imposed upon the plaintiff when Goss grasped the plaintiff's arm readily distinguishes this case from *Sweeney v. F. W. Woolworth Co.*, relied upon by the defendants.

In addition, as this court observed in the Jacques case, the 'honesty and veracity (of the plaintiff) had been openly challenged. If she had gone out before (exonerating herself), her departure well might have been interpreted by the lookers on as an admission of guilt, or of circumstances from which guilt might be inferred. The situation was in the control of the defendant. The restraint or duress

imposed by the mode of investigation the jury could say was for the accomplishment of the defendant's purpose, even if no threats of public exposure or of arrest
were made, and no physical restraint of (the plaintiff) was attempted.' For cases
in other jurisdictions, where the evidence tended to support the tort of false imprisonment.

The defendants next contend that the detention of the plaintiff was sanctioned by [a statute that] provides as follows: 'In an action for false arrest or false
imprisonment brought by any person by reason of having been detained for questioning on or in the immediate vicinity of the premises of a merchant, if such
person was detained in a reasonable manner and for not more than a reasonable
length of time by a person authorized to make arrests or by the merchant or his
agent or servant authorized for such purpose and if there were reasonable grounds
to believe that the person so detained was committing or attempting to commit
larceny of goods for sale on such premises, it shall be a defence to such action. If
such goods had not been purchased and were concealed on or amongst the be-
longings of a person so detained it shall be presumed that there were reasonable
grounds for such belief.'

The defendants argue in accordance with the conditions imposed in the statute that the plaintiff was detained in a reasonable manner for a reasonable length
of time and that Goss had reasonable grounds for believing that the plaintiff was
attempting to commit larceny of goods held for sale.

It is conceded that the detention was for a reasonable length of time. We need
not decide whether the detention was effected in a reasonable manner for we are
of opinion that there were no reasonable grounds for believing that the plaintiff
was committing larceny and, therefore, he should not have been detained at all.
However, we observe that Goss's failure to identify himself as an employee of
Kennedy's and to disclose the reasons for his inquiry and actions, coupled with
the physical restraint in a public place imposed upon the plaintiff, an elderly man,
who had exhibited no aggressive intention to depart, could be said to constitute
an unreasonable method by which to effect detention.

The pivotal question before us as in most cases of this character is whether the evidence shows that there were reasonable grounds for the detention. At common law in an action for false imprisonment, the defence of probable cause, as measured by the prudent and cautious man standard, was available to a merchant. In enacting [the statute], the Legislature inserted the words, 'reasonable grounds.' Historically, the words 'reasonable grounds' and 'probable cause' have been given the same meaning by the courts. In the case of *United States v. Walker,* it was said: "Probable cause' and 'reasonable grounds' are concepts having virtually the same meaning.' The following cases have expressly stated that the words may be used interchangeably and without distinction. In the case of *Lukas v. J. C. Penney Co.*, the Oregon Supreme Court construed the meaning of the words 'reasonable grounds' in its 'shoplifting statute' as having the same meaning as they have in a statute authorizing arrest without a warrant and applied the probable cause standard to the facts before it.

The defendants assert that the judge improperly instructed the jury in stating that 'grounds are reasonable when there is a basis which would appear to the reasonably prudent, cautious, intelligent person.' In their brief, they argue that the 'prudent and cautious man rule' is an objective standard and requires a more rigorous and restrictive standard of conduct than is contemplated by [the statute]. The defendants' requests for instructions, in effect, state that the proper test is a subjective one, whether the defendant Goss had an honest and strong suspicion that the plaintiff was committing or attempting to commit larceny.

We do not agree. As we have attempted to show, the words 'reasonable grounds' and 'probable cause' have traditionally been accorded the same meaning. In the case of *Terry v. Ohio*, involving the question whether a police officer must have probable cause within the Fourth Amendment to 'stop-and-frisk' a suspected individual, the Supreme Court of the United States held that the 'probable cause' requirement of the Fourth Amendment applies to a 'stop-and-frisk' and that a 'stop-and-frisk' must 'be judged against an objective standard: would the facts available to the officer at the moment 'warrant a man of reasonable caution in the belief' that the action taken was appropriate? Anything less would invite intrusions upon constitutionally guaranteed rights based on nothing more substantial than inarticulate hunches, a result this Court has consistently refused to sanction.'

If we adopt the subjective test as suggested by the defendants, the individual's right to liberty and freedom of movement would become subject to the 'honest suspicion' of a shopkeeper based on his own 'inarticulate hunches' without regard to any discernible facts. In effect, the result would be to afford the merchant even greater authority than that given to a police officer. In view of the well-established meaning of the words 'reasonable grounds' we believe that the Legislature intended to give these words their traditional meaning. This seems to us a valid conclusion since the Legislature has permitted an individual to be detained for a 'reasonable length of time.' This would be at least analogous to a 'stop' within the meaning of the *Terry* case.

We also note that an objective standard is the criterion for determining probable cause or reasonable grounds in malicious prosecution and false arrest cases. We see no valid reason to depart from this precedent in regard to cases involving false imprisonment.

Applying the standard of reasonable grounds as measured by the reasonably prudent man test to the evidence in the instant case, we are of opinion that the evidence warranted the conclusion that Goss was not reasonably justified in believing that the plaintiff was engaged in shoplifting. There was no error in denying the motion for directed verdicts and in the refusal to give the requested instructions.

Agis v. Howard Johnson Co., 371 Mass. 140 (1976)

This case involved the tort of intentional infliction of emotional distress. Consider the following:

- *What is the issue?*

- *What are the facts?*

- *What is the rationale for only permitting the tort of intentional infliction of emotion distress when there is resulting physical injury?*

- *What is the rationale for extending the tort to cases without physical injury?*

- *What are the elements of the tort?*

Opinion

This case raises the issue, expressly reversed in *George v. Jordan Marsh Co.*, whether a cause of action exists in this Commonwealth for the intentional or reckless infliction of severe emotional distress without resulting bodily injury. Counts 1 and 2 of this action were brought by the plaintiff Debra Agis against the Howard Johnson Company and Roger Dionne, manager of the restaurant in which she was employed, to recover damages for mental anguish and emotional distress allegedly caused by her summary dismissal from such employment. Counts 3 and 4 were brought by her husband, James Agis, against both defendants for loss of the services, love, affection and companionship of his wife. This case is before us on the plaintiffs' appeal from the dismissal of their complaint.

Briefly, the allegations in the plaintiffs' complaint, which we accept as true for purposes of ruling on this motion, *Hub Theatres, Inc. v. Massachusetts Port Authority*, are the following. Debra Agis was employed by the Howard Johnson Company as a waitress in a restaurant known as the Ground Round. On or about May 23, 1975, the defendant Dionne notified all waitresses that a meeting would be held at 3 P.M. that day. At the meeting, he informed the waitresses that 'there was some stealing going on,' but that the identity of the person or persons responsible was not known, and that, until the person or persons responsible were discovered, he would begin firing all the present waitresses in alphabetical order, starting with the letter 'A.' Dionne then fired Debra Agis.

The complaint alleges that, as a result of this incident, Mrs. Agis became greatly upset, began to cry, sustained emotional distress, mental anguish, and loss of wages and earnings. It further alleges that the actions of the defendants were reckless, extreme, outrageous and intended to cause emotional distress and anguish. In addition, the complaint states that the defendants knew or should have known that their actions would cause such distress.

The defendants moved to dismiss the complaint pursuant to Mass.R.Civ.P. 12(b)(6) on the ground that, even if true, the plaintiffs' allegations fail to state a claim upon which relief can be granted because damages for emotional distress are not compensable absent resulting physical injury. The judge allowed the motion, and the plaintiffs appealed.

Our discussion of whether a cause of action exists for the intentional or reckless infliction of severe emotional distress without resulting bodily injury starts with our decision in *George v. Jordan Marsh Co.* While in that case we found it unnecessary to address the precise question raised here, we did summarize the history of actions for emotional distress and concluded that the law of the Commonwealth should be, and is, 'that one who, without a privilege to do so, by extreme and outrageous conduct intentionally causes severe emotional distress to another, with bodily harm resulting from such distress, is subject to liability . . .' The question whether such liability should be extended to cases in which there is no resulting bodily injury was 'left until it arises,' and that question has arisen here.

In the *George* case, we discussed in depth the policy considerations underlying the recognition of a cause of action for intentional infliction of severe emotional distress with resulting physical injury, and we concluded that the difficulties presented in allowing such an action were outweighed by the unfair and illogical consequences of the denial of recognition of such an independent tort. In so doing, we examined the persuasive authority then recognizing such a cause of action, and we placed considerable reliance on the Restatement (Second) of Torts. Our examination of the policies underlying the extension of that cause of action to cases where there has been no bodily injury, and our review of the judicial precedent and the Restatement in this regard, lead us to conclude that such extension is both warranted and desirable.

The most often cited argument for refusing to extend the cause of action for intentional or reckless infliction of emotional distress to cases where there has been no physical injury is the difficulty of proof and the danger of fraudulent or frivolous claims. There has been a concern that 'mental anguish, standing alone, is too subtle and speculative to be measured by any known legal standard,' that 'mental anguish and its consequences are so intangible and peculiar and vary so much with the individual that they cannot reasonably be anticipated,' that a wide door might 'be opened not only to fictitious claims but to litigation over trivialities and mere bad manners as well,' and that there can be no objective measurement of the extent or the existence of emotional distress. There is a fear that '(i)t is easy to assert a claim of mental anguish and very hard to disprove it.'

While we are not unconcerned with these problems, we believe that 'the problems presented are not . . . insuperable' and that 'administrative difficulties do not justify the denial of relief for serious invasions of mental and emotional tranquility . . .' 'That some claims may be spurious should not compel those who administer justice to shut their eyes to serious wrongs and let them go without being brought to account. It is the function of courts and juries to determine whether claims are valid or false. This responsibility should not be shunned merely because the task may be difficult to perform.'

Furthermore, the distinction between the difficulty which juries may encounter in determining liability and assessing damages where no physical injury occurs and their performance of that same task where there has been resulting physical harm may be greatly overstated. 'The jury is ordinarily in a better position . . . to determine whether outrageous conduct results in mental distress than whether that distress in turn results in physical injury. From their own experience jurors are aware of the extent and character of the disagreeable emotions that may result from the defendant's conduct, but a difficult medical question is presented when it must be determined if emotional distress resulted in physical injury. . . . Greater proof that mental suffering occurred is found in the defendant's conduct designed to bring it about than in physical injury that may or may not have resulted therefrom.' We are thus unwilling to deny the existence of this cause of action merely because there may be difficulties of proof. Instead, we believe 'the door to recovery should be opened but narrowly and with due caution.'

In light of what we have said, we hold that one who, by extreme and outrageous conduct and without privilege, causes severe emotional distress to another is subject to liability for such emotional distress even though no bodily harm may result. However, in order for a plaintiff to prevail in a case for liability under this tort, four elements must be established. It must be shown (1) that the actor intended to inflict emotional distress or that he knew or should have known that emotional distress was the likely result of his conduct; (2) that the conduct was 'extreme and outrageous,' was 'beyond all possible bounds of decency' and was 'utterly intolerable in a civilized community'; (3) that the actions of the defendant were the cause of the plaintiff's distress; and (4) that the emotional distress sustained by the plaintiff was 'severe' and of a nature 'that no reasonable man could be expected to endure it.' These requirements are 'aimed at limiting frivolous suits and avoiding litigation in situations where only bad manners and mere hurt feelings are involved,' and we believe they are a 'realistic safeguard against false claims. . .'

Testing the plaintiff Debra Agis's complaint by the rules stated above, we hold that she makes out a cause of action and that her complaint is therefore legally sufficient. While many of her allegations are not particularly well stated, we believe that the '(p)laintiff has alleged facts and circumstances which reasonably could lead the trier of fact to conclude that defendant's conduct was extreme and outrageous, having a severe and traumatic effect upon plaintiff's emotional tranquility.' Because reasonable men could differ on these issues, we believe that 'it is for the jury, subject to the control of the court,' to determine whether there should be liability in this case. While the judge was not in error in dismissing the complaint under the then state of the law, we believe that, in light of what we have said, the judgment must be reversed and the plaintiff Debra Agis must be given an opportunity to prove the allegations which she has made.

Counts 3 and 4 of the complaint are brought by James Agis seeking relief for loss of consortium as a result of the mental distress and anguish suffered by his wife Debra. There is no question that an action for loss of consortium by either spouse may be maintained in this Commonwealth where such loss is shown to arise from personal injury to one spouse caused by the negligence of a third person. The question before us is whether an action for loss of consortium may be maintained where the acts complained of are intentional, and where the injuries to the spouse are emotional rather than physical.

Traditionally, where the right to sue for loss of consortium has been recognized, intentional invasions of the marriage relationship such as alienation of affections or adultery have been held to give rise to this cause of action. We see no reason not to apply the same rule to the tort of intentional or reckless infliction of severe emotional distress. Similarly, the fact that there is no physical injury should not bar the plaintiff's claim. In the Diaz case, we hinted that 'psychological injury' could provide the basis for a consortium action. In addition, the underlying purpose of such an action is to compensate for the loss of the companionship, affection and sexual enjoyment of one's spouse, and it is clear that these can be lost as a result of psychological or emotional injury as well as from actual physical harm. Accordingly, we hold that, where a person has a cause of action for intentional or reckless infliction of severe emotional distress, his or her spouse also has a cause of action for loss of consortium arising out of that distress.

The judgment entered in the Superior Court dismissing the plaintiffs' complaint is reversed.

Butterfield v. Forrester, 103 Eng. Rep. 926 (King's Bench 1809)

Butterfield v. Forrester *was an early negligence case. Please pay attention to how the court described the care that the plaintiff should have exercised. Consider the following:*

- *What does it mean to be careful?*

- *What difference would it have made had the plaintiff been careful?*

- *How did the plaintiff deviate from the standard of care?*

Opinion

This was an action . . . for obstructing a highway, by means of which obstruction the plaintiff, who was riding along the road, was thrown down with his horse, and injured, &c. At the trial before Bayley J. at Derby, it appeared that the defendant, for the purpose of making some repairs to his house, which was close by the road side at one end of the town, had put up a pole across this part of the road, a free passage being left by another branch or street in the same direction. That the plaintiff left a public house not far distant from the place in question at 8 o'clock in the evening in August, when they were just beginning to light candles, but while there was light enough left to discern the obstruction at 100 yards distance: and the witness, who proved this, said that if the plaintiff had not been riding very hard he might have observed and avoided it: the plaintiff however, who was riding violently, did not observe it, but rode against it, and fell with his horse and was much hurt in consequence of the accident; and there was no evidence of his being intoxicated at the time. On this evidence Bayley J. directed the jury, that if a person riding with reasonable and ordinary care could have seen and avoided the obstruction; and if they were satisfied that the plaintiff was riding along the street extremely hard, and without ordinary care, they should find a verdict for the defendant: which they accordingly did. ...

Bayley J. The plaintiff was proved to be riding as fast as his horse could go, and this was through the streets of Derby. If he had used ordinary care he must have seen the obstruction; so that the accident appeared to happen entirely from his own fault.

Lord Ellenborough C.J. A party is not to cast himself upon an obstruction which has been made by the fault of another, and avail himself of it, if he do not himself use common and ordinary caution to be in the right. In cases of persons riding upon what is considered to be the wrong side of the road, that would not authorise another purposely to ride up against them. One person being in fault will not dispense with another's using ordinary care for himself. Two things must concur to support this action, an obstruction in the road by the fault of the defendant, and no want of ordinary care to avoid it on the part of the plaintiff.

United States v. Carroll Towing, 159 F.2d 169 (2d Cir. 1947)

While reading Justice Learned Hand's opinion, consider the following:

- *It's confusing, but suffice that there was an accident concerning a barge.*

- *The issue concerns the sufficiency of the lines tying the barge to the pier.*

- *And, whether a "bargee" should have been present on the barge to reduce "sinking damages".*

- *What does this mean? "For this reason, the question arises whether a barge owner is slack in the care of his barge if the bargee is absent."*

- *What is the Hand Formula? What does the Hand Formula look like when applied to the facts of this case?*

- *How did the barge owner breach its duty of care?*

- *How did the breach cause the accident?*

Opinion

These appeals concern the sinking of the barge, 'Anna C,' on January 4, 1944, off Pier 51, North River. …

The tide and wind carried down the six barges, still holding together, until the 'Anna C' fetched up against a tanker, lying on the north side of the pier below- Pier 51- whose propeller broke a hole in her at or near her bottom. Shortly there- after: i.e., at about 2:15 P.M., she careened, dumped her cargo of flour and sank. The tug, 'Grace,' owned by the Grace Line, and the 'Carroll,' came to the help of the flotilla after it broke loose; and, as both had syphon pumps on board, they could have kept the 'Anna C' afloat, had they learned of her condition; but the bargee had left her on the evening before, and nobody was on board to observe that she was leaking.

[Was the absence of the bargeman on the 'Anna C' a breach of the duty of care? Was it negligent?]

On the other hand, if the bargee had been on board, and had done his duty to his employer, he would have gone below at once, examined the injury, and called for help from the 'Carroll' and the Grace Line tug. Moreover, it is clear that these tugs could have kept the barge afloat, until they had safely beached her, and saved her cargo. This would have avoided what we shall call the 'sinking damages.' Thus, if it was a failure in the Conner Company's proper care of its own barge, for the bargee to be absent, the company can recover only one third of the 'sink- ing' damages from the Carroll Company and one third from the Grace Line. For this reason the question arises whether a barge owner is slack in the care of his barge if the bargee is absent.

*   *   *

It appears ... that there is no general rule to determine when the absence of a bargee or other attendant will make the owner of the barge liable for injuries to other vessels if she breaks away from her moorings. ...

It becomes apparent why there can be no such general rule, when we consider the grounds for such a liability. Since there are occasions when every vessel will break from her moorings, and since, if she does, she becomes a menace to those about her; the owner's duty, as in other similar situations, to provide against resulting injuries is a function of three variables: **(1) The probability that she will break away; (2) the gravity of the resulting injury, if she does; (3) the burden of adequate precautions.** Possibly it serves to bring this notion into relief to state it in algebraic terms: if the probability be called P; the injury, L; and the burden, B; liability depends upon whether B is less than L multiplied by P: i.e., whether B less than PL.

Applied to the situation at bar, the likelihood that a barge will break from her fasts and the damage she will do, vary with the place and time; for example, if a storm threatens, the danger is greater; so it is, if she is in a crowded harbor where moored barges are constantly being shifted about. On the other hand, the barge must not be the bargee's prison, even though he lives aboard; he must go ashore at times. We need not say whether, even in such crowded waters as New York Harbor a bargee must be aboard at night at all; it may be that the custom is otherwise, as Ward, J., supposed in '*The Kathryn B. Guinan*,' and that, if so, the situation is one where custom should control. We leave that question open; but we hold that it is not in all cases a sufficient answer to a bargee's absence without excuse, during working hours, that he has properly made fast his barge to a pier, when he leaves her. In the case at bar the bargee left at five o'clock in the afternoon of January 3rd, and the flotilla broke away at about two o'clock in the afternoon of the following day, twenty-one hours afterwards. The bargee had been away all the time, and we hold that his fabricated story was affirmative evidence that he had no excuse for his absence. At the locus in quo- especially during the short January days and in the full tide of war activity- barges were being constantly 'drilled' in and out. Certainly it was not beyond reasonable expectation that, with the inevitable haste and bustle, the work might not be done with adequate care. In such circumstances we hold- and it is all that we do hold- that it was a fair requirement that the Conners Company should have a bargee aboard (unless he had some excuse for his absence), during the working hours of daylight.

Warner v. Santa Catalina Island Co., 44 Cal. 2d 310 (1955)

This negligence case involved consideration of the issue of causation. Consider the following:

- *What is the nature of the accident?*

- *What did the trial court decide?*

- *How does the court define "ordinary care"?*

- *How did the defendant breach its duty of care? In other words, what did the defendant do wrong? What should the defendant have done?*

- *How did the breach cause the injury to the plaintiff?*

Opinion

… Plaintiff, on July 18, 1947, was at a shooting gallery watching one of his party shoot at a target when a particle of a bullet ricocheted and entered his eye, causing him to lose the sight therein. The shooting gallery was owned and operated by Rushmore and Eckley; Nordlund, as their employee, was the actual operator of the concession. Cartridges containing bullets known as "Kant-Splash," used in the guns from which customers fired at various targets in the gallery, were manufactured by defendant Olin Industries.

Plaintiff alleged that Olin represented to the purchasers and users of its "Kant-Splash" bullets that they were designed for use in short range shooting galleries and to disintegrate upon striking a metal target or backstop; that Olin was negligent in the manufacture, testing and inspection of the bullets, as a result of which he was injured.

The record shows that there was a metal backstop the width of the gallery at the back .... Plaintiff was approximately 40 feet from the backstop at the time he received his injury.

... Plaintiff alleged that a portion of the Kant-Splash bullet caused his injury and there is no evidence to the contrary.

Plaintiff's evidence showed that defendant had been manufacturing Kant-Splash cartridges for use in shooting galleries since 1944; that underneath the name Kant-Splash on the package of cartridges appeared the following words: "These cartridges have special synthetic greased bullets designed to disintegrate upon striking a metal target or backstop"; that the bullets were advertised to the trade as those which would disintegrate into small particles with "splash-backs" reduced to an absolute minimum.

Mr. Doughan, the manager in charge of sales and distribution of the ammunition manufactured by defendant, testified (by deposition) that he was aware of the fact that when customers ordered shooting gallery cartridges, "particularly Kant-Splash" they were ordered so that they would disintegrate into powder or dust.

                    *   *   *

Mr. Frost, the manager of the Products Service Division for the defendant, testified (by deposition) that the only way of testing a bullet was after its manufacture; that out of 10,000 bullets "probably 24" would be tested; that 200,000 Kant-Splash bullets were made per day; that testing took place once a week; that the bullets tested were not "lotted" but were selected at random from the production; that the spatter-back tests were on approximately 100 bullets per week...

                    *   *   *

The trial court granted defendant's motion for a nonsuit because it was of the opinion that defendant was not guilty of any negligence in either the manufacture or inspection of its Kant-Splash cartridges; that no duty existed on defendant's part to warn the gallery operators of any inherent dangers in the cartridges; that even if such a duty existed, the defendant could not be expected to "reasonably anticipate the action of the gallery operators in continuing to operate that gallery as they did with full knowledge that these bullets did splash back or ricochet, and that they were inherently dangerous in the manner they were used in that particular gallery." **It was concluded [by the trial court] that the failure of defendant to give notice to the gallery operators "if there was any inherent danger in [the bullets]" was not a proximate cause of the plaintiff's injuries.**

*   *   *

A summary of plaintiff's evidence shows that defendant's Kant-Splash bullets were designed for, and sold for use in short range shooting galleries; that all testing of the bullets was done under ideal conditions in that a smooth, unpitted backstop was used; that at no time were any tests made under actual shooting gallery conditions with targets between the person doing the shooting and the backstop; that the test shooting was always done at a 90-degree angle; that no measurement was made of the size of the particles which spattered back or ricocheted from the metal backstop; that there was no way of ascertaining from which machine a bullet came; that even when tests were made under the above stated ideal conditions, each test showed a spatter-back which extended 30 to 40 feet from the backstop. Plaintiff's evidence showed that defendant sold its cartridges on the theory that when the bullets hit a metal surface, the bullets would disintegrate into powder or dust.

All persons are required to use ordinary care to prevent others being injured as the result of their acts; **ordinary care has been defined as that degree of care which people of ordinarily prudent behavior could be reasonably expected to exercise under the circumstances of a given case.** In other words, the care required must be in proportion to the danger to be avoided and the consequences that might reasonably be anticipated

The risk incident to dealing with fire, firearms, explosive or highly inflammable matters, corrosive or otherwise dangerous or noxious fluids requires a great deal of care to be exercised. In other words, the standard of care required of the reasonable person when dealing with such dangerous articles is so great that a slight deviation therefrom will constitute negligence.

There can be no doubt but that ammunition used in guns has propensities dangerous to human life. Plaintiff's evidence also established that defendant knew its ammunition was to be used in shooting galleries, that those galleries were usually found in crowded places; that the shooting was done in close proximity to other persons; that defendant's cartridges spattered back even though the testing was done under ideal conditions unlike those prevalent in most shooting galleries; that defendant's tests showed that its cartridges did not disintegrate into powder or dust, but into particles which ricocheted as far as 40 feet, the longest length of any shooting gallery. From this evidence and other evidence found in the record, the jury could have legitimately inferred that defendant was guilty of negligence in manufacturing and inspecting a product dangerous to human life in that it had deviated from the great degree of care required of one manufacturing an explosive article.

*   *   *

The issue of proximate cause is essentially one of fact. From the evidence, the trier of fact could have inferred that defendant knew of the dangerous propensities of its cartridges; that it knew that its product did not disintegrate into powder or dust upon striking even a smooth metal surface; that it knew the dangerous character of the cartridges became intensified when a pitted surface was present in the metal backstop; that defendant knew, or could in the exercise of reasonable care have known, that shooting gallery conditions were different from the ideal conditions under which its tests were conducted. ...

The danger of spattering, or ricocheting particles was precisely the danger defendant sought to minimize with its specially designed Kant-Splash bullets and any conduct tending to increase that danger should have been, in the exercise of reasonable care, foreseeable by defendant and the jury could have concluded that its tests should have been conducted with the end to be achieved in view.

*   *   *

In so doing it appears as heretofore set forth that plaintiff has made out a case for defendant's negligence as the proximate cause of his injury and that defendant's argument would be a matter of defense on the trial of the issues of negligence and proximate cause.

The judgment is reversed.

Petition of Kinsman Transit Co., 338 F.2d 708 (2d Cir. 1964) and Dellwo v. Pearson, 259 Minn. 452 (1961)

These two cases deal with causation in negligence cases. The first addresses a string of accidents on the Buffalo River all caused in fact by the unmooring of one ship. The question was whether the negligent actor with regard to that one ship could be held liable for everything that happened downstream. Resolution of this question required addressing two points: (1) did the owner of the ship owe a duty to those downstream, that is were those downstream "foreseeable plaintiffs" within the meaning of Palsgraf v. Long Island Railroad, *and (2) was the owner responsible for unforeseen consequences downstream, meaning does foreseeability have a role to play in proximate causation in negligence? Please be able to discuss the court's resolution of these two points.*

The court in the second case Dellwo v. Pearson *addresses the notion of foreseeability in proximate causation more directly. What does the court have to say on the matter? What does this mean "Consequences which follow in unbroken sequence, without an intervening efficient cause, from the original negligent act, are natural and proximate; and for such consequences the original wrongdoer is responsible, even though he could not have foreseen the particular results which did follow."*

Petition of Kinsman Transit Co., 338 F.2d 708 (2d Cir. 1964)

Opinion

[This case] arose out of a series of misadventures on a navigable portion of the Buffalo River during the night of January 21, 1959. ...

We see little similarity between the *Palsgraf* case and the situation before us. The point of *Palsgraf* was that the appearance of the newspaper-wrapped package gave no notice that its dislodgement could do any harm save to itself and those nearby, and this by impact, perhaps with consequent breakage, and not by explosion. In contrast, a ship insecurely moored in a fast flowing river is a known danger not only to herself but to the owners of all other ships and structures downriver, and to persons upon them. No one would dream of saying that a shipowner who 'knowingly and wilfully' failed to secure his ship at a pier on such a river 'would not have threatened' persons and owners of property downstream in some manner. The shipowner and the wharfinger in this case having thus owed a duty of care to all within the reach of the ship's known destructive power, the impossibility of advance identification of the particular person who would be hurt is without legal consequence.

Similarly the foreseeable consequences of the City's failure to raise the bridge were not limited to the Shiras and the Tewksbury. Collision plainly created a danger that the bridge towers might fall onto adjoining property, and the crash of two uncontrolled lake vessels, one 425 feet and the other 525 feet long, into a bridge over a swift ice-ridden stream, with a channel only 177 feet wide, could well result in a partial damming that would flood property upstream. As to the City also, it is useful to consider, by way of contrast, Chief Judge Cardozo's statement that the Long Island would not have been liable to Mrs. Palsgraf had the guard wilfully thrown the package down. If the City had deliberately kept the bridge closed in the face of the onrushing vessels, taking the risk that they might not come so far, no one would give house-room to a claim that it 'owed no duty' to those who later suffered from the flooding. Unlike Mrs. Palsgraf, they were within the area of hazard. ...

Since all the claimants here met the *Palsgraf* requirement of being persons to whom the actors owed a 'duty of care,' we are not obliged to reconsider whether that case furnishes as useful a standard for determining the boundaries of liability in admiralty for negligent conduct .... But this does not dispose of the alternative argument that the manner in which several of the claimants were harmed, particularly by flood damage, was unforeseeable and that recovery for this may not be had- whether the argument is put in the forthright form that unforeseeable damages are not recoverable or is concealed under a formula of lack of 'proximate cause.' ...

Foreseeability of danger is necessary to render conduct negligent; where as here the damage was caused by just those forces whose existence required the exercise of greater care than was taken- the current, the ice, and the physical mass of the Shiras, the incurring of consequences other and greater than foreseen does not make the conduct less culpable or provide a reasoned basis for insulation. The oft encountered argument that failure to limit liability to foreseeable consequences may subject the defendant to a loss wholly out of proportion to his fault seems scarcely consistent with the universally accepted rule that the defendant takes the plaintiff as he finds him and will be responsible for the full extent of the injury even though a latent susceptibility of the plaintiff renders this far more serious than could reasonably have been anticipated.

The weight of authority in this country rejects the limitation of damages to consequences foreseeable at the time of the negligent conduct when the consequences are 'direct,' and the damage, although other and greater than expectable, is of the same general sort that was risked. … Other American courts, purporting to apply a test of foreseeability to damages, extend that concept to such unforeseen lengths as to raise serious doubt whether the concept is meaningful ….

We see no reason why an actor engaging in conduct which entails a large risk of small damage and a small risk of other and greater damage, of the same general sort, from the same forces, and to the same class of persons, should be relieved of responsibility for the latter simply because the chance of its occurrence, if viewed alone, may not have been large enough to require the exercise of care. By hypothesis, the risk of the lesser harm was sufficient to render his disregard of it actionable; the existence of a less likely additional risk that the very forces against whose action he was required to guard would produce other and greater damage than could have been reasonably anticipated should inculpate him further rather than limit his liability. This does not mean that the careless actor will always be held for all damages for which the forces that he risked were a cause in fact. Somewhere a point will be reached when courts will agree that the link has become too tenuous- that what is claimed to be consequence is only fortuity. … Where the line will be drawn will vary from age to age; as society has come to rely increasingly on insurance and other methods of loss-sharing, the point may lie further off than a century ago. … We go only so far as to hold that where, as here, the damages resulted from the same physical forces whose existence required the exercise of greater care than was displayed and were of the same general sort that was expectable, unforeseeability of the exact developments and of the extent of the loss will not limit liability. Other fact situations can be dealt with when they arise.

*   *   *

Dellwo v. Pearson, 259 Minn. 452 (1961)

Opinion

This case arises out of a personal injury to Jeanette E. Dellwo, one of the plaintiffs. She and her husband, the other plaintiff, were fishing on one of Minnesota's numerous and beautiful lakes by trolling at a low speed with about 40 to 50 feet of line trailing behind the boat. Defendant, a 12-year-old boy, operating a boat with an outboard motor, crossed behind plaintiffs' boat. Just at this time Mrs. Dellwo felt a jerk on her line which suddenly was pulled out very rapidly. The line was knotted to the spool of the reel so that when it had run out the fishing rod was pulled downward, the reel hit the side of the boat, the reel came apart, and part of it flew through the lens of Mrs. Dellwo's glasses and injured her eye. Both parties then proceeded to a dock where inspection of defendant's motor disclosed 2 to 3 feet of fishing line wound about the propeller.

The case was fully tried to the court and jury and submitted to the jury upon instructions which, in so far as relevant here, instructed the jury that: (1) In considering the matter of negligence the duty to which defendant is held is modified because he is a child, a child not being held to the same standard of conduct as an adult and being required to exercise only that degree of care which ordinarily is exercised by children of like age, mental capacity, and experience under the same or similar circumstances; (2) 'A person guilty of negligence is liable for all consequences which might reasonably have been foreseen as likely to result from one's negligent act or omissions under the circumstances; * * *. A wrongdoer is not responsible for a consequence which is merely possible according to occasional experience, but only for a consequence which is probable according to ordinary and usual experience'; and (3) plaintiff could not recover if she was guilty of contributory negligence. Several hours after the jury retired it returned and asked for additional instructions with respect to 'foreseeable responsibility' and 'the responsibility of a youngster compared to a more mature person.' The court thereupon repeated the instructions relating to negligence, the standard of care, and proximate cause, including the language quoted above.

The jury returned a general verdict for defendant, and plaintiffs appeal. Plaintiffs contend that the trial court erred in its instruction that a defendant is not responsible for unforeseen consequences of negligence and in submitting the issue of contributory negligence to the jury.

The instruction of the trial court limiting liability for negligence to foreseeable consequences was a part of the instruction on proximate cause and, in effect, made foreseeability a test of proximate cause.

There is no subject in the field of law upon which more has been written with less elucidation than that of proximate cause. Cases discussing it are legion. It has challenged many of the most able commentators at one time or another. It is generally agreed that there is no simple formula for defining proximate cause, but this is assumed to be a difficulty peculiar to the law, which distinguishes between "proximate cause" and "cause in fact." However, examination of the literature suggests that neither scientists nor philosophers have been more successful than judges in providing a verbal definition for this concept. We can contrast the concept of cause with that of destiny and of chance, we can use it operationally and pragmatically, but we cannot formulate a precise, rigorous, or very satisfactory verbal definition. Cause seems to be one of those elemental concepts that defies refined analysis but is known intuitively to commonsense.

Although a rigorous definition of proximate cause continues to elude us, nevertheless it is clear, in this state at least, that it is not a matter of foreseeability. We are unable now to make any better statement on this issue than that of Mr. Justice Mitchell many years ago. Speaking for this court, he said:

> 'It is laid down in many cases and by some text writers that, in order to warrant a finding that negligence (not wanton) is the proximate cause of an injury, it must appear that the injury was the natural and probable consequence of the negligent act, and that it (the injury) was such as might

or ought, in the light of attending circumstances, to have been anticipated. … This mode of stating the law is misleading, if not positively inaccurate. It confounds and mixes the definition of 'negligence' with that of 'proximate cause.'

'What a man may reasonably anticipate is important, and may be decisive, in determining whether an act is negligent, but is not at all decisive in determining whether that act is the proximate cause of an injury which ensues. If a person had no reasonable ground to anticipate that a particular act would or might result in any injury to anybody, then, of course, the act would not be negligent at all; **but, if the act itself is negligent, then the person guilty of it is equally liable for all its natural and proximate consequences, whether he could have foreseen them or not.** Otherwise expressed, the law is that if the act is one which the party ought, in the exercise of ordinary care, to have anticipated was liable to result in injury to others, then he is liable for any injury proximately resulting from it, although he could not have anticipated the particular injury which did happen. **Consequences which follow in unbroken sequence, without an intervening efficient cause, from the original negligent act, are natural and proximate; and for such consequences the original wrongdoer is responsible, even though he could not have foreseen the particular results which did follow.'**

Although language may be found in some opinions dealing with the specific facts of particular cases that seems to be at variance with the statement of Mr. Justice Mitchell, this court has consistently through the years followed the doctrine thus enunciated. We now reaffirm that the doctrine of the *Christianson* case is still the law of Minnesota and, in the words of Mr. Justice Stone, decline the invitation of this case to add further to the already excessive literature of the law dealing, or attempting to deal, with the problem of proximate cause. It is enough to say that negligence is tested by foresight but proximate cause is determined by hindsight.

It follows that the trial court erred in making foreseeability a test of proximate cause. There can be no question that this was misleading to the jury and therefore prejudicial to the plaintiff, requiring reversal of the judgment.

*   *   *

Ford v. Trident Fisheries Co., 232 Mass. 400 (1919)

This negligence case also involves causation. Keep Palsgraf *in mind while reading it and consider the following:*

- *What is the issue?*

- *What is the claimed carelessness?*

- *What does it mean that the intestate was "connected to this boat for two months"? Why does it matter? How does this impact the defendant's duty of care as to the lack of a railing?*

- *What about the lifeboat? Did the defendant breach its duty of care there?*

- *If there was a breach, was it the* **cause** *of the plaintiff's death? Why or why not? What does the court say?*

Opinion

The plaintiff's intestate was drowned while employed as mate of the defendant's steam trawler, the Long Island. This action is to recover damages for his death.

On December 21, 1916, about 5 o'clock in the afternoon, the vessel left T wharf, Boston, bound for the 'Georges,' which are fishing banks in Massachusetts waters. About 6 o'clock, shortly after passing Boston Light, the plaintiff's intestate, Jerome Ford, came on deck to take charge of his watch as mate of the vessel. He came from the galley in the forecastle and walked aft on the starboard side. As he was ascending a flight of four steps leading from the deck to the pilot house, the vessel rolled and he was thrown overboard. At the time of the accident there was a fresh northwest breeze and the vessel was going before the wind; no cry was heard, no clothing was seen floating in the water, and Ford was not seen by any one from the time he fell overboard.

The negligence relied on was the absence of a guard or rail along the flight of four steps leading from the deck to the pilot house. The intestate 'had been connected with this particular boat for about two months,' as its mate, and during that time the stairs remained in the same condition-with no railing or guard upon them. **The employer was under no duty to the employee to change the obvious conditions of the vessel where the intestate was to perform his work, and the defendant was not negligent in continuing the arrangements as they were when the employment began.**

The plaintiff also contends that the boat which was lowered to pick up the intestate was lashed to the deck instead of being suspended from davits and in order to launch it the lashings had to be cut; that McCue, who manned it, had only one oar and was obliged to scull, instead of rowing as he might have done if he had had two oars. **Even if it be assumed that upon these facts it could have been found the defendant was negligent, there is nothing to show they in any way contributed to Ford's death. He disappeared when he fell from the trawler and it does not appear that if the boat had been suspended from davits and a different method of propelling it had been used he could have been rescued.**

As no evidence of the defendant's negligence is shown the plaintiff cannot recover in this action; it therefore becomes unnecessary to consider whether any sufficient notice was given the defendant or the question of evidence argued by the plaintiff.

*   *   *

Chapter 14: Introduction to Criminal Law

Introduction

Criminal law is the body of law that relates to crime and punishment. In many ways criminal law sets the boundaries of the individual's relationship with the state and other people. If a person crosses one of these boundaries, the state steps in with appropriate punishment. Criminal law generally prohibits conduct perceived as threatening, harmful, or otherwise endangering to the property, health, safety, and moral welfare of other people. Most criminal law is established by statute, which is to say that the laws are enacted by a legislature elected by the people. In contrast to civil law, criminal law is designed to punish and serve as a deterrent to others. In civil law, the emphasis is more on dispute resolution and victim compensation rather than on punishment (except when punitive damages are involved). Criminal procedure, which will be discussed in the next chapter, is the formalized process that the state must follow in order to punish individuals for crimes committed.

The central issue in all of criminal law is *intent*. That is, the requisite state of mind that a criminal defendant must have possessed in order to be properly convicted of a crime. This requirement is sometimes referred to as ***mens rea***, which is Latin for "guilty mind." Black's Law Dictionary defines *mens rea* as follows:

> The state of mind that the prosecution, to secure a conviction, must prove that a defendant had when committing a crime <the mens rea for theft is the intent to deprive the rightful owner of the property>. • Mens rea is the second of two essential elements of every crime at common law, the other being the actus reus. Under the Model Penal Code, the required levels of mens rea — expressed by the adverbs purposely, knowingly, recklessly, and negligently — are termed "culpability requirements."

MENS REA, Black's Law Dictionary (11th ed. 2019)

This chapter will predominantly discuss this idea of criminal intent.

Excerpt from William Blackstone, Commentaries on the Laws of England (ch. II, "The Persons Capable of Committing Crimes")

Here, Blackstone discusses the very essence of criminal law, the necessity of having both a culpable intent ("vicious will") and the commission of an unlawful act as a product of that will. Please note the three types of defects in will that Blackstone discusses at the end of the excerpt. What are they? How do they render a "vicious will" defective? What about the examples that he provides in his concluding sentence? How do they vitiate the required culpable or criminal intent?

Having, in the preceding chapter, considered in general the nature of crime, and punishment, we are next led, in the order of our distribution, to inquire what persons are, or are not, capable of committing crimes; who are exempted from the censures of the law upon the commission of acts, which in other persons would be severely punished. In the process of this inquiry, we must have recourse to particular and special exceptions: for the general rule is, that no person shall be excused from punishment for disobedience to the laws of his country, excepting such as are expressly defined and exempted by the laws themselves.

We have seen that a criminal act is one which affects prejudicially the public; it must also (subject to some few and peculiar exceptions) have proceeded from a guilty mind. So that the several pleas and excuses, which protect the committer of a forbidden act from the punishment which is otherwise annexed thereto, may in general be reduced to this single consideration, the want or defect of will. An involuntary act, as it has no claim to merit, so neither can it induce any guilt: the concurrence of the will, when it has its choice either to do or to avoid the fact in question, being the only thing that renders human action either praiseworthy or culpable. Indeed, to make a complete crime cognisable by human laws, there must be both a will and an act. For though, *in foro conscientiae*, a fixed design or will to do an unlawful act is almost as heinous as the commission of it, yet, as no temporal tribunal can search the heart, or fathom the intentions of the mind, otherwise than as they are demonstrated by outward actions, it therefore cannot punish for that which it cannot know. For which reason in all temporal jurisdictions an overt act, or some evidence of an intended crime, is necessary in order to demonstrate the depravity of the will, before the accused is liable to punishment. And, as a vicious will without a vicious act is no civil crime, so, on the other hand, an unwarrantable act without a vicious will may be no crime at all. So that to constitute a crime against human laws, there must in almost all cases be, first, a vicious will; and secondly, an unlawful act consequent upon such vicious will.

Now there are three cases, in which the will does not join with the act: **1.** Where there is a defect of understanding. For where there is no discernment, there is no choice; and where there is no choice, there can be no act of the will, which is nothing else but a determination of one's choice to do or to abstain from a particular action: he, therefore, who has no understanding, can have no will to guide his conduct. **2.** Where there is understanding and will sufficient, residing in the party; but not called forth and exerted at the time of the action done; as where an offence is committed by mischance or ignorance. Here the will sits neuter; and neither concurs with the act, nor disagrees to it. **3.** Where the action is constrained by some outward force and violence. Here the will counteracts the deed; and is so far from concurring with, that it loathes and disagrees to, what the man is obliged to perform. It will be the business of the present chapter, briefly to consider the several species of defect in will, as they fall under some one or other of these general heads: as infancy, idiocy, lunacy, and intoxication, which fall under the first class; misfortune, and ignorance, which may be referred to the second; and compulsion or necessity, which may properly rank in the third.

18 Pa. Con. Stat. Ann. Sec. 302 (General Requirements of Culpability)

Below is the Pennsylvania statute related to criminal culpability. Note the general admonition that a "a person is not guilty of an offense unless he acted intentionally, knowingly, recklessly or negligently, as the law may require, with respect to each material element of the offense." This describes various levels of criminal culpability and then those levels of culpability are defined. The substantive law regarding a crime will set forth the level of culpability required.

(a) Minimum requirements of culpability.--Except as provided in section 305 of this title (relating to limitations on scope of culpability requirements), a person is not guilty of an offense unless he acted intentionally, knowingly, recklessly or negligently, as the law may require, with respect to each material element of the offense.

(b) Kinds of culpability defined.—

(1) A person acts intentionally with respect to a material element of an offense when:

    (i)   if the element involves the nature of his conduct or a result thereof, it is his conscious object to engage in conduct of that nature or to cause such a result; and

    (ii)   if the element involves the attendant circumstances, he is aware of the existence of such circumstances or he believes or hopes that they exist.

(2) A person acts knowingly with respect to a material element of an offense when:

    (i)   if the element involves the nature of his conduct or the attendant circumstances, he is aware that his conduct is of that nature or that such circumstances exist; and

    (ii)   if the element involves a result of his conduct, he is aware that it is practically certain that his conduct will cause such a result.

(3) A person acts recklessly with respect to a material element of an offense when he consciously disregards a substantial and unjustifiable risk that the material element exists or will result from his conduct. The risk must be of such a nature and degree that, considering the nature and intent of the actor's conduct and the circumstances known to him, its disregard involves a gross deviation from the standard of conduct that a reasonable person would observe in the actor's situation.

(4) A person acts negligently with respect to a material element of an offense when he should be aware of a substantial and unjustifiable risk that the material element exists or will result from his conduct. The risk must be of such a nature and degree that the actor's failure to perceive it, considering the nature and intent of his conduct and the circumstances known to him, involves a gross deviation from the standard of care that a reasonable person would observe in the actor's situation.

(c) Culpability required unless otherwise provided.--When the culpability sufficient to establish a material element of an offense is not prescribed by law, such element is established if a person acts intentionally, knowingly or recklessly with respect thereto.

(d) Prescribed culpability requirement applies to all material elements.--When the law defining an offense prescribes the kind of culpability that is sufficient for the commission of an offense, without distinguishing among the material elements thereof, such provision shall apply to all the material elements of the offense, unless a contrary purpose plainly appears.

(e) Substitutes for negligence, recklessness and knowledge.--When the law provides that negligence suffices to establish an element of an offense, such element also is established if a person acts intentionally or knowingly. When acting knowingly suffices to establish an element, such element also is established if a person acts intentionally.

(f) Requirement of intent satisfied if intent is conditional.--When a particular intent is an element of an offense, the element is established although such intent is conditional, unless the condition negatives the harm or evil sought to be prevented by the law defining the offense.

(g) Requirement of willfulness satisfied by acting knowingly.--A requirement that an offense be committed willfully is satisfied if a person acts knowingly with respect to the material elements of the offense, unless a purpose to impose further requirements appears.

(h) Culpability as to illegality of conduct.--Neither knowledge nor reckless-ness or negligence as to whether conduct constitutes an offense or as to the existence, meaning or application of the law determining the elements of an offense is an element of such offense, unless the definition of the offense or this title so provides.

Regina v. Cunningham, 41 Crim. App. 155 (1957)

In this case, the defendant/appellant most certainly did something wrong; he intended to and did steal a gas meter. A seemingly unintended consequence was that his soon-to-be mother-in-law was almost asphyxiated by virtue of the leaking gas. What crimes has the defendant/appel-lant committed? Obviously, theft; he intended to and did steal the gas meter. But what about endangering his mother-in-law's life through use of a poison? Did he intend to do that?

What does it mean to act with malice? How did the defendant/appellant define malice? How did the trial court? What about the appellate court? Why is the conviction reversed ("quashed")?

Opinion

The appellant was convicted . . . upon an indictment framed under section 28 of the Offences against the Person Act which. . . charged that he unlawfully and maliciously caused to be taken by Sarah Wade a certain noxious thing, namely, coal gas, so as thereby to endanger the life of the said Sarah Wade.

The facts were that the appellant was engaged to be married and his prospec-tive mother-in-law was the tenant of a house, No. 7A, Bakes Street, Bradford, which was unoccupied, but which was to be occupied by the appellant after his marriage. Mrs. Wade and her husband, an elderly couple, lived in the house next door. At one time the two houses had been one, but when the building was con-verted into two houses a wall had been erected to divide the cellars of the two houses, and that wall was composed of rubble loosely cemented.

On the evening of January 17, 1957, the appellant went to the cellar of No. 7A, Bakes Street, wrenched the gas meter from the gas pipes and stole it, together with its contents, and in a second indictment he was charged with the larceny of the gas meter and its contents. To that indictment he pleaded guilty and was sentenced to six months' imprisonment. In respect of that matter he does not appeal.

The facts were not really in dispute, and in a statement to a police officer the appellant said: 'All right, I will tell you. I was short of money, I had been off work for three days, I got eight shillings from the gas meter. I tore it off the wall and threw it away.' Although there was a stop tap within two feet of the meter the appellant did not turn off the gas, with the result that a very considerable volume of gas escaped, some of which seeped through the wall of the cellar and partially asphyxiated Mrs. Wade, who was asleep in her bedroom next door, with the result that her life was endangered.

At the close of the case for the prosecution, Mr. Brodie, who appeared for the appellant at the trial and who has appeared for him again in this court, submitted that there was no case to go to the jury, but the judge, quite rightly in our opinion, rejected this submission. The appellant did not give evidence.

The act of the appellant was clearly unlawful **and therefore the real question for the jury was whether it was also malicious** within the meaning of section 23 of the Offences against the Person Act, 1861.

Before this court Mr. Brodie has taken three points, all dependent upon the construction of that section. Section 23 provides: "Whosoever shall unlawfully and maliciously administer to or cause to be administered to or taken by any other person any poison or other destructive or noxious thing, so as thereby to endanger the life of such person, or so as thereby to inflict upon such person any grievous bodily harm, shall be guilty of felony. . . ."

Mr. Brodie argued, first, that *mens rea* of some kind is necessary. Secondly, that the nature of the *mens rea* required is that the appellant must intend to do the particular kind of harm that was done, or, alternatively, that he must foresee that that harm may occur yet nevertheless continue recklessly to do the act. Thirdly, that the judge misdirected the jury as to the meaning of the word 'maliciously.

We have considered . . . the following principles. . . .:

In any statutory definition of a crime, malice must be taken not in the old vague sense of wickedness in general but as requiring either (1) An actual intention to do the particular kind of harm that in fact was done; or (2) recklessness as to whether such harm should occur or not (i.e., the accused has foreseen that the particular kind of harm might be done and yet has gone on to take the risk of it). It is neither limited to nor does it indeed require any ill will towards the person injured.

We think that this is an accurate statement of the law. . . . In our opinion the word 'maliciously' in a statutory crime postulates foresight of consequence.

In his summing-up Oliver J. directed the jury as follows:

> You will observe that there is nothing there about 'with intention that that person should take it.' He has not got to intend that it should be taken; it is sufficient that by his unlawful and malicious act he causes it to be taken. What you have to decide here, then, is whether, when he loosed that frightful cloud of coal gas into the house which he shared with this old lady, he caused her to take it by his unlawful and malicious action. 'Unlawful' does not need any definition. It is something forbidden by law. What about 'malicious'? 'Malicious' for this purpose means wicked - something which he has no business to do and perfectly well knows it. 'Wicked' is as good a definition as any other which you would get.

> The facts . . . are these . . . [T]he prisoner quite deliberately intended to steal the money that was in the meter, broke the gas meter away from the supply pipes and thus released the main supply of gas at large into that house. When he did that he knew that this old lady and her husband were living next door to him. The gas meter was in a cellar. The wall which divided his cellar from the cellar next door was a kind of honeycomb wall through which gas could very well, so that when he loosed that cloud of gas into that place he must have known perfectly well that gas would percolate all over the house. If it were part of this offence, which it is not, that he intended to poison the old lady, I should have left it to you to decided, and I should have told you that there was evidence on which you

could find that he intended that, since he did an action which he must have known would result in that. As I have already told you, it is not necessary to prove that he intended to do it; it is quite enough that what he did was done unlawfully and maliciously.

With the utmost respect to the learned judge, we think it is incorrect to say that the word 'malicious' in a statutory offence merely means wicked. We think the judge was, in effect, telling the jury that if they were satisfied that the appellant acted wickedly - and he had clearly acted wickedly in stealing the gas meter and its contents - they ought to find that he had acted maliciously in causing the gas to be taken by Mrs. Wade so as thereby to endanger her life.

In our view it should have been left to the jury to decide whether, even if the appellant did not intend the injury to Mrs. Wade, he foresaw that the removal of the gas meter might cause injury to someone but nevertheless removed it. We are unable to say that a reasonable jury, properly directed as to the meaning of the word 'maliciously' in the context of section 23, would without doubt have convicted.

In these circumstances this court has no alternative but to allow the appeal and quash the conviction.

Commonwealth v. Carroll, 412 Pa. 525 (1963)

In Carroll, *what were the defendant's arguments in favor of reducing his crime to second degree murder? How did the court define "intent" for the purpose of first degree murder? Does "intent" involve "evil intent"? How did defendant's conduct meet the definition of "intent" for the purpose of first degree murder?*

Opinion

The defendant, Carroll, pleaded guilty generally to an indictment charging him with the murder of his wife, and was tried by a Judge without a jury in the Court of Oyer and Terminer of Allegheny County. That Court found him guilty of first degree murder and sentenced him to life imprisonment. Following argument and denial of motions in arrest of judgment and for a new trial, defendant took this appeal. The only questions involved are thus stated by the appellant:

(1) Does not the evidence sustain a conviction no higher than murder in the second degree?

(2) Does not the evidence of defendant's good character, together with the testimony of medical experts, including the psychiatrist for the Behavior Clinic of Allegheny County, that the homicide was not premeditated or intentional, require the Court below to fix the degree of guilt of defendant no higher than murder in the second degree?

The defendant married the deceased in 1955, when he was serving in the Army in California. Subsequently he was stationed in Alabama, and later in Greenland. During the latter tour of duty, defendant's wife and two children lived with his parents in New Jersey. Because this arrangement proved incompatible, defendant returned to the United States on emergency leave in order to move his family to their own quarters. On his wife's insistence, defendant was forced first to secure a 'compassionate transfer' back to the States, and subsequently to resign from the Army in July of 1960, by which time he had attained the rank of Chief Warrant Officer. Defendant was a hard worker, earned a substantial salary and bore a very good reputation among his neighbors.

In 1958, decedent-wife suffered a fractured skull while attempting to leave defendant's car in the course of an argument. Allegedly this contributed to her mental disorder which was later diagnosed as a schizoid personality type. In 1959 she underwent psychiatric treatment at the Mental Hygiene Clinic in Aberdeen, Maryland. She complained of nervousness and told the examining doctor 'I feel like hurting my children.' This sentiment sometimes took the form of sadistic 'discipline' toward their very young children. Nevertheless, upon her discharge from the Clinic, the doctors considered her much improved. With this background we come to the immediate events of the crime.

In January, 1962, defendant was selected to attend an electronics school in Winston-Salem, North Carolina, for nine days. His wife greeted this news with violent argument. Immediately prior to his departure for Winston-Salem, at the suggestion and request of his wife, he put a loaded .22 calibre pistol on the window sill at the head of their common bed, so that she would feel safe. On the evening of January 16, 1962, defendant returned home and told his wife that he had been temporarily assigned to teach at a school in Chambersburg, which would necessitate his absence from home four nights out of seven for a ten week period. A violent and protracted argument ensued at the dinner table and continued until four o'clock in the morning.

Defendant's own statement after his arrest details the final moments before the crime: 'We went into the bedroom a little before 3 o'clock on Wednesday morning where we continued to argue in short bursts. Generally she laid with her back to me facing the wall in bed and would just talk over her shoulder to me. I became angry and more angry especially what she was saying about my kids and myself, and sometime between 3 and 4 o'clock in the morning I remembered the gun on the window sill over my head. I think she had dozed off. I reached up and grabbed the pistol and brought it down and shot her twice in the back of the head.'

Defendant's testimony at the trial elaborated this theme. He started to think about the children, 'seeing my older son's feet what happened to them. I could see the bruises on him and Michael's chin was split open, four stitches. I didn't know what to do. I wanted to help my boys. Sometime in there she said something in there, she called me some kind of name. I kept thinking of this. During this time I either thought or felt-I thought of the gun, just thought of the gun. I am not sure whether I felt my hand move toward the gun-I saw my hand move, the next thing-the only thing I can recollect after that is right after the shots or right during the shots I saw the gun in my hand just pointed at my wife's head. She was still lying on her back-I mean her side. I could smell the gunpowder and I could hear something-it sounded like running water. I didn't know what it was at first, didn't realize what I'd done at first. Then I smelled it. I smelled blood before.

Q. At the time you shot her, Donald, were you fully aware and intend to do what you did?

A. I don't know positively. All I remember hearing was two shots and feeling myself go cold all of a sudden.

Shortly thereafter defendant wrapped his wife's body in a blanket, spread and sheets, tied them on with a piece of plastic clothesline and took her down to the cellar. He tried to clean up as well as he could. That night he took his wife's body, wrapped in a blanket with a rug over it to a desolate place near a trash dump. He then took the children to his parents' home in Magnolia, New Jersey. He was arrested the next Monday in Chambersburg where he had gone to his teaching assignment.

Although defendant's brief is voluminous, the narrow and only questions which he raises on this appeal are as hereinbefore quoted. Both are embodied in his contention that the crime amounted only to second degree murder and that his conviction should therefore be reduced to second degree or that a new trial should be granted.

The applicable principles of law are well settled, but because they are so frequently misunderstood or misapplied or overlooked, we deem it wise to restate them. Many of them are set forth and reaffirmed in *Commonwealth v. Gooslin*, where the Court said: 'Murder in Pennsylvania was first authoritatively defined in the famous case of *Commonwealth v. Drum*, is defined as an unlawful killing of another with malice aforethought, express or implied.' The legislature divided murder into two classifications, murder in the first degree and murder in the second degree; and provided that **(1) all murder perpetrated by poison or lying in wait; or by any other kind of wilful, deliberate [and] premeditated killing, or any murder which shall be committed in the perpetration of or attempt to perpetrate certain specified felonies [arson, rape, robbery, burglary, or kidnapping], is murder in the first degree and (2) every other kind of murder is murder in the second degree.**

"Malice express or implied is [the hallmark] the criterion and absolutely essential ingredient of murder." Malice in its legal sense exists not only where there is a particular ill will, but also whenever there is a wickedness of disposition, hardness of heart, wanton conduct, cruelty, recklessness of consequences and a mind regardless of social duty. Legal malice may be inferred and found from the attending circumstances.

The test of the sufficiency of the evidence-irrespective of whether it is direct or circumstantial-is whether accepting as true all the evidence upon which, if believed, the jury could properly have based its verdict, it is sufficient in law to prove beyond a reasonable doubt that the defendant is guilty of the crime charged.

It has become customary for a defendant in his argument before an Appellate Court to base his claims and contentions upon his own testimony or that of his witnesses even after a jury has found him guilty. This, of course, is basic error. After a plea or verdict of guilty, 'we accept as true all of the Commonwealth's evidence upon which, if believed, the jury could have properly based its verdict. [citing numerous authorities].'

In *Commonwealth v. Kravitz*, the Court said: 'Proof by eye witnesses or direct evidence of the corpus delicti or of identity or of the commission by the defendant of the crime charged is not necessary.' It is clearly settled that a man may be convicted on circumstantial evidence alone, and a criminal intent may be inferred by the jury from facts and circumstances which are of such a nature as to prove defendant's guilt beyond a reasonable doubt.

In *Commonwealth v. Tyrrell*, the Court said: 'The essential difference in a non-felony murder-killing between murder in the first degree and murder in the second degree is that murder in the first degree requires a specific intent to take the life of another human being.'

The specific intent to kill which is necessary to constitute in a non-felony murder, murder in the first degree, may be found from a defendant's words or conduct or from the attendant circumstances together with all reasonable inferences therefrom, and may be inferred from the intentional use of a deadly weapon on a vital part of the body of another human being.

It is well settled that a jury or a trial Court can believe all or a part of or none of a defendant's statements, confessions or testimony, or the testimony of any witness.

If we consider only the evidence which is favorable to the Commonwealth, it is without the slightest doubt sufficient in law to prove first degree. However, even if we believe all of defendant's statements and testimony, there is no doubt that this killing constituted murder in the first degree. Defendant first urges that there was insufficient time for premeditation in the light of his good reputation. This is based on an isolated and oft repeated statement in *Commonwealth v. Drum*, that "no time is too short for a wicked man to frame in his mind the scheme of murder." Defendant argues that, conversely, a long time is necessary to find premeditation in a 'good man.' We find no merit in defendant's analogy or contention. As Chief Justice Maxey appropriately and correctly said in *Commonwealth v. Earnest*: 'Whether the intention to kill and the killing, that is, the premeditation and the fatal act, were within a brief space of time or a long space of time is immaterial if the killing was in fact intentional, wilful, deliberate and premeditated. As Justice Agnew said in *Com. v. Drum*: 'The law fixes upon no length of time as necessary to form the intention to kill, but leaves the existence of a fully formed intent as a fact to be determined by the jury, from all the facts and circumstances in the evidence.'

Defendant further contends that the time and place of the crime, the enormous difficulty of removing and concealing the body, and the obvious lack of an escape plan, militate against and make a finding of premeditation legally impossible. This is a 'jury argument'; it is clear as crystal that such circumstances do not negate premeditation. This contention of defendant is likewise clearly devoid of merit.

Defendant's most earnestly pressed contention is that the psychiatrist's opinion of what defendant's state of mind must have been and was at the time of the crime, clearly establishes not only the lack but also the legal impossibility of premeditation. Dr. Davis, a psychiatrist of the Allegheny County Behavior Clinic, testified that defendant was 'for a number of years passively going along with a situation which he [was] not controlling and he [was] not making any decisions, and finally a decision [was] forced on him. He had left the military to take this assignment, and he was averaging about nine thousand a year; he had a good job. He knew that if he didn't accept this teaching assignment in all probability he would be dismissed from the Government service, and at his age and his special training he didn't know whether he would be able to find employment. More critical to that was the fact that at this point, as we understand it, his wife issued an ultimatum that if he went and gave this training course she would leave him. He was so dependent upon her he didn't want her to leave. He couldn't make up his mind what to do. He was trapped.'

The doctor then gave his opinion that 'rage', 'desperation', and 'panic' produced 'an impulsive automatic reflex type of homicide, as opposed to an intentional premeditated type of homicide. Our feeling was that if this gun had fallen to the floor he wouldn't have been able to pick it up and consummate that homicide. And I think if he had to load the gun he wouldn't have done it. This is a matter of opinion, but this is our opinion about it.'

There are three answers to this contention. First, as we have hereinbefore stated, neither a Judge nor a jury has to believe all or any part of the testimony of the defendant or of any witness. Secondly, the opinion of the psychiatrists was based to a large extent upon statements made to them by the defendant, which need not be believed and which are in some instances opposed by the facts themselves. Thirdly, a psychiatrist's opinion of a defendant's impulse or lack of intent or state of mind is, in this class of case, entitled to very little weight, and this is especially so when defendant's own actions, or his testimony or confession, or the facts themselves, belie the opinion.

The rule regarding the weight of expert testimony in this class of case is well settled. [E]xpert testimony is entitled to little weight as against positive facts. Expert medical opinions are especially entitled to little or no weight when based upon insufficient or (partly) erroneous facts or a feigned state of mind or an inaccurate past history, or upon unreasonable deductions.

In *Commonwealth v. Woodhouse*, we held that the jury was free to disregard expert psychiatric testimony that defendant was insane at the time of commission of the killing,-which would have acquitted the defendant under the M'Naghten Rule-in the face of testimony by lay witnesses who actually observed him and considered him to be sane at times when he was allegedly insane. Mr. Justice Eagen, speaking for the Court, said: 'It must be kept in mind that an opinion is only an opinion. It creates no fact. Because of this, opinion evidence is considered of a low grade and not entitled to much weight against positive testimony of actual facts such as statements by the defendant and observations of his actions.'

Defendant's own statement after his arrest, upon which his counsel so strongly relies, as well as his testimony at his trial, clearly convict him of first degree murder and justify the finding and sentence of the Court below. Defendant himself described his actions at the time he killed his wife. From his own statements and from his own testimony, it is clear that, terribly provoked by his allegedly nagging, belligerent and sadistic wife, defendant remembered the gun, deliberately took it down, and deliberately fired two shots into the head of his sleeping wife. There is no doubt that this was a wilful, deliberate and premeditated murder.

While defendant makes no contention that he was insane at the commission of the murder or at any time, what this Court said in *Commonwealth v. Tyrrell*:

> 'Defendant's psychiatrist did not testify that the defendant was insane. What he did say was that because defendant's wife frequently picked on him and just before the killing insulted or goaded him, defendant had an emotional impulse to kill her which he could not resist.

> [S]ociety would be almost completely unprotected from criminals if the law permitted a blind or irresistible impulse or inability to control one's self, to excuse or justify a murder or to reduce it from first degree to second degree. In the times in which we are living, nearly every normal adult human being has moments or hours or days or longer periods when he or she is depressed and disturbed with resultant emotional upset feelings and so-called blind impulses; and the young especially have many uncontrolled emotions every day which are euphemistically called irresistible impulses. The Courts of Justice should not abdicate their function and duty of determining criminal responsibility to the psychiatrist. In such event, the test will differ not only with each psychiatrist but also with the prevailing psychiatric winds of the moment. Only a short time ago that concept [of irresistible impulse] was emphatically presented as an example of the 'uniform' opinion of psychiatrists on criminal responsibility; and yet today, 'irresistible impulse' is rejected by most psychiatrists as unsound.

Just as the Courts cannot abdicate to the psychiatrists the task of determining criminal responsibility in law, so also they cannot remit to psychiatrists the right to determine the intent or the state of mind of an accused at the time of the commission of a homicide.

Since this is a case of murder, we have carefully reviewed the record. It is crystal clear, from the record, that defendant was justifiably convicted of murder in the first degree.

Maher v. People, 10 Mich. 212 (1862)

In Maher, *how does "provocation" affect intent? Do you think that the defendant in the* Carroll *case above was sufficiently provoked such that his murder charge should have been reduced? Please explain why you think so.*

Opinion

The prisoner was charged with an assault with intent to kill and murder one Patrick Hunt. The evidence on the part of the prosecution was, that the prisoner entered the saloon of one Michael Foley, in the village of Houghton, where said Hunt was standing with several other persons; that prisoner entered through a back door and by a back way leading to it, in his shirt sleeves, in a state of great perspiration, and appearing to be excited; and on being asked if he had been at work, said he had been across the lake; that, on entering the saloon, he immediately passed nearly through it to where said Hunt was standing, and, on his way towards Hunt, said something, but it did not appear what, or to whom; that as soon as the prisoner came up to where Hunt was standing, he fired a pistol at Hunt, the charge of which took effect upon the head of Hunt, in and through the left ear, causing a severe wound thereon; by reason of which Hunt in a few moments fell to the floor, was partially deprived of his sense of hearing in that ear, and received a severe shock to his system which caused him to be confined to his bed for about a week, under the care of a physician; that immediately after the firing of the pistol prisoner left the saloon, nothing being said by Hunt or the prisoner. It did not appear how, or with what, the pistol was loaded. The prisoner offered evidence tending to show an adulterous intercourse between his wife and Hunt on the morning of the assault, and within less than half an hour previous; that the prisoner saw them going into the woods together about half an hour before the assault; that on their coming out of the woods the prisoner followed

them immediately (evidence having already been given that the prisoner had followed them to the woods); that, on their coming out of the woods, the prisoner
followed them and went after said Hunt into the saloon, where, on his arrival, the
assault was committed; that the prisoner on his way to the saloon, a few minutes
before entering it, was met by a friend who informed him that Hunt and the prisoner's wife had had sexual intercourse the day before in the woods. This evidence
was rejected by the court, and the prisoner excepted. **Was the evidence properly
rejected? This is the main question in the case, and its decision must depend upon the question whether the proposed evidence would have tended
to reduce the killing--had death ensued--from murder to manslaughter, or
rather, to have given it the character of manslaughter instead of murder?** If
the homicide--in case death had ensued--would have been but manslaughter, then
defendant could not be guilty of the assault with intent to murder, but only of a
simple assault and battery. The question therefore involves essentially the same
principles as where evidence is offered for a similar purpose in a prosecution for
murder; except that, in some cases of murder, an actual intention to kill need not
exist; but in a prosecution for an assault with intent to murder, the actual intention
to kill must be found, and that under circumstances which would make the killing
murder.

**Homicide, or the mere killing of one person by another, does not, of
itself, constitute murder; it may be murder, or manslaughter, or excusable,
or justifiable homicide, and therefore entirely innocent, according to the
circumstances, or the disposition or state of mind or purpose, which induced the act.** It is not, therefore, the act which constitutes the offense, or determines its character; but the *quo animo*, the disposition, or state of mind, with
which it is done. *Actus non facit reum nisi mens sit rea.*

To give the homicide the legal character of murder, all the authorities agree
that it must have been perpetrated with malice prepense or aforethought. This
malice is just as essential an ingredient of the offense as the act which causes the
death; without the concurrence of both, the crime cannot exist; and, as every man
is presumed innocent of the offense with which he is charged till he is proved to
be guilty, this presumption must apply equally to both ingredients of the offense-
-to the malice as well as to the killing. Hence, though the principle seems to have
been sometimes overlooked, the burden of proof, as to each, rests equally upon

the prosecution, though the one may admit and require more direct proof than the other; malice, in most cases, not being susceptible of direct proof, but to be established by inferences more or less strong, to be drawn from the facts and circumstances connected with the killing, and which indicate the disposition or state of mind with which it was done.

It is for the court to define the legal import of the term, malice aforethought, or, in other words, that state or disposition of mind which constitutes it; but the question whether it existed or not, in the particular instance, would, upon principle, seem to be as clearly a question of fact for the jury, as any other fact in the cause, and that they must give such weight to the various facts and circumstances accompanying the act, or in any way bearing upon the question, as in their judgment, they deserve: and that the court have no right to withdraw the question from the jury by assuming to draw the proper inferences from the whole, or any part of, the facts proved, as presumption of law. If courts could do this, juries might be required to find the fact of malice where they were satisfied from the whole evidence it did not exist. I do not here speak of those cases in which the death is caused in the attempt to commit some other offense, or in illegal resistance to public officers, or other classes of cases which may rest upon peculiar grounds of public policy, and which may or may not form an exception; but of ordinary cases, such as this would have been had death ensued. It is not necessary here to enumerate all the elements which enter into the legal definition of malice aforethought. It is sufficient to say that, within the principle of all the recognized definitions, the homicide must, in all ordinary cases, have been committed with some degree of coolness and deliberation, or, at least, under circumstances in which ordinary men, or the average of men recognized as peaceable citizens, would not be liable to have their reason clouded or obscured by passion; and the act must be prompted by, or the circumstances indicate that it sprung from, a wicked, depraved or malignant mind--a mind which, even in its habitual condition, and when excited by no provocation which would be liable to give undue control to passion in ordinary men, is cruel, wanton or malignant, reckless of human life, or regardless of social duty.

But if the act of killing, though intentional, be committed under the influence of passion or in heat of blood, produced by an adequate or reasonable provocation, and before a reasonable time has elapsed for the blood to cool and reason to resume its habitual control, and is the result of the temporary excitement, by which the control of reason was disturbed, rather than of any wickedness of heart or cruelty or recklessness of disposition; then the law, out of indulgence to the frailty of human nature, or rather, in recognition of the laws upon which human nature is constituted, very properly regards the offense as of a less heinous character than murder, and gives it the designation of manslaughter.

To what extent the passions must be aroused and the dominion of reason disturbed to reduce the offense from murder to manslaughter, the cases are by no means agreed; and any rule which should embrace all the cases that have been decided in reference to this point, would come very near obliterating, if it did not entirely obliterate, all distinction between murder and manslaughter in such cases. We must, therefore, endeavor to discover the principle upon which the question is to be determined. It will not do to hold that reason should be entirely dethroned, or overpowered by passion so as to destroy intelligent volition. Such a degree of mental disturbance would be equivalent to utter insanity, and, if the result of adequate provocation, would render the perpetrator morally innocent. But the law regards manslaughter as a high grade of offense; as a felony. On principle, therefore, the extent to which the passions are required to be aroused and reason obscured must be considerably short of this, and never beyond that degree within which ordinary men have the power, and are, therefore, morally as well as legally bound to restrain their passions. It is only on the idea of a violation of this clear duty, that the act can be held criminal. There are many cases to be found in the books in which this consideration, plain as it would seem to be in principle, appears to have been, in a great measure, overlooked, and a course of reasoning adopted which could only be justified on the supposition that the question was between murder and excusable homicide.

The principle involved in the question, and which I think clearly deducible from the majority of well considered cases, would seem to suggest as the true general rule, that reason should, at the time of the act, be disturbed or obscured by passion to an extent which might render ordinary men, of fair average disposition, liable to act rashly or without due deliberation or reflection, and from passion, rather than judgment.

To the question, what shall be considered in law a reasonable or adequate provocation for such state of mind, so as to give to a homicide, committed under its influence, the character of manslaughter? On principle, the answer, as a general rule, must be, anything the natural tendency of which would be to produce such a state of mind in ordinary men, and which the jury are satisfied did produce it in the case before them--not such a provocation as must, by the laws of the human mind, produce such an effect with the certainty that physical effects follow from physical causes; for then the individual could hardly be held morally accountable. Nor, on the other hand, must the provocation, in every case, be held sufficient or reasonable, because such a state of excitement has followed from it; for then, by habitual and long continued indulgence of evil passions, a bad man might acquire a claim to mitigation which would not be available to better men, and on account of that very wickedness of heart which, in itself, constitutes an aggravation both in morals and in law.

In determining whether the provocation is sufficient or reasonable, ordinary human nature, or the average of men recognized as men of fair average mind and disposition, should be taken as the standard--unless, indeed, the person whose guilt is in question be shown to have some peculiar weakness of mind or infirmity of temper, not arising from wickedness of heart or cruelty of disposition.

It is, doubtless, in one sense, the province of the court to define what, in law, will constitute a reasonable or adequate provocation, but not, I think, in ordinary cases, to determine whether the provocation proved in the particular case is sufficient or reasonable. This is essentially a question of fact, and to be decided with reference to the peculiar facts of each particular case. As a general rule, the court, after informing the jury to what extent the passions must be aroused and reason obscured to render the homicide manslaughter, should inform them that the provocation must be one, the tendency of which would be to produce such a degree of excitement and disturbance in the minds of ordinary men; and if they should find such provocation from the facts proved, and should further find that it did produce that effect in the particular instance, and that the homicide was the result of such provocation, it would give it the character of manslaughter. Besides the consideration that the question is essentially one of fact, jurors, from the mode of their selection, coming from the various classes and occupations of society, and conversant with the practical affairs of life, are, in my opinion, much better qualified to judge of the sufficiency and tendency of a given provocation, and much more likely to fix, with some degree of accuracy, the standard of what constitutes the average of ordinary human nature, than the judge whose habits and course of life give him much less experience of the workings of passion in the actual conflicts of life.

*   *   *

It remains only to apply these principles to the present case. The proposed evidence, in connection with what had already been given, would have tended strongly to show the commission of adultery by Hunt with the prisoner's wife, within half an hour before the assault; that the prisoner saw them going to the woods together, under circumstances calculated strongly to impress upon his mind the belief of the adulterous purpose; that he followed after them to the woods; that Hunt and the prisoner's wife were, not long after, seen coming from the woods, and that the prisoner followed them, and went in hot pursuit after Hunt to the saloon, and was informed by a friend on the way that they had committed adultery the day before in the woods. I can not resist the conviction that this would have been sufficient evidence of provocation to go to the jury, and from which, when taken in connection with the excitement and ""great perspiration" exhibited on entering the saloon, the hasty manner in which he approached and fired the pistol at Hunt, it would have been competent for the jury to find that the act was committed in consequence of the passion excited by the provocation, and in a state of mind which, within the principle already explained, would have given to the homicide, had death ensued, the character of manslaughter only. In holding otherwise the court below was doubtless guided by those cases in which courts have arbitrarily assumed to take the question from the jury, and to decide upon the facts or some particular fact of the case, whether a sufficient provocation had been shown, and what was a reasonable time for cooling.

*   *   *

The judgment should be reversed and a new trial granted.

*   *   *

Chapter 15: Introduction to Criminal Procedure

Introduction

Criminal law defines crimes and who may be punished for committing them. Criminal procedure, on the other hand, describes the process that the state must follow in apprehending, prosecuting, and punishing criminal defendants. Why is there a set process? Think about it like this. An alleged criminal or criminal defendant is subject to the power of the state in his arrest and faces the risk of a loss of liberty or life, again by virtue of the power of the state. This exercise of the power of the state over the individual requires the implementation of powerful safeguards to prevent state overreach.

These safeguards have their origin in the U.S. Constitution, particularly the Fourth, Fifth, and Sixth Amendments.

Text of the Fourth Amendment

The Fourth Amendment places a profound limitation on the ability of the state to apprehend individuals and collect evidence. It states that the people have a "right" to be free o "unreasonable searches and seizures." What's more, the state may not search a place nor seize a person or things without a warrant based on "probable cause." While there are exceptions to these rules, of course, they are a vital bulwark against the arbitrary application of state power.

"The right of the people to be secure in their persons, houses, papers, and effects, against unreasonable searches and seizures, shall not be violated, and no warrants shall issue, but upon probable cause, supported by oath or affirmation, and particularly describing the place to be searched, and the persons or things to be seized."

Text of the Fifth Amendment

This amendment mandates that a Grand Jury must deliver an indictment prior to any conviction of a defendant in a federal criminal matter. The Fifth Amendment also contains the Double Jeopardy clause, the right against self-incrimination, and a "takings" provision providing that the state may not take private property for public use without just compensation. It is from the "due process of law" provision of the Fifth Amendment that many procedural safeguards as to federal criminal defendants (and any other individual subject to federal power) derive. The Fourteenth Amendment has a similar due process provision that applies to the states.

"No person shall be held to answer for a capital, or otherwise infamous crime, unless on a presentment or indictment of a Grand Jury, except in cases arising in the land or naval forces, or in the Militia, when in actual service in time of War or public danger; nor shall any person be subject for the same offence to be twice put in jeopardy of life or limb; nor shall be compelled in any criminal case to be a witness against himself, nor be deprived of life, liberty, or property, without due process of law; nor shall private property be taken for public use, without just compensation."

Text of the Sixth Amendment

The Sixth Amendment mandates that all criminal defendants are entitled to a speedy and public trial by an impartial jury, to be confronted by the witnesses against him, and to the effective assistance of counsel.

"In all criminal prosecutions, the accused shall enjoy the right to a speedy and public trial, by an impartial jury of the State and district wherein the crime shall have been committed, which district shall have been previously ascertained by law, and to be informed of the nature and cause of the accusation; to be confronted with the witnesses against him; to have compulsory process for obtaining witnesses in his favor, and to have the Assistance of Counsel for his defence.

Mapp v. Ohio, 367 U.S. 643 (1961)

Mapp v. Ohio *is a Fourth Amendment case. How does the Court describe the importance of the Fourth Amendment and what it protects? Describe the nature of the illegal search and seizure here. Can you list everything the police did wrong?*

Specifically, this case involves application of the Exclusionary Rule to the states by virtue of the Fourteenth Amendment. The Exclusionary Rule is a rule that provides that evidence unlawfully obtained may not be used at trial. Prior to Mapp v. Ohio, *that rule restricted the federal government but not the states. This is an example of the "Incorporation Doctrine." The*

Incorporation Doctrine is a constitutional doctrine through which much of the first ten amend-ments of the United States Constitution are made applicable to the states through operation of the Due Process clause of the Fourteenth Amendment. Prior to the Fourteenth Amendment, the Bill of Rights restricted the Federal Government only. States could choose to adopt similar pro-tections, but were not required to.

Why is the Exclusionary Rule so important? Why does the Court decide that it must apply to the states in the same manner as it does to the federal government?

Opinion

Appellant stands convicted of knowingly having had in her possession and under her control certain lewd and lascivious books, pictures, and photographs ... . [T]he Supreme Court of Ohio found that her conviction was valid though "based primarily upon the introduction in evidence of lewd and lascivious books and pictures unlawfully seized during an unlawful search of defendant's home."

On May 23, 1957, three Cleveland police officers arrived at appellant's resi-dence in that city pursuant to information that 'a person (was) hiding out in the home, who was wanted for questioning in connection with a recent bombing, and that there was a large amount of policy paraphernalia being hidden in the home.' Miss Mapp and her daughter by a former marriage lived on the top floor of the two-family dwelling. Upon their arrival at that house, the officers knocked on the door and demanded entrance but appellant, after telephoning her attorney, re-fused to admit them without a search warrant. They advised their headquarters of the situation and undertook a surveillance of the house.

The officers again sought entrance some three hours later when four or more additional officers arrived on the scene. When Miss Mapp did not come to the door immediately, at least one of the several doors to the house was forcibly opened and the policemen gained admittance. Meanwhile Miss Mapp's attorney arrived, but the officers, having secured their own entry, and continuing in their defiance of the law, would permit him neither to see Miss Mapp nor to enter the house. It appears that Miss Mapp was halfway down the stairs from the upper floor to the front door when the officers, in this highhanded manner, broke into

the hall. She demanded to see the search warrant. A paper, claimed to be a warrant, was held up by one of the officers. She grabbed the 'warrant' and placed it
in her bosom. A struggle ensued in which the officers recovered the piece of paper
and as a result of which they handcuffed appellant because she had been 'belligerent' in resisting their official rescue of the 'warrant' from her person.

Running roughshod over appellant, a policeman 'grabbed' her, 'twisted (her)
hand,' and she 'yelled (and) pleaded with him' because 'it was hurting.' Appellant,
in handcuffs, was then forcibly taken upstairs to her bedroom where the officers
searched a dresser, a chest of drawers, a closet and some suitcases. They also
looked into a photo album and through personal papers belonging to the appellant. The search spread to the rest of the second floor including the child's bedroom, the living room, the kitchen and a dinette. The basement of the building
and a trunk found therein were also searched. The obscene materials for possession of which she was ultimately convicted were discovered in the course of that
widespread search.

At the trial no search warrant was produced by the prosecution, nor was the
failure to produce one explained or accounted for. At best, 'There is, in the record,
considerable doubt as to whether there ever was any warrant for the search of
defendant's home.' The Ohio Supreme Court believed a 'reasonable argument'
could be made that the conviction should be reversed 'because the 'methods' employed to obtain the (evidence) were such as to 'offend 'a sense of justice,'" but
the court found determinative the fact that the evidence had not been taken 'from
defendant's person by the use of brutal or offensive physical force against defendant.'

The State says that even if the search were made without authority, or otherwise unreasonably, it is not prevented from using the unconstitutionally seized
evidence at trial, citing *Wolf v. People of State of Colorado*, in which this Court did
indeed hold 'that in a prosecution in a State court for a State crime the Fourteenth
Amendment does not forbid the admission of evidence obtained by an unreasonable search and seizure.' On this appeal, of which we have noted probable jurisdiction, it is urged once again that we review that holding.

Seventy-five years ago, in *Boyd v. United States*, considering the Fourth and
Fifth Amendments as running 'almost into each other' on the facts before it, this

Court held that the doctrines of those Amendments **'apply to all invasions on the part of the government and its employees of the sanctity of a man's home and the privacies of life. It is not the breaking of his doors, and the rummaging of his drawers, that constitutes the essence of the offence; but it is the invasion of his indefeasible right of personal security, personal liberty and private property. Breaking into a house and opening boxes and drawers are circumstances of aggravation; but any forcible and compulsory extortion of a man's own testimony or of his private papers to be used as evidence to convict him of crime or to forfeit his goods, is within the condemnation (of those Amendments).'**

The Court noted that constitutional provisions for the security of person and property should be liberally construed. It is the duty of courts to be watchful for the constitutional rights of the citizen, and against any stealthy encroachments thereon.

In this jealous regard for maintaining the integrity of individual rights, the Court gave life to Madison's prediction that 'independent tribunals of justice will be naturally led to resist every encroachment upon rights expressly stipulated for in the Constitution by the declaration of rights. Concluding, the Court specifically referred to the use of the evidence there seized as 'unconstitutional.'

Less than 30 years after Boyd, this Court, in *Weeks v. United States*, stated that 'the 4th Amendment put the courts of the United States and Federal officials, in the exercise of their power and authority, under limitations and restraints (and) forever secure(d) the people, their persons, houses, papers, and effects, against all unreasonable searches and seizures under the guise of law and the duty of giving to it force and effect is obligatory upon all entrusted under our Federal system with the enforcement of the laws.'

Specifically dealing with the use of the evidence unconstitutionally seized, the Court concluded: 'If letters and private documents can thus be seized and held and used in evidence against a citizen accused of an offense, the protection of the Fourth Amendment declaring his right to be secure against such searches and seizures is of no value, and, so far as those thus placed are concerned, might as well be stricken from the Constitution. The efforts of the courts and their officials

Introduction to Criminal Procedure

to bring the guilty to punishment, praiseworthy as they are, are not to be aided by the sacrifice of those great principles established by years of endeavor and suffering which have resulted in their embodiment in the fundamental law of the land.'

Finally, the Court in that case clearly stated that use of the seized evidence involved 'a denial of the constitutional rights of the accused.' Thus, in the year 1914, in the Weeks case, this Court 'for the first time' held that 'in a federal prosecution the Fourth Amendment barred the use of evidence secured through an illegal search and seizure.' This Court has ever since required of federal law officers a strict adherence to that command which this Court has held to be a clear, specific, and constitutionally required—even if judicially implied—deterrent safeguard without insistence upon which the Fourth Amendment would have been reduced to 'a form of words.' It meant, quite simply, that 'conviction by means of unlawful seizures and enforced confessions should find no sanction in the judgments of the courts,' and that such evidence 'shall not be used at all.'

*   *   *

In 1949, 35 years after *Weeks* was announced, this Court, in *Wolf v. People of State of Colorado*, again for the first time, discussed the effect of the Fourth Amendment upon the States through the operation of the Due Process Clause of the Fourteenth Amendment. It said: '(W)e have no hesitation in saying that were a State affirmatively to sanction such police incursion into privacy it would run counter to the guaranty of the Fourteenth Amendment.'

Nevertheless, after declaring that the 'security of one's privacy against arbitrary intrusion by the police' is 'implicit in 'the concept of ordered liberty' and as such enforceable against the States through the Due Process Clause,' and announcing that it 'stoutly adhere(d)' to the *Weeks* decision, the Court decided that the *Weeks* exclusionary rule would not then be imposed upon the States as 'an essential ingredient of the right.'

*   *   *

Since the Fourth Amendment's right of privacy has been declared enforceable against the States through the Due Process Clause of the Fourteenth, it is enforceable against them by the same sanction of exclusion as is used against the Federal Government. Were it otherwise, then just as without the *Weeks* rule the assurance against unreasonable federal searches and seizures would be 'a form of words', valueless and undeserving of mention in a perpetual charter of inestimable human liberties, so too, without that rule the freedom from state invasions of privacy would be so ephemeral and so neatly severed from its conceptual nexus with the freedom from all brutish means of coercing evidence as not to merit this Court's high regard as a freedom 'implicit in 'the concept of ordered liberty." At the time that the Court held in *Wolf* that the Amendment was applicable to the States through the Due Process Clause, the cases of this Court, as we have seen, had steadfastly held that as to federal officers the Fourth Amendment included the exclusion of the evidence seized in violation of its provisions. Even *Wolf* 'stoutly adhered' to that proposition.

The right to privacy, when conceded operatively enforceable against the States, was not susceptible of destruction by avulsion of the sanction upon which its protection and enjoyment had always been deemed dependent .... Therefore, in extending the substantive protections of due process to all constitutionally unreasonable searches—state or federal—it was logically and constitutionally necessary that the exclusion doctrine—an essential part of the right to privacy—be also insisted upon as an essential ingredient of the right newly recognized by the *Wolf* case. In short, the admission of the new constitutional right by *Wolf* could not consistently tolerate denial of its most important constitutional privilege, namely, the exclusion of the evidence which an accused had been forced to give by reason of the unlawful seizure. To hold otherwise is to grant the right but in reality to withhold its privilege and enjoyment. Only last year the Court itself recognized that the purpose of the exclusionary rule 'is to deter—to compel respect for the constitutional guaranty in the only effectively available way—by removing the incentive to disregard it.'

*   *   *

Moreover, our holding that the exclusionary rule is an essential part of both the Fourth and Fourteenth Amendments is not only the logical dictate of prior cases, but it also makes very good sense. There is no war between the Constitution and common sense. Presently, a federal prosecutor may make no use of evidence illegally seized, but a State's attorney across the street may, although he supposedly is operating under the enforceable prohibitions of the same Amendment. Thus the State, by admitting evidence unlawfully seized, serves to encourage disobedience to the Federal Constitution which it is bound to uphold.

*   *   *

The criminal goes free, if he must, but it is the law that sets him free. Nothing can destroy a government more quickly than its failure to observe its own laws, or worse, its disregard of the charter of its own existence. As Mr. Justice Brandeis, dissenting, said in *Olmstead v. United St*ates: 'Our government is the potent, the omnipresent teacher. For good or for ill, it teaches the whole people by its example. If the government becomes a lawbreaker, it breeds contempt for law; it invites every man to become a law unto himself; it invites anarchy.' Nor can it lightly be assumed that, as a practical matter, adoption of the exclusionary rule fetters law enforcement. Only last year this Court expressly considered that contention and found that 'pragmatic evidence of a sort' to the contrary was not wanting.

The Court noted that: 'The federal courts themselves have operated under the exclusionary rule of Weeks for almost half a century; yet it has not been suggested either that the Federal Bureau of Investigation has thereby been rendered ineffective, or that the administration of criminal justice in the federal courts has thereby been disrupted. Moreover, the experience of the states is impressive. The movement towards the rule of exclusion has been halting but seemingly inexorable.'

*   *   *

Gideon v. Wainwright, 372 U.S. 335 (1963)

Gideon v. Wainwright *is another of the great "incorporation" cases, this one involving the Sixth Amendment's right to effective assistance of counsel in a criminal matter. Since the Supreme Court's ruling in* Johnson v. Zerbst, *304 U.S. 458 (1938), it had been the rule in federal court for all criminal trials that if a defendant could not afford an attorney, one would be appointed for him. The question in* Gideon *was whether the Sixth Amendment guarantee*

also applied to the states by virtue of the Fourteenth Amendment. The Court unanimously held
that it did. Please be able to discuss the Court's earlier decision in Betts v. Brady, *which the*
Court in Gideon *overruled. Why is the right to assistance of counsel deemed "fundamental"?*

Mr. Justice BLACK delivered the opinion of the Court.

Petitioner was charged in a Florida state court with having broken and entered a poolroom with intent to commit a misdemeanor. This offense is a felony under Florida law. Appearing in court without funds and without a lawyer, petitioner asked the court to appoint counsel for him, whereupon the following colloquy took place:

> The COURT: Mr. Gideon, I am sorry, but I cannot appoint Counsel to represent you in this case. Under the laws of the State of Florida, the only time the Court can appoint Counsel to represent a Defendant is when that person is charged with a capital offense. I am sorry, but I will have to deny your request to appoint Counsel to defend you in this case.

> The DEFENDANT: The United States Supreme Court says I am entitled to be represented by Counsel.

Put to trial before a jury, Gideon conducted his defense about as well as could be expected from a layman. He made an opening statement to the jury, cross-examined the State's witnesses, presented witnesses in his own defense, declined to testify himself, and made a short argument emphasizing his innocence to the charge contained in the Information filed in this case. The jury returned a verdict of guilty, and petitioner was sentenced to serve five years in the state prison. Later, petitioner filed in the Florida Supreme Court this habeas corpus petition attacking his conviction and sentence on the ground that the trial court's refusal to appoint counsel for him denied him rights guaranteed by the Constitution and the Bill of Rights by the United States Government. Treating the petition for habeas corpus as properly before it, the State Supreme Court, upon consideration thereof but without an opinion, denied all relief.

Since 1942, when *Betts v. Brady*, was decided by a divided Court, the problem of a defendant's federal constitutional right to counsel in a state court has been a continuing source of controversy and litigation in both state and federal courts. To give this problem another review here, we granted certiorari.

Since Gideon was proceeding *in forma pauperis*, we appointed counsel to represent him and requested both sides to discuss in their briefs and oral arguments the following: Should this Court's holding in *Betts v. Brady*, be reconsidered?

The facts upon which Betts [in *Betts v. Brady*] claimed that he had been unconstitutionally denied the right to have counsel appointed to assist him are strikingly like the facts upon which Gideon here bases his federal constitutional claim. Betts was indicted for robbery in a Maryland state court. On arraignment, he told the trial judge of his lack of funds to hire a lawyer and asked the court to appoint one for him. Betts was advised that it was not the practice in that county to appoint counsel for indigent defendants except in murder and rape cases. He then pleaded not guilty, had witnesses summoned, cross-examined the State's witnesses, examined his own, and chose not to testify himself. He was found guilty by the judge, sitting without a jury, and sentenced to eight years in prison. Like Gideon, Betts sought release by habeas corpus, alleging that he had been denied the right to assistance of counsel in violation of the Fourteenth Amendment. Betts was denied any relief, and on review this Court affirmed. It was held that a refusal to appoint counsel for an indigent defendant charged with a felony did not necessarily violate the Due Process Clause of the Fourteenth Amendment, which for reasons given the Court deemed to be the only applicable federal constitutional provision. The Court said:

> Asserted denial (of due process) is to be tested by an appraisal of the totality of facts in a given case. That which may, in one setting, constitute a denial of fundamental fairness, shocking to the universal sense of justice, may, in other circumstances, and in the light of other considerations, fall short of such denial.

Treating due process as a concept less rigid and more fluid than those envisaged in other specific and particular provisions of the Bill of Rights, the Court held that refusal to appoint counsel under the particular facts and circumstances in the *Betts* case was not so offensive to the common and fundamental ideas of fairness' as to amount to a denial of due process. Since the facts and circumstances of the two cases are so nearly indistinguishable, we think the *Betts v. Brady* holding if left standing would require us to reject Gideon's claim that the Constitution guarantees him the assistance of counsel. Upon full reconsideration we conclude that *Betts v. Brady* should be overruled.

The Sixth Amendment provides, 'In all criminal prosecutions, the accused shall enjoy the right to have the Assistance of Counsel for his defence.' We have construed this to mean that in federal courts counsel must be provided for defendants unable to employ counsel unless the right is competently and intelligently waived. Betts argued that this right is extended to indigent defendants in state courts by the Fourteenth Amendment. In response the Court stated that, while the Sixth Amendment laid down no rule for the conduct of the states, the question recurs whether the constraint laid by the amendment upon the national courts expresses a rule so fundamental and essential to a fair trial, and so, to due process of law, that it is made obligatory upon the states by the Fourteenth Amendment.

In order to decide whether the Sixth Amendment's guarantee of counsel is of this fundamental nature, the Court in *Betts* set out and considered relevant data on the subject afforded by constitutional and statutory provisions subsisting in the colonies and the states prior to the inclusion of the Bill of Rights in the national Constitution, and in the constitutional, legislative, and judicial history of the states to the present date. On the basis of this historical data the Court concluded that appointment of counsel is not a fundamental right, essential to a fair trial. It was for this reason the *Betts* Court refused to accept the contention that the Sixth Amendment's guarantee of counsel for indigent federal defendants was extended to or, in the words of that Court, made obligatory upon the states by the Fourteenth Amendment. Plainly, had the Court concluded that appointment of counsel for an indigent criminal defendant was a fundamental right, essential to a fair trial, it would have held that the Fourteenth Amendment requires appointment of counsel in a state court, just as the Sixth Amendment requires in a federal court.

We think the Court in *Betts* had ample precedent for acknowledging that those guarantees of the Bill of Rights which are fundamental safeguards of liberty immune from federal abridgment are equally protected against state invasion by the

Due Process Clause of the Fourteenth Amendment. This same principle was recognized, explained, and applied in *Powell v. Alabama*, a case upholding the right of counsel, where the Court held that despite sweeping language to the contrary in *Hurtado v. California*, the Fourteenth Amendment embraced those fundamental principles of liberty and justice which lie at the base of all our civil and political institutions, even though they had been specifically dealt with in another part of the Federal Constitution. In many cases other than *Powell* and *Betts*, this Court has looked to the fundamental nature of original Bill of Rights guarantees to decide whether the Fourteenth Amendment makes them obligatory on the States. Explicitly recognized to be of this fundamental nature and therefore made immune from state invasion by the Fourteenth, or some part of it, are the First Amendment's freedoms of speech, press, religion, assembly, association, and petition for redress of grievances. For the same reason, though not always in precisely the same terminology, the Court has made obligatory on the States the Fifth Amendment's command that private property shall not be taken for public use without just compensation, the Fourth Amendment's prohibition of unreasonable searches and seizures, and the Eighth's ban on cruel and unusual punishment.

On the other hand, this Court in *Palko v. Connecticut*, refused to hold that the Fourteenth Amendment made the double jeopardy provision of the Fifth Amendment obligatory on the States. In so refusing, however, the Court, speaking through Mr. Justice Cardozo, was careful to emphasize that 'immunities that are valid as against the federal government by force of the specific pledges of particular amendments have been found to be implicit in the concept of ordered liberty, and thus, through the Fourteenth Amendment, become valid as against the states' and that guarantees in their origin effective against the federal government alone had by prior cases been taken over from the earlier articles of the Federal Bill of Rights and brought within the Fourteenth Amendment by a process of absorption.

We accept *Betts v. Brady's* assumption, based as it was on our prior cases, that a provision of the Bill of Rights which is fundamental and essential to a fair trial is made obligatory upon the States by the Fourteenth Amendment. We think the Court in *Betts* was wrong, however, in concluding that the Sixth Amendment's guarantee of counsel is not one of these fundamental rights. Ten years before *Betts v. Brady*, this Court, after full consideration of all the historical data examined in

Betts, had unequivocally declared that the right to the aid of counsel is of this fundamental character. While the Court at the close of its *Powell* opinion did by its language, as this Court frequently does, limit its holding to the particular facts and circumstances of that case, its conclusions about the fundamental nature of the right to counsel are unmistakable. Several years later, in 1936, the Court reemphasized what it had said about the fundamental nature of the right to counsel in this language:

> We concluded that certain fundamental rights, safeguarded by the first eight amendments against federal action, were also safeguarded against state action by the due process of law clause of the Fourteenth Amendment, and among them the fundamental right of the accused to the aid of counsel in a criminal prosecution.

And again in 1938 this Court said:

> [The assistance of counsel] is one of the safeguards of the Sixth Amendment deemed necessary to insure fundamental human rights of life and liberty. [. . .] The Sixth Amendment stands as a constant admonition that if the constitutional safeguards it provides be lost, justice will not still be done.

In light of these and many other prior decisions of this Court, it is not surprising that the *Betts* Court, when faced with the contention that one charged with crime, who is unable to obtain counsel, must be furnished counsel by the state, conceded that (e)xpressions in the opinions of this court lend color to the argument. The fact is that in deciding as it did—that appointment of counsel is not a fundamental right, essential to a fair trial—the Court in *Betts v. Brady* made an abrupt break with its own well-considered precedents. In returning to these old precedents, sounder we believe than the new, we but restore constitutional principles established to achieve a fair system of justice. **Not only these precedents but also reason and reflection require us to recognize that in our adversary system of criminal justice, any person haled into court, who is too poor to hire a lawyer, cannot be assured a fair trial unless counsel is provided for him. This seems to us to be an obvious truth. Governments, both state and federal, quite properly spend vast sums of money to establish machinery to**

try defendants accused of crime. Lawyers to prosecute are everywhere deemed essential to protect the public's interest in an orderly society. Similarly, there are few defendants charged with crime, few indeed, who fail to hire the best lawyers they can get to prepare and present their defenses. That government hires lawyers to prosecute and defendants who have the money hire lawyers to defend are the strongest indications of the wide— spread belief that lawyers in criminal courts are necessities, not luxuries. The right of one charged with crime to counsel may not be deemed fundamental and essential to fair trials in some countries, but it is in ours. From the very beginning, our state and national constitutions and laws have laid great emphasis on procedural and substantive safeguards designed to assure fair trials before impartial tribunals in which every defendant stands equal before the law. This noble ideal cannot be realized if the poor man charged with crime has to face his accusers without a lawyer to assist him. A defendant's need for a lawyer is nowhere better stated than in the moving words of Mr. Justice Sutherland in *Powell v. Alabama*:

> The right to be heard would be, in many cases, of little avail if it did not comprehend the right to be heard by counsel. Even the intelligent and educated layman has small and sometimes no skill in the science of law. If charged with crime, he is incapable, generally, of determining for himself whether the indictment is good or bad. He is unfamiliar with the rules of evidence. Left without the aid of counsel he may be put on trial without a proper charge, and convicted upon incompetent evidence, or evidence irrelevant to the issue or otherwise inadmissible. He lacks both the skill and knowledge adequately to prepare his defense, even though he have a perfect one. He requires the guiding hand of counsel at every step in the proceedings against him. Without it, though he be not guilty, he faces the danger of conviction because he does not know how to establish his innocence.

The Court in *Betts v. Brady* departed from the sound wisdom upon which the Court's holding in *Powell v. Alabama* rested. Florida, supported by two other States, has asked that *Betts v. Brady* be left intact. Twenty-two States, as friends of the Court, argue that *Betts* was an anachronism when handed down and that it should now be overruled. We agree.

The judgment is reversed and the cause is remanded to the Supreme Court of Florida for further action not inconsistent with this opinion.

Miranda v. Arizona, 384 U.S. 436 (1963)

Miranda is a Supreme Court case that nearly everyone who has watched an American police drama will be familiar with. It's the case that mandated the issuance of a so-called "Miranda warning," which begins with the familiar refrain, "You have the right to remain silent …." The case though is not strictly about the warning, it's about the rights that the warning is designed to protect. What are those rights and why are they important? What is the origin of the rights involved, and how is the warning designed to protect them? What does the Court have to say about custodial police interrogations? Why does the Court feel the warning is necessary?

Mr. Chief Justice WARREN delivered the opinion of the Court.

The cases before us raise questions which go to the roots of our concepts of American criminal jurisprudence: the restraints society must observe consistent with the Federal Constitution in prosecuting individuals for crime. More specifically, we deal with the admissibility of statements obtained from an individual who is subjected to custodial police interrogation and the necessity for procedures which assure that the individual is accorded his privilege under the Fifth Amendment to the Constitution not to be compelled to incriminate himself.

We dealt with certain phases of this problem recently in *Escobedo v. State of Illinois.* There, as in the four cases before us, law enforcement officials took the defendant into custody and interrogated him in a police station for the purpose of obtaining a confession. The police did not effectively advise him of his right to remain silent or of his right to consult with his attorney. Rather, they confronted him with an alleged accomplice who accused him of having perpetrated a murder. When the defendant denied the accusation and said 'I didn't shoot Manuel, you did it,' they handcuffed him and took him to an interrogation room.

There, while handcuffed and standing, he was questioned for four hours until he confessed. During this interrogation, the police denied his request to speak to his attorney, and they prevented his retained attorney, who had come to the police station, from consulting with him. At his trial, the State, over his objection, introduced the confession against him. We held that the statements thus made were constitutionally inadmissible.

This case has been the subject of judicial interpretation and spirited legal debate since it was decided two years ago. Both state and federal courts, in assessing its implications, have arrived at varying conclusions. A wealth of scholarly material has been written tracing its ramifications and underpinnings. Police and prosecutor have speculated on its range and desirability. We granted certiorari in these cases, in order further to explore some facets of the problems, thus exposed, of applying the privilege against self-incrimination to in-custody interrogation, and to give concrete constitutional guidelines for law enforcement agencies and courts to follow.

We start here, as we did in *Escobedo*, with the premise that our holding is not an innovation in our jurisprudence, but is an application of principles long recognized and applied in other settings. We have undertaken a thorough re-examination of the *Escobedo* decision and the principles it announced, and we reaffirm it. That case was but an explication of basic rights that are enshrined in our Constitution—that 'No person shall be compelled in any criminal case to be a witness against himself,' and that 'the accused shall have the Assistance of Counsel'— rights which were put in jeopardy in that case through official overbearing. These precious rights were fixed in our Constitution only after centuries of persecution and struggle. And in the words of Chief Justice Marshall, they were secured 'for ages to come, and designed to approach immortality as nearly as human institutions can approach it,'

*   *   *

It was necessary in *Escobedo*, as here, to insure that what was proclaimed in the Constitution had not become but a form of words in the hands of government officials. And it is in this spirit, consistent with our role as judges, that we adhere to the principles of *Escobedo* today.

Our holding will be spelled out with some specificity in the pages which follow but briefly stated it is this: the prosecution may not use statements,

whether exculpatory or inculpatory, stemming from custodial interrogation of the defendant unless it demonstrates the use of procedural safeguards effective to secure the privilege against self-incrimination. By custodial interrogation, we mean questioning initiated by law enforcement officers after a person has been taken into custody or otherwise deprived of his freedom of action in any significant way. As for the procedural safeguards to be employed, unless other fully effective means are devised to inform accused persons of their right of silence and to assure a continuous opportunity to exercise it, the following measures are required. **Prior to any questioning, the person must be warned that he has a right to remain silent, that any statement he does make may be used as evidence against him, and that he has a right to the presence of an attorney, either retained or appointed. The defendant may waive effectuation of these rights, provided the waiver is made voluntarily, knowingly and intelligently.** If, however, he indicates in any manner and at any stage of the process that he wishes to consult with an attorney before speaking there can be no questioning. Likewise, if the individual is alone and indicates in any manner that he does not wish to be interrogated, the police may not question him. The mere fact that he may have answered some questions or volunteered some statements on his own does not deprive him of the right to refrain from answering any further inquiries until he has consulted with an attorney and thereafter consents to be questioned.

The constitutional issue we decide in each of these cases is the admissibility of statements obtained from a defendant questioned while in custody or otherwise deprived of his freedom of action in any significant way. In each, the defendant was questioned by police officers, detectives, or a prosecuting attorney in a room in which he was cut off from the outside world. In none of these cases was the defendant given a full and effective warning of his rights at the outset of the interrogation process. In all the cases, the questioning elicited oral admissions, and in three of them, signed statements as well which were admitted at their trials. They all thus share salient features—incommunicado interrogation of individuals in a police-dominated atmosphere, resulting in self-incriminating statements without full warnings of constitutional rights.

An understanding of the nature and setting of this in-custody interrogation is essential to our decisions today. The difficulty in depicting what transpires at such interrogations stems from the fact that in this country they have largely taken place incommunicado. From extensive factual studies undertaken in the early 1930's, including the famous Wickersham Report to Congress by a Presidential Commission, it is clear that police violence and the 'third degree' flourished at that time. In a series of cases decided by this Court long after these studies, the police resorted to physical brutality—beatings, hanging, whipping—and to sustained and protracted questioning incommunicado in order to extort confessions. The Commission on Civil Rights in 1961 found much evidence to indicate that 'some policemen still resort to physical force to obtain confessions.' The use of physical brutality and violence is not, unfortunately, relegated to the past or to any part of the country. Only recently in Kings County, New York, the police brutally beat, kicked and placed lighted cigarette butts on the back of a potential witness under interrogation for the purpose of securing a statement incriminating a third party.

The examples given above are undoubtedly the exception now, but they are sufficiently widespread to be the object of concern. Unless a proper limitation upon custodial interrogation is achieved—such as these decisions will advance—there can be no assurance that practices of this nature will be eradicated in the foreseeable future. The conclusion of the Wickersham Commission Report, made over 30 years ago, is still pertinent:

> 'To the contention that the third degree is necessary to get the facts, the reporters aptly reply in the language of the present Lord Chancellor of England (Lord Sankey): 'It is not admissible to do a great right by doing a little wrong. * * * It is not sufficient to do justice by obtaining a proper result by irregular or improper means.' Not only does the use of the third degree involve a flagrant violation of law by the officers of the law, but it involves also the dangers of false confessions, and it tends to make police and prosecutors less zealous in the search for objective evidence. As the New York prosecutor quoted in the report said, 'It is a short cut and makes the police lazy and unenterprising.' Or, as another official quoted remarked: 'If you use your fists, you are not so likely to use your wits.' We agree with the conclusion expressed in the report, that 'The third degree brutalizes the police, hardens the prisoner against society, and lowers the esteem in which the administration of justice is held by the public.''

*   *   *

In the cases before us today, given this background, we concern ourselves primarily with this interrogation atmosphere and the evils it can bring. In ... *Miranda v. Arizona*, the police arrested the defendant and took him to a special interrogation room where they secured a confession. ...

In these cases, we might not find the defendants' statements to have been involuntary in traditional terms. Our concern for adequate safeguards to protect precious Fifth Amendment rights is, of course, not lessened in the slightest. In each of the cases, the defendant was thrust into an unfamiliar atmosphere and run through menacing police interrogation procedures. The potentiality for compulsion is forcefully apparent, for example, in *Miranda*, where the indigent Mexican defendant was a seriously disturbed individual with pronounced sexual fantasies.... The fact remains that in none of these cases did the officers undertake to afford appropriate safeguards at the outset of the interrogation to insure that the statements were truly the product of free choice.

It is obvious that such an interrogation environment is created for no purpose other than to subjugate the individual to the will of his examiner. This atmosphere carries its own badge of intimidation. To be sure, this is not physical intimidation, but it is equally destructive of human dignity. The current practice of incommunicado interrogation is at odds with one of our Nation's most cherished principles—that the individual may not be compelled to incriminate himself. Unless adequate protective devices are employed to dispel the compulsion inherent in custodial surroundings, no statement obtained from the defendant can truly be the product of his free choice.

From the foregoing, we can readily perceive an intimate connection between the privilege against self-incrimination and police custodial questioning. It is fitting to turn to history and precedent underlying the Self-Incrimination Clause to determine its applicability in this situation.

We sometimes forget how long it has taken to establish the privilege against self-incrimination, the sources from which it came and the fervor with which it was defended. Its roots go back into ancient times. ...

We have recently noted that the privilege against self-incrimination—the essential mainstay of our adversary system—is founded on a complex of values. All these policies point to one overriding thought: the constitutional foundation underlying the privilege is the respect a government—state or federal—must accord to the dignity and integrity of its citizens. To maintain a 'fair state-individual balance,' to require the government 'to shoulder the entire load,' [T]o respect the inviolability of the human personality, our accusatory system of criminal justice demands that the government seeking to punish an individual produce the evidence against him by its own independent labors, rather than by the cruel, simple expedient of compelling it from his own mouth. In sum, the privilege is fulfilled only when the person is guaranteed the right 'to remain silent unless he chooses to speak in the unfettered exercise of his own will.'

*   *   *

Today, then, there can be no doubt that the Fifth Amendment privilege is available outside of criminal court proceedings and serves to protect persons in all settings in which their freedom of action is curtailed in any significant way from being compelled to incriminate themselves. We have concluded that without proper safeguards the process of in-custody interrogation of persons suspected or accused of crime contains inherently compelling pressures which work to undermine the individual's will to resist and to compel him to speak where he would not otherwise do so freely. In order to combat these pressures and to permit a full opportunity to exercise the privilege against self-incrimination, the accused must be adequately and effectively apprised of his rights and the exercise of those rights must be fully honored.

It is impossible for us to foresee the potential alternatives for protecting the privilege which might be devised by Congress or the States in the exercise of their creative rule-making capacities. Therefore we cannot say that the Constitution necessarily requires adherence to any particular solution for the inherent compulsions of the interrogation process as it is presently conducted. Our decision in no way creates a constitutional straitjacket which will handicap sound efforts at reform, nor is it intended to have this effect. We encourage Congress and the States to continue their laudable search for increasingly effective ways of protecting the rights of the individual while promoting efficient enforcement of our criminal laws. However, unless we are shown other procedures which are at least as effective in apprising accused persons of their right of silence and in assuring a continuous opportunity to exercise it, the following safeguards must be observed.

At the outset, if a person in custody is to be subjected to interrogation, he must first be informed in clear and unequivocal terms that he has the right to remain silent. For those unaware of the privilege, the warning is needed simply to make them aware of it—the threshold requirement for an intelligent decision as to its exercise. More important, such a warning is an absolute prerequisite in overcoming the inherent pressures of the interrogation atmosphere. It is not just the subnormal or woefully ignorant who succumb to an interrogator's imprecations, whether implied or expressly stated, that the interrogation will continue until a confession is obtained or that silence in the face of accusation is itself damning and will bode ill when presented to a jury. Further, the warning will show the individual that his interrogators are prepared to recognize his privilege should he choose to exercise it. ...

The warning of the right to remain silent must be accompanied by the explanation that anything said can and will be used against the individual in court. This warning is needed in order to make him aware not only of the privilege, but also of the consequences of forgoing it. It is only through an awareness of these consequences that there can be any assurance of real understanding and intelligent exercise of the privilege. Moreover, this warning may serve to make the individual more acutely aware that he is faced with a phase of the adversary system—that he is not in the presence of persons acting solely in his interest.

The circumstances surrounding in-custody interrogation can operate very quickly to overbear the will of one merely made aware of his privilege by his interrogators. Therefore, the right to have counsel present at the interrogation is indispensable to the protection of the Fifth Amendment privilege under the system we delineate today. Our aim is to assure that the individual's right to choose between silence and speech remains unfettered throughout the interrogation process. ...

*   *   *

Chapter 16: Legal Ethics

Introduction

In the United States, lawyers are subject to rules of ethics or conduct that are set forth by the state in which they are licensed to practice. For example, a lawyer licensed to practice in the state of New York is subject to the New York Rules of Professional Conduct.

The cases in this chapter discuss various problems in legal ethics. While reading the cases, think about both the importance and purpose of the relevant ethics rule.

The cases deal with the following topics.

- *People v. Belge*: This case is about a lawyer's duty of confidentiality. Why is it so important that a lawyer keep his client's secrets? Why is it so important that criminal defendants receive the effective assistance of counsel? Did the lawyers here do the right thing?

- *People v. Meredith*: This case is a about an attorney's obligations with regard to evidence. What did the attorney do wrong and what was the consequence? How was the attorney client privilege partially waived?

- *In re Himmel*: This case is a about an attorney's obligation to report misconduct committed by other lawyers. Why do attorneys have such an obligation? What did the attorney here do wrong and what was the consequence?

- *Bates v. State Bar of Arizona*: This case deals with lawyer advertising. Is lawyer advertising important? Why would states try to limit or ban lawyer advertising?

- *Sanford v. Commonwealth of Virginia:* This case deals with conflicts of interest between current clients. Why was there a conflict in this case? How was the lawyer materially limited in representing all his clients competently? Why was the consent of the clients insufficient?

- *Westinghouse v. Gulf:* This case is also about conflicts of interest, but this time involving conflicts between current and former clients. What is the nature of the conflict here? What role did confidential information play in the court's analysis?

People v. Belge, 372 N.Y.S.2d 798 (1975)

Opinion

In the summer of 1973 Robert F. Garrow, Jr. stood charged in Hamilton County with the crime of MURDER. The Defendant was assigned two attorneys, Frank H. Armani and Francis R. Belge. A defense of insanity discussions between Garrow and his two counsel, three other murders were admitted by Garrow, one being in Onondaga County. On or about September of 1973 Mr. Belge conducted his own investigation based upon what his client had told him and with the assistance of a friend the location of the body of Alicia Hauck was found in Oakwood Cemetery in Syracuse. Mr. Belge personally inspected the body and was satisfied, presumably, that this was the Alicia Hauck that his client had told him that he murdered.

This discovery was not disclosed to the authorities, but became public during the trial of Mr. Garrow in June of 1974, when to affirmatively establish the defense of insanity, these three other murders were brought before the jury by the defense in the Hamilton County trial. Public indignation reached the fever pitch; statements were made by the District Attorney of Onondaga County relative to the situation and he caused the Grand Jury of Onondaga County, then sitting, to conduct a thorough investigation. As a result of this investigation Frank Armani was No Billed by the Grand Jury but Indictment No. 75—55 was returned as against Francis R. Belge, Esq., accusing him of having violated § 4200(1) of the Public Health Law, which, in essence, requires that a decent burial be accorded the dead, and § 4143 of the Public Health Law, which, in essence, requires anyone knowing of the death of a person without medical attendance, to report the same to the proper authorities. Defense counsel moves for a dismissal of the Indictment on the grounds that a confidential, privileged communication existed between him and Mr. Garrow, which should excuse the attorney from making full disclosure to the authorities.

The National Association of Criminal Defense Lawyers, as Amicus Curiae, citing *Times Publishing Co. v. Williams*, succinctly state the issue in the following language:

> If this indictment stands,
>
> The attorney-client privilege will be effectively destroyed. No defendant will be able to freely discuss the facts of his case with his attorney. No attorney will be able to listen to those facts without being faced with the Hobson's choice of violating the law or violating his professional code of Ethics.

Initially in England the practice of law was not recognized as a profession, and certainly some people are skeptics today. However, the practice of learned and capable men appearing before the Court on behalf of a friend or an acquaintance became more and more demanding. Consequently, the King granted a privilege to certain of these men to engage in such practice. There had to be rules governing their duties. These came to be known as 'Canons'. The King has, in this country, been substituted by a democracy, but the 'Canons' are with us today, having been honed and refined over the years to meet the changes of time. Most are constantly being studied and revamped by the American Bar Association and by the bar associations of the various states. While they are, for the most part, general by definition, they can be brought to bear in a particular situation. Among those is the following cited in *United States v. Funk*:

> Confidential communications between an attorney and his client are privileged from disclosure . . . as a rule of necessity in the administration of justice.

In the most recent issue of the New York State Bar Journal (June 1975) there is an article by Jack B. Weinstein, entitled 'Educating Ethical Lawyers'. In a sub-caption to this article is the following language which is pertinent:

> The most difficult ethical dilemmas result from the frequent conflicts between the obligation to one's client and those to the legal system and to society. It is in this area that legal education has its greatest responsibility, and can have its greatest effects.

In the course of his article Mr. Weinstein states that there are three major types of pressure facing a practicing lawyer. He uses the following language to describe these:

> First, there are those that originate in the attorney's search for his own well-being. Second, pressures arise from the attorney's obligation to his client. Third, the lawyer has certain obligations to the courts, the legal system, and society in general.

Our system of criminal justice is an adversary system and the interests of the state are not absolute, or even paramount. The dignity of the individual is respected to the point that even when the citizen is known by the state to have committed a heinous offense, the individual is nevertheless accorded such rights as counsel, trial by jury, due process, and the privilege against self-incrimination.

A trial is in part a search for truth, but it is only partly a search for truth. The mantle of innocence is flung over the defendant to such an extent that he is safeguarded by rules of evidence which frequently keep out absolute truth, much to the chagrin of juries. Nevertheless, this has been a part of our system since our laws were taken from the laws of England and over these many years has been found to best protect a balance between the rights of the individual and the rights of society.

The concept of the right to counsel has again been with us for a long time, but since the decision of *Gideon v. Wainwright*, it has been extended more and more so that at the present time a defendant is entitled to have counsel at a parole hearing or a probation violation hearing.

The effectiveness of counsel is only as great as the confidentiality of its client-attorney relationship. If the lawyer cannot get all the facts about the case, he can only give his client half of a defense. This, of necessity, involves the client telling his attorney everything remotely connected with the crime.

Apparently, in the instant case, after analyzing all the evidence, and after hearing of the bizarre episodes in the life of their client, they decided that the only possibility of salvation was in a defense of insanity. For the client to disclose not only everything about this particular crime but also everything about other crimes which might have a bearing upon his defense, requires the strictest confidence in, and on the part of, the attorney.

When the facts of the other homicides became public, as a result of the defendant's testimony to substantiate his claim of insanity, 'Members of the public were shocked at the apparent callousness of these lawyers, whose conduct was seen as typifying the unhealthy lack of concern of most lawyers with the public interest and with simple decency.' A hue and cry went up from the press and other news media suggesting that the attorneys should be found guilty of such crimes as obstruction of justice or becoming an accomplice after the fact. From a layman's standpoint, this certainly was a logical conclusion. However, the constitution of the United States of America attempts to preserve the dignity of the individual and to do that guarantees him the services of an attorney who will bring to the bar and to the bench every conceivable protection from the inroads of the state against such rights as are vested in the constitution for one accused of crime. Among those substantial constitutional rights is that a defendant does not have to incriminate himself. His attorneys were bound to uphold that concept and maintain what has been called a sacred trust of confidentiality.

The following language from the brief of the Amicus Curiae further points up the statements just made:

> The client's Fifth Amendment rights cannot be violated by his attorney. There is no viable distinction between the personal papers and criminal evidence in the hands or mind of the client. Because the discovery of

the body of Alicia Hauck would have presented 'a significant link in a chain of evidence tending to establish his guilt,'

Garrow was constitutionally exempt from any statutory requirement to disclose the location of the body. And Attorney Belge, as Garrow's attorney, was not only equally exempt, but under a positive stricture precluding such disclosure. Garrow, although constitutionally privileged against a requirement of compulsory disclosure, was free to make such a revelation if he chose to do so. Attorney Belge was affirmatively required to withhold disclosure. The criminal defendant's self-incrimination rights become completely nugatory if compulsory disclosure can be exacted through his attorney.

In the recent and landmark case of *United States v. Nixon*, the Court stated:

> The constitutional need for production of relevant evidence in a criminal proceeding is specific and neutral to the fair adjudication of a particular criminal case in the administration of justice. Without access to specific facts a criminal prosecution may be totally frustrated.

In the case at bar we must weigh the importance of the general privilege of confidentiality in the performance of the defendant's duties as an attorney, against the inroads of such a privilege, on the fair administration of criminal justice as well as the heart tearing that went on in the victim's family by reason of their uncertainty as to the whereabouts of Alicia Hauck. In this type situation the Court must balance the rights of the individual against the rights of society as a whole. There is no question but Attorney Belge's failure to bring to the attention of the authorities the whereabouts of Alicia Hauck when he first verified it, prevented bringing Garrow to the immediate bar of justice for this particular murder. This was in a sense, obstruction of justice. This duty, I am sure, loomed large in the mind of Attorney Belge. However, against this was the Fifth Amendment right of his client, Garrow, not to incriminate himself. If the Grand Jury had returned an indictment charging Mr. Belge with obstruction of justice under a proper statute, the work of this Court would have been much more difficult than it is.

There must always be a conflict between the obstruction of the administration of criminal justice and the preservation of the right against self-incrimination which permeates the mind of the attorney as the alter ego of his client. But that is not the situation before this Court. We have the Fifth Amendment right, derived from the constitution, on the one hand, as against the trivia of a pseudo-criminal statute on the other, which has seldom been brought into play. Clearly the latter is completely out of focus when placed alongside the client-attorney privilege. An examination of the Grand Jury testimony sheds little light on their reasoning. The testimony of Mr. Armani added nothing new to the facts as already presented to the Grand Jury. He and Mr. Belge were co-counsel. Both were answerable to the Canons of professional ethics. The Grand Jury chose to indict one and not the other. It appears as if that body were grasping at straws.

It is the decision of this Court that Francis R. Belge conducted himself as an officer of the Court with all the zeal at his command to protect the constitutional rights of his client. Both on the grounds of a privileged communication and in the interests of justice the Indictment is dismissed.

People v. Meredith, 631 P.2d 46 (Cal. 1981)

Opinion

Defendants Frank Earl Scott and Michael Meredith appeal from convictions for the first degree murder and first degree robbery of David Wade. Meredith's conviction rests on eyewitness testimony that he shot and killed Wade. Scott's conviction, however, depends on the theory that Scott conspired with Meredith and a third defendant, Jacqueline Otis, to bring about the killing and robbery. To support the theory of conspiracy the prosecution sought to show the place where the victim's wallet was found, and, in the course of the case this piece of evidence became crucial. The admissibility of that evidence comprises the principal issue on this appeal.

At trial the prosecution called Steven Frick, who testified that he observed the victim's partially burnt wallet in a trash can behind Scott's residence. Scott's trial counsel then adduced that Frick served as a defense investigator. Scott himself had told his former counsel that he had taken the victim's wallet, divided the money with Meredith, attempted to burn the wallet, and finally put it in the trash can. At counsel's request, Frick then retrieved the wallet from the trash can. Counsel examined the wallet and then turned it over to the police.

The defense acknowledges that the wallet itself was properly admitted into evidence. The prosecution in turn acknowledges that the attorney-client privilege protected the conversations between Scott, his former counsel, and counsel's investigator. Indeed the prosecution did not attempt to introduce those conversations at trial. The issue before us, consequently, focuses upon a narrow point: whether under the circumstances of this case Frick's observation of the location of the wallet, the product of a privileged communication, finds protection under the attorney-client privilege.

This issue, one of first impression in California, presents the court with competing policy considerations. On the one hand, to deny protection to observations arising from confidential communications might chill free and open communication between attorney and client and might also inhibit counsel's investigation of his client's case. On the other hand, we cannot extend the attorney-client privilege so far that it renders evidence immune from discovery and admission merely because the defense seizes it first.

Balancing these considerations, we conclude that an observation by defense counsel or his investigator, which is the product of a privileged communication, may not be admitted unless the defense by altering or removing physical evidence has precluded the prosecution from making that same observation.

In the present case the defense investigator, by removing the wallet, frustrated any possibility that the police might later discover it in the trash can. The conduct of the defense thus precluded the prosecution from ascertaining the crucial fact of the location of the wallet. Under these circumstances, the prosecution was entitled to present evidence to show the location of the wallet in the trash can; the trial court did not err in admitting the investigator's testimony.

The other contentions presented by Scott, and all contentions raised by codefendant Meredith, were fully addressed in the Court of Appeal opinion. We affirm the convictions, as modified, for the reasons stated in that opinion.

We first summarize the evidence other than that relating to the discovery and location of the victim's wallet. Our summary is based upon the testimony of Jacqueline Otis and Laurie Ann Sam, the key prosecution witnesses, upon the statement given the police by defendant Scott, and upon Scott's trial testimony.

On the night of April 3, 1976, Wade (the victim) and Jacqueline Otis, a friend of the defendants, entered a club known as Rich Jimmy's. Defendant Scott remained outside by a shoeshine stand. A few minutes later codefendant Meredith arrived outside the club. He told Scott he planned to rob Wade, and asked Scott to go into the club, find Jacqueline Otis, and ask her to get Wade to go out to Wade's car parked outside the club.

In the meantime, Wade and Otis had left the club and walked to a liquor store to get some beer. Returning from the store, they left the beer in a bag by Wade's car and reentered the club. Scott then entered the club also and, according to the testimony of Laurie Ann Sam (a friend of Scott's who was already in the club), Scott asked Otis to get Wade to go back out to his car so Meredith could "knock him in the head."

When Wade and Otis did go out to the car, Meredith attacked Wade from behind. After a brief struggle, two shots were fired; Wade fell, and Meredith, witnessed by Scott and Sam, ran from the scene.

Scott went over to the body and, assuming Wade was dead, picked up the bag containing the beer and hid it behind a fence. Scott later returned, retrieved the bag, and took it home where Otis and Meredith joined him.

We now recount the evidence relating to Wade's wallet, basing our account primarily on the testimony of James Schenk, Scott's first appointed attorney. Schenk visited Scott in jail more than a month after the crime occurred and solicited information about the murder, stressing that he had to be fully acquainted with the facts to avoid being "sandbagged" by the prosecution during the trial. In response, Scott gave Schenk the same information that he had related earlier to the police. In addition, however, Scott told Schenk something Scott had not revealed to the police: that he had seen a wallet, as well as the paper bag, on the ground near Wade. Scott said that he picked up the wallet, put it in the paper bag, and placed both behind a parking lot fence. He also said that he later retrieved the bag, took it home, found $100 in the wallet and divided it with Meredith, and then tried to burn the wallet in his kitchen sink. He took the partially burned wallet, Scott told Schenk, placed it in a plastic bag, and threw it in a burn barrel behind his house.

Schenk, without further consulting Scott, retained Investigator Stephen Frick and sent Frick to find the wallet. Frick found it in the location described by Scott and brought it to Schenk. After examining the wallet and determining that it contained credit cards with Wade's name, Schenk turned the wallet and its contents over to Detective Payne, investigating officer in the case. Schenk told Payne only that, to the best of his knowledge, the wallet had belonged to Wade.

The prosecution subpoenaed Attorney Schenk and Investigator Frick to testify at the preliminary hearing. When questioned at that hearing, Schenk said that he received the wallet from Frick but refused to answer further questions on the ground that he learned about the wallet through a privileged communication. Eventually, however, the magistrate threatened Schenk with contempt if he did not respond "yes" or "no" when asked whether his contact with his client led to disclosure of the wallet's location. Schenk then replied "yes," and revealed on further questioning that this contact was the sole source of his information as to the wallet's location.

At the preliminary hearing Frick, the investigator who found the wallet, was then questioned by the district attorney. Over objections by counsel, Frick testified that he found the wallet in a garbage can behind Scott's residence.

Prior to trial, a third attorney, Hamilton Hintz, was appointed for Scott. Hintz unsuccessfully sought an in limine ruling that the wallet of the murder victim was inadmissible and that the attorney-client privilege precluded the admission of testimony concerning the wallet by Schenk or Frick.

At trial Frick, called by the prosecution, identified the wallet and testified that he found it in a garbage can behind Scott's residence. On cross-examination by Hintz, Scott's counsel, Frick further testified that he was an investigator hired by Scott's first attorney, Schenk, and that he had searched the garbage can at Schenk's request. Hintz later called Schenk as a witness: Schenk testified that he told Frick to search for the wallet immediately after Schenk finished talking to Scott. Schenk also stated that Frick brought him the wallet on the following day; after examining its contents Schenk delivered the wallet to the police. Scott then took the stand and testified to the information about the wallet that he had disclosed to Schenk.

The jury found both Scott and Meredith guilty of first degree murder and first degree robbery. It further found that Meredith, but not Scott, was armed with a deadly weapon. Both defendants appeal from their convictions.

Defendant Scott concedes, and we agree, that the wallet itself was admissible in evidence. Scott maintains, however, that Evidence Code section 954 bars the testimony of the investigator concerning the location of the wallet. We consider, first, whether the California attorney-client privilege codified in that section extends to observations which are the product of privileged communications. We then discuss whether that privileged status is lost when defense conduct may have frustrated prosecution discovery.

Section 954 provides, "(T)he client ... has a privilege to refuse to disclose, and to prevent another from disclosing, a confidential communication between client and lawyer ...." Under that section one who seeks to assert the privilege must establish that a confidential communication occurred during the course of the attorney-client relationship.

Scott's statements to Schenk regarding the location of the wallet clearly fulfilled the statutory requirements. Moreover, the privilege did not dissolve when Schenk disclosed the substance of that communication to his investigator, Frick. Under Evidence Code section 912, subdivision (d), a disclosure which is "reasonably necessary" to accomplish the purpose for which the attorney has been consulted does not constitute a waiver of the privilege. If Frick was to perform the investigative services for which Schenk had retained him, it was "reasonably necessary," that Schenk transmit to Frick the information regarding the wallet. Thus, Schenk's disclosure to Frick did not waive the statutory privilege.

The statutes codifying the attorney-client privilege do not, however, indicate whether that privilege protects facts viewed and observed as a direct result of confidential communication. To resolve that issue, we turn first to the policies which underlie the attorney-client privilege, and then to the cases which apply those policies to observations arising from a protected communication.

The fundamental purpose of the attorney-client privilege is, of course, to encourage full and open communication between client and attorney. "Adequate legal representation in the ascertainment and enforcement of rights or the prosecution or defense of litigation compels a full disclosure of the facts by the client to his attorney.... Given the privilege, a client may make such a disclosure without fear that his attorney may be forced to reveal the information confided to him."

In the criminal context, as we have recently observed, these policies assume particular significance: " 'As a practical matter, if the client knows that damaging information could more readily be obtained from the attorney following disclosure than from himself in the absence of disclosure, the client would be reluctant to confide in his lawyer and it would be difficult to obtain fully informed legal advice.' ... Thus, if an accused is to derive the full benefits of his right to counsel, he must have the assurance of confidentiality and privacy of communication with his attorney."

Judicial decisions have recognized that the implementation of these important policies may require that the privilege extend not only to the initial communication between client and attorney but also to any information which the attorney or his investigator may subsequently acquire as a direct result of that communication. In a venerable decision involving facts analogous to those in the instant case, the Supreme Court of West Virginia held that the trial court erred in admitting an attorney's testimony as to the location of a pistol which he had discovered as the result of a privileged communication from his client. That the attorney had observed the pistol, the court pointed out, did not nullify the privilege: "All that the said attorney knew about this pistol, or where it was to be found, he knew only from the communications which had been made to him by his client confidentially and professionally, as counsel in this case. And it ought therefore, to have been entirely excluded from the jury. It may be, that in this particular case this evidence tended to the promotion of right and justice, but as was well said in *Pearce v. Pearce*: 'Truth like all other good things may be loved unwisely, may be pursued too keenly, may cost too much.'"

This unbearable cost, the Douglass court concluded, could not be entirely avoided by attempting to admit testimony regarding observations or discoveries made as the result of a privileged communication, while excluding the communication itself. Such a procedure, Douglass held, "was practically as mischievous in all its tendencies and consequences, as if it has required (the attorney) to state everything, which his client had confidentially told him about this pistol. It would be a slight safeguard indeed, to confidential communications made to counsel, if he was thus compelled substantially, to give them to a jury, although he was required not to state them in the words of his client."

More recent decisions reach similar conclusions. In *State v. Olwell*, the court reviewed contempt charges against an attorney who refused to produce a knife he obtained from his client. The court first observed that "(t)o be protected as a privileged communication ... the securing of the knife ... must have been the direct result of information given to Mr. Olwell by his client." The court concluded that defense counsel, after examining the physical evidence, should deliver it to the prosecution, but should not reveal the source of the evidence; "(b)y thus allowing the prosecution to recover such evidence, the public interest is served, and by refusing the prosecution an opportunity to disclose the source of the evidence, the client's privilege is preserved and a balance reached between these conflicting interests."

Finally, we note the decisions of the New York courts in *People v. Belge*. Defendant, charged with one murder, revealed to counsel that he had committed three others. Counsel, following defendant's directions, located one of the bodies. Counsel did not reveal the location of the body until trial, 10 months later, when he exposed the other murders to support an insanity defense.

Counsel was then indicted for violating two sections of the New York Public Health Law for failing to report the existence of the body to proper authorities in order that they could give it a decent burial. The trial court dismissed the indictment; the appellate division affirmed, holding that the attorney-client privilege shielded counsel from prosecution for actions which would otherwise violate the Public Health Law.

The foregoing decisions demonstrate that the attorney-client privilege is not strictly limited to communications, but extends to protect observations made as a consequence of protected communications. We turn therefore to the question whether that privilege encompasses a case in which the defense, by removing or altering evidence, interferes with the prosecution's opportunity to discover that evidence.

In some of the cases extending the privilege to observations arising from protected communications the defense counsel had obtained the evidence from his client or in some other fashion removed it from its original location. None of the decisions, however, confronts directly the question whether such removal or alteration should affect the defendant's right to assert the attorney-client privilege as a bar to testimony concerning the original location or condition of the evidence.

When defense counsel alters or removes physical evidence, he necessarily deprives the prosecution of the opportunity to observe that evidence in its original condition or location. As the amicus Appellate Committee of the California District Attorneys Association points out, to bar admission of testimony concerning the original condition and location of the evidence in such a case permits the defense in effect to "destroy" critical information; it is as if, he explains, the wallet in this case bore a tag bearing the words "located in the trash can by Scott's residence," and the defense, by taking the wallet, destroyed this tag. To extend the attorney-client privilege to a case in which the defense removed evidence might encourage defense counsel to race the police to seize critical evidence.

We therefore conclude that courts must craft an exception to the protection extended by the attorney-client privilege in cases in which counsel has removed or altered evidence. Indeed, at oral argument defense counsel acknowledged that such an exception might be necessary in a case in which the police would have inevitably discovered the evidence in its original location if counsel had not removed it. Counsel argued, however, that the attorney-client privilege should protect observations of evidence, despite subsequent defense removal, unless the prosecution could prove that the police probably would have eventually discovered the evidence in the original site.

We have seriously considered counsel's proposal, but have concluded that a test based upon the probability of eventual discovery is unworkably speculative. Evidence turns up not only because the police deliberately search for it, but also because it comes to the attention of policemen or bystanders engaged in other business. In the present case, for example, the wallet might have been found by the trash collector. Moreover, one physical evidence (the wallet) is turned over to the police, they will obviously stop looking for it; to ask where, how long, and how carefully they would have looked is obviously to compel speculation as to theoretical future conduct of the police.

We therefore conclude that whenever defense counsel removes or alters evidence, the statutory privilege does not bar revelation of the original location or condition of the evidence in question. We thus view the defense decision to remove evidence as a tactical choice. If defense counsel leaves the evidence where he discovers it, his observations derived from privileged communications are insulated from revelation. If, however, counsel chooses to remove evidence to examine or test it, the original location and condition of that evidence loses the protection of the privilege. Applying this analysis to the present case, we hold that the trial court did not err in admitting the investigator's testimony concerning the location of the wallet.

*   *   *

In re Himmel, 533 N.E.2d 790 (Ill. 1988)

Opinion

This is a disciplinary proceeding against respondent, James H. Himmel. On January 22, 1986, the Administrator of the Attorney Registration and Disciplinary Commission (the Commission) filed a complaint with the Hearing Board, alleging that respondent violated Rule 1-103(a) of the Code of Professional Responsibility (the Code) by failing to disclose to the Commission information concerning attorney misconduct. On October 15, 1986, the Hearing Board found that respondent had violated the rule and recommended that respondent be reprimanded. The Administrator filed exceptions with the Review Board. The Review Board issued its report on July 9, 1987, finding that respondent had not violated a disciplinary rule and recommending dismissal of the complaint. We granted the Administrator's petition for leave to file exceptions to the Review Board's report and recommendation.

We will briefly review the facts, which essentially involve three individuals: respondent, James H. Himmel, licensed to practice law in Illinois on November 6, 1975; his client, Tammy Forsberg, formerly known as Tammy McEathron; and her former attorney, John R. Casey.

The complaint alleges that respondent had knowledge of John Casey's conversion of Forsberg's funds and respondent failed to inform the Commission of this misconduct. The facts are as follows.

In October 1978, Tammy Forsberg was injured in a motorcycle accident. In June 1980, she retained John R. Casey to represent her in any personal injury or property damage claim resulting from the accident. Sometime in 1981, Casey negotiated a settlement of $35,000 on Forsberg's behalf. Pursuant to an agreement between Forsberg and Casey, one-third of any monies received would be paid to Casey as his attorney fee.

In March 1981, Casey received the $35,000 settlement check, endorsed it, and deposited the check into his client trust fund account. Subsequently, Casey converted the funds.

Between 1981 and 1983, Forsberg unsuccessfully attempted to collect her $23,233.34 share of the settlement proceeds. In March 1983, Forsberg retained respondent to collect her money and agreed to pay him one-third of any funds recovered above $23,233.34.

Respondent investigated the matter and discovered that Casey had misappropriated the settlement funds. In April 1983, respondent drafted an agreement in which Casey would pay Forsberg $75,000 in settlement of any claim she might have against him for the misappropriated funds. By the terms of the agreement, Forsberg agreed not to initiate any criminal, civil, or attorney disciplinary action against Casey. This agreement was executed on April 11, 1983. Respondent stood to gain $17,000 or more if Casey honored the agreement. In February 1985, respondent filed suit against Casey for breaching the agreement, and a $100,000 judgment was entered against Casey. If Casey had satisfied the judgment, respondent's share would have been approximately $25,588.

The complaint stated that at no time did respondent inform the Commission of Casey's misconduct. According to the Administrator, respondent's first contact with the Commission was in response to the Commission's inquiry regarding the lawsuit against Casey.

In April 1985, the Administrator filed a petition to have Casey suspended from practicing law because of his conversion of client funds and his conduct involving moral turpitude in matters unrelated to For berg's claim. Casey was subsequently disbarred on consent on November 5, 1985.

A hearing on the complaint against the present respondent was held before the Hearing Board of the Commission on June 3, 1986. In its report, the Hearing Board noted that the evidence was not in dispute. The evidence supported the allegations in the complaint and provided additional facts as follows.

Before retaining respondent, Forsberg collected $5,000 from Casey. After being retained, respondent made inquiries regarding Casey's conversion, contacting the insurance company that issued the settlement check, its attorney, Forsberg, her mother, her fiance and Casey. Forsberg told respondent that she simply wanted her money back and specifically instructed respondent to take no other action. Because of respondent's efforts, Forsberg collected another $10,400 from Casey. Respondent received no fee in this case.

The Hearing Board found that respondent received unprivileged information that Casey converted Forsberg's funds, and that respondent failed to relate the information to the Commission in violation of Rule 1-103(a) of the Code. The Hearing Board noted, however, that respondent had been practicing law for 11 years, had no prior record of any complaints, obtained as good a result as could be expected in the case, and requested no fee for recovering the $23,233.34. Accordingly, the Hearing Board recommended a private reprimand.

Upon the Administrator's exceptions to the Hearing Board's recommendation, the Review Board reviewed the matter. The Review Board's report stated that the client had contacted the Commission prior to retaining respondent and, therefore, the Commission did have knowledge of the alleged misconduct. Further, the Review Board noted that respondent respected the client's wishes regarding not pursuing a claim with the Commission. Accordingly, the Review Board recommended that the complaint be dismissed.

The Administrator now raises three issues for review: (1) whether the Review Board erred in concluding that respondent's client had informed the Commission of misconduct by her former attorney; (2) whether the Review Board erred in concluding that respondent had not violated Rule 1-103(a); and (3) whether the proven misconduct warrants at least a censure.

As to the first issue, the Administrator contends that the Review Board erred in finding that Forsberg informed the Commission of Casey's misconduct prior to retaining respondent. In support of this contention, the Administrator cites to testimony in the record showing that while Forsberg contacted the Commission and received a complaint form, she did not fill out the form, return it, advise the Commission of the facts, or name whom she wished to complain about. The Administrator further contends that even if Forsberg had reported Casey's misconduct to the Com- mission, such an action would not have relieved respondent of his duty to report under Rule 1-103(a). Additionally, the Administrator argues that no evidence exists to prove that respondent failed to report because he assumed that Forsberg had already reported the matter.

Respondent argues that the record shows that Forsberg did contact the Commission and was forwarded a complaint form, and that the record is not clear that Forsberg failed to disclose Casey's name to the Commission. Respondent also argues that Forsberg directed respondent not to pursue the claim against Casey, a claim she had already begun to pursue.

We begin our analysis by examining whether a client's complaint of attorney misconduct to the Commission can be a defense to an attorney's failure to report the same misconduct. Respondent offers no authority for such a defense and our research has disclosed none. Common sense would dictate that if a lawyer has a duty under the Code, the actions of a client would not relieve the attorney of his own duty. Accordingly, while the parties dispute whether or not respondent's client in- formed the Commission, that question is irrelevant to our inquiry in this case. We have held that the canons of ethics in the Code constitute a safe guide for profession- al conduct, and attorneys may be disciplined for not observing them. The question is, then, whether or not respondent violated the Code, not whether Forsberg informed the Commission of Casey's misconduct.

As to respondent's argument that he did not report Casey's misconduct because his client directed him not to do so, we again note respondent's failure to suggest any legal support for such a defense. A lawyer, as an officer of the court, is duty-bound to uphold the rules in the Code. The title of Canon 1 reflects this observation: "A lawyer should assist in maintaining the integrity and competence of the legal profession." A lawyer may not choose to circumvent the rules by simply asserting that his client asked him to do so.

As to the second issue, the Administrator argues that the Review Board erred in concluding that respondent did not violate Rule 1-103(a). The Administrator urges acceptance of the Hearing Board's finding that respondent had unprivileged knowledge of Casey's conversion of client funds, and that respondent failed to disclose that information to the Commission. The Administrator states that respondent's knowledge of Casey's conversion of client funds was knowledge of illegal conduct involving moral turpitude under *In re Stillo*.

Further, the Administrator argues that the information respondent received was not privileged under the definition of privileged information articulated by this court in *People v. Adam* (1972).

Therefore, the Administrator concludes, respondent violated his ethical duty to report misconduct under Rule 1-103(a). According to the Administrator, failure to disclose the information deprived the Commission of evidence of serious misconduct, evidence that would have assisted in the Commission's investigation of Casey.

Respondent contends that the information was privileged information received from his client, Forsberg, and therefore he was under no obligation to disclose the matter to the Commission. Respondent argues that his failure to report Casey's misconduct was motivated by his respect for his client's wishes, not by his desire for financial gain. To support this assertion, respondent notes that his fee agreement with Forsberg was contingent upon her first receiving all the money Casey originally owed her. Further, respondent states that he has received no fee for his representation of Forsberg.

Our analysis of this issue beings with a reading of the applicable disciplinary rules. Rule 1-103(a) of the Code states:

> (a) A lawyer possessing unprivileged knowledge of a violation of Rule 1-102(a)(3) or (4) shall report such knowledge to a tribunal or other authority empowered to investigate or act upon such violation.

Rule 1-102 of the Code states:

> (a) A lawyer shall not
> (1) violate a disciplinary rule;
> (2) circumvent a disciplinary rule through actions of another;
> (3) engage in illegal conduct involving moral turpitude;
> (4) engage in conduct involving dis- honesty, fraud, deceit, or misrepresentation; or
> (5) engage in conduct that is prejudicial to the administration of justice.

These rules essentially track the language of the American Bar Association Model Code of Professional Responsibility, upon which the Illinois Code was modeled. Therefore, we find instructive the opinion of the American Bar Association's Committee on Ethics and Professional Responsibility that discusses the Model Code's Disciplinary Rule 1-103. Informal Opinion 1210 states that under DR 1-103(a) it is the duty of a lawyer to report to the proper tribunal or authority any unprivileged knowledge of a lawyer's perpetration of any misconduct listed in Disciplinary Rule 1-102. The opinion states that "the Code of Professional Responsibility through its Disciplinary Rules necessarily deals directly with reporting of lawyer misconduct or misconduct of others directly observed in the legal practice or the administration of justice."

This court has also emphasized the importance of a lawyer's duty to report misconduct. In the case *In re Anglin* because of the petitioner's refusal to answer questions regarding his knowledge of other persons' misconduct, we denied a petition for reinstatement to the roll of attorneys licensed to practice in Illinois. We stated, "Under Disciplinary Rule 1-103 a lawyer has the duty to report the misconduct of other lawyers. Petitioner's belief in a code of silence indicates to us that he is not at present fully rehabilitated or fit to practice law."

Thus, if the present respondent's conduct did violate the rule on reporting misconduct, imposition of discipline for such a breach of duty is mandated.

The question whether the information that respondent possessed was protected by the attorney-client privilege, and thus exempt from the reporting rule, requires application of this court's definition of the privilege. We have stated that "'(1) [w]here legal advice of any kind is sought (2) from a professional legal adviser in his capacity as such, (3) the communications relating to that purpose, (4) made in confidence (5) by the client, (6) are at his instance permanently protected (7) from dis- closure by himself or by the legal adviser, (8) except the protection be waived.'" We agree with the Administrator's argument that the communication regarding Casey's conduct does not meet this definition. The record does not suggest that this information was communicated by Forsberg to the respondent in confidence. We have held that information voluntarily disclosed by a client to an attorney, in the presence of third parties who are not agents of the client or attorney, is not privileged information. In this case, Forsberg dis- cussed the matter with respondent at various times while her mother and her fiancé were present. Consequently, unless the mother and fiance were agents of respondent's client, the information communicated was not privileged. Moreover, we have also stated that matters intended by a client for disclosure by the client's attorney to third parties, who are not agents of either the client or the attorney, are not privileged. The record shows that respondent, with Forsberg's consent, discussed Casey's conversion of her funds with the insurance company involved, the insurance company's lawyer, and with Casey himself. Thus, under *Werhollick* and probably *Williams*, the information was not privileged.

Though respondent repeatedly asserts that his failure to report was motivated not by financial gain but by the request of his client, we do not deem such an argument relevant in this case. This court has stated that discipline may be appropriate even if no dishonest motive for the misconduct exists. In addition, we have held that client approval of an attorney's action does not immunize an attorney from disciplinary action. We have already dealt with, and dismissed, respondent's assertion that his conduct is acceptable because he was acting pursuant to his client's directions.

Respondent does not argue that Casey's conversion of Forsberg's funds was not illegal conduct involving moral turpitude under Rule 1-102(a)(3) or conduct involving dishonesty, fraud, deceit, or misrepresentation under Rule 1-102(a)(4). It is clear that conversion of client funds is, indeed, conduct involving moral turpitude. We conclude, then, that respondent possessed unprivileged know edge of Casey's conversion of client funds, which is illegal conduct involving moral turpitude, and that respondent failed in his duty to report such misconduct to the Commission. Because no defense exists, we agree with the Hearing Board's finding that respondent has violated Rule 1-103(a) and must be disciplined.

The third issue concerns the appropriate quantum of discipline to be imposed in this case. The Administrator contends that respondent's misconduct warrants at least a censure, although the Hearing Board recommended a private reprimand and the Review Board recommended dismissal of the matter entirely. In support of the request for a greater quantum of discipline, the Administrator cites to the purposes of attorney discipline, which include maintaining the integrity of the legal profession and safeguarding the administration of justice. The Administrator argues that these purposes will not be served unless respondent is publicly disciplined so that the profession will be on notice that a violation of Rule 1-103(a) will not be tolerated. The Administrator argues that a more severe sanction is necessary because respondent deprived the Commission of evidence of another attorney's conversion and thereby interfered with the Commission's investigative function under Supreme Court Rule 752 filed against Casey, the Administrator notes that Casey converted many clients' funds after respondent's duty to report Casey arose. The Administrator also argues that both respondent and his client behaved in contravention of the Criminal Code's prohibition against compounding a crime by agreeing with Casey not to report him, in exchange for settlement funds.

In his defense, respondent reiterates his arguments that he was not motivated by desire for financial gain. He also states that Forsberg was pleased with his performance on her behalf. According to respondent, his failure to report was a "judgment call" which resulted positively in Forsberg's regaining some of her funds from Casey.

In evaluating the proper quantum of discipline to impose, we note that it is this court's responsibility to determine appropriate sanctions in attorney disciplinary cases. We have stated that while recommendations of the Boards are to be considered, this court ultimately bears responsibility for deciding an appropriate sanction. We reiterate our statement that "'[w]hen determining the nature and extent of discipline to be imposed, the respondent's actions must be viewed in relationship "to the underlying purposes of our disciplinary process, which purposes are to maintain the integrity of the legal profession, to protect the administration of justice from reproach, and to safeguard the public."

Bearing these principles in mind, we agree with the Administrator that public discipline is necessary in this case to carry out the purposes of attorney discipline. While we have considered the Boards' recommendations in this matter, we cannot agree with the Review Board that respondent's conduct served to rectify a wrong and did not injure the bar, the public, or the administration of justice. Though we agree with the Hearing Board's assessment that respondent violated Rule 1-103 of the Code, we do not agree that the facts warrant only a private reprimand. As previously stated, the evidence proved that respondent possessed unprivileged knowledge of Casey's conversion of client funds, yet respondent did not report Casey's misconduct.

This failure to report resulted in interference with the Commission's investigation of Casey, and thus with the administration of justice. Perhaps some members of the public would have been spared from Casey's misconduct had respondent reported the information as soon as he knew of Casey's conversions of client funds. We are particularly disturbed by the fact that respondent chose to draft a settlement agreement with Casey rather than report his misconduct. As the Administrator has stated, by this conduct, both respondent and his client ran afoul of the Criminal Code's prohibition against compounding a crime, which states in section 32-1:

> (a) A person compounds a crime when he receives or offers to another any consideration for a promise not to prosecute or aid in the prosecution of an offender.
>
> (b) Sentence. Compounding a crime is a petty offense.

Both respondent and his client stood to gain financially by agreeing not to prose- cute or report Casey for conversion. According to the settlement agreement, respondent would have received $17,000 or more as his fee. If Casey had satisfied the judgment entered against him for failure to honor the settlement agreement, respondent would have collected approximately $25,588.

We have held that fairness dictates consideration of mitigating factors in disciplinary cases. Therefore, we do consider the fact that Forsberg recovered $10,400 through respondent's services, that respondent has practiced law for 11 years with no record of complaints, and that he requested no fee for minimum collection of Forsberg's funds. However, these considerations do not outweigh the serious nature of respondent's failure to report Casey, the resulting interference with the Commission's investigation of Casey, and respondent's ill-advised choice to settle with Casey rather than report his misconduct.

Accordingly, it is ordered that respondent be suspended from the practice of law for one year.

Bates v. State Bar of Arizona, 433 U.S. 350 (1977)

Mr. Justice Blackmun delivered the opinion of the Court.

The issue presently before us is a narrow one. First, we need not address the peculiar problems associated with advertising claims relating to the *quality* of legal services. Such claims probably are not susceptible of precise measurement or verification and, under some circumstances, might well be deceptive or misleading to the public, or even false. Appellee does not suggest, nor do we perceive, that appellants' advertisement contained claims, extravagant or otherwise, as to the quality of services. Accordingly, we leave that issue for another day. Second, we also need not resolve the problems associated with in-person solicitation of clients - at the hospital room or the accident site, or in any other situation that breeds undue influence - by attorneys or their agents or "runners." Activity of that kind might well pose dangers of overreaching and misrepresentation not encountered in newspaper announcement advertising. Hence, this issue also is not before us. Third, we note that appellee's criticism of advertising by attorneys does not apply with much force to some of the basic factual content of advertising: information as to the attorney's name, address, and telephone number, office hours, and the like. The American Bar Association itself has a provision in its current Code of Professional Responsibility that would allow the disclosure of such information, and more, in the classified section of the telephone directory. We recognize, however, that an advertising diet limited to such spartan fare would provide scant nourishment.

The heart of the dispute before us today is whether lawyers also may constitutionally advertise the *prices* at which certain routine services will be performed. Numerous justifications are proffered for the restriction of such price advertising. We consider each in turn:

1. *The Adverse Effect on Professionalism.*

Appellee places particular emphasis on the adverse effects that it feels price advertising will have on the legal profession. The key to professionalism, it is argued, is the sense of pride that involvement in the discipline generates. It is claimed that price advertising will bring about commercialization, which will undermine the attorney's sense of dignity and self-worth. The hustle of the marketplace will adversely affect the profession's service orientation, and irreparably damage the delicate balance between the lawyer's need to earn and his obligation selflessly to serve. Advertising is also said to erode the client's trust in his attorney: Once the client perceives that the lawyer is motivated by profit, his confidence that the attorney is acting out of a commitment to the client's welfare is jeopardized. And advertising is said to tarnish the dignified public image of the profession.

We recognize, of course, and commend the spirit of public service with which
the profession of law is practiced and to which it is dedicated. The present Members of this Court, licensed attorneys all, could not feel otherwise. And we would
have reason to pause if we felt that our decision today would undercut that spirit.
But we find the postulated connection between advertising and the erosion of
true professionalism to be severely strained. At its core, the argument presumes
that attorneys must conceal from themselves and from their clients the real-life
fact that lawyers earn their livelihood at the bar. We suspect that few attorneys
engage in such self-deception. And rare is the client, moreover, even one of the
modest means, who enlists the aid of an attorney with the expectation that his
services will be rendered free of charge. In fact, the American Bar Association
advises that an attorney should reach 'a clear agreement with his client as to the
basis of the fee charges to be made,' and that this is to be done '(a)s soon as
feasible after a lawyer has been employed.' If the commercial basis of the relationship is to be promptly disclosed on ethical grounds, once the client is in the office,
it seems inconsistent to condemn the candid revelation of the same information
before he arrives at that office.

Moreover, the assertion that advertising will diminish the attorney's reputation in the community is open to question. Bankers and engineers advertise, and
yet these professions are not regarded as undignified. In fact, it has been suggested
that failure of lawyers to advertise creates public disillusionment with the profession. The absence of advertising may be seen to reflect the profession's failure to
reach out and serve the community: Studies reveal that many persons do not obtain counsel even when they perceive a need because of the feared price of services or because of an inability to locate a competent attorney. Indeed, cynicism
with regard to the profession may be created by the fact that it long has publicly
eschewed advertising, while condoning the actions of the attorney who structures
his social or civic associations so as to provide contacts with potential clients.

It appears that the ban on advertising originated as a rule of etiquette and not
as a rule of ethics. Early lawyers in Great Britain viewed the law as a form of
public service, rather than as a means of earning a living, and they looked down
on "trade" as unseemly. Eventually, the attitude toward advertising fostered by
this view evolved into an aspect of the ethics of the profession. But habit and

tradition are not in themselves an adequate answer to a constitutional challenge. In this day, we do not belittle the person who earns his living by the strength of his arm or the force of his mind. Since the belief that lawyers are somehow "above" trade has become an anachronism, the historical foundation for the advertising restraint has crumbled.

*   *   *

3. *The Adverse Effect on the Administration of Justice.*

Advertising is said to have the undesirable effect of stirring up litigation. The judicial machinery is designed to serve those who feel sufficiently aggrieved to bring forward their claims. Advertising, it is argued, serves to encourage the assertion of legal rights in the courts, thereby undesirably unsettling societal repose. There is even a suggestion of barratry.

But advertising by attorneys is not an unmitigated source of harm to the administration of justice. It may offer great benefits. Although advertising might increase the use of the judicial machinery, we cannot accept the notion that it is always better for a person to suffer a wrong silently than to redress it by legal action. As the bar acknowledges, 'the middle 70% of our population is not being reached or served adequately by the legal profession.' Among the reasons for this underutilization is fear of the cost, and an inability to locate a suitable lawyer. Advertising can help to solve this acknowledged problem: Advertising is the traditional mechanism in a free-market economy for a supplier to inform a potential purchaser of the availability and terms of exchange. The disciplinary rule at issue likely has served to burden access to legal services, particularly for the not-quite-poor and the unknowledgeable. A rule allowing restrained advertising would be in accord with the bar's obligation to 'facilitate the process of intelligent selection of lawyers, and to assist in making legal services fully available.'

*   *   *

It is at least somewhat incongruous for the opponents of advertising to extol the virtues and altruism of the legal profession at one point, and, at another, to assert that its members will seize the opportunity to mislead and distort. We suspect that, with advertising, most lawyers will behave as they always have: They will abide by their solemn oaths to uphold the integrity and honor of their profession and of the legal system. For every attorney who overreaches through advertising, there will be thousands of others who will be candid and honest and straightforward. And, of course, it will be in the latter's interest, as in other cases of misconduct at the bar, to assist in weeding out those few who abuse their trust.

In sum, we are not persuaded that any of the proffered justifications rise to the level of an acceptable reason for the suppression of all advertising by attorneys.

Sanford v. Commonwealth of Virginia, 687 F. Supp. 2d 591 (E.D. Va. 2009)

Opinion

[Charles Sanford died while a patient at the Medical College of Virginia, where he was recovering from surgery in which a kidney was removed. Sanford was mentally and physically disabled. In the days following his surgery, he was often delirious and hallucinating. On the day of his death, plaintiffs argue Sanford became delirious as a consequence of the medications he had been prescribed by physicians at the hospital. Nurses at the hospital then called the police. The police restrained Sanford, handcuffed him, and forced him to the ground. Nurses then injected Sanford with a sedative. Thirty minutes later Sanford was dead.]

[The plaintiffs have brought claims against three groups of defendants and two individuals: the police, the physicians, the nurses, the police chief, and the nurses' supervisor. The claims against the police are based on excessive use of force; those against the physicians are medical malpractice claims for negligently prescribing Sanford's medication; those against the nurses are for their role in restraining Sanford and injecting him with the sedative; and those against the police chief and the nurses' supervisor are for negligent failure to train their respective employees].

[The same lawyer represents all of the police defendants and the police chief **("the police defendants")**. Another lawyer represents the physicians, nurses, and the nurses' supervisor **("the hospital defendants")**.]

[Plaintiffs have filed a motion to disqualify the lawyers representing the police defendants and the hospital defendants].

The motion to disqualify defense counsel is based upon Virginia State Bar Rule of Professional Conduct 1.7, entitled "Conflict of Interest." Rule 1.7 provides that:

> (a) except as provided in paragraph (b), a lawyer shall not represent a client if the representation involves a concurrent conflict of interest. A concurrent conflict of interest exists if:
>
> * * *
>
> (2) there is significant risk that the representation of one or more clients will be materially limited by the lawyers' responsibilities to another client, a former client or a third person or by personal interest of the lawyer.

Note [8] [to Rule 1.7] provides that:

> Loyalty to a client is also impaired when a lawyer cannot consider, recommend or carry out an appropriate course of action for the client because of the lawyer's other responsibilities or interests. The conflict in effect forecloses alternatives that would otherwise be available to the client. A possible conflict does not preclude the representation. The critical questions are the likelihood that a conflict will eventuate, and if it does, whether it will materially interfere with the lawyer's independent professional judgment in considering alternatives or courses of action that reasonably should be pursued on behalf of the client.

*   *   *

Counsel for both sets of defendants represent that [they] met with their respective clients and, pursuant to Rule 1.7(b), secured the consent of each client to the joint representation. Each lawyer has expressed the view that he will "be able to provide competent and diligent representation to each affected client." Under Rule 1.7, joint representation can be permitted.

The Plaintiffs contend that Note [19] operates to negate the consent. The rule provides:

> However, when a disinterested lawyer would conclude that the client should not agree to the representation under the circumstances, the lawyer involved cannot properly ask for such agreement or provide representation on the basis of the client's consent.

Note [23] provides that:

> An impermissible conflict may exist by reason of substantial discrepancy in the parties' testimony, incompatibility in positions in relation to an opposing party or the fact that there are substantially different possibilities of settlement of the claims or liabilities in question.

According to counsel for the Plaintiffs, the current conflicts exist by reason of substantial discrepancy in the parties' testimony and the incompatibility in positions in relation to opposing parties. Further, it appears that there are substantially different possibilities of settlement of the claims or liabilities in question as to different defendants and that too is a topic that must be examined.

*   *   *

[The Police Defendants]

First, there is, according to the Plaintiffs, the conflict between Colonel Fuller and all of the subordinate VCU police officers respecting the adequacy of training for dealing with hospital patients. Colonel Fuller has admitted that VCUPD officers receive no special training about how to deal with restraining hospital patients. In sum, it is the position of Colonel Fuller that his officers are adequately trained to deal with hospital patients because their general training about how to deal with handcuffed persons includes instruction to check for signs of physical distress and for difficulty in breathing.

The testimony of Officer LaVigne is that subordinate officers received no training for handling patients in a health care setting and Officer Carter testifies that she is not trained to look for signs of distress or difficulty in breathing. Officer Carter's testimony clearly conflicted with Colonel Fuller's testimony on that point. Officer LaVigne's does not. However, LaVigne's testimony would permit an argument that he engaged in no misconduct, and that the lack of training respecting how to deal with hospital patients, not his conduct, was the cause of Sanford's death. Officer Pryor testified that he did not monitor Sanford during the period when he was handcuffed and that places his testimony also at odds with the position of Colonel Fuller respecting the adequacy of training.

Thus, on this topic, the adequacy of training, there appears to be a substantial discrepancy in the testimony of the VCUPD officer defendants and an incompatibility in positions that the VCUPD officer defendants occupy vis-à-vis Colonel Fuller. The possibilities for settlement also appear to be substantially different on the claims and liabilities in question as to Colonel Fuller, on one hand, and the VCUPD officer defendants, on the other.

It is also asserted by the Plaintiffs that there is conflict between the VCUPD officer defendants who initially responded to the summons to Sanford's room and effectuated the seizure by handcuffing Sanford and keeping him facedown on the floor, and those officers who arrived on the scene later. This conflict arises out of the undisputed evidence that the accepted protocol for the VCUPD in situations such as the one here at issue is that the first responding officer provides the lead and that subsequently responding officers follow the instructions of the lead officer. Officer Bailey was the lead responder and the other defendants, Officers Pryor, LaVigne, and Carter, followed his lead, as specified by the departmental protocol. Further, it appears also that Officers Pryor and Carter followed explicit directions given by Officer Bailey after they arrived at the scene. Thus, the objective evidence is that Officer Bailey took the action which resulted in handcuffing Sanford and in maintaining him in a prone position and that Officers Pryor and Carter acted pursuant to his explicit direction in doing what they did and that Officer LaVigne followed Officer Bailey's lead in accord with the departmental protocol.

These largely undisputed facts present a somewhat clearer incompatibility in the positions occupied by Officer Bailey, on the one hand, and Officers Pryor, Carter and LaVigne, on the other. The latter would be able to assert that their conduct was governed by protocol, which had been set in place when they arrived upon the scene and by the instructions of Officer Bailey. Thus, they could argue that the reasonableness of their conduct, which lies at the heart of their ability to defend a number of the claims against them, must be assessed differently than the conduct of Officer Bailey who was the one who first laid hands on Sanford and who also dictated that Sanford be kept in handcuffs and be kept facedown in the prone position. The positional incompatibility in presenting a defense is obvious. In addition to the incompatibility of positions in relation to Sanford, the same facts give rise to a considerably different possibility for settlement with respect to Officers LaVigne, Pryor, and Carter on the one hand and Officer Bailey on the other.

Lastly, the Plaintiffs point to a conflict created by an order that was issued by Corporal Branch, the superior of all of the other VCU police officers (excepting Colonel Fuller). Corporal Branch arrived after the other officers had arrived and acted. It was undisputed that Sanford was calm by the time that Corporal Branch arrived upon the scene. It was further undisputed that Corporal Branch gave an order to Officer Bailey and the other officers to keep Sanford in the restraints until stronger restraints arrived from the psychiatric ward (such restraints having been sent for by the nursing staff at the direction of the VCU police officer defendants). Corporal Branch has said that he intended his order to mean that Officer Bailey and the others should keep Sanford handcuffed and prone until the stronger restraints arrived. After issuing that order, Corporal Branch left the scene. It also appears that Sanford died during this phase of the restraint.

The testimony of Corporal Branch in this regard gives rise to a potential positional conflict between Officer Bailey and Branch, and also between Colonel Fuller and Corporal Branch. Because of the sequence in which depositions were taken, it is not clear that there is a positional conflict between Branch and Officer Carter.

A lawyer representing the officers other than Corporal Branch might reasonably be expected to argue to the jury that the conduct of those officers was quite reasonable in view of Corporal Branch's instruction. Of course, the mere fact that they were following Corporal Branch's instructions would not present a legal defense, but it would present a significant basis for differentiating the reasonableness of the conduct of Corporal Branch on the one hand and the other officers on the other. Further, the evidence respecting Corporal Branch's instruction gives rise to significantly different possibilities of settlement of the claims and liabilities in question.

Moreover, the situation confronting Officers LaVigne, Pryor, and Carter must be measured in perspective of Officer Bailey's conduct (handcuffing Sanford and keeping him prone) and Corporal Branch's order (to keep him that way). Thus, it is rather clear that to defend the reasonableness of their conduct, as well as the rightness of their conduct, Officers LaVigne, Carter, and Prior would want to point to the conduct of Officer Bailey and Corporal Branch as the cause of Sanford's death, rather than the action they took in doing what they were told to do by the departmental protocol, by Officer Bailey and Corporal Branch.

[The Hospital Defendants]

The motion asserts several conflicts among the VCU medical defendants. First, Dr. Meguid diagnosed Sanford's condition as opium withdrawal rather than delirium, a condition which Dr. Meguid stated might be present in Sanford only in its waning stages. Several defense experts (a pharmacist, a toxicologist, and a psychiatrist) have expressed the opinion that Sanford's symptoms were consistent with delirium, not with opium withdrawal. The Plaintiffs intend to offer evidence that Dr. Meguid's diagnosis was erroneous and that, as a consequence of the misdiagnosis, certain of Sanford's medications were resumed without the necessary, precedent tests. As a consequence, it will be said by other expert witnesses that certain drug levels reached toxic levels and created episodes of delirium which led to the decision to restrain Sanford and hence to his death.

In other words, the expert opinions of the defense experts will support the conclusion that Dr. Meguid misdiagnosed Sanford. There is a medical malpractice claim against Dr. Meguid and an attorney representing Dr. Meguid would certainly want to present expert testimony that Dr. Meguid's diagnosis was correct. However, there appears to be no such evidence offered on his behalf and, indeed, the defense experts render opinions which make it quite difficult for Dr. Meguid to assert that his diagnosis was a correct one. On this record, there is a significant incompatibility in position between Dr. Meguid and the other medical professionals on this issue. In addition, the existence of the testimony of these other medical experts on behalf of the medical defendants other than Dr. Meguid presents a substantially different possibility for settlement of the claims and liabilities in question.

Second, it is undisputed that Dr. Meguid made a medical note that Haldol should be avoided for Sanford, if possible. Further, Dr. Meguid recognized that Haldol might not be appropriate for a patient with Biemond's Syndrome and that the drug could have adverse cardiac side effects. Dr. Maiberger, however, prescribed Haldol and Nurse Brown or Nurse Ferguson administered Haldol. Neither of the three were aware of Dr. Meguid's cautions respecting the use of Haldol for Sanford. At oral argument on the disqualification motion, counsel for the medical defendants asserted that it was the position of Dr. Maiberger and Nurse Brown that they had no reason to be aware of Dr. Meguid's caution because Dr. Meguid had not entered his note in the computerized system which, in turn, would have alerted the nurses to Dr. Meguid's cautionary advice. That failure is a further indictment of Dr. Meguid.

Quite clearly there are conflicting positions presented by the testimony. Dr. Meguid certainly is entitled to present, as part of his defense, that he cautioned against the use of Haldol. At the same time, Dr. Maiberger and the nurses intend to say that they had no reason to know of this caution because Dr. Meguid did not act in accord with established procedure at the Hospital to take the necessary actions to alert them to his caution. Counsel for Dr. Maiberger and the nurses, therefore, would certainly want to point the finger of fault toward Dr. Meguid as part of the means of defending Dr. Maiberger and the nurses.

Neither Dr. Maiberger nor the nurses have asserted the position (Dr. Meguid's failure to enter the note in the computer) that quite logically might assist in exonerating them from liability, if supported by the evidence and if accepted by the jury. Also, there is a positional incompatibility between Dr. Maiberger and Nurse Brown, on the one hand, and Dr. Meguid, on the other as respects the propriety of using Haldol to sedate Sanford. Additionally, the factual differences presented by the potential different defenses present substantially different possibilities of settlement of the claims and liabilities in question.

Third, it is alleged that there exists a conflict between CNO Crosby and Nurse Brown on the issue of training. CNO Crosby asserts that Nurse Brown was properly trained in every respect and, in particular, in the restraint policy that CNO Crosby says that she established. It is beyond dispute that Nurse Brown violated the restraint policy as it is understood by CNO Crosby. Thus, as the Plaintiffs contend, if CNO Crosby properly trained Nurse Brown to follow the policy, then Nurse Brown ignored that training and that fact would certainly be pertinent in making out a defense for Chief Nurse Crosby. On the other hand, if Nurse Brown complied with her training, then a reasonable juror could conclude, and counsel representing Nurse Brown would want to argue, that she was not properly trained and that her actions were reasonable ones. Here too, there is a positional conflict between these two defendants.

Fourth, it is alleged that there is a likely conflict between Dr. Grob, the urologist who performed the surgery and under whose care Sanford was at the time of the incident, and Dr. Koo, an attending physician. Dr. Grob was on vacation at the time of Sanford's death, and had delegated the task of post-operatively caring for Sanford to Dr. Koo. Dr. Koo is a newly added defendant, and he has not been deposed so it is uncertain what his position will be. The claims against Dr. Grob include failing to recognize signs of Sanford's delirium, failing to supervise residents, failing properly to communicate with consultant physicians and failing properly to communicate with the attending physician who was covering for Dr. Grob. That physician is Dr. Koo.

Dr. Grob has fastened his defense on the fact that he was on a holiday vacation, and that he had turned all of the responsibility for Sanford's care to Dr. Koo as a covering attendant physician. Thus, it appears rather likely that there is a conflict between Dr. Grob and Dr. Koo. The conflict is positional in nature and has a significant impact on the settlement possibilities, particularly as to Dr. Grob.

Finally, it is alleged that Dr. Maiberger was not properly advised of the facts by Nurse Brown at the time that he had prescribed the administration of Haldol for Sanford. Dr. Maiberger prescribed the use of Haldol without seeing Sanford and did so on the basis of a description given by Nurse Brown over the telephone to the effect that Sanford's conduct was such that it took six officers to hold Sanford down. The record simply does not support the version of facts communicated by Nurse Brown to Dr. Maiberger. Indeed, there is evidence that only two people were involved in handcuffing Sanford; that the task was accomplished relatively quickly; and that Sanford was in fact calm well before Haldol was administered. It seems rather clear that the defense of Dr. Maiberger requires a showing that his conduct was reasonable in perspective of the information that he was given by Nurse Brown. And, of course, if that information was wrong, then Dr. Maiberger would have a defense, the existence of which would require the lawyer defending Dr. Maiberger to point at Nurse Brown's inadequate information as a means of exonerating Dr. Maiberger. That evidence would point necessarily, in an inculpatory fashion, to Nurse Brown. That conflict is positional and is pertinent to settlement issues.

The Legal Principles

… As noted above, Rule 1.7 prohibits a lawyer from representing a client if the representation involves a concurrent conflict of interest, which exists if "there is a significant risk that the representation of one or more clients will be materially limited by the lawyer's responsibilities to another client." The notes to Rule 1.7 make clear that "[l]oyalty and independent judgment are essential elements in the lawyer's relationship to a client." Rule 1.7, Note [1]. This assessment ought to be undertaken at the beginning of the representation of multiple clients in the same action, but the rules make clear that if the conflict arises after the representation has been undertaken, it is the obligation of the lawyer to withdraw from the representation.

"Loyalty to a client is also impaired when a lawyer cannot consider, recommend or carry out an appropriate course of action for the client because of the lawyer's other responsibilities or interests. The conflict in effect forecloses alternatives that otherwise would be available to the client." It is also important to note that "[s]imultaneous representation of parties whose interests in litigation may conflict, such as co-plaintiffs or co-defendants, is governed by paragraph (a)(2)" of Rule 1.7. "An impermissible conflict may exist by reason of substantial discrepancy in the parties' testimony, incompatibility in positions in relation to an opposing party or the fact that there are substantially different possibilities of settlement of the claims or liabilities in question."

*   *   *

It is, of course, important in our system of justice that parties be free to retain counsel of their choice. "However, this Court has held that the right of one to retain counsel of his choosing is 'secondary in importance to the Court's duty to maintain the highest ethical standards of professional conduct to insure and preserve trust in the integrity of the bar.'" Accordingly, "[t]here must be a balance between the client's free choice of counsel and the maintenance of the highest and ethical and professional standards in the legal community." Moreover, the party seeking disqualification has a high standard of proof to show that disqualification is warranted. These principles are well settled.

*   *   *

As explained above, the conflicts that are presented here are real conflicts. They exist now and they have existed throughout the course of the case. They have significant impact on the conduct of the trial respecting how best to serve the interests of the individual defendants who are affected by the extant conflicts.

Furthermore, the conflicts here raise the serious prospect that the trial could fall into disarray. This prospect has actually manifested itself in the motions for summary judgment presented by the defendants and in the presentation of expert testimony, including several contentions of law and opinion favoring the interest of one defendant while presenting the prospect of real harm to others.

It is obvious [that defense counsel] have staked out defensive positions that they think are the best positions for the defense side of the case considered as a whole. It does not appear, however, that counsel have considered, or that they appreciate, how the assertion of those positions could affect the ability of each individual defendant to defend herself or himself by presenting arguments that other defendants are really responsible for Sanford's tragic death even though another defendant may have had some involvement in the circumstances leading up to that death. ...

Having conferred with counsel on the issues in this case on a number of occasions in connection with motions to dismiss and discovery issues and having studied the briefs in support of motions for summary judgment made by all of the defendants, as well as a motion for summary judgment made by the plaintiffs, and having examined the expert opinions in the case filed by both sides, the Court must conclude that the conflicts alleged here are real ones that are currently in existence. The conflicts also present very real risks of serious, adverse consequences for the rights of the litigants, mostly the defendants, but also those of the plaintiffs.

*   *   *

Counsel for each group of defendants asserts that disqualification is not required because all of the defendants have consented to multiple representations. It is true that Rule 1.7(b) provides that the written consent of the client may allow counsel to represent clients who otherwise would not be representable under Rule 1.7(a)(2). However, there are four conditions to a representation under the consent process: (1) the lawyer must reasonably believe that he will be able to provide competent representation to each affected client; (2) the representation must not be prohibited by law; (3) the representation does not involve the assertion of a claim by one client against another; and (4) the waiver of conflict must be in writing. Rule 1.7(b). The second and third conditions above do not present any problems for the counsel in this case. As will be explained below, the fourth condition, for purposes of the Plaintiff's motion, is not dispositive, and the Court will assume compliance therewith. However, the Court cannot conclude that any lawyer reasonably could believe, as the first condition requires, that he would be able to provide competent and diligent representation to each of the affected clients identified in the foregoing discussion of conflicts.

*   *   *

For consent to be effective under Rule 1.7(b), it must be meaningful and that, in turn, necessitates that the clients be advised clearly about the conflicts that might very well arise.

*   *   *

Although counsel for these defendants asserts that the consent was provided knowingly and voluntarily, there is no basis in the record to conclude that the affected defendants had the very real conflicts described to them thoroughly and accurately. And, such a showing is essential especially where, as here, the conflicts are so patent and so numerous and have such potentially adverse consequences for many of the defendant clients. The absence of that showing alone renders the record on consent here insufficient to animate the exception permitted by Rule 1.7(b).

*   *   *

Westinghouse Elec. Corp. v. Gulf Oil Corp., 588 F.2d 221 (7th Cir. 1978)

Opinion

In this case we review the propriety of a district court's refusal to grant a motion to disqualify opposing counsel. The issues presented are whether there is a sufficient relationship between matters presented by the pending litigation and matters which the lawyers in question worked on in behalf of the party now seeking disqualification and whether the party seeking disqualification has given legally sufficient consent to the dual representation.

This case arises as one aspect of the complex litigation filed by Westinghouse against a number of parties engaged in, or having interests in, the mining of uranium. That suit alleged that increases in the price of uranium, which had encouraged Westinghouse to default on long-term uranium supply contracts, resulted from an international cartel which was alleged to have "fixed and increased the price of uranium to purchasers within the United States; . . . allocated, divided and curtailed the supply of, and market for, uranium; . . . boycotted certain uranium purchasers . . . ; and . . . otherwise eliminated competition among defendants. . . ." The movant here, Gulf Oil Corporation (Gulf), and the respondent, United Nuclear Corporation (UNC) are two of the named defendants in this action. UNC is being represented by the Santa Fe, New Mexico firm of Bigbee, Stephenson, Carpenter & Crout (Bigbee), which had previously performed legal work on behalf of Gulf. Gulf, accordingly, moved to disqualify the Bigbee firm.

The history of the relationship between Gulf and Bigbee had its origin in 1968, when substantial reserves of uranium ore were discovered on tracts of land located near Grant, New Mexico. By 1971 Gulf owned a substantial majority interest in a joint venture which had acquired a portion, designated as the Mt. Taylor properties, of these uranium reserves. After having acquired its interests, Gulf retained the Bigbee firm to represent it on legal matters relating to Gulf's uranium operations in New Mexico. During a five year period of representation from 1971 through 1976, the Bigbee firm through nine of its twelve attorneys performed numerous services for Gulf including the patenting of fifty-nine mining claims, drafting leases required for uranium exploration, representing Gulf in litigation involving title disputes, counseling Gulf in relation to the resolution of certain problems relating to mine waters, and lobbying on behalf of Gulf in front of the New Mexico state legislature on tax and environmental matters. One of Bigbee's name partners, G. Stanley Crout, alone spent over 2,000 hours working on behalf of Gulf.

Gulf argued before the district court that these matters on which Bigbee represented Gulf were substantially related to the matters raised in the Westinghouse litigation. Gulf delineated this relationship by arguing that since the Mt. Taylor properties constituted Gulf's largest supply of uranium and was not currently in production, the reasons for Gulf's failure to produce from this property would be material to the allegation of the Westinghouse suit that Gulf, as well as the other defendants, withheld uranium supplies from the market. Further, Gulf argued, in relation to Bigbee's prior representation of Gulf, Gulf had entrusted Bigbee with confidential information relating to the quantity and quality of uranium reserves in the Mt. Taylor properties. Finally, even though Bigbee represented UNC, a co-defendant in Westinghouse, the position between the two parties was adverse because UNC was attempting to exculpate itself by inculpating Gulf.

The district court accepted Gulf's argument of actual adverseness but nonetheless declined to disqualify the Bigbee firm. The court concluded that Bigbee "certainly did gain knowledge of Gulf's uranium properties during its work" but reasoned that nevertheless there was not a substantial relationship between the matters encompassed by the prior representation and those of the Westinghouse litigation, because the prior representation "focused on real estate transactions connected with Gulf's untapped and undeveloped uranium reserves," whereas the "heart of the complaint" details a price-fixing conspiracy, the evidence of which "will focus on meetings and communications among the alleged co-conspirators, as well as evidence on uranium prices, terms and conditions of sale, and market availability." Thus, the court concluded that there was no substantial relationship between the matters.

The district court set out and attempted to apply what is clearly settled as the relevant test in disqualification matters: where an attorney represents a party in a matter in which the adverse party is that attorney's former client, the attorney will be disqualified if the subject matter of the two representations are "substantially related."

The substantial relationship test had its federal court genesis in *T. C. Theatre Corp. v. Warner Bros. Pictures, Inc.* The Second Circuit continues to apply the test. That circuit has also developed the "peripheral representation" exception. This circuit has also adopted the substantial relationship test.

*   *   *

The substantial relationship test is not a rule of substantive law but a measure of the quantum of evidence required for proof of the existence of the professional obligation. The evidence need only establish the scope of the legal representation and not the actual receipt of the allegedly relevant confidential information. Then only where it is clearly discernible, "that the issues involved in a current case do not relate to matters in which the attorney formerly represented the adverse party will the attorney's present representation be treated as measuring up to the standard of legal ethics." Doubts as to the existence of an asserted conflict of interest should be resolved in favor of disqualification.

*   *   *

Essentially then, disqualification questions require three levels of inquiry. Initially, the trial judge must make a factual reconstruction of the scope of the prior legal representation. Second, it must be determined whether it is reasonable to infer that the confidential information allegedly given would have been given to a lawyer representing a client in those matters. Finally, it must be determined whether that information is relevant to the issues raised in the litigation pending against the former client.

Although the district court properly identified this rule of law, it erred in its application. First, we accept Judge Marshall's factual reconstruction of the scope of Bigbee's prior representation. It was established that Bigbee prepared numerous mining patents and handled real estate transactions relating to Gulf uranium properties. Given this reconstruction, the second step in the analysis is to inquire whether it is reasonable to presume that Gulf would have transmitted to the Bigbee firm the class of confidential information allegedly given.

Gulf alleges that three types of confidential information were imparted: 1) that relating to the quantity and quality of uranium reserves at Mt. Taylor, 2) the reasons for delaying the production of those reserves, and 3) information detailing Gulf's relationship with one of the joint owners of the properties. Regardless of the reasonableness of inferring knowledge of the reasons for production delay from the scope of the former representation, we think it is clearly reasonable to presume that the information regarding quantity and quality of uranium was given. Indeed, it seems difficult to believe that Bigbee would not have acquired rather detailed information relating to the quantity and quality of the uranium reserves in the course of its filing of mining patents and resolution of conflicting claims.4 Judge Marshall concluded that the firm "did gain knowledge of Gulf's uranium properties during its work."

Having established the presumption that this information was given, disqualification must result if that information is relevant to the issues in the suit pending against Gulf. Relevance must be gauged by the violations alleged in the complaint and assessment of the evidence useful in establishing those allegations. Judge Marshall did not consider the information allegedly given to Bigbee to be relevant to the cartel litigation. He reasoned that the violation charged was essentially price fixing, not conspiratorial control of uranium production. Further, he concluded that the price-fixing charge would be proven by evidence of "meetings and communications among the alleged co-conspirators, as well as evidence on uranium prices, terms and conditions of sale, and market availability."

The lower court erred, both in identifying the issues raised by an allegation of price fixing, and in assessing the relevance of circumstantial economic evidence to proof of a price fixing conspiracy. The lower court found that the "heart of the (Westinghouse) complaint is directed at alleged price-fixing arrangements."

However, an agreement to restrict the production of uranium unquestionably is a price fixing arrangement. "Price fixing" is a characterization which extends to all conspiracies designed to manipulate the price of goods. In fact, all serious attempts to establish a supracompetitive price must necessarily include an agreement to restrict output. Otherwise the monopoly price could never be maintained. Thus, the lower court's view that conspiracy to fix prices and conspiracy to restrict output are distinct offenses is in error. The lower court's reliance on the fact that the complaint contains only a "few scanty references to the alleged conspiratorial control of uranium production" is misplaced. Westinghouse's general allegation of price fixing is sufficient to make evidence tending to establish a conspiracy to restrict uranium production relevant to the litigation.

The lower court also erred in its determination of what evidence was relevant to proof of the alleged price fixing conspiracy. The judge found that evidence of Gulf's quantity and quality of uranium reserves was not sufficiently relevant, reasoning that the conspiracy would be proven through direct evidence of agreement among the conspirators. Relevance, however, must be measured against the potential avenues of proof and not against the expected. Price fixing can be established by direct evidence of agreement or through circumstantial evidence of conduct.

If sufficient evidence is obtained to prove the existence of an agreement to fix prices directly, it is true that information revealing the quantity and quality of Gulf uranium reserves would not ever be needed, but Westinghouse need not establish the charged violation by this course.

Most price fixing conspiracies are established through circumstantial evidence. Proof that Gulf was restricting its output of uranium would be highly relevant circumstantial evidence if its competitors were behaving in a parallel fashion. Although evidence of parallel behavior alone may not be sufficient to establish conspiracy, it is given great weight. Furthermore, it has been suggested that proof that an individual competitor has un-utilized productive capacity in excess of demand may in itself suggest collusive behavior within an industry. Information possibly demonstrating that Gulf had uranium reserves available for production which were not brought on to the market would be central to this mode of proof. Thus, even though Westinghouse could prove its claim of price fixing solely through direct evidence of collusive agreements, evidence of Gulf's quantity and quality of uranium reserves could serve as a central element in an alternative method of proof of the Section One Sherman Act violation alleged. Certainly the complaint would not prevent Westinghouse from establishing the restraint of trade through use of this inferential economic evidence. Therefore the incentives to disclose and abuse the confidential information are present, and disqualification is required.

In one of the most recent Second Circuit cases, a lawyer upon graduation from law school became associated with a firm representing Cook Industries, which was being sued in connection with a shipment of soybeans from Louisiana to Taiwan which was 254 tons short of the amount stated on the bills of lading and weight certificates. After putting in more than 100 hours over three years on behalf of Cook, the young lawyer left his firm and became associated with another firm where he was assigned to represent the government of India which was suing Cook Industries for delivery of grain of inferior quality and grade and of short weight. Although the two representations involved different shipments at different times to different parties, they shared similar loading and weighing procedures of Cook to which the lawyer had become privy in his first representation. The Second Circuit concluded that "(i)t would be difficult to think of a closer nexus between issues."

Here it could reasonably be said that during the former representation the attorneys might have acquired information related to the subject matter of the subsequent representation, that the former representation was lengthy and pervasive, that the former representation was more than peripheral, and that the relationship between the two matters is sufficiently close to bring the later representation within the prohibition of the canons. Therefore there was clearly a substantial relationship between the two representations.

*   *   *

About the Author

Steve Donweber is a lecturer at Boston University School of Law, where he teaches Professional Responsibility, Evidence, Introduction to American Law, Contracts for LLMs, Civil Procedure for LLMs, and sometimes Federal Civil Practice and Discovery Theory and Practice. He has also taught various courses related to legal research and writing. Steve is a dedicated and enthusiastic professor. Devoted to his students, he brings energy, wit, clear explanations, and even multimedia to the subjects he teaches.

Prior to joining the full-time faculty at Boston University School of Law in the summer of 2016, Steve served the BU Law community as a senior research librarian and adjunct faculty member. Prior to that, he was a litigator at a large law firm in Philadelphia, Pennsylvania.

Steve is the 2019 recipient of the Michael Melton award for teaching excellence at BU Law and the 2019 inaugural recipient of the Mark Pettit teaching award given to the faculty member voted as the 3L class' favorite professor.

Other books by Steve include *Federal Civil Practice, Cases and Materials on Discovery Practice in the Federal Courts, The Law Student's Quick Guide to Legal Citation,* and *Researching the Law* (with other research librarians at BU Law).

Steve lives in Boston with his wife and son.

Made in United States
North Haven, CT
05 November 2023

43645067R00261